D1199293

DUNGEONS & DRAGONS®

ADVENTURER'S VAULT™ 2
Arms and Equipment for All Classes

ROLEPLAYING GAME SUPPLEMENT

Rob Heinsoo • Eytan Bernstein • Logan Bonner • Peter Schaefer

CREDITS

Design
Rob Heinsoo (lead),
Eytan Bernstein, Logan Bonner,
Stephen Radney-MacFarland

Additional Design
Rob Donoghue

Development
Peter Schaefer (lead),
Stephen Schubert, Logan Bonner

Additional Development
Rodney Thompson, Rob Watkins

Editing
Cal Moore (lead),
Jennifer Clarke Wilkes, Jeremy Crawford,
Scott Fitzgerald Gray, M. Alexander Jurkat

Managing Editing
Kim Mohan

Director of D&D R&D and Book Publishing
Bill Slavicsek

D&D Creative Manager
Christopher Perkins

D&D Design Manager
James Wyatt

D&D Development and Editing Manager
Andy Collins

Art Director
Kate Irwin

Cover Illustration
Wayne Reynolds

Graphic Designers
Keven Smith, Leon Cortez, Lisa Hanson

Interior Illustrations
Kalman Andrasofszky, Jeff Carlisle, Ed Cox, Thomas
Denmark, Wayne England, Jason A. Engle, Howard
Lyon, Sean "Muttonhead" Murray, Lucio Parrillo,
Chris Seaman, Matias Tapia, Eric L. Williams,
Kieran Yanner

Publishing Production Specialist
Angelika Lokotz

Prepress Manager
Jefferson Dunlap

Imaging Technicians
Ashley Brock

Production Manager
Cynda Callaway

Game rules based on the original DUNGEONS & DRAGONS®
rules created by **E. Gary Gygax** and **Dave Arneson**, and
the later editions by **David "Zeb" Cook** (2nd Edition);
Jonathan Tweet, Monte Cook, Skip Williams, Richard
Baker, and **Peter Adkison** (3rd Edition); and **Rob**
Heinsoo, Andy Collins, and **James Wyatt** (4th Edition).

620-24177720-001 HB
9 8 7 6 5 4 3 2 1
First Printing: August 2009
ISBN: 978-0-7869-5204-5

U.S., CANADA, ASIA, PACIFIC,
& LATIN AMERICA
Wizards of the Coast LLC
P.O. Box 707
Renton WA 98057-0707
+1-800-324-6496

EUROPEAN HEADQUARTERS
Hasbro UK Ltd
Caswell Way
Newport, Gwent NP9 0YH
GREAT BRITAIN
Please keep this address for your records

WIZARDS OF THE COAST, BELGIUM
Industrialaan 1
1702 Groot-Bijgaarden
Belgium
+32.070.233.277

DUNGEONS & DRAGONS, D&D, d20, d20 System, WIZARDS OF THE COAST, *Adventurer's Vault, Player's Handbook, Dungeon Master's Guide, Monster Manual,* D&D Insider, all other
Wizards of the Coast product names, and their respective logos are trademarks of Wizards of the Coast in the U.S.A. and other countries. All Wizards characters and the
distinctive likenesses thereof are property of Wizards of the Coast LLC. This material is protected under the copyright laws of the United States of America. Any reproduction or
unauthorized use of the material or artwork contained herein is prohibited without the express written permission of Wizards of the Coast LLC. Any similarity to actual people,
organizations, places, or events included herein is purely coincidental. Printed in the U.S.A. ©2009 Wizards of the Coast LLC

VISIT OUR WEBSITE AT WWW.WIZARDS.COM/DND

Introduction

Adventurer's Vault 2 is a successor and a companion to the *Adventurer's Vault* supplement. In it you'll find a wide selection of magic items to augment those presented in its predecessor as well as in the *Player's Handbook®*, *Player's Handbook 2*, and other sources.

More than just a continuation, though, *Adventurer's Vault 2* puts forth a few advances in the way that magic items are presented and conceptualized.

More Magic Items

Chapter 1: Magic Items gives players and DMs even more choices for gear and goodies to outfit characters and to serve as treasure. In addition to the usual categories (armor, weapons, rings, and so forth), this chapter has sections for two kinds of implements—tomes and totems—that have been added to the game since *Adventurer's Vault* was published. It also breaks new ground with lair items, which bring new meaning to the term "comforts of home"; tattoos, for those who want the ultimate in portability for their magic; and immurements, a form of consumable item that enables its owner to actually reshape the battlefield.

Sidebars throughout this chapter highlight particular items, providing flavor in the form of background stories and offering one or two ideas for how the item can be worked into an adventure plot. Magic items can be more than just possessions—they can be the stuff of which entire campaigns are built.

Item Sets

Chapter 2: Item Sets takes the idea of magic items as flavor devices one step further. Each of the more than 30 sections in this chapter tells the story of a group of items that have a common origin or theme. Each item is tailored for one of the three tiers of play—heroic, paragon, or epic. Although any of these items can be used individually, a character who owns and uses more than one item of a set gains an additional benefit beyond what the items themselves impart.

Alternatively, an item might be part of a group set. These collections of items are special because they provide additional benefits based on how many different members of an adventuring party wield one or more of the items in the set.

Item Tables

Finally, no book of this sort would be complete without a collection of tables to summarize its contents. The tables in the appendix of *Adventurer's Vault 2* are organized by level and by types of items within each level, so that a DM looking to fill out a treasure parcel and a player making up a wish list can both easily find what they need.

Contents

CHAPTER 1

MAGIC ITEMS

WHEREVER ONE travels throughout the world (and beyond), magic items are highly sought after for their benefits both small and large.

Adventurers seek out magical treasures to help them achieve their goals. Many of those treasures have histories that inspire rumors and spawn quests.

This chapter presents more magic items to fill out adventurers' wish lists.

+ **Armor:** Strong materials and protective magic keep blades and arrows away from your flesh.
+ **Weapons:** Strike fear into your enemies when you wield a weapon of power.
+ **Ammunition:** Arrows, bolts, and sling stones give you a combat edge at range.
+ **Implements:** Holy symbols, orbs, rods, staffs, tomes, totems, and wands channel your magic and grant special benefits.
+ **Arms Slot Items:** Shields to guard you and bracers to smite your foes.
+ **Feet Slot Items:** When you need to move quicker, jump farther, or dodge better, step into one of these items.
+ **Hands Slot Items:** Magic gloves and gauntlets not only keep your hands warm but keep you alive.
+ **Head Slot Items:** Magic to bolster the mind, body, and spirit.
+ **Neck Slot Items:** Improve your defenses in style!
+ **Rings:** Jewelry imbued with powerful and varied enchantments.
+ **Waist Slot Items:** These items can improve your health and increase your skills—as well as hold your pants up.
+ **Wondrous Items:** Strange and fantastic items with a wide range of uses.
+ **Lair Items:** New wondrous items to enhance your base of operations.
+ **Tattoos:** The best thing about magic of the flesh is that it's inseparable from you.
+ **Consumables:** Use these one-shot items to get out of a tough situation.

Several of the item descriptions are augmented by sidebars that offer lore or background about the item, plus one or more adventure hooks involving the item and how the characters might acquire it.

HOWARD LYON

ARMOR

No attack is too devastating to be turned aside.

Armor is an integral part of any adventurer's gear. From the wizard's robes and the barbarian's hide to the bard's chainmail and the paladin's plate, armor's protection is available to every hero.

Enchantments improve the wearer's Armor Class, whether by filling plate armor's gaps with shields of force or hardening leather armor into something that can stop a ballista shot. Seasoned adventurers can depend on magic armor to protect them even from the teeth of an ancient wyrm.

At least some of the time.

Armor of Aegis Expansion — Level 2+

Flecks of magical force swirl around this light armor, coalescing to deflect attacks against you and your companions.

Lvl 2	+1	520 gp	Lvl 17	+4	65,000 gp
Lvl 7	+2	2,600 gp	Lvl 22	+5	325,000 gp
Lvl 12	+3	13,000 gp	Lvl 27	+6	1,625,000 gp

Armor: Cloth, leather
Enhancement: AC
Power (Encounter): Immediate Interrupt. *Trigger:* A creature you have marked with your *aegis of shielding* power targets you and at least one of your allies with an attack. *Effect:* The damage of the triggering creature's attack damage is reduced by 5 + the armor's enhancement bonus.
Level 12 or 17: 10 + enhancement bonus.
Level 22 or 27: 15 + enhancement bonus.

Armor of Dark Deeds — Level 14+

Swirling with shadows, this armor masks you from your enemies.

Lvl 14	+3	21,000 gp	Lvl 24	+5	525,000 gp
Lvl 19	+4	105,000 gp	Lvl 29	+6	2,625,000 gp

Armor: Leather, hide
Enhancement: AC
Property: When you attack an enemy that is granting combat advantage to you, you gain concealment until the end of your next turn.

Armor of Enduring Health — Level 23+

While wearing this armor, you can draw more deeply on your inner resources.

Lvl 23	+5	425,000 gp	Lvl 28	+6	2,125,000 gp

Armor: Hide, chain
Enhancement: AC
Property: You can use your second wind one additional time per encounter.

Armor of Shared Health — Level 30

This golden chainmail glows with divine energy that heals you when you help others.

Lvl 30	+6	3,125,000 gp

Armor: Chain
Enhancement: AC
Property: When you use a healing power that benefits an ally, you also regain hit points equal to one-half the hit points that ally regains.

Armor of Shared Valor — Level 15+

When you exhort your allies to find courage, you find it yourself.

Lvl 15	+3	25,000 gp	Lvl 25	+5	625,000 gp
Lvl 20	+4	125,000 gp	Lvl 30	+6	3,125,000 gp

Armor: Leather, chain
Enhancement: AC
Property: When you use a power that grants an ally a bonus to any defense, you gain an equal bonus of the same type to the same defense. This bonus lasts until the power's effect ends or until the end of your next turn.

Armor of Sudden Recovery — Level 3+

You shrug off deadly conditions easily in this supple armor.

Lvl 3	+1	680 gp	Lvl 18	+4	85,000 gp
Lvl 8	+2	3,400 gp	Lvl 23	+5	425,000 gp
Lvl 13	+3	17,000 gp	Lvl 28	+6	2,125,000 gp

Armor: Cloth, leather
Enhancement: AC
Property: You gain a +1 item bonus to saving throws against ongoing damage.
Power (Daily ✦ Healing): Minor Action. You can use this power when you're taking ongoing damage. The ongoing damage ends, and you gain regeneration equal to the amount of the ongoing damage until the end of the encounter.

Bastion Armor — Level 7+

This blocky armor, usually crafted in the dwarven style, is a favorite of dwarven defenders.

Lvl 7	+2	2,600 gp	Lvl 22	+5	325,000 gp
Lvl 12	+3	13,000 gp	Lvl 27	+6	1,625,000 gp
Lvl 17	+4	65,000 gp			

Armor: Scale, plate
Enhancement: AC
Power (Encounter): Minor Action. You end a mark on you or an ally adjacent to you.

Blackflock Robe — Level 12+

Wrapped in this tattered black cloth, you can briefly transform into a flock of ravens.

Lvl 12	+3	13,000 gp	Lvl 22	+5	325,000 gp
Lvl 17	+4	65,000 gp	Lvl 27	+6	1,625,000 gp

Armor: Cloth
Enhancement: AC
Power (Daily): Immediate Reaction. *Trigger:* You take damage from an attack. *Effect:* You fly 8 squares and become insubstantial until the start of your next turn.

Coruscating Armor
Level 2+

This glittering steel armor masks your exact location from enemies that would impede you.

Lvl 2	+1	520 gp	Lvl 17	+4	65,000 gp
Lvl 7	+2	2,600 gp	Lvl 22	+5	325,000 gp
Lvl 12	+3	13,000 gp	Lvl 27	+6	1,625,000 gp

Armor: Scale, plate
Enhancement: AC
Power (Daily): Minor Action. Until the end of your next turn, you don't provoke opportunity attacks and can't be grabbed. This power doesn't end an existing grab.

Counterstrike Armor
Level 10+

The warding on this armor punishes the first enemy to strike you in battle.

Lvl 10	+2	5,000 gp	Lvl 25	+5	625,000 gp
Lvl 15	+3	25,000 gp	Lvl 30	+6	3,125,000 gp
Lvl 20	+4	125,000 gp			

Armor: Cloth, leather, hide
Enhancement: AC
Property: The first enemy that hits you during an encounter takes ongoing 5 damage (save ends).
Level 20, 25, or 30: Ongoing 10 damage (save ends).

Dazzling Plate
Level 4+

Favored by paladins of Pelor, this shining suit of polished mithral plate strengthens your spirit and dazzles your foes.

Lvl 4	+1	840 gp	Lvl 19	+4	105,000 gp
Lvl 9	+2	4,200 gp	Lvl 24	+5	525,000 gp
Lvl 14	+3	21,000 gp	Lvl 29	+6	2,625,000 gp

Armor: Plate
Enhancement: AC
Property: You gain a +2 item bonus to all defenses against charm, fear, and psychic effects.
Power (Daily): Minor Action. Each enemy adjacent to you takes a –2 penalty to attack rolls (save ends).

Death's Brink Armor
Level 7+

This black metal armor has the image of an outthrust hand emblazoned on its breast.

Lvl 7	+2	2,600 gp	Lvl 22	+5	325,000 gp
Lvl 12	+3	13,000 gp	Lvl 27	+6	1,625,000 gp
Lvl 17	+4	65,000 gp			

Armor: Scale, plate
Enhancement: AC
Property: While you're dying, you don't die until you fail four death saving throws.
Power (Daily): No Action. *Trigger:* You roll a death saving throw and dislike the result. *Effect:* You gain a +2 bonus to the saving throw.
Level 12 or 17: +3 bonus.
Level 22 or 27: +4 bonus.

ARMOR OF SHARED VALOR

The ballad of Velira is also the legend of the *armor of shared valor*. A bard who came from across the sea when the waters of the world were ice and the land was still unformed, Velira brought the magic of fire and music to the scattered tribes of humanoids and helped defend them against all invaders. Her most powerful tool was the armor she created for herself: As she shielded an entire tribe with the magic of her songs, she too became a more powerful protector.

Suits of *armor of shared valor* exist today, but they're thought to be lesser copies of the original.

Persuade a Bardic College: Bardic colleges usually craft and control distribution of *armor of shared valor*. An adventurer who seeks such an item must convince the organization of his or her worthiness. True bardic colleges are few and far between, but loose fellowships of wandering bards are often called colleges as well. Obtaining their approval requires getting references and traveling to meet with scattered members.

Velira's People: The ballad of Velira is regarded as a fantasy by most, but it has a kernel of truth. The tribes spoken of in it might yet exist, huddled along fjords and wandering in arctic regions. Adventurers who locate such a hidden people might learn the secret of creating *armor of shared valor*, or perhaps acquire a suit that has been stashed away since ancient times.

Armor of shared valor

THOMAS DENMARK

Gambit armor

Gallant Armor

Level 27

This magnificent suit of plate mail rewards you for selflessly tending your companions.

Lvl 27   +6   1,625,000 gp

Armor: Plate

Enhancement: AC

Property: When you use the *lay on hands* power on an ally, you also regain hit points equal to one-half your healing surge value.

Gambit Armor

Level 13+

Made for those who like to take chances in battle, this armor lets you risk your own safety for a better chance to harm your foes.

Lvl 13	+3	17,000 gp	Lvl 23	+5	425,000 gp
Lvl 18	+4	85,000 gp	Lvl 28	+6	2,125,000 gp

Armor: Cloth, leather

Enhancement: AC

Property: When an enemy scores a critical hit against you, you can score a critical hit on a roll of 17-20 on your next attack against that enemy before the end of your next turn.

Power (Daily ✦ Stance): Minor Action. Until the stance ends, you grant combat advantage and any creature you attack grants combat advantage to you.

Gambler's Suit

Level 6

Luck is fickle, and this stylish set of leathers plays both sides of the coin.

Lvl 6	+2	1,800 gp	Lvl 21	+5	225,000 gp
Lvl 11	+3	9,000 gp	Lvl 26	+6	1,125,000 gp
Lvl 16	+4	45,000 gp			

Armor: Leather

Enhancement: AC

Property: When you make at least two saving throws, you can choose to gain a +2 bonus to the first saving throw and take a -2 penalty to the second.

Power (Daily): Immediate Interrupt. *Trigger:* An enemy hits you with an attack. *Effect:* The triggering enemy rerolls the attack roll and must use the second result. If that result is a hit, the attack scores a critical hit.

Genasi Soul Armor

Level 4+

Elemental energies ripple through this armor, said to contain the life energy of a genasi.

Lvl 4	+1	840 gp	Lvl 19	+4	105,000 gp
Lvl 9	+2	4,200 gp	Lvl 24	+5	525,000 gp
Lvl 14	+3	21,000 gp	Lvl 29	+6	2,625,000 gp

Armor: Leather, hide

Enhancement: AC

Property: This armor is attuned to one genasi elemental manifestation (*Forgotten Realms Player's Guide*, page 10) chosen at the time the armor is created.

Power (Daily): Minor Action. Until the end of the encounter, you can use the racial encounter power associated with the armor's elemental manifestation. If you already have that racial power, you can use it a second time during this encounter.

Demonscale

Level 9+

Piecemeal skins, scales, and exoskeletons of demons form a frightful but sturdy suit of scale armor.

Lvl 9	+2	4,200 gp	Lvl 24	+5	525,000 gp
Lvl 14	+3	21,000 gp	Lvl 29	+6	2,625,000 gp
Lvl 19	+4	105,000 gp			

Armor: Scale

Enhancement: AC

Power (Encounter): Immediate Interrupt. *Trigger:* You take acid, cold, fire, or lightning damage. *Effect:* You gain resist 5 to the triggering damage type until the end of the encounter.

Level 14 or 19: Resist 10.

Level 24 or 29: Resist 15.

Formidable Armor

Level 14+

When you activate this armor, even the mightiest blow can do little more than scratch your skin.

Lvl 14	+3	21,000 gp	Lvl 24	+5	525,000 gp
Lvl 19	+4	105,000 gp	Lvl 29	+6	2,625,000 gp

Armor: Hide, chain

Enhancement: AC

Power (Daily): Immediate Interrupt. *Trigger:* An attack hits you and doesn't score a critical hit. *Effect:* The triggering attack deals the minimum damage.

HOWARD LYON

Great Cat Armor — Level 19+

In this sleek suit of hide armor, you bound around the battlefield like a powerful feline.

Lvl 19	+4	105,000 gp	Lvl 29	+6	2,625,000 gp
Lvl 24	+5	525,000 gp			

Armor: Hide
Enhancement: AC
Property: When you shift, you can shift 1 additional square.
Power (Daily): Move Action. You shift a number of squares equal to twice the armor's enhancement bonus.

Healer's Armor — Level 5+

This sturdy armor enhances your ability to heal your allies.

Lvl 5	+1	1,000 gp	Lvl 20	+4	125,000 gp
Lvl 10	+2	5,000 gp	Lvl 25	+5	625,000 gp
Lvl 15	+3	25,000 gp	Lvl 30	+6	3,125,000 gp

Armor: Hide, chain
Enhancement: AC
Property: When you use a healing power, the target regains additional hit points equal to the armor's enhancement bonus.

HOLY RADIANCE ARMOR

Xelfide was a den of iniquity, sin, and debauchery. The town, inhabited by villains, leeches, and other low characters, existed outside the realm of law and decency. In such a place, good had little chance to flourish.

Fifty years ago, a traveling cleric of Pelor known as Koslin came to Xelfide with the intention of purifying it. His first attempt was met with outright resistance, violence, and theft. After that disaster, the cleric's resolve faltered—until he received a vision from Pelor that showed him standing in the town square at noon and praying.

Koslin went to the square, obeying what he saw as a mission from his god. At first, he attracted sneers and laughs, but as he continued to pray, his armor began to glow with increasing brilliance. This demonstration of divine blessing won Koslin many converts to the worship of Pelor. Tragically, the cleric was slain by those who still clung to their evil ways, but not before the town had turned to a righteous path. *Holy radiance armor* memorializes this sacred act.

Purify Xelfide, Again: In the years since the death of Koslin, Xelfide has slowly returned to its old ways. The corrupt town leaders hold Koslin's armor and keep it hidden in their stronghold. If a worthy hero can recover the armor and wear it again in Pelor's name, the town might return to the good.

Remnants of the Underbelly: A few of Xelfide's most evil citizens fled to the frontier when Koslin converted the town to the worship of Pelor. Before they left, they managed to murder the cleric and plunder his armor, which they buried in their encampment. Now, they plague the town, paralyzing trade, and stealing and killing with no remorse. The citizens seek aid from heroes who walk the same path as Koslin.

Hero's Armor — Level 2+

This shirt of glimmering chainmail fortifies those who take bold action in battle.

Lvl 2	+1	520 gp	Lvl 17	+4	65,000 gp
Lvl 7	+2	2,600 gp	Lvl 22	+5	325,000 gp
Lvl 12	+3	13,000 gp	Lvl 27	+6	1,625,000 gp

Armor: Chain
Enhancement: AC
Property: When you spend an action point to take an extra action, you also gain a +2 bonus to all defenses until the end of your next turn.
Power (Daily ✦ Healing): Free Action. *Trigger:* You spend an action point. *Effect:* You forgo the bonus to all defenses granted by the armor's property. Instead, an ally within 5 squares of you uses his or her second wind as a free action.

Holy Adversary's Armor — Level 3+

When you swear an oath against your prey, divine grace permeates this armor, protecting you against that creature's attacks.

Lvl 3	+1	680 gp	Lvl 18	+4	85,000 gp
Lvl 8	+2	3,400 gp	Lvl 23	+5	425,000 gp
Lvl 13	+3	17,000 gp	Lvl 28	+6	2,125,000 gp

Armor: Cloth
Enhancement: AC
Power (Daily): Minor Action. Until the end of the encounter, you gain resistance to all damage against attacks by your current *oath of enmity* target equal to the armor's enhancement bonus.

Holy Radiance Armor — Level 15+

This gleaming chainmail glows with the radiance of the sun.

Lvl 15	+3	25,000 gp	Lvl 25	+5	625,000 gp
Lvl 20	+4	125,000 gp	Lvl 30	+6	3,125,000 gp

Armor: Chain
Enhancement: AC
Power (Daily ✦ Healing): Minor Action. You expend your use of a Channel Divinity power for this encounter and shed bright light 20 squares in all directions. While within the light, you and each ally gain regeneration 3 while bloodied and a +2 power bonus to saving throws.

Kemstone Armor — Level 8+

Fashioned with the strong but light kemras stone found in various dominions of the Astral Sea, this armor stabilizes its wearer's essence.

Lvl 8	+2	3,400 gp	Lvl 23	+5	425,000 gp
Lvl 13	+3	17,000 gp	Lvl 28	+6	2,125,000 gp
Lvl 18	+4	85,000 gp			

Armor: Scale, plate
Enhancement: AC
Property: You gain a +4 item bonus to all defenses against polymorph effects.

Lifefont Armor · Level 4+

Embedded with ancient and powerful primal symbols, this armor has saved the life of more than one warden.

Lvl 4	+1	840 gp	Lvl 19	+4	105,000 gp
Lvl 9	+2	4,200 gp	Lvl 24	+5	525,000 gp
Lvl 14	+3	21,000 gp	Lvl 29	+6	2,625,000 gp

Armor: Hide
Enhancement: AC
Property: When you make saving throws at the start of your turn using the Font of Life class feature, you gain a +1 item bonus to each saving throw.
Power (Daily): No Action. *Trigger:* You start your turn and have the Font of Life class feature. *Effect:* You make a saving throw against each effect that a save can end instead of just one.

RAT KILLER'S COAT

The reclusive mage Sarkudo hid his laboratory deep under the capital city out of a desire for privacy. To his chagrin, he discovered that by plying his trade in the sewers, he had invited a dungeon to his doorstep. Dealing with slimes, molds, vermin, giant bugs, and the like was so frustrating and time-consuming that Sarkudo almost gave up and left.

Sarkudo had long observed one of the city's rat catchers and was baffled as to how the man had survived so long in such a dangerous place, armed with only a sharp stick and a small but vicious dog. The wizard asked him what his secret was. The rat catcher opened Sarkudo's eyes by revealing the secret lore of the sewers and how to live in harmony with the unique environment. Sarkudo was so impressed that he hired the rat catcher to help redesign his lab, and in short order, it was attracting much less trouble.

The wizard also made a protective coat for his assistant, which the rat catcher in turn passed on to his heir. The child aspired to a grander career, namely adventuring. The coat served its wearer so well in battle that fellow adventurers made versions of their own, and *rat killer's coats* soon became popular.

The King of Cats: The King of Cats is a very specialized shop, carrying special items such as silver weaponry, rat poison, and exotic tools. Ruffians are extorting protection money from the owner, who seeks assistance in stopping them. She offers a *rat killer's coat* as a reward.

The Grieving Family: Sven is a hunter of vermin and a minor adventurer. He entered the sewers over a week ago and hasn't been seen since. His wife has given up hope but wants someone to recover the body for a proper burial. Whoever accomplishes this task can keep the tools of Sven's trade, including his magic coat, if he's really dead.

Magnetic Armor · Level 9+

Studded with lodestones, this heavy armor pulls creatures into your reach.

Lvl 9	+2	4,200 gp	Lvl 24	+5	525,000 gp
Lvl 14	+3	21,000 gp	Lvl 29	+6	2,625,000 gp
Lvl 19	+4	105,000 gp			

Armor: Scale, plate
Enhancement: AC
Power (Daily): Minor Action. You pull one creature within 3 squares of you 3 squares. If you pull it into a square adjacent to you, it's also immobilized (save ends).
Level 14 or 19: One creature within 5 squares.
Level 24 or 29: One creature within 10 squares, and you pull it 5 squares.

Marauder's Armor · Level 7+

This heavy, fur-lined armor is favored by barbarian pirates who rush into the fray.

Lvl 7	+2	2,600 gp	Lvl 22	+5	325,000 gp
Lvl 12	+3	13,000 gp	Lvl 27	+6	1,625,000 gp
Lvl 17	+4	65,000 gp			

Armor: Leather, hide
Enhancement: AC
Property: When you charge, you gain a +1 bonus to AC until the end of your next turn.
Level 12 or 17: +2 bonus.
Level 22 or 27: +3 bonus.
Power (Daily ✦ Healing): Free Action. *Trigger:* You hit with a charge attack. *Effect:* You make a saving throw with a bonus equal to the armor's enhancement bonus, or you spend a healing surge and regain additional hit points equal to the armor's enhancement bonus.

Mind Armor · Level 23+

At a moment's notice, you can surround this adamantine armor with a psychic field that protects you from mental attacks.

Lvl 23	+5	425,000 gp	Lvl 28	+6	2,125,000 gp

Armor: Scale, plate
Enhancement: AC
Property: You gain resist 15 psychic.
Power (Daily): Minor Action. Until the end of the encounter, any enemy that attacks you with a charm, fear, illusion, psychic, or sleep power rolls the attack roll twice and must use the lower result.

Moon Armor · Level 3+

This armor is made from deposits of a strange ore that some believe came from the moon.

Lvl 3	+1	680 gp	Lvl 18	+4	85,000 gp
Lvl 8	+2	3,400 gp	Lvl 23	+5	425,000 gp
Lvl 13	+3	17,000 gp	Lvl 28	+6	2,125,000 gp

Armor: Chain
Enhancement: AC
Property: While you're in darkness or dim light (including starlight), you gain a +1 bonus to AC.

Nightmare Ward Armor Level 3+

The glistening black material of this armor, strangely cold to the touch, reliably deflects mental attacks.

Lvl 3	+1	680 gp	Lvl 18	+4	85,000 gp
Lvl 8	+2	3,400 gp	Lvl 23	+5	425,000 gp
Lvl 13	+3	17,000 gp	Lvl 28	+6	2,125,000 gp

Armor: Leather, hide
Enhancement: AC
Property: You gain resist 5 psychic.
  Level 13 or 18: Resist 10 psychic.
  Level 23 or 28: Resist 15 psychic.
Property: You gain a +2 item bonus to saving throws against charm, fear, or psychic effects.

Parchment Armor Level 4+

This armor is made of magically reinforced parchment inscribed with arcane writings.

Lvl 4	+1	840 gp	Lvl 19	+4	105,000 gp
Lvl 9	+2	4,200 gp	Lvl 24	+5	525,000 gp
Lvl 14	+3	21,000 gp	Lvl 29	+6	2,625,000 gp

Armor: Cloth, leather
Enhancement: AC
Property: This armor contains a number of arcane charges equal to its enhancement bonus. Recharging the armor requires an extended rest.
Power (At-Will): Free Action. *Trigger:* You use an arcane power and make an attack roll. *Effect:* You spend any number of unused charges from this armor and gain a power bonus to the attack roll for the triggering power equal to the number of charges spent.

Predator's Hide Level 3+

This tiger's hide clearly marks you as a formidable hunter.

Lvl 3	+1	680 gp	Lvl 18	+4	85,000 gp
Lvl 8	+2	3,400 gp	Lvl 23	+5	425,000 gp
Lvl 13	+3	17,000 gp	Lvl 28	+6	2,125,000 gp

Armor: Hide
Enhancement: AC
Property: When you hit a target you have designated with your Hunter's Quarry class feature, you gain a +1 bonus to all defenses against attacks by the designated quarry until the end of your next turn.
  Level 13 or 18: +2 bonus.
  Level 23 or 28: +3 bonus.

Rat Killer's Coat Level 2+

This fur-trimmed jacket is favored by all who must deal with dangerous vermin.

Lvl 2	+1	520 gp	Lvl 17	+4	65,000 gp
Lvl 7	+2	2,600 gp	Lvl 22	+5	325,000 gp
Lvl 12	+3	13,000 gp	Lvl 27	+6	1,625,000 gp

Armor: Cloth, leather
Enhancement: AC
Property: You gain resist 5 against damage from swarms' attacks. In addition, you can move through a space occupied by a swarm, and your movement doesn't provoke opportunity attacks from swarms.
  Level 12 or 17: Resist 10.
  Level 22 or 27: Resist 15.

Parchment armor

Robe of Avoidance Level 3+

When an enemy's attack misses you, this billowing robe confuses the foe so that you can get away.

Lvl 3	+1	680 gp	Lvl 18	+4	85,000 gp
Lvl 8	+2	3,400 gp	Lvl 23	+5	425,000 gp
Lvl 13	+3	17,000 gp	Lvl 28	+6	2,125,000 gp

Armor: Cloth
Enhancement: AC
Power (Encounter): Immediate Reaction. *Trigger:* An enemy misses you with a melee attack. *Effect:* You shift 1 square.

CHRIS SEAMAN

SANGUINE VESTMENTS

Avengers wear these magic robes to proclaim their enmity for their chosen prey. *Sanguine vestments* are dyed deep red, not only symbolizing the blood of those the wearer slays but often incorporating it. However, the garment often has sleeves or trim of pure white. After a battle, the avenger wipes the foe's blood from his or her weapon onto the white to demonstrate victory. This action also reinforces the avenger's commitment to destroy all enemies of his or her god.

Prove Yourself Worthy: The first step in acquiring *sanguine vestments* is to earn them through suitable actions. The guardians of the monasteries that train avengers bestow such a garment only on someone who defeats a great enemy.

Red Thread of Bel Yasura: Far from any civilization, across a dry, dangerous scrubland, stands the Bel Yasura monastery. Here, priests, monks, and avengers-in-training craft beautiful *sanguine vestments* as a form of meditation, using a unique type of red thread. Only those who swear the order's vows of asceticism and immerse themselves relentlessly in service to the god can learn the secret of creating this raiment of the faithful.

Runic Armor — Level 3+

The arcane sigils engraved on this armor glow in the presence of magical emanations.

Lvl 3	+1	680 gp	Lvl 18	+4	85,000 gp
Lvl 8	+2	3,400 gp	Lvl 23	+5	425,000 gp
Lvl 13	+3	17,000 gp	Lvl 28	+6	2,125,000 gp

Armor: Any
Enhancement: AC
Property: You gain an item bonus to Arcana checks equal to the armor's enhancement bonus.
Property: When you use your second wind, you also gain a bonus to damage rolls with arcane attack powers equal to the armor's enhancement bonus until the end of your next turn.

Sanguine Vestments — Level 3+

The blood of wounded enemies only strengthens this deep red garment.

Lvl 3	+1	680 gp	Lvl 18	+4	85,000 gp
Lvl 8	+2	3,400 gp	Lvl 23	+5	425,000 gp
Lvl 13	+3	17,000 gp	Lvl 28	+6	2,125,000 gp

Armor: Cloth
Enhancement: AC
Property: You gain a +1 bonus to all defenses while your *oath of enmity* target is bloodied.

Scale of the Serpent — Level 4+

Forged by fomorians from a strange green ore of the Feywild, this armor makes you as slippery as a snake.

Lvl 4	+1	840 gp	Lvl 19	+4	105,000 gp
Lvl 9	+2	4,200 gp	Lvl 24	+5	525,000 gp
Lvl 14	+3	21,000 gp	Lvl 29	+6	2,625,000 gp

Armor: Scale
Enhancement: AC
Property: You gain a +5 item bonus to checks to escape a grab.
Power (Daily): Immediate Reaction. *Trigger:* An effect dazes, immobilizes, slows, or stuns you. *Effect:* You make a saving throw against the triggering effect. On a save, that effect ends.

Serpentine Armor — Level 4+

Metallic snakes writhe along the surface of this armor, ready to strike at any foe that tries to get by you.

Lvl 4	+1	840 gp	Lvl 19	+4	105,000 gp
Lvl 9	+2	4,200 gp	Lvl 24	+5	525,000 gp
Lvl 14	+3	21,000 gp	Lvl 29	+6	2,625,000 gp

Armor: Scale
Enhancement: AC
Property: You gain resist 5 poison.
Level 14 or 19: Resist 10 poison.
Level 24 or 29: Resist 15 poison.
Power (Daily): Free Action. *Trigger:* An enemy adjacent to you shifts. *Effect:* The triggering enemy takes damage equal to 5 + the armor's enhancement bonus.
Level 14 or 19: 10 + enhancement bonus.
Level 24 or 29: 15 + enhancement bonus.

Shadow Hound Armor — Level 7+

Crafted from the hide of a massive shadow hound, this armor lets you fade away from danger when you suffer a grievous wound.

Lvl 7	+2	2,600 gp	Lvl 22	+5	325,000 gp
Lvl 12	+3	13,000 gp	Lvl 27	+6	1,625,000 gp
Lvl 17	+4	65,000 gp			

Armor: Hide
Enhancement: AC
Power (Daily): Immediate Reaction. *Trigger:* You become bloodied. *Effect:* You become insubstantial until the end of your next turn.

Shadow Warlock Armor — Level 10+

While wearing this suit of black leather, you can cloud the mind of a cursed enemy so that your attack strikes true.

Lvl 10	+2	5,000 gp	Lvl 25	+5	625,000 gp
Lvl 15	+3	25,000 gp	Lvl 30	+6	3,125,000 gp
Lvl 20	+4	125,000 gp			

Armor: Leather
Enhancement: AC
Property: While you have concealment from your Shadow Walk class feature, any creature affected by your Warlock's Curse grants combat advantage to you.

Slime Armor — Level 8+

You can cause this heavy armor to drip with acidic ooze that burns those who touch it.

Lvl 8	+2	3,400 gp	Lvl 23	+5	425,000 gp
Lvl 13	+3	17,000 gp	Lvl 28	+6	2,125,000 gp
Lvl 18	+4	85,000 gp			

Armor: Scale, plate
Enhancement: AC
Power (Daily ✦ Acid): Minor Action. Until the end of your next turn, any creature that hits you with a melee attack takes ongoing 5 acid damage (save ends).
Level 13 or 18: Ongoing 10 acid damage (save ends).
Level 23 or 28: Ongoing 15 acid damage (save ends).

Snaketongue Robe — Level 13+

A pattern of tiny, scintillating scales covers the surface of this loose garment, granting you the qualities of a serpent.

Lvl 13	+3	17,000 gp	Lvl 23	+5	425,000 gp
Lvl 18	+4	85,000 gp	Lvl 28	+6	2,125,000 gp

Armor: Cloth
Enhancement: AC
Property: You gain a +2 item bonus to Bluff checks.
Property: You gain resist 5 poison.
Power (Daily): Move Action. You shift a number of squares equal to the armor's enhancement bonus.

Spectral Plate — Level 20+

This dull black plate armor is made of iron plates infused with Shadowfell essence, granting you wraithlike properties.

Lvl 20	+4	125,000 gp	Lvl 30	+6	3,125,000 gp
Lvl 25	+5	625,000 gp			

Armor: Plate
Enhancement: AC
Property: You ignore the speed and skill check penalties for wearing plate armor.
Power (Daily): Move Action. You move your speed. In addition, you become insubstantial and gain phasing until the end of your turn.

Spiderweb Robes — Level 8+

This light, thin robe is woven from spider silk and carries a hint of the power of arachnids.

Lvl 8	+2	3,400 gp	Lvl 23	+5	425,000 gp
Lvl 13	+3	17,000 gp	Lvl 28	+6	2,125,000 gp
Lvl 18	+4	85,000 gp			

Armor: Cloth
Enhancement: AC
Property: You gain resist 5 poison.
Level 13 or 18: Resist 10 poison.
Level 23 or 28: Resist 15 poison.
Power (Daily): Immediate Reaction. *Trigger:* An enemy adjacent to you hits you with a melee attack. *Effect:* The triggering enemy is restrained until the end of its next turn.

Spiked Jacket — Level 3+

Hidden razor-sharp spikes spring out from the elbows, shoulders, and sides of this jacket when something grabs you.

Lvl 3	+1	680 gp	Lvl 18	+4	85,000 gp
Lvl 8	+2	3,400 gp	Lvl 23	+5	425,000 gp
Lvl 13	+3	17,000 gp	Lvl 28	+6	2,125,000 gp

Armor: Leather, hide
Enhancement: AC
Power (Daily): Standard Action. *Trigger:* You are grabbed. *Effect:* You escape the grab, and the enemy that was grabbing you takes 1d6 damage per plus.

Spirit Armor — Level 14+

This suit of fine chain has a ghostly sheen, and its mesh protects you from the denizens of the spirit world.

Lvl 14	+3	21,000 gp	Lvl 24	+5	525,000 gp
Lvl 19	+4	105,000 gp	Lvl 29	+6	2,625,000 gp

Armor: Chain
Enhancement: AC
Power (At-Will): Immediate Reaction. *Trigger:* An insubstantial enemy adjacent to you hits you. *Effect:* The triggering enemy loses the insubstantial quality (save ends). You become insubstantial until the triggering enemy saves against this effect.

Supporting Armor — Level 4+

This heavy iron armor absorbs the shock of jarring attacks.

Lvl 5	+1	1,000 gp	Lvl 20	+4	125,000 gp
Lvl 10	+2	5,000 gp	Lvl 25	+5	625,000 gp
Lvl 15	+3	25,000 gp	Lvl 30	+6	3,125,000 gp

Armor: Scale, plate
Enhancement: AC
Power (Daily): No Action. *Trigger:* An effect dazes or stuns you. *Effect:* You make a saving throw against the triggering effect. On a save, the effect ends.

SNAKETONGUE ROBE

Human worshipers of the serpent god Zehir, known as snaketongue cultists, perform dreadful rituals to transform themselves into more snakelike forms. *Snaketongue robes* enhance the efficacy of these rituals. Yuan-ti create the robes for cultists who have performed exceptional deeds in Zehir's name.

Celebrants of Zehir: Some snaketongue celebrants (*Monster Manual*, page 273) wear *snaketongue robes* to even more closely resemble the serpent god and his yuan-ti emissaries. These cultists are of high rank and are protected by many snaketongue zealots and warriors.

Serpent Crypt: Yuan-ti have been weaving *snaketongue robes* since their empire was in full bloom. The garments were originally worn only by nobles, and royal crypts within ruined yuan-ti cities or under ancient pyramids still hold these treasures of former rulers.

Time link armor

Teleporting Armor

Level 12+

A small teleportation circle is emblazoned on the breastplate of this armor.

Lvl 12	+3	13,000 gp	Lvl 22	+5	325,000 gp
Lvl 17	+4	65,000 gp	Lvl 27	+6	1,625,000 gp

Armor: Scale, plate
Enhancement: AC
Power (Daily ✦ Teleportation): Move Action. You teleport a number of squares equal to twice the armor's enhancement bonus.

Time Link Armor

Level 4+

Woven from shimmering crystal, this light chain suit improves your reaction time.

Lvl 4	+1	840 gp	Lvl 19	+4	105,000 gp
Lvl 9	+2	4,200 gp	Lvl 24	+5	525,000 gp
Lvl 14	+3	21,000 gp	Lvl 29	+6	2,625,000 gp

Armor: Chain
Enhancement: AC
Property: You gain an item bonus to initiative checks equal to the armor's enhancement bonus.
Power (Daily): No Action. *Trigger:* You roll initiative and dislike the result. *Effect:* You reroll initiative but must use the second result.

Translocating Armor

Level 14+

A field of planar energy surrounds this armor. If an enemy fails to hit you, you can teleport out of its reach.

Lvl 14	+3	21,000 gp	Lvl 24	+5	525,000 gp
Lvl 19	+4	105,000 gp	Lvl 29	+6	2,625,000 gp

Armor: Any
Enhancement: AC
Power (Encounter ✦ Teleportation): Immediate Reaction. *Trigger:* An enemy misses you with an attack. *Effect:* You teleport 3 squares.

Wall Armor

Level 3+

This armor seems far heavier than its constituent material. It becomes as unforgiving as a brick wall at a moment's notice.

Lvl 3	+1	680 gp	Lvl 18	+4	85,000 gp
Lvl 8	+2	3,400 gp	Lvl 23	+5	425,000 gp
Lvl 13	+3	17,000 gp	Lvl 28	+6	2,125,000 gp

Armor: Any
Enhancement: AC
Power (Daily): Immediate Reaction. *Trigger:* An enemy hits or misses you with a bull rush or charge attack. *Effect:* The triggering enemy takes 1d6 damage per plus and is knocked prone.

Warmage's Uniform

Level 3+

These decorated greatcoats come in a variety of styles, but all lend military might to their wearers.

Lvl 3	+1	680 gp	Lvl 18	+4	85,000 gp
Lvl 8	+2	3,400 gp	Lvl 23	+5	425,000 gp
Lvl 13	+3	17,000 gp	Lvl 28	+6	2,125,000 gp

Armor: Cloth, leather
Enhancement: AC
Power (Daily): Free Action. *Trigger:* You hit an enemy with an arcane attack power. *Effect:* Until the end of your next turn, one ally within 5 squares of that enemy gains a power bonus to attack rolls against the enemy equal to the armor's enhancement bonus.

Winged Armor

Level 13+

Glorious angelic wings sprout from this armor at your command.

Lvl 13	+3	17,000 gp	Lvl 23	+5	425,000 gp
Lvl 18	+4	85,000 gp	Lvl 28	+6	2,125,000 gp

Armor: Any
Enhancement: AC
Property: You gain an item bonus to Athletics checks to jump equal to the armor's enhancement bonus.
Power (Daily): Move Action. You fly your speed. You must begin and end this move on a solid surface. You also gain a +2 power bonus to all defenses until the end of your next turn.

KALMAN ANDRASOFSZKY

WEAPONS

There's no protection in the world that can stop this cutting edge. Or out of the world, for that matter.

Along with armor and neck slot items, weapons are central to an adventurer's gear. Even the most diplomatic adventurer knows that when defense isn't enough, there's no substitute for a good offense.

Aegis Blade — Level 3+

This blade allows you to place your aegis on all nearby foes with a single word of power.

Lvl 3	+1	680 gp	Lvl 18	+4	85,000 gp
Lvl 8	+2	3,400 gp	Lvl 23	+5	425,000 gp
Lvl 13	+3	17,000 gp	Lvl 28	+6	2,125,000 gp

Weapon: Heavy blade, light blade
Enhancement: Attack rolls and damage rolls
Critical: +1d6 damage per plus
Power (Daily): Minor Action. Mark each enemy within a close burst 3 (save ends). If you have the Swordmage Aegis class feature, treat each mark as if you applied it with your chosen aegis.

ALFSAIR SPEAR

Where the Dayforge Mountains meet the pines of the Winterbole Forest, small copses of strange twisting coniferous trees called alfsairs grow in remote glens. Sometimes called wisewood by the druids and shamans of the north, the light and remarkably strong wood of this tree constantly exudes a sticky, sweet-smelling sap that some tribes use for primal communion.

Druids carefully harvest and prepare the warped branches of these trees and shape them into seemingly awkward but surprisingly functional spears. Through clever crafting and enchanting, wielders are able to control the flow of the sap, focusing it for their own benefit and to their enemies' detriment.

Vanishing Wisdom: An old shaman is in trouble. He's slowly being driven insane by a tormenting trio of spirits only he can see. According to the shaman, the tormenting spirits can be banished only by the touch of an *alfsair spear*. He will be grateful to any adventurer who can come to his aid with one of these spears.

Roof of the World: *Alfsair spears* are mystical weapons. Legends tell that the most powerful aren't crafted at all, but grow from the top of the world's highest mountain. As the story goes, every 76 years, on the longest day of the year and when the Dragontooth wandering star is visible in the night sky, a new *alfsair spear* appears on the summit of the Roof of the World Mountain.

Aftershock Weapon — Level 2+

This weapon sends ripples of force toward nearby foes.

Lvl 2	+1	520 gp	Lvl 17	+4	65,000 gp
Lvl 7	+2	2,600 gp	Lvl 22	+5	325,000 gp
Lvl 12	+3	13,000 gp	Lvl 27	+6	1,625,000 gp

Weapon: Any
Enhancement: Attack rolls and damage rolls
Critical: +1d6 damage per plus, and each enemy adjacent to the target of the critical hit is knocked prone.

Alfsair Spear — Level 3+

This spear is a favorite druid weapon.

Lvl 3	+1	680 gp	Lvl 18	+4	85,000 gp
Lvl 8	+2	3,400 gp	Lvl 23	+5	425,000 gp
Lvl 13	+3	17,000 gp	Lvl 28	+6	2,125,000 gp

Weapon: Spear
Enhancement: Attack rolls and damage rolls
Critical: +1d8 psychic and poison damage per plus
Property: You gain an item bonus to Nature checks equal to the spear's enhancement bonus.
Property: Classes that use totems can use this spear as an implement for class powers and paragon path powers.
Power (Daily ✦ Poison, Psychic): No Action. *Trigger:* You score a critical hit against an enemy with this spear. *Effect:* The enemy hit by the triggering attack is dazed until the end of its next turn.

Aura Killer Weapon — Level 3+

The dark purple magic trailing in this weapon's wake shuts down your enemy's subtle spells and instinctive powers.

Lvl 3	+1	680 gp	Lvl 18	+4	85,000 gp
Lvl 8	+2	3,400 gp	Lvl 23	+5	425,000 gp
Lvl 13	+3	17,000 gp	Lvl 28	+6	2,125,000 gp

Weapon: Any melee
Enhancement: Attack rolls and damage rolls
Critical: +1d6 damage per plus
Power (Daily): Free Action. *Trigger:* You use this weapon to hit an enemy that has an aura. *Effect:* The enemy's aura ends, and the enemy can't reactivate it (save ends).

Avalanche Hammer — Level 4+

Enchanted with the essence of elemental earth, this hammer strikes foes like an avalanche.

Lvl 4	+1	840 gp	Lvl 19	+4	105,000 gp
Lvl 9	+2	4,200 gp	Lvl 24	+5	525,000 gp
Lvl 14	+3	21,000 gp	Lvl 29	+6	2,625,000 gp

Weapon: Hammer
Enhancement: Attack rolls and damage rolls
Critical: +1d10 damage per plus, and the target is knocked prone.
Property: When you charge an enemy and hit with a melee basic attack using this weapon, the attack deals 1[W] extra damage.

Battle spirit weapon

Battle Spirit Weapon — Level 15+

Infused with the sprit of a savage warrior, this weapon gives you ghostly powers when charging.

| Lvl 15 | +3 | 25,000 gp | Lvl 25 | +5 | 625,000 gp |
| Lvl 20 | +4 | 125,000 gp | Lvl 30 | +6 | 3,125,000 gp |

Weapon: Axe, flail, hammer, heavy blade, mace, spear
Enhancement: Attack rolls and damage rolls
Critical: +1d6 damage per plus, or +1d10 damage per plus on a charge
Property: While charging, you are insubstantial and can move through squares occupied by enemies. Your movement provokes opportunity attacks as normal.

Blood Drinker — Level 9+

You know when to feed your weapon, because it growls when it's hungry.

Lvl 9	+2	4,200 gp	Lvl 24	+5	525,000 gp
Lvl 14	+3	21,000 gp	Lvl 29	+6	2,625,000 gp
Lvl 19	+4	105,000 gp			

Weapon: Axe, heavy blade
Enhancement: Attack rolls and damage rolls
Critical: +1d6 damage per plus
Property: If you make an attack using this weapon and miss all targets, the *blood drinker* deals 5 damage to you, and the next attack you make before the end of your next turn deals 2d6 extra damage to the first target it hits.
Level 14 or 19: The weapon deals 10 damage to you, and your next attack deals 3d6 extra damage.
Level 24 or 29: The weapon deals 15 damage to you, and your next attack deals 4d8 extra damage.

BATTLE SPIRIT WEAPON

Sometimes a warrior's legacy is so potent, her deeds so extraordinary, that some part of her spirit lives on after death. These spirit fragments are sometimes drawn to the weapon the warrior used in life, or some similar martial instrument. Often they cling to the weapon, infusing it with power without need of a ritual or outside intervention. When the connection is weaker, a ritual can be used to fuse a spirit into steel.

Once fused, the spirit fragment allows the wielder of the *battle spirit weapon* to transform into a ghostly mist when charging. Barbarians believe that this transformation allows a warrior to step briefly into the realm of the ancestors, and many warriors claim to have received life-changing visions and messages from their ancestors while charging into battle.

The Reforging: A barbarian tribe has carried a particular *battle spirit weapon* since the days of its founding. Infused with the spirit of the tribe's founder, the weapon was the symbol of the chief's power and led the tribe to many victories. Recently, an evil warlock stole into the tribe's camp, slew the chief, and sundered the weapon. He bound the founder's spirit fragment into another vessel and is using it to guide a construct he created that is now ravaging the countryside. According to the tribe's beliefs, the person who can free the spirit from the construct and reforge the weapon will earn the right to wield it.

Banishing Spellblade — Level 14+

A powerful enchantment placed on this blade allows you to sequester a foe for a short amount of time.

| Lvl 14 | +3 | 21,000 gp | Lvl 24 | +5 | 525,000 gp |
| Lvl 19 | +4 | 105,000 gp | Lvl 29 | +6 | 2,625,000 gp |

Weapon: Heavy blade, light blade
Enhancement: Attack rolls and damage rolls
Critical: +1d6 damage per plus, or +1d8 per plus when used as an implement for an arcane power
Power (Daily ✦ Teleportation): Free Action. *Trigger:* Using this weapon, you hit an enemy with an arcane attack power that pulls, pushes, slides, or teleports the target. *Effect:* Instead of being pushed, pulled, slid, or teleported, that enemy disappears. At the end of the enemy's next turn, it reappears in the space it left. If that space is occupied, it appears in the nearest unoccupied space (your choice).

MATIAS TAPIA

Blood Fury Weapon — Level 3+

Often decorated with bloodstones, these blades or axes are favored by dragonborn barbarians.

Lvl 3	+1	680 gp	Lvl 18	+4	85,000 gp
Lvl 8	+2	3,400 gp	Lvl 23	+5	425,000 gp
Lvl 13	+3	17,000 gp	Lvl 28	+6	2,125,000 gp

Weapon: Axe, heavy blade
Enhancement: Attack rolls and damage rolls
Critical: +1d8 damage per plus, or +1d12 damage while you're bloodied
Power (Encounter): Minor Action. You are considered bloodied for all purposes (including beneficial effects such as the Dragonborn Fury racial trait) until the end of your next turn.

Boltshard Crossbow — Level 7+

You pull the trigger, spraying shards at your foes.

Lvl 7	+2	2,600 gp	Lvl 22	+5	325,000 gp
Lvl 12	+3	13,000 gp	Lvl 27	+6	1,625,000 gp
Lvl 17	+4	65,000 gp			

Weapon: Crossbow
Enhancement: Attack rolls and damage rolls
Critical: +1d6 damage per plus
Power (Daily): Standard Action. Make a ranged basic attack using this crossbow against each creature in a close blast 3.
Level 17 or 22: Close blast 5; a creature hit is also pushed 2 squares.
Level 27: Close blast 7; a creature hit is also pushed 2 squares.

Challenge-Seeking Weapon — Level 1+

This weapon is always eager to be introduced to a fresh enemy.

Lvl 1	+1	360 gp	Lvl 16	+4	45,000 gp
Lvl 6	+2	1,800 gp	Lvl 21	+5	225,000 gp
Lvl 11	+3	9,000 gp	Lvl 26	+6	1,125,000 gp

Weapon: Any melee
Enhancement: Attack rolls and damage rolls
Critical: None
Property: You deal 1d6 extra damage when you hit enemies that are at maximum hit points with this weapon.
Level 11 or 16: Deal 2d6 extra damage.
Level 21 or 26: Deal 3d6 extra damage.

Death Mark Weapon — Level 23+

This weapon knows when you kill a hated foe, letting you shift away to face a new enemy.

Lvl 23	+5	425,000 gp	Lvl 28	+6	2,125,000 gp

Weapon: Any
Enhancement: Attack rolls and damage rolls
Critical: +1d6 damage per plus, or +1d12 damage per plus against an enemy marked by you
Power (At-Will): Free Action. *Trigger:* You use this weapon to reduce an enemy that is marked by you to 0 hit points.
Effect: You shift a number of squares up to your speed.

Duelist's Bow — Level 2+

With this mighty weapon humming as you release arrow after arrow, enemy archers face certain defeat.

Lvl 2	+1	520 gp	Lvl 17	+4	65,000 gp
Lvl 7	+2	2,600 gp	Lvl 22	+5	325,000 gp
Lvl 12	+3	13,000 gp	Lvl 27	+6	1,625,000 gp

Weapon: Bow
Enhancement: Attack rolls and damage rolls
Critical: +1d6 damage per plus
Property: When you hit an enemy with this weapon, that enemy takes a -2 penalty to ranged and area attack rolls until the end of your next turn.

Earth-Wrought Hammer — Level 1+

This hammer appears to be carved from a single piece of stone, though it's no heavier than a normal weapon. But it hits your enemies like a battering ram.

Lvl 1	+1	360 gp	Lvl 16	+4	45,000 gp
Lvl 6	+2	1,800 gp	Lvl 21	+5	225,000 gp
Lvl 11	+3	9,000 gp	Lvl 26	+6	1,125,000 gp

Weapon: Hammer
Enhancement: Attack rolls and damage rolls
Critical: The target is knocked prone.

Echoing Songblade — Level 4+

The echoes of your spells reverberate in the blade, hoping to be unleashed.

Lvl 4	+1	840 gp	Lvl 19	+4	105,000 gp
Lvl 9	+2	4,200 gp	Lvl 24	+5	525,000 gp
Lvl 14	+3	21,000 gp	Lvl 29	+6	2,625,000 gp

Weapon: Heavy blade, light blade
Enhancement: Attack rolls and damage rolls
Critical: +1d6 damage per plus, and if the attack was a bard encounter power, you can use that power one more time on your next turn against a single target with a -2 penalty to the attack roll (you must still use the appropriate action to use the power).
Property: Bards can use this weapon as an implement for bard powers and bard paragon path powers.

Entrapping Weapon — Level 2+

An arrow fired from this weapon keeps your enemy from wandering off.

Lvl 2	+1	520 gp	Lvl 17	+4	65,000 gp
Lvl 7	+2	2,600 gp	Lvl 22	+5	325,000 gp
Lvl 12	+3	13,000 gp	Lvl 27	+6	1,625,000 gp

Weapon: Bow, crossbow
Enhancement: Attack rolls and damage rolls
Critical: +1d6 damage per plus, or the target is restrained until the end of your next turn.

Farbond Spellblade — Level 2+

When bonded to you, this spellblade returns to your hand faster and from farther distances.

Lvl 2	+1	520 gp	Lvl 17	+4	65,000 gp
Lvl 7	+2	2,600 gp	Lvl 22	+5	325,000 gp
Lvl 12	+3	13,000 gp	Lvl 27	+6	1,625,000 gp

Weapon: Heavy blade, light blade
Enhancement: Attack rolls and damage rolls
Critical: +1d6 damage per plus, or +1d8 per plus when used as an implement for an arcane power
Property: This weapon can be used as a heavy thrown weapon with a range of 5/10. If you have the Swordbond class feature, you can call this weapon to your hand from up to a mile away.

Flesh Grinder — Level 3+

This weapon screeches as its serrated edge bites through flesh, bone, and steel.

Lvl 3	+1	680 gp	Lvl 18	+4	85,000 gp
Lvl 8	+2	3,400 gp	Lvl 23	+5	425,000 gp
Lvl 13	+3	17,000 gp	Lvl 28	+6	2,125,000 gp

Weapon: Axe, heavy blade, polearm
Enhancement: Attack rolls and damage rolls
Critical: +1d10 damage per plus
Power (Daily): Free Action. *Trigger:* You make an attack with this weapon that targets AC. *Effect:* The triggering attack targets Fortitude instead and deals 1d6 extra damage on a hit.
Level 13 or 18: 2d6 extra damage.
Level 23 or 28: 3d6 extra damage.

FARBOND SPELLBLADE

There's an ancient story about a war between an enclave of eladrin and a kingdom of dragonborn. Much of the war is forgotten, and its cause is obscured by allusion and misinformation, but how it ends is the stuff of legend.

During the last days of the war, an eladrin prince and his escort approached the dragonborn king's fortress and called for parley. The prince claimed to have the authority to negotiate a stalemate that would restore the peace and the borders before the war. The king invited the eladrin embassy into his fortress. Once inside, the eladrin were assaulted, blinded, and thrown into the dungeon.

The dragonborn king had hoped to ransom the prince's life for political gain, but the prince and his fellow prisoners arranged their own "ransom" the first night. The prince and his companions, all elite swordmages trained in the art of blind fighting, called their *farbond spellblades* from beyond the walls of the fortress and fought their way free. The treacherous dragonborn king didn't survive the night.

Benefit of Membership: A conclave of swordmages connected to the local wizards' college grants a *farbond spellblade* to each new member as a symbol of acceptance. Membership isn't easily gained. Applicants must first prove their worth by passing three tests and accomplishing at least one great deed chosen by the masters of the college.

A Strange Find: Rumors say that if you search the grounds around a tyrant's castle, you might find a *farbond spellblade* secreted behind a bush or under a rock.

Hideous weapon

Frost Fury Waraxe — Level 3+

When this weapon's wielder is bloodied, the axe blade becomes icy and promises a cold death with each swing.

Lvl 3	+1	680 gp	Lvl 18	+4	85,000 gp
Lvl 8	+2	3,400 gp	Lvl 23	+5	425,000 gp
Lvl 13	+3	17,000 gp	Lvl 28	+6	2,125,000 gp

Weapon: Axe
Enhancement: Attack rolls and damage rolls
Critical: +1d6 cold damage per plus, or +1d10 cold damage per plus while you're bloodied
Property: While you're bloodied, this axe deals extra cold damage equal to your Constitution modifier.

Great Hunger Weapon — Level 3+

This weapon's normal low keening tones build into a great howl when it engages in battle.

Lvl 3	+1	680 gp	Lvl 18	+4	85,000 gp
Lvl 8	+2	3,400 gp	Lvl 23	+5	425,000 gp
Lvl 13	+3	17,000 gp	Lvl 28	+6	2,125,000 gp

Weapon: Any melee
Enhancement: Attack rolls and damage rolls
Critical: +1d8 damage per plus
Property: When you score a critical hit using this weapon scores, the damage of the next critical hit you score with this weapon increases by 1[W]. This effect is cumulative until the end of the encounter.
Power (Daily): Immediate Reaction. *Trigger:* An enemy adjacent to you scores a critical hit against you. *Effect:* Roll this weapon's critical damage dice (including any extra damage from the weapon's property) and deal that much damage to the triggering enemy.

KIERAN YANNER

FLESH GRINDER

A horrific weapon created from nightmare, the *flesh grinder* is alive with malevolence, filled with an unspeakable thirst for blood and flesh. A *flesh grinder* has the general shape and size of an ordinary weapon of its make, but in place of a smooth cutting edge, it has a toothy row of jagged barbs. Old blood mixed with dark grease oozes from the barbs, and when the weapon is swung in battle, the serrated edge rocks back and forth to chew through flesh and bone, spewing noxious smoke into the air.

Flesh grinder weapons were born in the bowels of the Abyss, fashioned by demonic hands and infused with all the hate, bile, and violence bubbling up from that dire realm. The demons hoped to use these weapons to cut through the eldritch chains binding a forgotten god long confined to the plane's shadowy depths. Some believe that the *flesh grinders* in the world are remnants of the ancient demonic weapons, and even those fashioned by mortal hands are in fact the demon-created weapons reborn in form. Legend holds that when a certain number (the exact quantity is lost to history) of *flesh grinder* weapons are recovered, the chains binding the dark god will loosen and unleash an evil the world has never before seen.

Defeat the Twisted Spiral Cult: The Chained God locked away in the Abyss has numerous cults and servants in the mortal world, many of which assume a variety of names and attribute innumerable personas to the Chained God, each more frightful and insane than the last. Cults devoted to this fallen god seek items associated with his dread name and prize the *flesh grinder* as a physical symbol of their deity's malicious intent against those who stand against his designs. Finding and eliminating one of these cults is bound to reveal a *flesh grinder* weapon.

Navigate the Endless Maze: Baphomet rules the Endless Maze in the Abyss, a near-infinite layer of tunnels, passages, traps, and horrors, each of which lie in wait to snatch a hapless traveler and subject him to indescribable torments. Simply surviving the Endless Maze is an achievement in its own right, but actually navigating its tricks, traps, and guardians provides a nearly certain means to obtain all sorts of sinister items, including a *flesh grinder*. This said, such weapons are rarely left lying about, and adventurers will likely have to pry them from the cold, dead fingers of their previous owners.

Guardian's Brand | Level 3+

This weapon burns white with hatred when it's near a warden's marked enemy.

Lvl 3	+1	680 gp	Lvl 18	+4	85,000 gp
Lvl 8	+2	3,400 gp	Lvl 23	+5	425,000 gp
Lvl 13	+3	17,000 gp	Lvl 28	+6	2,125,000 gp

Weapon: Any melee

Enhancement: Attack rolls and damage rolls

Critical: +1d6 fire damage, or +1d10 fire damage while you're in a guardian form

Power (Daily ✦ Fire): Free Action. *Trigger:* You hit an enemy with your *warden's fury* power using this weapon. *Effect:* That enemy takes ongoing fire damage equal to 5 + your Strength modifier.
Level 13 or 18: Ongoing fire damage equal to 10 + your Strength modifier.
Level 23 or 28: Ongoing fire damage equal to 15 + your Strength modifier.

Guardian's Call | Level 2+

Decorated with the sigils of the wind and the oak, this weapon increases your defenses while you're in your guardian form.

Lvl 2	+1	520 gp	Lvl 17	+4	65,000 gp
Lvl 7	+2	2,600 gp	Lvl 22	+5	325,000 gp
Lvl 12	+3	13,000 gp	Lvl 27	+6	1,625,000 gp

Weapon: Any melee

Enhancement: Attack rolls and damage rolls

Critical: +1d6 damage per plus, or +1d10 damage per plus while you're in a guardian form

Property: When you assume a guardian form, pick one defense other than AC. You gain a +2 bonus to that defense while you're in that guardian form.

Harmonic Songblade | Level 2+

As well as channeling your bard spells, this blade gives off music that swirls away to encircle and empower one of your allies.

Lvl 2	+1	520 gp	Lvl 17	+4	65,000 gp
Lvl 7	+2	2,600 gp	Lvl 22	+5	325,000 gp
Lvl 12	+3	13,000 gp	Lvl 27	+6	1,625,000 gp

Weapon: Heavy blade, light blade

Enhancement: Attack rolls and damage rolls

Critical: +1d6 damage per plus

Property: Bards can use this weapon as an implement for bard powers and bard paragon path powers.

Power (Daily): Minor Action. One ally within 5 squares of you gains a +2 power bonus to attack rolls and all defenses until the start of your next turn.

Hideous Weapon | Level 8+

The only thing that looks worse than this ugly weapon is your enemy when you're done with it.

Lvl 8	+2	3,400 gp	Lvl 23	+5	425,000 gp
Lvl 13	+3	17,000 gp	Lvl 28	+6	2,125,000 gp
Lvl 18	+4	85,000 gp			

Weapon: Flail, hammer, pick

Enhancement: Attack rolls and damage rolls

Critical: +1d6 damage per plus

Property: You gain an item bonus to Intimidate checks equal to this weapon's enhancement bonus.

Power (Daily ✦ Fear, Weapon): Free Action. *Trigger:* You use this weapon to reduce an enemy to 0 hit points. *Effect:* You make an attack against each enemy in a close burst 2: Charisma + 2 + the weapon's enhancement bonus vs. Will; on a hit, the target takes a –2 penalty to attack rolls and if the target ends its turn in a square adjacent to you, it becomes dazed until the end of its next turn (save ends both).

Impaler's Pick   Level 4+

This barbed weapon can leave a short-lived magical replica of itself in your enemy to keep it pinned down.

Lvl 4	+1	840 gp	Lvl 19	+4	105,000 gp
Lvl 9	+2	4,200 gp	Lvl 24	+5	525,000 gp
Lvl 14	+3	21,000 gp	Lvl 29	+6	2,625,000 gp

Weapon: Pick
Enhancement: Attack rolls and damage rolls
Critical: +1d6 damage per plus, and the target is restrained by a magical duplicate of this weapon (save ends).
Aftereffect: 10 damage.
Level 14 or 19: Aftereffect: 15 damage.
Level 24 or 29: Aftereffect: 20 damage.

Incisive Dagger   Level 9+

You cut through space as easily as you cut through flesh.

Lvl 9	+2	4,200 gp	Lvl 24	+5	525,000 gp
Lvl 14	+3	21,000 gp	Lvl 29	+6	2,625,000 gp
Lvl 19	+4	105,000 gp			

Weapon: Dagger
Enhancement: Attack rolls and damage rolls
Critical: +1d6 damage per plus
Property: You can use this weapon as a focus when performing a travel ritual that involves creating and moving through portals. You can add the dagger's enhancement bonus as an item bonus to any skill checks related to the ritual's performance.
Property: When you use a teleportation power, the distance you can teleport increases by a number of squares equal to the dagger's enhancement bonus.
Power (Daily ✦ Teleportation): Minor Action. You teleport 5 squares.
Level 14 or 19: 10 squares.
Level 24 or 29: 10 squares, and you don't need to be able to see the destination square.

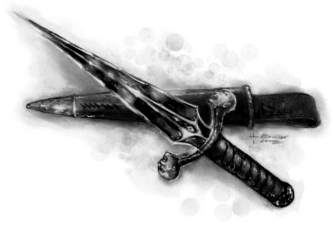

Incisive dagger

INCISIVE DAGGER

This stiletto's blue-black blade is razor-sharp and extends from a guard that resembles two screaming faces twisted in pain. The handle is short, as if designed for a small hand, and bloodstained leather covers its cold steel. The pommel is a smooth orb of black stone with golden flecks that glitter in the moonlight.

Modeled on a more powerful knife said to be able to cut through anything, the *incisive dagger* lacks that famed blade's superior cutting ability. It does help its wielder move through space and access different portals.

Defeat the Ghost Thief: In the hands of the wrong person, an *incisive dagger* can prove an invaluable tool for criminal enterprises. Such a weapon came into the possession of an ambitious thief whose exploits earned her the moniker "Ghost Thief." The authorities have no clues to how the elusive thief manages her daring crimes, because no one has ever spotted her and no security measure has proved secure enough to stop her. But someone must know something, since there is general agreement that the Ghost Thief is a female.

Intensifying Weapon   Level 4+

This weapon blazes with inner power that enhances your ongoing effects.

Lvl 4	+1	840 gp	Lvl 19	+4	105,000 gp
Lvl 9	+2	4,200 gp	Lvl 24	+5	525,000 gp
Lvl 14	+3	21,000 gp	Lvl 29	+6	2,625,000 gp

Weapon: Any
Enhancement: Attack rolls and damage rolls
Critical: +1d6 damage per plus, or +1d10 damage per plus on attacks that deal ongoing damage
Property: When you use this weapon to hit with an attack that deals ongoing damage, the ongoing damage increases by an amount equal to the weapon's enhancement bonus.

Master's Blade   Level 4+

Seemingly impossible feats are possible for master warriors, and for those who wield this perfectly designed weapon.

Lvl 4	+1	840 gp	Lvl 19	+4	105,000 gp
Lvl 9	+2	4,200 gp	Lvl 24	+5	525,000 gp
Lvl 14	+3	21,000 gp	Lvl 29	+6	2,625,000 gp

Weapon: Heavy blade, light blade
Enhancement: Attack rolls and damage rolls
Critical: +1d6 damage per plus
Property: While you're using a stance power, you gain a +1 bonus to attack rolls on melee basic attacks and at-will attacks with this weapon.
Power (Daily): Minor Action. Until the end of the encounter, while you wield this weapon, you can have two stances active at the same time.

Maw of the Guardian   Level 4+

Engraved with the primal rune of the devourer, this weapon increases your damage while you're in a guardian form.

Lvl 4	+1	840 gp	Lvl 19	+4	105,000 gp
Lvl 9	+2	4,200 gp	Lvl 24	+5	525,000 gp
Lvl 14	+3	21,000 gp	Lvl 29	+6	2,625,000 gp

Weapon: Any melee
Enhancement: Attack rolls and damage rolls
Critical: +1d6 damage per plus
Property: This weapon deals extra damage equal to your Constitution modifier while you're in a guardian form.

ED COX

Quicksilver Blade
Level 2+

This weapon seems to move too quickly to be seen, and it imparts that ability to you.

Lvl 2	+1	520 gp	Lvl 17	+4	65,000 gp
Lvl 7	+2	2,600 gp	Lvl 22	+5	325,000 gp
Lvl 12	+3	13,000 gp	Lvl 27	+6	1,625,000 gp

Weapon: Light blade

Enhancement: Attack rolls and damage rolls

Critical: +1d6 damage per plus

Property: You gain an item bonus to initiative checks equal to the blade's enhancement bonus.

Power (Daily): Free Action. *Trigger:* You score a critical hit with this weapon. *Effect:* You gain a move action that you must use before the end of your turn.

Ravenclaw Warblade
Level 8+

This sword becomes more powerful when its wielder or his enemies are at death's door.

Lvl 8	+2	3,400 gp	Lvl 23	+5	425,000 gp
Lvl 13	+3	17,000 gp	Lvl 28	+6	2,125,000 gp
Lvl 18	+4	85,000 gp			

Weapon: Heavy blade

Enhancement: Attack rolls and damage rolls

Critical: +1d6 damage per plus, or +1d10 damage per plus while you're bloodied

Property: When you use this weapon to reduce a non-minion enemy to 0 hit points, you can either spend a healing surge or make a saving throw.

Rebounding Weapon
Level 2+

You meant to do that. No, really.

Lvl 2	+1	520 gp	Lvl 17	+4	65,000 gp
Lvl 7	+2	2,600 gp	Lvl 22	+5	325,000 gp
Lvl 12	+3	13,000 gp	Lvl 27	+6	1,625,000 gp

Weapon: Any ranged

Enhancement: Attack rolls and damage rolls

Critical: +1d6 damage per plus

Power (Encounter): Free Action. *Trigger:* You attack an enemy with this weapon and miss. *Effect:* You make a ranged basic attack against a different enemy within 5 squares of that enemy.

Runic Weapon
Level 5+

This weapon is engraved with numerous arcane runes and sigils that glow when magical emanations are near.

Lvl 5	+1	1,000 gp	Lvl 20	+4	125,000 gp
Lvl 10	+2	5,000 gp	Lvl 25	+5	625,000 gp
Lvl 15	+3	25,000 gp	Lvl 30	+6	3,125,000 gp

Weapon: Any

Enhancement: Attack rolls and damage rolls

Critical: +1d6 damage per plus

Property: When you hit with an arcane power using this weapon, you gain temporary hit points equal to the weapon's enhancement bonus.

Screaming Bow
Level 4+

What begins as a low moan rises to an earsplitting shriek as the arrow seeks out its mark.

Lvl 4	+1	840 gp	Lvl 19	+4	105,000 gp
Lvl 9	+2	4,200 gp	Lvl 24	+5	525,000 gp
Lvl 14	+3	21,000 gp	Lvl 29	+6	2,625,000 gp

Weapon: Bow

Enhancement: Attack rolls and damage rolls

Critical: +1d6 thunder damage per plus

Property: When you use this weapon to hit an enemy with an attack power that doesn't have a damage type, the attack deals thunder damage, and the enemy is deafened until the end of your next turn.

Power (Daily): Free Action. *Trigger:* You hit an enemy with this weapon. *Effect:* That enemy gains vulnerable 5 thunder (save ends). Each creature adjacent to that enemy is deafened and gains vulnerable 5 thunder until the end of your next turn.

Level 14 or 19: The enemy gains vulnerable 10 thunder (save ends).

Level 24 or 29: The enemy gains vulnerable 20 thunder (save ends).

Shadowrift Blade
Level 12+

You can pass through the Shadowfell to a nearby location when you use this blade, but doing so costs you a bit of your life force.

| Lvl 12 | +3 | 13,000 gp | Lvl 22 | +5 | 325,000 gp |
| Lvl 17 | +4 | 65,000 gp | Lvl 27 | +6 | 1,625,000 gp |

Weapon: Light blade

Enhancement: Attack rolls and damage rolls

Critical: +1d6 damage per plus

Power (At-Will ✦ Teleportation): Free Action. *Trigger:* You hit an enemy that is granting you combat advantage. *Effect:* You take 5 damage and teleport 2 squares.

Level 17 or 22: Take 10 damage and teleport 3 squares.

Level 27: Take 15 damage and teleport 4 squares.

Shrieking Songbow
Level 13+

The sound of unbridled fear travels along with each of your shots.

| Lvl 13 | +3 | 17,000 gp | Lvl 23 | +5 | 425,000 gp |
| Lvl 18 | +4 | 85,000 gp | Lvl 28 | +6 | 2,125,000 gp |

Weapon: Bow, crossbow

Enhancement: Attack rolls and damage rolls

Critical: +1d6 damage per plus

Property: Bards can use this weapon as an implement for bard powers and bard paragon path powers.

Power (Daily ✦ Fear): Free Action. *Trigger:* You hit an enemy with a bard attack power using this weapon. *Effect:* That enemy moves a number of squares away from you equal to your Charisma modifier, avoiding opportunity attacks and unsafe squares if possible.

Screaming bow

SCREAMING BOW

Assembled from overlapping pieces of yew, lemonwood, horn, and other materials bound together with *sovereign glue*, a *screaming bow* would pass for any other high-quality longbow except for the silver eagle talons mounted at either end to hold its golden bowstring taut. Arrows fitted onto the string and drawn are transformed, the arrowhead stretching and contorting into the likeness of a screaming eagle's head. Once the arrow flies, it sounds a high-pitched screech that grows louder the closer it comes to its target until suddenly becoming silent on impact.

Each *screaming bow* is said to contain a soul fragment from an elf warrior slain in battle, who, through Corellon's grace, was given another chance to carry on the lifelong struggle against his or her people's enemies. Only those chosen to reside in Arvandor with their god can provide a portion of their soul to reside within a *screaming bow*, and then only when the bow is fashioned by an eladrin or elf mage.

Aerie of Griffons: Local legend claims that a band of heroes ascended into the mountains to assault a mountain fastness and defeat a tyrannical giant who dwelled there. Of those who ascended, none returned, but tales are still told around hearths about these lost heroes and the *screaming bow* that one of them possessed.

Avenge the Elven People: Orcs, goblins, and other despicable humanoids wage war against the sylvan folk in both the mortal world and the Feywild beyond. Many communities see to their own defenses and resent interference from outsiders, but a hero who proves herself an ally and fights in the name of good folk might gain a *screaming bow* as a token of friendship.

Songbow of Lullabies — Level 9+

The projectile fired from this weapon sings softly in a voice that its target finds most soothing.

Lvl 9	+2	4,200 gp	Lvl 24	+5	525,000 gp
Lvl 14	+3	21,000 gp	Lvl 29	+6	2,625,000 gp
Lvl 19	+4	105,000 gp			

Weapon: Bow, crossbow
Enhancement: Attack rolls and damage rolls
Critical: +1d6 damage per plus
Property: Bards can use this weapon as an implement for bard powers and bard paragon path powers.
Power (Daily ✦ Charm): Free Action. *Trigger:* You hit an enemy with a bard charm power using this weapon. *Effect:* That enemy is slowed (save ends). *First Failed Saving Throw:* The enemy is immobilized (save ends). *Second Failed Saving Throw:* The enemy is knocked unconscious (save ends).

Songbow of Summoning — Level 15+

When this weapon fires, an ancient paean sung by conquering peoples rings out and calls your allies in for the kill.

| Lvl 15 | +3 | 25,000 gp | Lvl 25 | +5 | 625,000 gp |
| Lvl 20 | +4 | 125,000 gp | Lvl 30 | +6 | 3,125,000 gp |

Weapon: Bow, crossbow
Enhancement: Attack rolls and damage rolls
Critical: +1d6 damage per plus
Property: Bards can use this weapon as an implement for bard powers and bard paragon path powers.
Power (Daily ✦ Teleportation): Free Action. *Trigger:* You hit an enemy with a bard power using this weapon. *Effect:* Each ally within 5 squares of you or within 5 squares of that enemy can teleport to a square adjacent to the enemy as a free action.

CHRIS SEAMAN

Songbow of Vanishment — Level 3+

Your magic whispers in the minds of your foes, convincing them you're elsewhere.

Lvl 3	+1	680 gp	Lvl 18	+4	85,000 gp
Lvl 8	+2	3,400 gp	Lvl 23	+5	425,000 gp
Lvl 13	+3	17,000 gp	Lvl 28	+6	2,125,000 gp

Weapon: Bow, crossbow

Enhancement: Attack rolls and damage rolls

Critical: +1d6 damage per plus

Property: Bards can use this weapon as an implement for bard powers and bard paragon path powers.

Power (Daily ✦ Illusion): Free Action. *Trigger:* You hit an enemy with a bard power using this weapon. *Effect:* You're invisible to that enemy until the end of your next turn.

Soul Drinker Weapon — Level 14+

If this weapon doesn't make a kill, it takes its frustration out on you.

| Lvl 14 | +3 | 21,000 gp | Lvl 24 | +5 | 525,000 gp |
| Lvl 19 | +4 | 105,000 gp | Lvl 29 | +6 | 2,625,000 gp |

Weapon: Any melee

Enhancement: Attack rolls and damage rolls

Critical: +1d6 necrotic damage per plus

Power (Encounter ✦ Necrotic): Free Action. *Trigger:* You hit an enemy with this weapon. *Effect:* You deal 2d10 extra necrotic damage to that enemy. If this hit doesn't reduce the enemy to 0 hit points, you take 2d12 damage.

Level 24 or 29: Deal 3d10 necrotic damage, and take 3d12 damage if the hit doesn't reduce the enemy to 0 hit points.

Space-Bending Weapon — Level 19+

This weapon always seems farther away than it actually is.

| Lvl 19 | +4 | 105,000 gp | Lvl 29 | +6 | 2,625,000 gp |
| Lvl 24 | +5 | 525,000 gp | | | |

Weapon: Heavy blade, light blade

Enhancement: Attack rolls and damage rolls

Critical: +1d6 damage per plus

Power (Daily): Minor Action. The next enemy you target with this weapon can be up to 5 squares away from you; you attack that enemy as if you were adjacent to it.

Level 24 or 29: Up to 10 squares away.

Stormbiter Warblade — Level 4+

Glistening with electric-blue eldritch energy, this weapon's blade packs a stormy punch.

Lvl 4	+1	840 gp	Lvl 19	+4	105,000 gp
Lvl 9	+2	4,200 gp	Lvl 24	+5	525,000 gp
Lvl 14	+3	21,000 gp	Lvl 29	+6	2,625,000 gp

Weapon: Heavy blade, light blade

Enhancement: Attack rolls and damage rolls

Critical: +1d6 thunder and lightning damage per plus

Power (Daily ✦ Lightning): Free Action. *Trigger:* You hit an enemy with a lightning power or a thunder power using this weapon. *Effect:* That enemy is knocked prone. It's also deafened and takes ongoing 5 lightning damage (save ends both).

Level 14 or 19: Deafened and ongoing 10 lightning damage (save ends both).

Level 24 or 29: Deafened and ongoing 15 lightning damage (save ends both).

Shadowrift blade

SHADOWRIFT BLADE

Eladrin and even some elves consider it distasteful—almost taboo—to carry a *shadowrift blade*. The reason for this prohibition is unclear, because no three eladrin can agree on it.

Some claim that the blades are treacherous gifts of the drow. Others that the strange gray-green metal of the weapons comes from a corner of the Far Realm where time and space conspire to produce spiraling insanity. And a few hint that the secrets of making *shadowrift blades* were given to the eladrin by an exarch of Gruumsh.

Whatever origin one might favor, eladrin sages and elders agree that these weapons are somehow cursed or corrupted, existing only to bleed the Shadowfell into the Feywild. To those who use a *shadowrift blade*, the eladrin's claims serve as the only evidence for any taint.

Zerth's New Blade: A rogue githzerai zerth has been tormenting a small, peaceful settlement. The leader of the town describes the powerful teleporting sword the zerth wields and promises that the blade's value alone is worth the effort of getting rid of his githzerai problem.

Save My Daughter (the Hard Way): An eladrin scholar is worried about her daughter, an errant swordmage. She has picked up a *shadowrift blade* to aid in her endeavors, ignoring her people's concerns about such weapons. The scholar is looking for someone to convince her daughter to give up the blade and is afraid that a sword duel—a combat in which the winner takes the sword of the vanquished—might be the only way.

THOMAS DENMARK

Stormbiter warblade

Targeting Weapon — Level 3+

When the bolt flies from your weapon, it shows the way to victory.

Lvl 3	+1	680 gp	Lvl 18	+4	85,000 gp
Lvl 8	+2	3,400 gp	Lvl 23	+5	425,000 gp
Lvl 13	+3	17,000 gp	Lvl 28	+6	2,125,000 gp

Weapon: Bow, crossbow

Enhancement: Attack rolls and damage rolls

Critical: +1d6 damage per plus, and the target grants combat advantage until the end of your next turn.

Power (Daily): Free Action. *Trigger:* You hit an enemy with an attack using this weapon. *Effect:* Until the end of your next turn, you and your allies can roll twice on attack rolls against that enemy and use either result.

Totemic Spear — Level 2+

This spear's power extends into the spirit world.

Lvl 2	+1	520 gp	Lvl 17	+4	65,000 gp
Lvl 7	+2	2,600 gp	Lvl 22	+5	325,000 gp
Lvl 12	+3	13,000 gp	Lvl 27	+6	1,625,000 gp

Weapon: Spear

Enhancement: Attack rolls and damage rolls

Critical: +1d6 damage per plus

Property: Shamans can use this weapon as an implement for shaman powers and shaman paragon path powers.

Property: You can target any enemy within 2 squares of your spirit companion with attacks that have a range of "Melee spirit."

Supreme Skirmisher's Bow — Level 10+

Perfectly balanced and blessed with powers that help shape each of your motions, this bow allows you to fight with unmatched grace.

Lvl 10	+2	5,000 gp	Lvl 25	+5	625,000 gp
Lvl 15	+3	25,000 gp	Lvl 30	+6	3,125,000 gp
Lvl 20	+4	125,000 gp			

Weapon: Bow

Enhancement: Attack rolls and damage rolls

Critical: +1d6 damage per plus

Power (Encounter): Free Action. *Trigger:* You make a ranged basic attack using this weapon. *Effect:* You make a ranged at-will attack using this weapon instead.

Supremely Vicious Weapon — Level 2+

Pure lethality.

Lvl 2	+1	520 gp	Lvl 17	+4	65,000 gp
Lvl 7	+2	2,600 gp	Lvl 22	+5	325,000 gp
Lvl 12	+3	13,000 gp	Lvl 27	+6	1,625,000 gp

Weapon: Any

Enhancement: Attack rolls and damage rolls

Critical: +1d8 damage per plus, and you can choose to reroll any or all of your critical damage dice, but you must take the second result of each die.

STORMBITER WARBLADE

Heur-Ket, a vicious primordial of gale and thunder, was defeated in the first war, but echoes of the primordial's howling winds live on. The primordial's essence was scattered throughout the world, the Shadowfell, and the Feywild.

According to the histories and legends of early empires, certain locations retained Heur-Ket's stormy nature. Weapons created near those locations became infused with the primordial's essence, becoming the first *stormbiter warblades*. Now the formula for making these weapons is commonly known, but the most potent of them are those first made after Heur-Ket's fall at a site where the entity's essence collected, or those crafted using a piece of one of the original weapons as a focus for the ritual.

Artificer's Endeavor: Artificers and others interested in the creation of magic weapons are always on the look-out for fragments of the original *stormbiter warblades*, or for a location where Heur-Ket's essence is present. Often they purchase this information with the promise of a weapon crafted from Heur-Ket's power.

Forge of the Landfall: Deep in the Feywild's Under-dark is a cyclops forge built on a site containing Heur-Ket's essence. The cyclopes are difficult to deal with and stingy with their creations, so the Court of Stars often commissions raids to plunder the site, and even provides teleportation magic to aid in these raids.

KIERAN YANNER

Totemic Warclub · Level 2+

Some of the power invested in your spirit companion also flows through this warclub.

Lvl 2	+1	520 gp	Lvl 17	+4	65,000 gp
Lvl 7	+2	2,600 gp	Lvl 22	+5	325,000 gp
Lvl 12	+3	13,000 gp	Lvl 27	+6	1,625,000 gp

Weapon: Mace
Enhancement: Attack rolls and damage rolls
Critical: +1d6 damage per plus
Property: Shamans can use this weapon as an implement for shaman powers and shaman paragon path powers.
Property: When you use this weapon as an implement for a power that has a range of "Melee spirit," you can choose to use your square as the origin square of the power.

Unforgettable Cudgel · Level 8+

A well-placed strike with this mace goes a long way toward showing an enemy the error of its ways.

Lvl 8	+2	3,400 gp	Lvl 23	+5	425,000 gp
Lvl 13	+3	17,000 gp	Lvl 28	+6	2,125,000 gp
Lvl 18	+4	85,000 gp			

Weapon: Mace
Enhancement: Attack rolls and damage rolls
Critical: +1d6 damage per plus, or the target is dazed (save ends)
Property: Divine characters can use this mace as a holy symbol implement for divine powers.
Property: You can score a critical hit with this weapon on a roll of 19-20 when it is used as a weapon or an implement for a divine melee attack power.

Weapon of Oaths Fulfilled · Level 4+

As your weapon slays your deity's enemy, you feel a surge of vitality that allows you to keep fighting.

Lvl 4	+1	840 gp	Lvl 19	+4	105,000 gp
Lvl 9	+2	4,200 gp	Lvl 24	+5	525,000 gp
Lvl 14	+3	21,000 gp	Lvl 29	+6	2,625,000 gp

Weapon: Any melee
Enhancement: Attack rolls and damage rolls
Critical: +1d6 damage per plus
Property: Avengers can use this weapon as an implement for avenger powers and avenger paragon path powers.
Property: When you reduce the target of your *oath of enmity* to 0 hit points, the next attack you make with this weapon before the end of your next turn deals 1d6 extra damage per plus.

Whistling Songbow · Level 2+

Projectiles launched from this weapon whistle as they streak toward their target.

Lvl 2	+1	520 gp	Lvl 17	+4	65,000 gp
Lvl 7	+2	2,600 gp	Lvl 22	+5	325,000 gp
Lvl 12	+3	13,000 gp	Lvl 27	+6	1,625,000 gp

Weapon: Bow, crossbow
Enhancement: Attack rolls and damage rolls
Critical: +1d6 damage per plus
Property: Bards can use this weapon as an implement for bard powers and bard paragon path powers.
Power (Daily): Free Action. *Trigger:* You attack an enemy with a bard attack power using this weapon. *Effect:* Each ally within 5 squares of that enemy gains a +2 power bonus to attack rolls against the enemy until the end of your next turn.

UNFORGETTABLE CUDGEL

An *unforgettable cudgel* features a sturdy haft cut from hickory and wrapped with red cord around a handle capped in iron wrought to resemble a stern face with a spadelike beard. The business end is a flanged mace head capped with a smoothed, convex steel ferrule. Each flange forms a wedge-shaped point, and there are seven flanges in all.

The weapon is fashioned as a religious icon in the image of a weapon wielded by an ancient saint, a righteous servant of the gods who fought against tyranny and injustice and sought the rule of divine law. It contains a portion of his holy essence, making it a highly sought-after item by divine servants the world over. Clerics and other divine heroes seek out the *unforgettable cudgel* for its ability to pass divine judgment by reminding those it strikes of their past crimes and wicked deeds. Few have the courage to withstand such a psychic assault.

Atonement: The gods of order and goodness sometimes bestow holy objects to those who have walked the road of shadow and resisted its temptations, returning to the light with all the fervor of the most devoted paladins. It takes a great act of self-sacrifice and penance for the gods to bequeath such an item, but those who truly and deeply atone might find themselves gifted with an icon such as an *unforgettable cudgel*.

Writhing Vine Weapon · Level 8+

Living vines writhe and constrict around this weapon when it's at rest, but they grasp at and harry your foes with each swing.

Lvl 8	+2	3,400 gp	Lvl 23	+5	425,000 gp
Lvl 13	+3	17,000 gp	Lvl 28	+6	2,125,000 gp
Lvl 18	+4	85,000 gp			

Weapon: Any melee
Enhancement: Attack rolls and damage rolls
Critical: +1d6 damage per plus
Property: When you immobilize a target with a melee attack using this weapon, that target grants combat advantage to you until the end of your next turn.
Power (Daily): Minor Action. Make an attack: Close burst 3; target one enemy in burst; Constitution + this weapon's enhancement bonus vs. Fortitude; on a hit, you pull that enemy 3 squares.

AMMUNITION

The effectiveness of a ranged weapon depends on aim, but don't discount its payload.

Enchanted arrows, bolts, and sling bullets can be activated and fired from ranged weapons to achieve exceptional results. You must load magic ammunition before you can activate and fire it (spending whatever action is necessary to do so), and it's used up when fired. When used with powers that target multiple enemies, magic ammunition affects only the first attack roll or target after it's loaded. In certain circumstances (such as when loading is a free action), however, a ranged attacker can load more magic ammunition during an attack against multiple targets if desired.

Ammunition applies an enhancement bonus to an attack roll and damage roll when used. If the projectile weapon is magical, use the ammunition's enhancement bonus in place of the weapon's enhancement bonus. The weapon's critical bonus and the properties from both the weapon and the ammunition still apply. Using magic ammunition doesn't prevent you from activating a magic weapon's powers.

You can fire magic ammunition without activating it, using your weapon's enhancement bonus and receiving no benefit from the ammunition's magic. The ammunition is still expended.

Ammunition names are keyed to certain ammunition types, but any of the enchantments described in this section can be placed on any type of ammunition; for instance, it's possible to create or acquire an arrow or a sling bullet that has the attributes of a *bolt of clumsiness*.

Arrow of Revelation | Level 9+
Ioun's eye marks this bright yellow arrow.

Lvl 9	+2	160 gp	Lvl 24	+5	21,000 gp
Lvl 14	+3	800 gp	Lvl 29	+6	105,000 gp
Lvl 19	+4	4,200 gp			

Ammunition
Enhancement: Attack rolls and damage rolls
Property: When you hit an enemy with an attack using this ammunition, that enemy doesn't benefit from invisibility until the end of your next turn.

Attention-Stealing Bullet | Level 3+
This bright red sling stone draws your target's immediate attention.

Lvl 3	+1	30 gp	Lvl 18	+4	3,400 gp
Lvl 8	+2	125 gp	Lvl 23	+5	17,000 gp
Lvl 13	+3	650 gp	Lvl 28	+6	85,000 gp

Ammunition
Enhancement: Attack rolls and damage rolls
Property: When you hit an enemy with an attack using this ammunition, you mark that enemy until the end of its next turn. While marked by you in this manner, when the enemy makes an attack that doesn't include you as a target, the ammunition strikes that target again for 1d6 damage per plus.

Bending Bullet | Level 5+
Whisper a direction to this warped bullet, and it bends around obstacles.

Lvl 5	+1	50 gp	Lvl 20	+4	5,000 gp
Lvl 10	+2	200 gp	Lvl 25	+5	25,000 gp
Lvl 15	+3	1,000 gp	Lvl 30	+6	125,000 gp

Ammunition
Enhancement: Attack rolls and damage rolls
Property: While you have line of effect to a square adjacent to an enemy, you can attack that enemy using this ammunition. Treat the enemy as having cover.

Bolt of Clumsiness | Level 8+
A victim of this malformed quarrel is too ungainly to avoid inviting attacks.

Lvl 8	+2	125 gp	Lvl 23	+5	17,000 gp
Lvl 13	+3	650 gp	Lvl 28	+6	85,000 gp
Lvl 18	+4	3,400 gp			

Ammunition
Enhancement: Attack rolls and damage rolls
Property: When you hit an enemy with an attack using this ammunition, that enemy can't shift until the end of its next turn.

Bolt of Transit | Level 8+
Use this lightning-shaped bolt to move closer to your target.

Lvl 8	+2	125 gp	Lvl 23	+5	17,000 gp
Lvl 13	+3	650 gp	Lvl 28	+6	85,000 gp
Lvl 18	+4	3,400 gp			

Ammunition
Enhancement: Attack rolls and damage rolls
Property: When you hit an enemy with an attack using this ammunition, you can teleport to a space adjacent to that enemy.

Dispelling Bolt | Level 8+
This flat-black quarrel extinguishes conjurations and zones.

Lvl 8	+2	125 gp	Lvl 23	+5	17,000 gp
Lvl 13	+3	650 gp	Lvl 28	+6	85,000 gp
Lvl 18	+4	3,400 gp			

Ammunition
Enhancement: Attack rolls and damage rolls
Property: When you hit an enemy with an attack using this ammunition, you can end one conjuration or zone that enemy has created.

Firestorm Arrow | Level 3+
The charred wood of this arrow seems to shimmer with heat.

Lvl 3	+1	30 gp	Lvl 18	+4	3,400 gp
Lvl 8	+2	125 gp	Lvl 23	+5	17,000 gp
Lvl 13	+3	650 gp	Lvl 28	+6	85,000 gp

Ammunition
Enhancement: Attack rolls and damage rolls
Property: When you hit an enemy with an attack using this ammunition, that enemy and each creature adjacent to it take 1d6 extra fire damage per plus.

Forbiddance Bolt | Level 9+
Teleportation becomes more difficult when this bolt strikes its mark.

Lvl 9	+2	160 gp	Lvl 24	+5	21,000 gp
Lvl 14	+3	800 gp	Lvl 29	+6	105,000 gp
Lvl 19	+4	4,200 gp			

Ammunition
Enhancement: Attack rolls and damage rolls
Property: When you hit an enemy with an attack using this ammunition, that enemy can't teleport until the end of its next turn, and no creature can teleport to a space within 2 squares of that target until the end of its next turn.

Phasing arrow

Freezing Arrow — Level 3+

The shaft of this arrow is shaved from unmelting ice.

Lvl 3	+1	30 gp	Lvl 18	+4	3,400 gp
Lvl 8	+2	125 gp	Lvl 23	+5	17,000 gp
Lvl 13	+3	650 gp	Lvl 28	+6	85,000 gp

Ammunition

Enhancement: Attack rolls and damage rolls

Property: When you hit an enemy with an attack using this ammunition, that enemy takes 1d6 extra cold damage per plus and is slowed until the end of its next turn.

Lightning Arrow — Level 3+

This arrow's blue and white streaks thrum with energy.

Lvl 3	+1	30 gp	Lvl 18	+4	3,400 gp
Lvl 8	+2	125 gp	Lvl 23	+5	17,000 gp
Lvl 13	+3	650 gp	Lvl 28	+6	85,000 gp

Ammunition

Enhancement: Attack rolls and damage rolls

Property: When you hit an enemy with an attack using this ammunition, that enemy takes 1d6 extra lightning damage per plus and is dazed until the end of its next turn.

Onslaught Arrow — Level 2+

This black arrow trails a bright pennant, flagging its target.

Lvl 2	+1	25 gp	Lvl 17	+4	2,600 gp
Lvl 7	+2	100 gp	Lvl 22	+5	13,000 gp
Lvl 12	+3	500 gp	Lvl 27	+6	65,000 gp

Ammunition

Enhancement: Attack rolls and damage rolls

Property: When you hit an enemy with an attack using this ammunition, each ally that can see that enemy gains a +1 item bonus to attack rolls against it until the end of your next turn.

Phasing Arrow — Level 25+

Ephemeral in flight, this arrow strikes its target solidly.

Lvl 25	+5	25,000 gp	Lvl 30	+6	125,000 gp

Ammunition

Enhancement: Attack rolls and damage rolls

Property: When you attack using this ammunition, you don't need line of effect to the target, and your attack roll takes no penalty from cover or superior cover.

Space-Shifting Bolt — Level 8+

Wrought in an eladrin design, this sizzling bolt teleports those it hits.

Lvl 8	+2	125 gp	Lvl 23	+5	17,000 gp
Lvl 13	+3	650 gp	Lvl 28	+6	85,000 gp
Lvl 18	+4	3,400 gp			

Ammunition

Enhancement: Attack rolls and damage rolls

Property: When you hit an enemy with an attack using this ammunition, you teleport that enemy 1 square.

Spider Bolt — Level 3+

This web-strewn quarrel envelops the enemy when it hits.

Lvl 3	+1	30 gp	Lvl 18	+4	3,400 gp
Lvl 8	+2	125 gp	Lvl 23	+5	17,000 gp
Lvl 13	+3	650 gp	Lvl 28	+6	85,000 gp

Ammunition

Enhancement: Attack rolls and damage rolls

Property: When you hit an enemy with an attack using this ammunition, that enemy and each enemy adjacent to it is slowed until the end of your next turn.

THOMAS DENMARK

Summoning Bullet
Level 8+

Use this magnetic bullet to bring an ally closer to your foe.

Lvl 8	+2	125 gp	Lvl 23	+5	17,000 gp
Lvl 13	+3	650 gp	Lvl 28	+6	85,000 gp
Lvl 18	+4	3,400 gp			

Ammunition

Enhancement: Attack rolls and damage rolls

Property: When you hit an enemy with an attack using this ammunition, one ally within 3 squares of that enemy can teleport to a space adjacent to it.

Surprise Bullet
Level 3+

This winking bullet blinks in and out, so your target can't see it coming.

Lvl 3	+1	30 gp	Lvl 18	+4	3,400 gp
Lvl 8	+2	125 gp	Lvl 23	+5	17,000 gp
Lvl 13	+3	650 gp	Lvl 28	+6	85,000 gp

Ammunition

Enhancement: Attack rolls and damage rolls

Property: When you attack an enemy using this ammunition, that enemy grants combat advantage to you for that attack.

HOLY SYMBOLS

Whatever form it takes, the symbol of a god has power. Of course, an enchanted holy symbol has even more power.

A holy symbol represents your deity and takes the shape of an aspect of the god. Whatever the symbol itself says about its wielder, enchantments are neutral and can be transferred from one holy symbol to another to better suit a new owner (see the Transfer Enchantment ritual, page 199 of *Adventurer's Vault*).

If you are a member of a class that can use a holy symbol as an implement, you can apply the symbol's enhancement bonus to the attack rolls and the damage rolls of any of your powers from that class that have the implement keyword, and you can use a symbol's properties and powers. Members of other classes gain no benefit from wearing or holding a holy symbol.

You can't make melee attacks with a holy symbol.

Unlike other implements, you need only wear a holy symbol for its property or power to function. If you are wearing or holding more than one holy symbol, none of your symbols function.

Convert's Symbol
Level 13

This symbol is a carving of a hand grasping an arcane implement. It allows you to convert some of your arcane power into healing.

Lvl 13	+3	17,000 gp	Lvl 23	+5	425,000 gp
Lvl 18	+4	85,000 gp	Lvl 28	+6	2,125,000 gp

Implement (Holy Symbol)

Enhancement: Attack rolls and damage rolls

Critical: +1d6 damage per plus

Property: Arcane casters can wield this holy symbol in one hand to use it as an implement for arcane powers. Choose the type of arcane implement when the symbol is created.

Power (Daily ✦ Healing): Minor Action. You expend an arcane daily attack power. One ally you can see within 10 squares of you regains hit points as though he or she had spent a healing surge, plus additional hit points equal to the level of the expended power.

Ioun Stone of Divine Knowledge
Level 25+

This amber sphere with a red gem in its center slowly orbits your head, leaving a trail of twinkling golden lights.

Lvl 25	+5	625,000 gp	Lvl 30	+6	3,125,000 gp

Implement (Holy Symbol)

Item Slot: Head

Enhancement: Attack rolls and damage rolls

Critical: +1d6 damage per plus

Property: Divine characters can use this item as a holy symbol implement for divine powers.

Property: You gain an item bonus to Insight checks and Religion checks equal to the symbol's enhancement bonus, and an item bonus to other Intelligence-based skill checks equal to one-half its enhancement bonus.

Power (Daily): Free Action. *Trigger:* You hit an enemy with a divine attack power using this holy symbol. *Effect:* You learn whether each of the other defenses of that enemy is higher or lower than the defense hit by this attack. In addition, the enemy grants combat advantage (save ends).

Ioun-Blessed Symbol
Level 2+

This symbol, blessed with Ioun's love of knowledge, is a slender length of ivory with only a suggestion of her icon.

Lvl 2	+1	520 gp	Lvl 17	+4	65,000 gp
Lvl 7	+2	2,600 gp	Lvl 22	+5	325,000 gp
Lvl 12	+3	13,000 gp	Lvl 27	+6	1,625,000 gp

Implement (Holy Symbol)

Enhancement: Attack rolls and damage rolls

Critical: +1d8 damage per plus

Property: Arcane characters can wield this holy symbol in one hand to use it as a wand implement for arcane powers.

IOUN STONE OF DIVINE KNOWLEDGE

The most powerful worshipers of Ioun use enchanted floating stones as holy symbols. The small number of these stones that exist in the world were passed down by Ioun herself, and a small fragment of her knowledge permeates each one. Some historians consider them to be the first, or at least the only true, *Ioun stones*.

Become an Exalted Eye: Ioun's most prominent priests are known as the Exalted Eyes of Ioun, and each wears an *Ioun stone of divine knowledge*. A hero who proves his or her valor to Ioun by reclaiming vast stores of lost knowledge or uncovering secrets held by Vecna's followers might be allowed into the ranks of the Exalted Eyes.

Undertake Ioun's Test: Ioun keeps many *Ioun stones of divine knowledge* within her swan tower Kerith-Ald, but they're reserved for only the most worthy and most knowledgeable. One who performs great deeds can earn an audience with Ioun or one of her aspects but must still prove that he or she has earned such a magnificent gift.

Symbol of Branding — Level 12+

As you utter a prayer, this symbol flares to sear your god's icon into the forehead of your foe.

| Lvl 12 | +3 | 13,000 gp | Lvl 22 | +5 | 325,000 gp |
| Lvl 17 | +4 | 65,000 gp | Lvl 27 | +6 | 1,625,000 gp |

Implement (Holy Symbol)
Enhancement: Attack rolls and damage rolls
Critical: +1d6 radiant damage per plus
Power (Daily): Free Action. *Trigger:* You hit an enemy with a divine attack power using this holy symbol. *Effect:* Until the end of the encounter, when that enemy takes radiant damage from your *divine challenge* or divine sanction, it takes 5 extra radiant damage.
Level 22 or 27: 10 extra radiant damage.

Symbol of Brawn — Level 3+

Physical strength and holy devotion are both enhanced by this adamantine holy symbol.

Lvl 3	+1	680 gp	Lvl 18	+4	85,000 gp
Lvl 8	+2	3,400 gp	Lvl 23	+5	425,000 gp
Lvl 13	+3	17,000 gp	Lvl 28	+6	2,125,000 gp

Implement (Holy Symbol)
Enhancement: Attack rolls and damage rolls
Critical: +1d6 damage per plus
Power (Daily): Free Action. *Trigger:* You hit with a divine attack power using this holy symbol. *Effect:* Make a melee basic attack. If the attack hits a creature marked by you, it deals 1d10 extra damage.
Level 13 or 18: 2d10 extra damage.
Level 23 or 28: 3d10 extra damage.

Symbol of Daring — Level 5+

When you wield this symbol, your allies are inspired to strike boldly.

Lvl 5	+1	1,000 gp	Lvl 20	+4	125,000 gp
Lvl 10	+2	5,000 gp	Lvl 25	+5	625,000 gp
Lvl 15	+3	25,000 gp	Lvl 30	+6	3,125,000 gp

Implement (Holy Symbol)
Enhancement: Attack rolls and damage rolls
Critical: +1d6 damage per plus, or +1d12 radiant damage per plus with attacks made when you spend an action point
Property: When any ally within 5 squares of you spends an action point to make an attack, he or she gains a bonus to damage rolls on that attack equal to the symbol's enhancement bonus.

Symbol of Defense — Level 18+

On command, this symbol generates a mantle of force to defend a comrade.

| Lvl 18 | +4 | 85,000 gp | Lvl 28 | +6 | 2,125,000 gp |
| Lvl 23 | +5 | 425,000 gp | | | |

Implement (Holy Symbol)
Enhancement: Attack rolls and damage rolls
Critical: +1d6 force damage per plus
Power (Daily): Immediate Interrupt. *Trigger:* An attack hits an ally you can see. *Effect:* The ally gains a +5 power bonus to all defenses against the triggering attack.

Symbol of Divine Force — Level 2+

Through this symbol, you batter foes with your relentless conviction.

Lvl 2	+1	520 gp	Lvl 17	+4	65,000 gp
Lvl 7	+2	2,600 gp	Lvl 22	+5	325,000 gp
Lvl 12	+3	13,000 gp	Lvl 27	+6	1,625,000 gp

Implement (Holy Symbol)
Enhancement: Attack rolls and damage rolls
Critical: +1d6 force damage per plus
Power (Daily): Free Action. *Trigger:* You hit an enemy with a divine attack power using this holy symbol. *Effect:* You push that enemy a number of squares equal to the symbol's enhancement bonus.

Symbol of Divine Light — Level 17+

The fierce radiance of this symbol is the bane of foul creatures that can't bear sunlight.

| Lvl 17 | +4 | 65,000 gp | Lvl 27 | +6 | 1,625,000 gp |
| Lvl 22 | +5 | 325,000 gp | | | |

Implement (Holy Symbol)
Enhancement: Attack rolls and damage rolls
Critical: +1d6 radiant damage per plus
Property: Any creature within 5 squares of you that has vulnerability to radiant damage has that vulnerability increased by 5.

CONVERT'S SYMBOL

Legend tells of a lone warlock named Celia, usually said to be human but sometimes a halfling, who quested deep in the Astral Sea for secrets left over from the wars of creation. Celia wasn't following the commands of any divine patron; she served only herself, fascinated by the powers that had fought long ago. Her quests reaped a treasury of ancient knowledge, which she hoarded jealously.

During her adventures, Celia often received welcome and shelter. At some point, not even realizing she had changed, she decided to repay such kindness with some of the knowledge she had gained in her quests. Celia used her hard-won secrets to help her friends: anything from curing a plague to finding an astral weapon to fighting off the ships of githyanki raiders.

Years passed in this way. During a later journey, Celia overheard people in one of her adopted homes speaking of the "wandering saint," a woman who served Ioun by finding hidden items and bringing them to where they were most needed. With a shock, Celia realized they were talking about her. Recognizing the truth laid before her, she adopted Ioun as her divine patron.

The final piece of the legend states that Celia opened a way for other practitioners of arcane power to touch the divine, through the *convert's symbol*.

Rampaging Cultists: Cultists of Vecna are terrorizing people within a few days' journey of one of their hidden temples, mutilating innocents by cutting one eye and one hand from each. The cultists have made the mistake of attacking one of the communities that used to be under Celia's protection. A priest of Ioun asks for aid, offering a *convert's symbol* to help in the cause.

Symbol of Fire and Fury
Level 9+

This symbol is made of red iron streaked with fiery, bright metal. While you wear it, you can blast your foes with righteous flame.

Lvl 9	+2	4,200 gp	Lvl 24	+5	525,000 gp
Lvl 14	+3	21,000 gp	Lvl 29	+6	2,625,000 gp
Lvl 19	+4	105,000 gp			

Implement (Holy Symbol)

Enhancement: Attack rolls and damage rolls

Critical: +1d6 fire damage per plus, and each other enemy within 5 squares of you takes fire damage equal to your Charisma modifier.

Property: When you hit an enemy marked by you with a divine attack power using this holy symbol, that enemy takes 1d6 extra fire damage, or 1d10 fire damage while you're bloodied.
Level 19 or 24: 2d6 or 2d10 extra fire damage.
Level 29: 3d6 or 3d10 extra fire damage.

Symbol of Foe Turning
Level 7+

Through this symbol, you can punish specific enemies of your faith as well as vile undead.

Lvl 7	+2	2,600 gp	Lvl 22	+5	325,000 gp
Lvl 12	+3	13,000 gp	Lvl 27	+6	1,625,000 gp
Lvl 17	+4	65,000 gp			

Implement (Holy Symbol)

Enhancement: Attack rolls and damage rolls

Critical: +1d6 damage per plus

Property: When this item is created, choose angel, demon, devil, dragon, or giant. When you use your *turn undead* power, you can target creatures of the chosen kind instead of undead creatures.

Symbol of Prayers Recovered
Level 18+

Your prayers are rarely wasted while you wear this holy symbol.

| Lvl 18 | +4 | 85,000 gp | Lvl 28 | +6 | 2,125,000 gp |
| Lvl 23 | +5 | 425,000 gp | | | |

Implement (Holy Symbol)

Enhancement: Attack rolls and damage rolls

Critical: +1d6 damage per plus

Power (Daily): Free Action. *Trigger:* You miss all targets with a divine encounter attack power using this holy symbol. *Effect:* The power isn't expended.

Symbol of Protection
Level 10+

This symbol allows you to shield a companion from the threats of your foes.

Lvl 10	+2	5,000 gp	Lvl 25	+5	625,000 gp
Lvl 15	+3	25,000 gp	Lvl 30	+6	3,125,000 gp
Lvl 20	+4	125,000 gp			

Implement (Holy Symbol)

Enhancement: Attack rolls and damage rolls

Critical: +1d6 damage per plus

Power (Daily): Free Action. *Trigger:* You hit an enemy with a divine attack power using this holy symbol. *Effect:* Choose one ally within 5 squares of you. Until the end of your next turn, the enemy you hit can't attack that ally.

Symbol of Reflection
Level 24+

As you present this glittering symbol, divine power turns your enemies' attacks back against them.

| Lvl 24 | +5 | 525,000 gp | Lvl 29 | +6 | 2,625,000 gp |

Implement (Holy Symbol)

Enhancement: Attack rolls and damage rolls

Critical: +1d8 damage per plus

Power (Daily): Immediate Interrupt. *Trigger:* An enemy targets you with a ranged attack. *Effect:* You gain a +3 power bonus to all defenses against the triggering enemy's attack. If the attack misses you, the triggering enemy repeats the attack against itself.

Symbol of Shared Healing
Level 7+

While you wear this symbol, your can heal an ally even as you tend to your own wounds.

Lvl 7	+2	2,600 gp	Lvl 22	+5	325,000 gp
Lvl 12	+3	13,000 gp	Lvl 27	+6	1,625,000 gp
Lvl 17	+4	65,000 gp			

Implement (Holy Symbol)

Enhancement: Attack rolls and damage rolls

Critical: +1d6 damage per plus

Power (Daily ✦ Healing): Free Action. *Trigger:* You use your second wind, or you use a power that allows you to spend a healing surge to regain hit points. *Effect:* One ally within 5 squares of you can spend a healing surge.

SYMBOL OF THE RADIANT FLAME

Eons ago, a faith existed whose adherents followed both the paths set forth by the gods and the lore of natural powers. Known as the followers of the Radiant Flame, they rejected the idea of a strict division between primal and divine power.

Other priests considered their beliefs blasphemous and tried to strike down the Radiant Flame. The followers of that faith responded by creating magic symbols that embodied their ideals. In the great battle that followed, they bore this symbol to proclaim that all power in the world came from the same source. Even today, the *symbol of the Radiant Flame* unites small sects of worshipers who hold both the divine and the primal in equal reverence.

Reconcile the Faiths: A conclave is gathering to celebrate the Radiant Flame. Its members have invited members of other faiths to witness the ceremony but fear reprisal from those offended by their religious syncretism. They plan to bestow *symbols of the Radiant Flame* upon those who demonstrate openness to new possibilities.

Protect the Faithful: Followers of the Radiant Flame are being assassinated and harassed by those who disagree with their beliefs. The survivors are looking for champions of faith and conviction to protect them and are willing to reward their defenders with a *symbol of the Radiant Flame.*

Symbol of the champion's code

SYMBOL OF THE CHAMPION'S CODE

Every paladin follows a code, whether written or internalized. The *symbol of the champion's code* was designed to help paladins keep their code in mind at all times. It mystically enforces whatever oath is written upon it, making the paladin's challenge even more painful to refuse.

Introspective paladins follow a personal code, believing that only through adherence to the tenets of faith can one truly follow a deity's path. When such a paladin wears this holy symbol, he or she radiates firmness and resolve. Dogmatic paladins believe that their code should apply to everyone, not just themselves, and they enforce its tenets no matter what resistance they face. On them, this symbol magnifies an already intimidating aspect.

Oaths of Aggression: A hobgoblin paladin has sent forth goblin warriors loyal to him, ordering them to kill in Bane's name. He carries a *symbol of the champion's code* covered with sinister oaths to foment war and wrath. Those who can defeat him might be able to erase the stain of his cruel acts by transforming his symbol into one holding less destructive precepts.

Symbol of the Self: Although any ritual caster can learn to craft a *symbol of the champion's code*, doing so is an intense, personal experience. The creator gathers materials and tools that are important to his or her faith and conducts the ritual in a private, sacred place. For example, a paladin of Bahamut might craft a symbol from platinum gathered from a dragon's hoard, while a follower of Corellon might perform the ritual at the top of a giant tree in the deep forest where it reaches into the Feywild. A quest to locate the proper materials and site might encompass many adventures.

Symbol of the Champion's Code			Level 8+

A code of honor is inscribed on this symbol, reinforcing your commitment to your god and making your challenge irresistible.

Lvl 8	+2	3,400 gp	Lvl 23	+5	425,000 gp
Lvl 13	+3	17,000 gp	Lvl 28	+6	2,125,000 gp
Lvl 18	+4	85,000 gp			

Implement (Holy Symbol)
Enhancement: Attack rolls and damage rolls
Critical: +1d6 damage per plus
Property: When a creature takes radiant damage from your *divine challenge* or divine sanction, it takes extra radiant damage equal to the symbol's enhancement bonus.
Power (Daily): Minor Action. You choose an enemy marked by you. Until the end of your next turn, that enemy can't make an attack that includes any creature other than you as a target.

Symbol of the First Spirits			Level 2+

An oath of dedication to the natural spirits of the world is inscribed in fine script upon this wooden holy symbol.

Lvl 2	+1	520 gp	Lvl 17	+4	65,000 gp
Lvl 7	+2	2,600 gp	Lvl 22	+5	325,000 gp
Lvl 12	+3	13,000 gp	Lvl 27	+6	1,625,000 gp

Implement (Holy Symbol)
Enhancement: Attack rolls and damage rolls
Critical: +1d8 damage per plus
Property: Primal characters can wield this holy symbol in one hand to use it as a totem implement for primal powers.

SYMBOL OF FIRE AND FURY

The dwarven city Cloudgate, built deep inside a fog-shrouded mountain, and the human settlement South Gwyvar, in the valley below the mountain, had a long history of animosity. But when word arrived that a hobgoblin army was marching on them, the two cities banded together. Dwarf clerics of Moradin and human champions of Kord worked together to turn the cities' longstanding conflict to a positive end, creating *symbols of fire and fury*.

Find a Priest-Smith: The art of making *symbols of fire and fury* is practiced mainly by dwarf priest-smiths. Trained in both item crafting and religious lore, they have preserved the details of creating these special symbols. Locating a priest-smith can be difficult, because they usually live in secluded villages and monasteries.

Take the Test of Two: A few scriptures detail the Test of Two, devised by the clerics of Cloudgate and South Gwyvar. This challenge identifies those worthy of carrying *symbols of fire and fury* against threats similar in scope to the hobgoblin invasion. Only a candidate filled with both divine might and great endurance and physical strength can pass the test. By finding a cleric to administer the trial, a hero might be able to win a *symbol of fire and fury*.

ED COX

Symbol of the holy nimbus

Symbol of the Holy Nimbus — Level 4+

This symbol combines the images of sun and moon. When you speak a word of healing, you and your allies are bathed in restoring light.

Lvl 4	+1	840 gp	Lvl 19	+4	105,000 gp
Lvl 9	+2	4,200 gp	Lvl 24	+5	525,000 gp
Lvl 14	+3	21,000 gp	Lvl 29	+6	2,625,000 gp

Implement (Holy Symbol)
Enhancement: Attack rolls and damage rolls
Critical: +1d6 damage per plus, and you or an ally within 5 squares of you can spend a healing surge.
Property: When you use the *healing word* power during a combat encounter, you and each ally within 5 squares of you also gain temporary hit points equal to your Charisma modifier + the symbol's enhancement bonus.

Symbol of the Radiant Flame — Level 8+

This symbol appears to be made of brilliant living fire hung on a chain of molten metal, but it doesn't burn your skin.

Lvl 8	+2	3,400 gp	Lvl 23	+5	425,000 gp
Lvl 13	+3	17,000 gp	Lvl 28	+6	2,125,000 gp
Lvl 18	+4	85,000 gp			

Implement (Holy Symbol)
Enhancement: Attack rolls and damage rolls
Critical: +1d6 fire and radiant damage per plus, and each ally within 5 squares of you gains a bonus to damage rolls equal to the symbol's enhancement bonus until the end of your next turn. The bonus damage is fire and radiant.
Property: Primal characters can wield this holy symbol in one hand to use it as a totem implement for primal powers.
Power (Daily): Free Action. *Trigger:* You score a critical hit with an attack power using this holy symbol. *Effect:* The bonus to allies' damage rolls when you score a critical hit with this symbol lasts until the end of the encounter.

Symbol of Unified Defense — Level 9+

This symbol is engraved with several rings linked in a circle, representing the interdependence of you and your comrades.

Lvl 9	+2	4,200 gp	Lvl 24	+5	525,000 gp
Lvl 14	+3	21,000 gp	Lvl 29	+6	2,625,000 gp
Lvl 19	+4	105,000 gp			

Implement (Holy Symbol)
Enhancement: Attack rolls and damage rolls
Critical: +1d6 damage per plus
Power (Daily): Immediate Interrupt. *Trigger:* An enemy targets you and at least one ally with an attack. *Effect:* You and your allies' defense against the triggering enemy's attack is the highest appropriate score among all of you being attacked. For example, if the attack is against Reflex and the highest Reflex among you and your allies is 25, you all have Reflex 25 against the attack.

Symbol of Vigor — Level 7+

This symbol rewards your good health with divine might.

Lvl 7	+2	2,600 gp	Lvl 22	+5	325,000 gp
Lvl 12	+3	13,000 gp	Lvl 27	+6	1,625,000 gp
Lvl 17	+4	65,000 gp			

Implement (Holy Symbol)
Enhancement: Attack rolls and damage rolls
Critical: +1d6 damage per plus, or +1d12 damage per plus while you're at maximum hit points
Property: You gain a +1 bonus to attack rolls made using this holy symbol while you're at maximum hit points.

ORBS

Above all else, be careful not to set your orb down on a flat, inclined surface.

The orb represents clarity of will, fine control of magic, and command over the creatures you target with magic. Wizards who want to ensure that their magic endures wield orbs, and the additional enchantments on most magic orbs aid that goal.

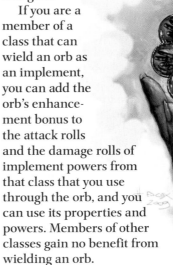

If you are a member of a class that can wield an orb as an implement, you can add the orb's enhancement bonus to the attack rolls and the damage rolls of implement powers from that class that you use through the orb, and you can use its properties and powers. Members of other classes gain no benefit from wielding an orb.

ED COX (2)

Orb of Accuracy — Level 14+

Though your opponent attempts to hide, this silver-caged, crystalline orb enables you to perceive its location.

| Lvl 14 | +3 | 21,000 gp | Lvl 24 | +5 | 525,000 gp |
| Lvl 19 | +4 | 105,000 gp | Lvl 29 | +6 | 2,625,000 gp |

Implement (Orb)

Enhancement: Attack rolls and damage rolls

Critical: +1d6 damage per plus, or +1d12 per plus against enemies that are invisible or that have concealment or total concealment from you

Property: When you use an arcane attack power through this orb, you take a -1 penalty (instead of -2) to attack rolls against enemies that have concealment from you, and a -3 penalty (instead of -5) to attack rolls against enemies that have total concealment from you.

Orb of Distance Denial — Level 20+

Composed of numerous smaller orbs fused into one spherical mass, this orb hampers an enemy's ranged attacks.

| Lvl 20 | +4 | 125,000 gp | Lvl 30 | +6 | 3,125,000 gp |
| Lvl 25 | +5 | 625,000 gp | | | |

Implement (Orb)

Enhancement: Attack rolls and damage rolls

Critical: +1d6 damage per plus

Power (Daily): Free Action. *Trigger:* You hit an enemy with an arcane attack power using this orb. *Effect:* That enemy can't target any creature more than 3 squares away from it (save ends).

Orb of Heightened Imposition — Level 12+

This green quartz orb extends the duration of powerful spells.

| Lvl 12 | +3 | 13,000 gp | Lvl 22 | +5 | 325,000 gp |
| Lvl 17 | +4 | 65,000 gp | Lvl 27 | +6 | 1,625,000 gp |

Implement (Orb)

Enhancement: Attack rolls and damage rolls

Critical: +1d6 damage per plus

Property: Your Orb of Imposition class feature can extend the duration of an effect created by an encounter power you use through this orb that would otherwise end at the end of your current turn. The effect instead ends at the end of your next turn. You can still use Orb of Imposition only once per encounter.

Orb of Petrification — Level 20+

This dull gray granite orb grasps your enemies in a stony embrace.

| Lvl 20 | +4 | 125,000 gp | Lvl 30 | +6 | 3,125,000 gp |
| Lvl 25 | +5 | 625,000 gp | | | |

Implement (Orb)

Enhancement: Attack rolls and damage rolls

Critical: +1d6 damage per plus, and the target is slowed until the end of your next turn.

Power (Daily): Free Action. *Trigger:* You hit an enemy with an arcane attack power using this orb. *Effect:* That enemy is petrified (save ends).

Orb of visionary protection

Orb of Repeated Imposition — Level 13+

This etched turquoise orb increases the frequency of your arcane imposition.

| Lvl 13 | +3 | 17,000 gp | Lvl 23 | +5 | 425,000 gp |
| Lvl 18 | +4 | 85,000 gp | Lvl 28 | +6 | 2,125,000 gp |

Implement (Orb)

Enhancement: Attack rolls and damage rolls

Critical: +1d8 damage per plus

Power (Daily): Free Action. *Trigger:* You hit an enemy with an arcane attack power using this orb. *Effect:* You regain the use of your Orb of Imposition class feature if you have already used it during this encounter.

Orb of Resilient Tenacity — Level 2+

The constant buzzing whisper that issues from this amethyst orb reinforces your will.

Lvl 2	+1	520 gp	Lvl 17	+4	65,000 gp
Lvl 7	+2	2,600 gp	Lvl 22	+5	325,000 gp
Lvl 12	+3	13,000 gp	Lvl 27	+6	1,625,000 gp

Implement (Orb)

Enhancement: Attack rolls and damage rolls

Critical: +1d6 damage per plus, and you or an ally within 5 squares of you gains a power bonus to saving throws equal to the enhancement bonus of the orb against one effect until that effect ends.

Power (Daily): Minor Action. You or an ally within 5 squares of you gains a power bonus to saving throws equal to the enhancement bonus of the orb against one effect until that effect ends.

MATIAS TAPIA

Orb of Supplementary Force — Level 3+

This sphere of scarlet glass pulses with barely controlled energy.

Lvl 3	+1	680 gp	Lvl 18	+4	85,000 gp
Lvl 8	+2	3,400 gp	Lvl 23	+5	425,000 gp
Lvl 13	+3	17,000 gp	Lvl 28	+6	2,125,000 gp

Implement (Orb)

Enhancement: Attack rolls and damage rolls

Critical: +1d6 force damage per plus, and the target is knocked prone.

Power (Daily): Minor Action. Until the end of your turn, each enemy you hit with an arcane close blast attack power using this orb is knocked prone after all other effects of the attack are resolved.

Orb of Visionary Protection — Level 12+

This translucent orb swirls with potential futures, each waiting for you to grasp and bend it to your will.

| Lvl 12 | +3 | 13,000 gp | Lvl 22 | +5 | 325,000 gp |
| Lvl 17 | +4 | 65,000 gp | Lvl 27 | +6 | 1,625,000 gp |

Implement (Orb)

Enhancement: Attack rolls and damage rolls

Critical: +1d6 damage per plus

Power (Daily): Immediate Interrupt. *Trigger:* You are subjected to an effect that a save can end. *Effect:* You can expend your Orb of Imposition class feature to make a saving throw against that effect instead of gaining the feature's normal benefit.

RODS

Heavier than a wand, smaller than a staff. If you have to ask what makes it different, you'll never know.

Warlocks, invokers, and artificers channel their power through rods. Some rods identify their intended users clearly by referencing specific class features or powers. Others have a broader appeal.

Except in rare cases, a rod is not robust enough to be used as a weapon. If a rod can function as either a weapon or an implement, that fact is noted in the item's description.

If you are a member of a class that can wield a rod as an implement, you can add the rod's enhancement bonus to the attack rolls and the damage rolls of implement powers from that class that you use through the rod, and you can use its properties and powers. Members of other classes gain no benefit from wielding a rod.

Battle-Pact Rod — Level 18+

This heavy cudgel can be used as both a warlock's rod and a weapon.

| Lvl 18 | +4 | 85,000 gp | Lvl 28 | +6 | 2,125,000 gp |
| Lvl 23 | +5 | 425,000 gp | | | |

Implement (Rod)

Enhancement: Attack rolls and damage rolls

Critical: +1d8 damage per plus

Property: This rod can be used as a melee weapon, functioning as a mace. You add its enhancement bonus to attack rolls and damage rolls of melee weapon attacks.

Power (Daily): Free Action. *Trigger:* You place your Warlock's Curse on an enemy. *Effect:* That enemy is also marked until the end of the encounter. When a creature marked by you in this way makes an attack that doesn't include you as a target, it takes your Warlock's Curse extra damage.

Darkspiral Rod — Level 4+

The darkspiral aura that exemplifies your devotion to the dark pact coalesces into a black cloud around this implement.

Lvl 4	+1	840 gp	Lvl 19	+4	105,000 gp
Lvl 9	+2	4,200 gp	Lvl 24	+5	525,000 gp
Lvl 14	+3	21,000 gp	Lvl 29	+6	2,625,000 gp

Implement (Rod)

Enhancement: Attack rolls and damage rolls

Critical: +1d6 necrotic and psychic damage per plus

Property: When you hit an enemy affected by your Warlock's Curse with a warlock attack power using this rod, you deal extra damage equal to the value of your Darkspiral Aura class feature to the enemy.

Hexer's Rod — Level 3+

Crafted by goblins, this rod channels their tricky, underhanded magic.

Lvl 3	+1	680 gp	Lvl 18	+4	85,000 gp
Lvl 8	+2	3,400 gp	Lvl 23	+5	425,000 gp
Lvl 13	+3	17,000 gp	Lvl 28	+6	2,125,000 gp

Implement (Rod)

Enhancement: Attack rolls and damage rolls

Critical: +1d6 damage per plus

Power (Daily): Free Action. *Trigger:* You hit an enemy with an attack power using this rod. *Effect:* The next time that enemy misses you with an attack, you can shift 3 squares as an immediate reaction, and you gain concealment against that enemy until the end of your next turn.

Rod of Burgeoning Memory — Level 2+

The astral essence in this rod ties you more tightly to your earlier lives as a deva.

Lvl 2	+1	520 gp	Lvl 17	+4	65,000 gp
Lvl 7	+2	2,600 gp	Lvl 22	+5	325,000 gp
Lvl 12	+3	13,000 gp	Lvl 27	+6	1,625,000 gp

Implement (Rod)

Enhancement: Attack rolls and damage rolls

Critical: +1d6 damage per plus

Property: When you use your *memory of a thousand lifetimes* racial power to improve the attack roll of a divine attack power you use through this rod, add +1 to the d6 roll.

An invoker with plenty of rods at the ready

Rod of Obliterating Wrath — Level 9+

Crafted to create as much destruction as possible, this rod lets you pierce your foes' defenses and destroy groups of enemies.

Lvl 9	+2	4,200 gp	Lvl 24	+5	525,000 gp
Lvl 14	+3	21,000 gp	Lvl 29	+6	2,625,000 gp
Lvl 19	+4	105,000 gp			

Implement (Rod)

Enhancement: Attack rolls and damage rolls

Critical: +1d6 damage per plus

Property: When an enemy's resistances reduce the damage of any invoker attack power you use through this rod, that enemy's resistance to that attack is reduced by an amount equal to this rod's enhancement bonus until the end of your next turn.

Power (Daily): Minor Action. You gain a +2 power bonus to attack rolls with the next invoker attack power you use through this rod.

Rod of Silver Rain — Level 15+

This rod appears to be made from molten silver. It can create clouds that rain silver upon the battlefield.

| Lvl 15 | +3 | 25,000 gp | Lvl 25 | +5 | 625,000 gp |
| Lvl 20 | +4 | 125,000 gp | Lvl 30 | +6 | 3,125,000 gp |

Implement (Rod)

Enhancement: Attack rolls and damage rolls

Critical: +1d8 damage per plus, or +1d12 damage per plus against fey creatures

Power (Daily): Minor Action. Make an attack: Area burst 3 within 20 squares. Each enemy in the burst that is affected by your Warlock's Curse takes ongoing 10 damage and grants combat advantage (save ends both). If the target is a fey creature, add your Charisma modifier to the ongoing damage.
Level 25 or 30: Ongoing 15 damage.

Rod of Stolen Starlight — Level 7+

At your command, this rod infuses your spell with light from mysterious stars.

Lvl 7	+2	2,600 gp	Lvl 22	+5	325,000 gp
Lvl 12	+3	13,000 gp	Lvl 27	+6	1,625,000 gp
Lvl 17	+4	65,000 gp			

Implement (Rod)

Enhancement: Attack rolls and damage rolls

Critical: +1d6 radiant and necrotic damage per plus

Property: When you hit an undead enemy affected by your Warlock's Curse with an attack power using this rod, you deal an extra die of Warlock's Curse damage against that enemy.

Power (At-Will ✦ Radiant): Minor Action. The next necrotic or poison power you use through this rod deals radiant damage instead of necrotic damage or poison damage.

Rod of Devilry — Level 10+

Infernal power flows through this rod, scouring your foes with hellfire.

Lvl 10	+2	5,000 gp	Lvl 25	+5	625,000 gp
Lvl 15	+3	25,000 gp	Lvl 30	+6	3,125,000 gp
Lvl 20	+4	125,000 gp			

Implement (Rod)

Enhancement: Attack rolls and damage rolls

Critical: +1d6 fire damage per plus, or +1d10 fire damage per plus against a bloodied target

Property: If you're a tiefling, when you use an attack power through this rod, your bonus to attack rolls from your *bloodhunt* racial trait increases by 1.

Property: When you hit a bloodied enemy affected by your Warlock's Curse with an attack power using this rod, it takes extra fire damage equal to this rod's enhancement bonus.

Rod of Divinity — Level 3+

This delicate silver rod lets you channel your deity's power back to yourself.

Lvl 3	+1	680 gp	Lvl 18	+4	85,000 gp
Lvl 8	+2	3,400 gp	Lvl 23	+5	425,000 gp
Lvl 13	+3	17,000 gp	Lvl 28	+6	2,125,000 gp

Implement (Rod)

Enhancement: Attack rolls and damage rolls

Critical: +1d6 damage per plus

Power (Daily): Free Action. *Trigger:* You hit with a divine attack power using this rod. *Effect:* You gain one extra use of your Channel Divinity class feature during this encounter.

ERIC L. WILLIAMS

ROD OF SILVER RAIN

Every fifty years, a supernatural rain falls across the Fey-wild. It coats the land in silver, causing feelings of great celebration among the goodly fey, who see it as an auspicious sign, and feelings of dread among the wicked, malicious dark fey, who hate the silver rain.

At one point, an eladrin warlock named Suzasha decided to collect the rain and transform it into a rod, using it as a tool to both celebrate the land and fight against the fomorians and other dark fey. The rod created a silver cloud that burned the minds of Suzasha's foes and aided her allies. Not surprisingly, the evil fey crafted a plan to remove the threat of the rod.

The fomorians dispatched their lackeys to steal the rod from Suzasha under cover of night. The thieves were successful and returned the rod to their dark stronghold, where the fomorians unsuccessfully attempted to disenchant the item. Pained by its proximity, they cast it into the Shadowfell. Lesser copies have been created, but the eladrin have been searching for the original ever since.

Shadowfell Search: Adventurers have sought the original rod in the Shadowfell to no avail. Only one creature knows where it lies hidden—a fomorian wretch named Kruvthos. He claims to have been banished from the fomorian realms and is threatening to gain revenge by revealing the rod's location to those who will help him. But none so far have been willing to trust the fomorian, since lies and deception are a part of a fomorian's very essence, and any help that Kruvthos gives will come at a cost.

The Queen of Air and Darkness: The Queen of Air and Darkness, an evil ruler of wicked fey, lives in exile, holding a *rod of silver rain* in her court. She keeps it in a vault that shields her courtiers from its harmful effects. Rumors suggest that the Queen is away petitioning to return to the Feywild, making this the perfect time to steal her rod.

Rod of the Fickle Servant — Level 2+

This special rod gives you access to a different vestige when you need it.

Lvl 2	+1	520 gp	Lvl 17	+4	65,000 gp
Lvl 7	+2	2,600 gp	Lvl 22	+5	325,000 gp
Lvl 12	+3	13,000 gp	Lvl 27	+6	1,625,000 gp

Implement (Rod)
Enhancement: Attack rolls and damage rolls
Critical: +1d6 damage per plus
Power (Daily): Free Action. *Trigger:* You hit an enemy affected by your Warlock's Curse with an attack power using this rod. *Effect:* You make one of your primary vestiges your active vestige (*Arcane Power*, page 72).

Rod of the Hag — Level 14+

This slender obsidian rod is topped with a hag's eye that opens when you use your powers, terrifying your foe.

| Lvl 14 | +3 | 21,000 gp | Lvl 24 | +5 | 525,000 gp |
| Lvl 19 | +4 | 105,000 gp | Lvl 29 | +6 | 2,625,000 gp |

Implement (Rod)
Enhancement: Attack rolls and damage rolls
Critical: +1d6 psychic damage per plus
Power (Daily): Free Action. *Trigger:* You hit an enemy affected by your Warlock's Curse with an attack power using this rod. *Effect:* That enemy takes extra damage equal to this rod's enhancement bonus and is dazed until the end of your next turn.

Rod of the Pactbinder — Level 4+

An oath inscribed on this rod gives you quick access to one of your vestige patrons.

Lvl 4	+1	840 gp	Lvl 19	+4	105,000 gp
Lvl 9	+2	4,200 gp	Lvl 24	+5	525,000 gp
Lvl 14	+3	21,000 gp	Lvl 29	+6	2,625,000 gp

Implement (Rod)
Enhancement: Attack rolls and damage rolls
Critical: +1d6 damage per plus
Property: When you acquire a rod of this sort, choose one daily power you know that has a vestige pact entry; this choice can't be changed later. The vestige associated with that power becomes bound to this rod.
Power (Daily): Free Action. *Trigger:* You hit an enemy affected by your Warlock's Curse with an attack power using this rod. *Effect:* The vestige bound to the rod becomes your active vestige.

ROD OF STOLEN STARLIGHT

When a drow city was beset by hordes of undead, even the most powerful dark pact warlocks found their spells ineffective. Willing to go to any lengths to stop the invasion, these warlocks sent false diplomats to find star pact warlocks from whom they could steal power. With their newfound knowledge, they created the first *rods of stolen starlight*, which were powerful weapons in the battle against undead.

Scions of the Stars: Sometimes, the remains of dedicated star pact warlocks develop cysts that swell until creatures of the Far Realm burst forth. Rumors abound of places where this has happened and aberrant creatures are attacking the local populace. Heroes who follow these rumors and defeat those creatures might find a *rod of stolen starlight*.

The Demon Prince's Drow: Some drow take up the worship of Orcus, which displeases the powers of darkness. Followers of those entities might give a *rod of stolen starlight* to a group of heroes to help them destroy these Orcus-worshiping drow and their undead followers.

Torch of misery

Spider Rod — Level 13+

This gray metal rod is covered with a web of mithral studded with black onyx spiders.

Lvl 13	+3	17,000 gp	Lvl 23	+5	425,000 gp
Lvl 18	+4	85,000 gp	Lvl 28	+6	2,125,000 gp

Implement (Rod)
Enhancement: Attack rolls and damage rolls
Critical: Ongoing 10 poison damage (save ends)
  Level 23 or 28: Ongoing 15 poison damage (save ends)
Property: When you hit with an attack that deals ongoing necrotic or ongoing poison damage using this rod, the ongoing damage increases by an amount equal to the rod's enhancement bonus.
Power (Daily ✦ Poison): Minor Action. You choose an enemy within 20 squares of you that is affected by an effect you created that a save can end. The effect gains *"Aftereffect:* The target takes ongoing 5 poison damage (save ends)."
  Level 23 or 28: Ongoing 10 poison damage (save ends).

Rod of the Risen Dead — Level 27

This delicate crystal rod allows you to take control of the mind and body of a slain foe.

Lvl 27	+6	1,625,000 gp

Implement (Rod)
Enhancement: Attack rolls and damage rolls
Critical: +1d6 psychic damage per plus
Power (Daily ✦ Charm): Free Action. *Trigger:* You use this rod to reduce an enemy affected by your Warlock's Curse to 0 hit points. *Effect:* That enemy is dominated until the end of its next turn. After that, the enemy is killed or knocked unconscious, as normal.

Torch of Misery — Level 10+

Flames encircle the end of this black and gold wand.

Lvl 10	+2	5,000 gp	Lvl 25	+5	625,000 gp
Lvl 15	+3	25,000 gp	Lvl 30	+6	3,125,000 gp
Lvl 20	+4	125,000 gp			

Implement (Rod)
Enhancement: Attack rolls and damage rolls
Critical: +1d6 fire damage per plus
Property: When you hit an enemy with a fire or radiant attack power using this rod and deal damage to it, that enemy grants combat advantage to you on your next attack against it.
Power (At-Will): Minor Action. Green flame bursts from the end of the rod, illuminating the area around you like a torch. You can end this effect as a free action.

TORCH OF MISERY

Both infernal warlocks and star pact warlocks use *torches of misery*, which are created to mock the warmth and comfort of light and flame. These rods carry a legacy of torture and death. They gained infamy in the hands of cambion warlocks called the Princes of Misery, who used them to terrorize the enemies of the Nine Hells.

Hellish Trophies: Devils hate few things more than those who use the devils' own power against them. In the Nine Hells (or other devilish enclaves), the implements of infernal pact warlocks who fought against the devils are used as decoration. The devils convert them into *torches of misery* to light their halls, usually pinning the former owner's dismembered head or hand to the wall with the implement. Any heroes brave enough to venture into one of these domains can claim one of these rods and put its former owner to rest.

Prince Gorzia's Torch: Gorzia the Despised, one of the Princes of Misery, was defeated by a group of human wizards working in concert. His *torch of misery* is said to rest in his tower on the inhospitable Hailblight Peak. Whoever survives the dangerous journey to the peak, passes the defenses left by the wizard, and contends with the occupant (who might be living, dead, or undead) can find Gorzia's powerful implement.

STAFFS

A guideline in the Graywatch manual on dealing with prisoners reads, "Never leave an old man or a traveler his staff. No exceptions."

A traditional implement for old, wise spellcasters, the staff serves as a perfect channel for power, yet remains seemingly innocuous. It can be difficult to take a walking staff from someone who looks harmless.

Beyond their enhancement bonuses, staffs often hold defensive powers, as befits their inoffensive appearance, but they're by no means limited to defensive magic.

If you are a member of a class that can wield a staff as an implement, you can add the staff's enhancement bonus to the attack rolls and the damage rolls of implement powers from that class that you use through the staff, and you can use its properties and powers. Members of other classes gain no benefit from wielding a staff.

ED COX

MOONSILVER STAFF

Hundreds of years ago, the evil gods conspired to cover the world in darkness. Their followers unleashed magic from powerful items, masking the sun and the moon from view. The plants began to die, and people grew sick. The darkness drove lycanthropes into a supernatural madness. They rampaged across the land, slaughtering anyone they encountered.

A sorcerer and devotee of Sehanine quested to recover an ancient staff sacred to her deity. Her band braved countless dangers before they found a sacred glade. When they arrived, a shaft of moonlight pierced the deep blackness, leaving a staff behind where it had struck the ground.

With the help of the staff, the band destroyed many of the wild lycanthropes, as well as the objects that had plunged the world into darkness. Its task complete, the staff turned into moonlight once again, waiting to be rediscovered by a mortal in need. It has since reappeared from time to time, in forms of varying power.

Darkness Returns: The forces of evil conspire to bathe the land in darkness once again. Heroes are needed to find a holy place of Sehanine where a *moonsilver staff* waits and banish this evil.

Society of Silver: The Society of Silver, an organization made up of members of many races, has been fighting a drawn-out, bloody campaign to eliminate lycanthropes. They continually seek new adventurers to join their cause and have been known to award a *moonsilver staff* to those who prove themselves worthy.

Blastwarp Staff — Level 10+

The crownpiece of silver and gold that tops this staff extends arcane power around its wielder.

Lvl 10	+2	5,000 gp	Lvl 25	+5	625,000 gp
Lvl 15	+3	25,000 gp	Lvl 30	+6	3,125,000 gp
Lvl 20	+4	125,000 gp			

Implement (Staff)

Enhancement: Attack rolls and damage rolls

Critical: +1d6 force damage per plus

Property: When you hit at least three targets with a close attack power using this staff, you gain combat advantage on your next attack before the end of your next turn.

Power (Daily): Free Action. *Trigger:* You use an arcane close blast attack power through this staff. *Effect:* The attack becomes a close burst 2 squares smaller than the blast, to a minimum of 1 (for example, a close blast 5 becomes a close burst 3).

Moonsilver Staff — Level 7+

This pale wood staff is topped with a moonstone sphere. It harms lycanthropes with radiant energy.

Lvl 7	+2	2,600 gp	Lvl 22	+5	325,000 gp
Lvl 12	+3	13,000 gp	Lvl 27	+6	1,625,000 gp
Lvl 17	+4	65,000 gp			

Implement (Staff)

Enhancement: Attack rolls and damage rolls

Critical: +1d6 radiant damage per plus

Property: Treat this staff as silvered (*Player's Handbook*, page 220) for the purpose of implement and weapon attack powers made using it.

Power (Daily): Free Action. *Trigger:* You hit an enemy with an arcane radiant power and deal damage to it using this staff. *Effect:* That enemy takes extra radiant damage equal to 5 + the staff's enhancement bonus.

Spellshaper's Staff — Level 18+

This mahogany staff ends in a complex series of precisely angled bends.

| Lvl 18 | +4 | 85,000 gp | Lvl 28 | +6 | 2,125,000 gp |
| Lvl 23 | +5 | 425,000 gp | | | |

Implement (Staff)

Enhancement: Attack rolls and damage rolls

Critical: +1d6 damage per plus

Power (Daily): Free Action. *Trigger:* You use an arcane area burst attack power through this staff. *Effect:* The attack becomes an area wall in a number of squares equal to the burst's size + 5 (for example, an area burst 2 within 20 becomes an area wall 7 within 20). The wall is 2 squares high. This effect doesn't change the duration or other attributes of the power.

Staff of Divinity — Level 2+

The glowing symbol of a deity rests atop this majestic staff.

Lvl 2	+1	520 gp	Lvl 17	+4	65,000 gp
Lvl 7	+2	2,600 gp	Lvl 22	+5	325,000 gp
Lvl 12	+3	13,000 gp	Lvl 27	+6	1,625,000 gp

Implement (Staff)

Enhancement: Attack rolls and damage rolls

Critical: +1d8 damage per plus

Property: Divine characters can use this staff as a holy symbol implement for divine powers.

Staff of Iron Infusion — Level 4+

With the aid of this iron staff, your healing artifices also toughen your ally's skin, making it resistant to damage.

Lvl 4	+1	840 gp	Lvl 19	+4	105,000 gp
Lvl 9	+2	4,200 gp	Lvl 24	+5	525,000 gp
Lvl 14	+3	21,000 gp	Lvl 29	+6	2,625,000 gp

Implement (Staff)

Enhancement: Attack rolls and damage rolls

Critical: +1d6 damage per plus

Property: When you use your Healing Infusion class feature on an ally, that ally gains resistance to all damage equal to the staff's enhancement bonus until the end of your next turn.

Power (Daily): Minor Action. An ally within 10 squares of you gains resistance to all damage equal to your Wisdom modifier + the staff's enhancement bonus until the end of your next turn.

A wizard and his collection of staffs

Staff of Knives — Level 2+

This steel-gray wooden staff transforms into a steel-hard wooden dagger on command.

Lvl 2	+1	520 gp	Lvl 17	+4	65,000 gp
Lvl 7	+2	2,600 gp	Lvl 22	+5	325,000 gp
Lvl 12	+3	13,000 gp	Lvl 27	+6	1,625,000 gp

Implement (Staff)

Enhancement: Attack rolls and damage rolls

Critical: +1d6 damage per plus, or +1d12 damage per plus when used as a melee weapon

Power (At-Will): Minor Action. You transform this item from a staff into a dagger or from a dagger into a staff.

Staff of Luck and Skill — Level 23+

Whoever wields this blond yew staff capitalizes on both luck and skill.

Lvl 23	+5	425,000 gp	Lvl 28	+6	2,125,000 gp

Implement (Staff)

Enhancement: Attack rolls and damage rolls

Critical: +1d6 damage per plus, and you gain a cumulative +1 bonus (up to a maximum of the staff's enhancement bonus) to all defenses each time you score a critical hit until the end of the encounter.

Power (Daily): Minor Action. The first time you roll an attack roll of 17 or higher with an attack power using this staff before the end of the encounter, you score a critical hit with that attack.

Staff of Resilience — Level 3+

This black ash staff can absorb some of your life force and turn it into a protective aura.

Lvl 3	+1	680 gp	Lvl 18	+4	85,000 gp
Lvl 8	+2	3,400 gp	Lvl 23	+5	425,000 gp
Lvl 13	+3	17,000 gp	Lvl 28	+6	2,125,000 gp

Implement (Staff)

Enhancement: Attack rolls and damage rolls

Critical: +1d6 damage per plus

Power (Daily): Minor Action. You spend a healing surge but regain no hit points. Instead, you gain temporary hit points equal to twice your healing surge value.

Staff of Sleep and Charm — Level 3+

The crystal eye atop this dusky birch staff enhances spells that target the mind.

Lvl 3	+1	680 gp	Lvl 18	+4	85,000 gp
Lvl 8	+2	3,400 gp	Lvl 23	+5	425,000 gp
Lvl 13	+3	17,000 gp	Lvl 28	+6	2,125,000 gp

Implement (Staff)

Enhancement: Attack rolls and damage rolls

Critical: +1d6 damage per plus

Property: You gain a +1 item bonus to attack rolls with arcane charm or sleep attack powers.
Level 13 or 18: +2 item bonus.
Level 23 or 28: +3 item bonus.

JEFF CARLISLE

STAFF OF SPELL BLASTING

Morgrale the Brilliant was an ogre of rare wisdom. It was said that he could curse in four languages and even sign his own name. He was such a prodigy that he sought training in matters arcane. As the story goes, he found Tucius, a dark wizard who was amused by the idea of a spellcasting ogre and took Morgrale as an apprentice. In time, Tucius came to regret that decision.

When Tucius had taught the ogre all he cared to, he sent Morgrale away. Soon, the ogre became a lieutenant for an oni warlord, establishing a reputation as a mighty combat leader. A staff of his own invention became a symbol of fear among his enemies, for he was equally adept at calling down magical fire as he was at leaping into melee and blasting foes up close.

When Morgrale's master commanded him to conquer Tucius's estate, the ogre didn't hesitate. After a successful conquest, Morgrale gained riches and contentment. No longer desiring to venture into battle, he became lord of a number of slaves and warriors. He reproduced his magic staff and granted copies to his underlings, sending them out to pillage and subjugate others in his name.

Morgrale's Grasp: Nearby ogres have come under the command of an oni mage carrying a standard of Morgrale. They're invading their neighbors in the name of their master. There are too many ogres to turn away; only taking the fight to Morgrale, who still keeps the original *staff of spell blasting*, will end his ambitions.

Vengeance Before Death: The wizard Gharlteban the Betrayer got his nickname from turning his back on Morgrale. Years after swearing fealty to the ogre, Gharlteban switched sides and began worked against his former master. He has grown old and frail, however, and now seeks Morgrale's final defeat before he is no longer able to appreciate it fully. He's looking for others to accomplish this task and is offering his *staff of spell blasting* in exchange.

Staff of Spell Blasting — Level 14+

Bound in silver, this polished pale elm staff violently channels arcane energy.

| Lvl 14 | +3 | 21,000 gp | Lvl 24 | +5 | 525,000 gp |
| Lvl 19 | +4 | 105,000 gp | Lvl 29 | +6 | 2,625,000 gp |

Implement (Staff)
Enhancement: Attack rolls and damage rolls
Critical: +1d6 damage per plus
Property: When you use an arcane ranged or area attack power through this staff, you don't provoke opportunity attacks from enemies adjacent to you that are targeted by the attack.
Power (Daily): Free Action. *Trigger:* You use an at-will arcane ranged attack power. *Effect:* The attack becomes a close blast 3 instead.

Staff of the Faithful Arcanist — Level 8+

This alabaster staff is topped with a deity's symbol for those who consider their powers to be a gift from their god.

Lvl 8	+2	3,400 gp	Lvl 23	+5	425,000 gp
Lvl 13	+3	17,000 gp	Lvl 28	+6	2,125,000 gp
Lvl 18	+4	85,000 gp			

Implement (Staff)
Prerequisite: You must have the Initiate of the Faith feat.
Enhancement: Attack rolls and damage rolls
Critical: +1d6 damage per plus
Power (Daily ✦ Divine, Healing): Minor Action. As the cleric's *healing word* power (*Player's Handbook*, page 62).

Staff of Wind — Level 5+

This feather-light staff of cloudy crystal allows you to command the air.

Lvl 5	+1	1,000 gp	Lvl 20	+4	125,000 gp
Lvl 10	+2	5,000 gp	Lvl 25	+5	625,000 gp
Lvl 15	+3	25,000 gp	Lvl 30	+6	3,125,000 gp

Implement (Staff)
Enhancement: Attack rolls and damage rolls
Critical: +1d6 damage per plus
Power (Daily): Minor Action. Make an attack: Close blast 5; targets each creature in blast; Intelligence or Charisma vs. Fortitude; on a hit, the target is pushed a number of squares equal to the enhancement bonus of the staff and knocked prone.

Summoner's Staff — Level 7+

This hawthorn staff is engraved with the images of dozens of different creatures.

Lvl 7	+2	2,600 gp	Lvl 22	+5	325,000 gp
Lvl 12	+3	13,000 gp	Lvl 27	+6	1,625,000 gp
Lvl 17	+4	65,000 gp			

Implement (Staff)
Enhancement: Attack rolls and damage rolls
Critical: +1d6 damage per plus, or +1d10 damage per plus if a creature you summoned scored the critical hit
Property: When an enemy attacks a creature you summoned and misses, you or an ally within 5 squares of the summoned creature gains temporary hit points equal to 5 + the staff's enhancement bonus.
Power (Daily): Immediate Interrupt. *Trigger:* An enemy hits a creature you summoned. *Effect:* The triggering enemy rerolls the attack roll and must use the second result.

Verdant Staff — Level 2+

This writhing staff is composed of thin vines that constantly flourish and wither.

Lvl 2	+1	520 gp	Lvl 17	+4	65,000 gp
Lvl 7	+2	2,600 gp	Lvl 22	+5	325,000 gp
Lvl 12	+3	13,000 gp	Lvl 27	+6	1,625,000 gp

Implement (Staff)
Enhancement: Attack rolls and damage rolls
Critical: +1d8 damage per plus
Property: Primal characters can use this staff as a totem implement for primal powers.

TOMES

Secrets are bound within these pages that only the true masters of magic can know.

Most tomes contain one or more wizard spells, often supplemented by information on improving the spells' effectiveness. You can't make melee attacks with a tome.

If you are a member of a class that can wield a tome as an implement, you can add the tome's enhancement bonus to the attack rolls and the damage rolls of implement powers from that class that you use through the tome, and you can use its properties and powers. Members of other classes gain no benefit from wielding a tome.

Confounding Tome — Level 28

The cloth cover of this tome is inscribed with a repeating maze-like pattern.

Lvl 28	+6	2,125,000 gp

Implement (Tome)
Enhancement: Attack rolls and damage rolls
Critical: +1d6 psychic damage per plus
Property: When you use the *maze* power through this tome, the target rolls twice when making Intelligence checks to escape the maze and can escape only if both checks succeed.
Power (Daily): Free Action. You expend an unused wizard daily attack power of level 25 or higher and gain the use of the *maze* power (*Player's Handbook*, page 168). The power is lost if you don't use it before the end of the encounter.

Deck of Spells — Level 14+

All your spells are written on these cards, whose illustrations depict you crushing foes with your potent arcane arsenal.

Lvl 14	+3	21,000 gp	Lvl 24	+5	525,000 gp
Lvl 19	+4	105,000 gp	Lvl 29	+6	2,625,000 gp

Implement (Tome)
Enhancement: Attack rolls and damage rolls
Critical: +1d6 damage per plus
Property: Wizards can use this tome as a spellbook.
Property: When you prepare your arcane powers, you can choose one wizard daily attack power from your spellbook at random. You must prepare the randomly chosen power before you prepare any others. You gain a +2 bonus to attack rolls with that power until you take an extended rest.
Power (Daily): Free Action. You choose a wizard daily attack power in your spellbook that you didn't prepare today and expend an unused wizard daily attack power of an equal or higher level. You gain the use of the chosen power, with a +2 bonus to attack rolls with that power, until the end of the encounter. The power is lost if you don't use it before the end of the encounter.

Dispelling Tome — Level 7+

This thin tome helps you unbind magical creations.

Lvl 7	+2	2,600 gp	Lvl 22	+5	325,000 gp
Lvl 12	+3	13,000 gp	Lvl 27	+6	1,625,000 gp
Lvl 17	+4	65,000 gp			

Implement (Tome)
Enhancement: Attack rolls and damage rolls
Critical: +1d6 damage per plus
Property: When you use the *dispel magic* power through this tome, you can target two conjurations or zones instead of one, and you gain a +2 item bonus to attack rolls to destroy them.
Power (Daily): Free Action. You expend an unused wizard utility power of level 6 or higher and gain the use of the *dispel magic* power (*Player's Handbook*, page 162). The power is lost if you don't use it before the end of the encounter.

Frozen Tome — Level 18+

The cover of this thick tome appears to be made from solid ice. It's cool to the touch but doesn't melt.

Lvl 18	+4	85,000 gp	Lvl 28	+6	2,125,000 gp
Lvl 23	+5	425,000 gp			

Implement (Tome)
Enhancement: Attack rolls and damage rolls
Critical: +1d6 cold damage per plus
Property: When you use the *wall of ice* power through this tome, the wall can be up to 15 squares long and 10 squares high.
Power (Daily): Free Action. You expend an unused wizard utility power of level 15 or higher and gain the use of the *wall of ice* power (*Player's Handbook*, page 165). The power is lost if you don't use it before the end of the encounter.

DECK OF SPELLS

Although wizards have a reputation for being ponderous and analytical, not all of them are sensible or sane. Amproemus was one most kindly described as eccentric, and his inventions are a testament to the best and worst traits of humanity. His *deck of spells* can bestow great power on a wielder, but it can't be controlled.

No authoritative story tells how the deck came to be. Some say that Amproemus meant to create a spellbook that let its user cast spells more often and that randomness was a side effect, while others claim the item was the product of a deranged mind. A few believe Amproemus simply lost a bet.

The Unassuming Deck: There are many *decks of spells* in the world, and not all are possessed by wizards. In fact, someone who doesn't understand arcane magic might be using one simply as an ornate deck for card games. Gamblers swear by them as "lucky decks"—some might give them up for money, but a superstitious gambler might demand a contest of *Three-Dragon Ante* or another game of chance.

Gossamer Tome — Level 8+

This tome is covered in webs infested by myriad tiny spiders that swarm over your hands but never bite.

Lvl 8	+2	3,400 gp	Lvl 23	+5	425,000 gp
Lvl 13	+3	17,000 gp	Lvl 28	+6	2,125,000 gp
Lvl 18	+4	85,000 gp			

Implement (Tome)

Enhancement: Attack rolls and damage rolls

Critical: +1d6 damage per plus

Property: When you use the *web* power through this tome, any creature that ends its move in the zone of webs is restrained instead of immobilized.

Power (Daily): Free Action. You expend an unused wizard utility power of level 5 or higher and gain the use of the *web* power (*Player's Handbook*, page 161). The power is lost if you don't use it before the end of the encounter.

Mordenkainen's Tome — Level 13+

This tome's cover is inscribed with a shimmering silver sword.

| Lvl 13 | +3 | 17,000 gp | Lvl 23 | +5 | 425,000 gp |
| Lvl 18 | +4 | 85,000 gp | Lvl 28 | +6 | 2,125,000 gp |

Implement (Tome)

Enhancement: Attack rolls and damage rolls

Critical: +1d6 force damage per plus

Property: When you use the *Mordenkainen's sword* power through this tome, the sword deals extra force damage equal to the tome's enhancement bonus.

Power (Daily): Free Action. You expend an unused wizard utility power of level 9 or higher and gain the use of the *Mordenkainen's sword* power (*Player's Handbook*, page 163). The power is lost if you don't use it before the end of the encounter.

GOSSAMER TOME

Drow spellcasters have perfected a technique of crafting magic tomes from spider webs. They fold layer after layer of webbing into sheets, then treat the pages with alchemical substances. These tomes enhance the creation of magical webs and are highly prized among wizards.

Gossamer tomes have become a symbol of the Venom Tongue, a cabal of mostly drow wizards who transform their bodies into vessels through dark rituals. Their preserved flesh hosts swarms of grotesque, blood-gorged spiders.

Web Weaver Contest: A local wizard's guild is holding an annual competition to determine who can make best use of the *web* spell. Competitors might create webs to trap rats, to confine other contestants in a maze, or simply to support the most weight. The winner receives a *gossamer tome* stolen from the drow (who might want to get it back).

Drow Bandits: Some Venom Tongue drow have been raiding shipments traveling between towns that lie above a drow city. Their handiwork is easy to see: They leave behind the caravan merchants and guards, suffocated or starved, tangled in thick sticky webs. The people of the towns want the dark elves rooted out and slain.

Tome of Crushing Force — Level 9+

This jet black tome is inset with several moonstones and radiates power.

Lvl 9	+2	4,200 gp	Lvl 24	+5	525,000 gp
Lvl 14	+3	21,000 gp	Lvl 29	+6	2,625,000 gp
Lvl 19	+4	105,000 gp			

Implement (Tome)

Enhancement: Attack rolls and damage rolls

Critical: +1d6 force damage per plus

Property: When you use a wizard force power through this tome that attacks Reflex, you can choose to have the power attack Fortitude instead.

Property: This tome contains two wizard daily force powers. Both powers must be of a level equal to or lower than that of the tome. You must choose these powers when you acquire the tome; they can't be changed later. You can add these powers to your spellbook.

Power (Daily): Free Action. You choose a power contained in the tome and expend an unused wizard daily attack power of an equal or higher level. You gain the use of the chosen power. The power is lost if you don't use it before the end of the encounter.

Tome of Enduring Creation — Level 14+

Your summoned creatures are more durable when you wield this leather-bound tome.

| Lvl 14 | +3 | 21,000 gp | Lvl 24 | +5 | 525,000 gp |
| Lvl 19 | +4 | 105,000 gp | Lvl 29 | +6 | 2,625,000 gp |

Implement (Tome)

Enhancement: Attack rolls and damage rolls

Critical: +1d6 damage per plus

Property: When you hit with a wizard attack power using this tome, a creature you summoned gains temporary hit points equal to 2 + the tome's enhancement bonus.

Power (Daily): Free Action. *Trigger:* You use a wizard summoning power. *Effect:* A creature you summoned gains a +2 power bonus to all defenses until the end of the encounter or until the creature is dismissed.

Tome of Striking Lightning — Level 4+

Sparks leap between the covers of this copper-bound tome.

Lvl 4	+1	840 gp	Lvl 19	+4	105,000 gp
Lvl 9	+2	4,200 gp	Lvl 24	+5	525,000 gp
Lvl 14	+3	21,000 gp	Lvl 29	+6	2,625,000 gp

Implement (Tome)

Enhancement: Attack rolls and damage rolls

Critical: +1d6 lightning damage per plus

Property: When you use a wizard lightning attack power through this tome, you can score a critical hit on a roll of 19–20.

Property: This tome contains two wizard daily lightning powers. Both powers must be of a level equal to or lower than that of the tome. You must choose these powers when you acquire the tome; they can't be changed later. You can add these powers to your spellbook.

Power (Daily): Free Action. You choose a power contained in the tome and expend an unused wizard daily attack power of an equal or higher level. You gain the use of the chosen power. The power is lost if you don't use it before the end of the encounter.

Toxic Tome | Level 24+

This snakeskin-bound tome gives off a slight acrid scent.

| Lvl 24 | +5 | 525,000 gp | Lvl 29 | +6 | 2,625,000 gp |

Implement (Tome)
Enhancement: Attack rolls and damage rolls
Critical: +1d6 poison damage per plus
Property: When you use the *cloudkill* power through this tome, you can move the cloud 3 squares as part of the minor action to sustain the power.
Power (Daily): Free Action. You expend an unused wizard utility power of level 19 or higher and gain the use of the *cloudkill* power (*Player's Handbook*, page 166). The power is lost if you don't use it before the end of the encounter.

TOTEMS

Cougar bone, python hide, werewolf toes—and dead foes.

A totem is a short length of wood or bone carved to resemble patron spirits, which are generally ancestors or animals. Strips of hides, teeth, small bones, and the like hang from one end. The symbolism of the carved image, combined with the attached items, give the totem its power. You can't make melee attacks with a totem.

If you are a member of a class that can wield a totem as an implement, you can add the totem's enhancement bonus to the attack rolls and the damage rolls of implement powers from that class that you use through the totem, and you can use its properties and powers. Members of other classes gain no benefit from wielding a totem.

Avalanche's Wake Totem | Level 19+

Your spirit companion draws power from this jagged stone totem to become as unstoppable as a landslide.

| Lvl 19 | +4 | 105,000 gp | Lvl 29 | +6 | 2,625,000 gp |
| Lvl 24 | +5 | 525,000 gp |

Implement (Totem)
Enhancement: Attack rolls and damage rolls
Critical: +1d6 damage per plus, and you push the target 1 square per plus.
Property: Your spirit companion ignores difficult terrain when it moves.
Power (Daily): Free Action. *Trigger:* You hit with an attack through your spirit companion using this totem. *Effect:* Each enemy adjacent to your spirit companion is slowed until the end of your next turn.

Bloodhunter Totem | Level 5+

This totem is carved from a petrified heart, which beats when the totem is close to wounded prey.

Lvl 5	+1	1,000 gp	Lvl 20	+4	125,000 gp
Lvl 10	+2	5,000 gp	Lvl 25	+5	625,000 gp
Lvl 15	+3	25,000 gp	Lvl 30	+6	3,125,000 gp

Implement (Totem)
Enhancement: Attack rolls and damage rolls
Critical: +1d6 damage per plus, or +1d10 damage per plus against a bloodied target
Property: You gain a +1 bonus to attack rolls using this totem against bloodied creatures.

Boar's Charge Totem | Level 3+

When you grasp this boar's tusk, your heart races with feral excitement and you throw yourself headlong into battle.

Lvl 3	+1	680 gp	Lvl 18	+4	85,000 gp
Lvl 8	+2	3,400 gp	Lvl 23	+5	425,000 gp
Lvl 13	+3	17,000 gp	Lvl 28	+6	2,125,000 gp

Implement (Totem)
Enhancement: Attack rolls and damage rolls
Critical: +1d6 damage per plus
Property: When charging while you are in beast form, you gain a +1 bonus to speed.
Power (Daily): Free Action. *Trigger:* You hit an enemy with a charge attack using this totem while you are in beast form. *Effect:* You push that enemy 1 square and can shift into the space it vacated.

Bronzewood Coils Totem | Level 13+

With this knotted serpent totem crafted of bronzewood, you can grant your spirit companion an aspect of the World Serpent.

| Lvl 13 | +3 | 17,000 gp | Lvl 23 | +5 | 425,000 gp |
| Lvl 18 | +4 | 85,000 gp | Lvl 28 | +6 | 2,125,000 gp |

Implement (Totem)
Enhancement: Attack rolls and damage rolls
Critical: +1d6 damage per plus
Power (Daily): Free Action. *Trigger:* You hit an enemy with the *spirit's fangs* power (*Player's Handbook 2*, page 120) using this totem. *Effect:* That enemy is grabbed by your spirit companion. When the enemy attempts to escape the grab, you can have it make the Acrobatics check or Athletics check against your Will instead of your Fortitude or Reflex.

Dire Totem | Level 10+

As you undergo the transformation into beast form, your body grows larger, heavier, and far more dangerous.

Lvl 10	+2	5,000 gp	Lvl 25	+5	625,000 gp
Lvl 15	+3	25,000 gp	Lvl 30	+6	3,125,000 gp
Lvl 20	+4	125,000 gp

Implement (Totem)
Enhancement: Attack rolls and damage rolls
Critical: +1d6 damage per plus
Power (Daily): Free Action. *Trigger:* You use your *wild shape* power (*Player's Handbook 2*, page 84) to assume your beast form. *Effect:* While you are in beast form, your size is Large, and you gain a power bonus to damage rolls using beast form powers through this totem equal to the totem's enhancement bonus.

Earthfall Totem
Level 7+

Attacks with this rough-hewn stone totem pack a powerful punch.

Lvl 7	+2	2,600 gp		Lvl 22	+5	325,000 gp
Lvl 12	+3	13,000 gp		Lvl 27	+6	1,625,000 gp
Lvl 17	+4	65,000 gp				

Implement (Totem)
Enhancement: Attack rolls and damage rolls
Critical: +1d6 damage per plus
Property: When you use a primal attack power through this totem that pushes or slides a creature or knocks a creature prone, you deal 1d6 extra damage to each creature that was pushed, slid, or knocked prone.
Level 17, 22, or 27: 2d6 extra damage.

Fell Beast Totem
Level 3+

This totem is infused with venom extracted from corrupt predators of the swamp.

Lvl 3	+1	680 gp		Lvl 18	+4	85,000 gp
Lvl 8	+2	3,400 gp		Lvl 23	+5	425,000 gp
Lvl 13	+3	17,000 gp		Lvl 28	+6	2,125,000 gp

Implement (Totem)
Enhancement: Attack rolls and damage rolls
Critical: +1d6 poison damage per plus
Power (Daily ✦ Poison): Free Action. The next time you use a primal attack power through this totem during this turn, each creature hit by the attack takes ongoing 5 poison damage (save ends).
Level 13 or 18: Ongoing 10 poison damage (save ends).
Level 23 or 28: Ongoing 15 poison damage (save ends).

Flameheart Totem
Level 10+

A constantly smoldering mote of flame dangles from this totem and infuses your evocations with fiery power.

Lvl 10	+2	5,000 gp		Lvl 25	+5	625,000 gp
Lvl 15	+3	25,000 gp		Lvl 30	+6	3,125,000 gp
Lvl 20	+4	125,000 gp				

Implement (Totem)
Enhancement: Attack rolls and damage rolls
Critical: +1d6 fire damage per plus
Property: When you hit a creature that is granting combat advantage to you using a primal attack power through this totem, that creature takes 1d6 extra fire damage.
Power (Daily ✦ Fire): Free Action. The next time you use a primal attack power through this totem during this turn, each creature hit by the attack takes ongoing 5 fire damage (save ends).
Level 15 or 20: Ongoing 10 fire damage (save ends).
Level 25 or 30: Ongoing 15 fire damage (save ends).

Iron Bear Totem
Level 8+

This black iron rod, bound with bear fur, empowers your spirit companion to bolster nearby allies.

Lvl 8	+2	3,400 gp		Lvl 23	+5	425,000 gp
Lvl 13	+3	17,000 gp		Lvl 28	+6	2,125,000 gp
Lvl 18	+4	85,000 gp				

Implement (Totem)
Enhancement: Attack rolls and damage rolls
Critical: +1d6 damage per plus
Power (Daily): Minor Action. Until the end of your next turn, any ally gains a +2 bonus to all defenses while adjacent to your spirit companion.

Life River Totem
Level 13+

While you're armed with this green wood totem, your group enjoys great vitality even in the face of deadly adversity.

Lvl 13	+3	17,000 gp		Lvl 23	+5	425,000 gp
Lvl 18	+4	85,000 gp		Lvl 28	+6	2,125,000 gp

Implement (Totem)
Enhancement: Attack rolls and damage rolls
Critical: +1d6 damage per plus
Property: When you hit with a primal attack power using this totem, you or any ally adjacent to you who spends a healing surge before the end of your next turn regains additional hit points equal to the totem's enhancement bonus.

Nine Furies Totem
Level 20+

This totem is crafted of horn, wood, and sinew. It flares with power as warrior spirits invigorate your comrades in battle.

Lvl 20	+4	125,000 gp		Lvl 30	+6	3,125,000 gp
Lvl 25	+5	625,000 gp				

Implement (Totem)
Enhancement: Attack rolls and damage rolls
Critical: +1d6 damage per plus
Property: When you grant temporary hit points to your allies with a shaman power, one ally gains additional temporary hit points equal to the totem's enhancement bonus.
Power (Daily): Immediate Reaction. *Trigger:* An ally you can see becomes bloodied. *Effect:* Each ally you can see gains temporary hit points equal to twice the totem's enhancement bonus. These temporary hit points stack with any existing temporary hit points.

TOTEM OF NEW BEGINNINGS

Civilization's bones litter the world: crumbling cities, fallen towers, and moss-covered stones that were once statues celebrating mighty heroes. Nature eventually reclaims the resources that mortals have stolen, and something new always arises from the wreckage of the old. This is life's cycle. New growth and new possibilities can exist only through death.

A *totem of new beginnings* draws power from this natural rhythm. In a wielder's hand, the totem briefly spurs innovation and creativity, those sensations withering soon after they bloom. Experienced wielders learn to harness this ebb and flow to channel primal energy at the right moment.

Returning Home: As a unique event, a hero might discover a *totem of new beginnings* growing in a hard-to-reach location associated with his or her previous life. For instance, if a hero lived for several years in an urban or built-up area that has since been reclaimed by the wilderness, especially as a consequence of war or a battle with primal powers, that hero might stumble upon a living branch that can function as a *totem of new beginnings* while returning to visit the ruined homeland. Perhaps it's growing from a ruined doorframe of an old home or at the grave of the hero's parents.

Panther Totem — Level 9+

Carved in the shape of a panther and adorned with fangs, this totem grants its user feline stealth.

Lvl 9	+2	4,200 gp	Lvl 24	+5	525,000 gp
Lvl 14	+3	21,000 gp	Lvl 29	+6	2,625,000 gp
Lvl 19	+4	105,000 gp			

Implement (Totem)
Enhancement: Attack rolls and damage rolls
Critical: +1d6 damage per plus, or +1d10 damage per plus against a target granting combat advantage to you
Power (Daily ✦ Illusion): Minor Action. Until the end of your next turn, you are invisible to enemies more than 5 squares away from you.

Razor Talon Totem — Level 14+

Festooned with talons, claws, and fangs, this totem makes your attacks in beast form more dangerous.

| Lvl 14 | +3 | 21,000 gp | Lvl 24 | +5 | 525,000 gp |
| Lvl 19 | +4 | 105,000 gp | Lvl 29 | +6 | 2,625,000 gp |

Implement (Totem)
Enhancement: Attack rolls and damage rolls
Critical: +1d6 damage per plus, or +1d8 damage per plus while you are in beast form
Property: When you use a beast form attack power through this totem, you can score a critical hit on a roll of 19-20.

NINE FURIES TOTEM

On the Stormkissed Plain, in the shadow of the Moon Peaks, nine warriors stood. They were called the Nine Furies; each was the greatest of his or her tribe and gifted with quickness, talent, wisdom, and strength. They gathered to confront Borstod the Blasphemer, a catastrophic dragon of great age and power. As the dragon neared, the Furies' peoples fled into the mountains, depending on their champions to buy them time to escape.

For nine days and nights the Furies fought the ancient wyrm, each dawn marking a champion's end until only one remained. Although that champion's companions no longer lived, their devoted spirits continued the fight at her side. With their support, she spent her remaining life force in a final attack and drove her axe into the dragon's skull. The cruel voice of the dragon was silenced forever.

A *Nine Furies totem* captures the noble deeds of these mighty champions. Each totem contains the essence of one Fury, and on moonless nights its wielder might just spy a spectral hero and dragon battling in the sky. Those who brandish one of these totems in battle can draw on a measure of that fabled power to aid them against superior foes.

The Centaurs' Secrets: Some sages believe that the centaurs were the first to craft these totems and that they alone know the method of their manufacture. To acquire such an item, a hero must seek out a tribe of centaurs and prove his or her worth by defeating a dragon in battle. Success earns not only a *Nine Furies totem*, but also the potential to unearth other long-guarded secrets and forgotten lore.

Ninth Fury: Conventional legend holds that all the champions perished, but some tales suggest that the ninth survived and might live still. If she can be found, she might grant her totem to a worthy bearer.

Roaring Bear Totem — Level 2+

Carved from the great claw of a dire bear, this totem growls like that mighty beast when you channel primal power through it.

Lvl 2	+1	520 gp	Lvl 17	+4	65,000 gp
Lvl 7	+2	2,600 gp	Lvl 22	+5	325,000 gp
Lvl 12	+3	13,000 gp	Lvl 27	+6	1,625,000 gp

Implement (Totem)
Enhancement: Attack rolls and damage rolls
Critical: +1d6 damage per plus
Power (Daily): Free Action. *Trigger:* You hit an enemy with a primal attack power using this totem. *Effect:* You knock the enemy prone.

Totem of Nature's Balm — Level 10+

When you wave this totem, decorated with dried herbs, healing light streams from your spirit companion into your allies.

Lvl 10	+2	5,000 gp	Lvl 25	+5	625,000 gp
Lvl 15	+3	25,000 gp	Lvl 30	+6	3,125,000 gp
Lvl 20	+4	125,000 gp			

Implement (Totem)
Enhancement: Attack rolls and damage rolls
Critical: +1d6 damage per plus, and one ally you can see within 10 squares of you can spend a healing surge.
Power (Daily): Free Action. *Trigger:* You hit with a primal attack power using this totem. *Effect:* Each ally within 2 squares of you or your spirit companion makes a saving throw with a power bonus equal to the totem's enhancement bonus.

Totem of New Beginnings — Level 14+

This bone totem gradually changes color in your hands, shifting from green to gray to black to green again.

| Lvl 14 | +3 | 21,000 gp | Lvl 24 | +5 | 525,000 gp |
| Lvl 19 | +4 | 105,000 gp | Lvl 29 | +6 | 2,625,000 gp |

Implement (Totem)
Enhancement: Attack rolls and damage rolls
Critical: +1d6 damage per plus
Power (Daily): No Action. *Trigger:* You use a primal daily attack power through this totem and miss all targets. *Effect:* One ally within 5 squares of you regains the use of an expended encounter power of the totem's level or lower.

Totem of the Awakened Bear — Level 13+

Carved in the form of a yawning beast, this totem rouses your spirit companion against opponents that draw your attention.

| Lvl 13 | +3 | 17,000 gp | Lvl 23 | +5 | 425,000 gp |
| Lvl 18 | +4 | 85,000 gp | Lvl 28 | +6 | 2,125,000 gp |

Implement (Totem)
Enhancement: Attack rolls and damage rolls
Critical: +1d6 damage per plus, or +1d10 damage per plus while you're bloodied
Power (Daily): Free Action. *Trigger:* You hit an enemy with your *spirit's shield* power (*Player's Handbook 2*, page 121). *Effect:* That enemy grants combat advantage until the end of your next turn.

Totem of the Crashing Tide   Level 15+

Moisture continually beads over the conch shell that forms this totem and then evaporates, reflecting the tides in which it once lived.

Lvl 15	+3	25,000 gp	Lvl 25	+5	625,000 gp
Lvl 20	+4	125,000 gp	Lvl 30	+6	3,125,000 gp

Implement (Totem)
Enhancement: Attack rolls and damage rolls
Critical: +1d6 damage per plus, and you push the target 1
   square per plus.
Property: When you push a creature with a primal attack
   power using this totem, the distance of the push increases
   by 1 square.
Power (Daily): Free Action. *Trigger:* You push an enemy
   with a primal attack power using this totem. *Effect:* That
   enemy grants combat advantage until the end of your
   next turn.

Totem of the Harrier's Claws   Level 12+

This totem, covered in owl feathers and talons, grants you the ferocity of a hunting bird against weakened prey.

Lvl 12	+3	13,000 gp	Lvl 22	+5	325,000 gp
Lvl 17	+4	65,000 gp	Lvl 27	+6	1,625,000 gp

Implement (Totem)
Enhancement: Attack rolls and damage rolls
Critical: +1d6 damage per plus
Property: Creatures taking ongoing damage grant combat
   advantage to you.

TOTEM OF THE NIGHT

The Endless Swamp is so large and its growth so lush that the canopy in its deepest sections blocks the light of day. In those dark places the spirits of night are strongest. From there the legendary Circle of the Bat protects the land and gains strange powers of augury from the swamp spirits the Circle members revere.

Although *totems of the night* are made of cypress wood, the druids and shamans of the Circle claim that they're actually the bodies of bats that live deep within the Endless Swamp. According to this tale, a bat sometimes flies too high during daylight and breaks through the thick canopy. When touched by the rays of the sun, it turns to wood and falls to the swamp floor, where its body is harvested to create one of these totems.

The Hag's Coven: A group of hags dwelling at the southern end of the Endless Swamp is constantly at war with the Circle of the Bat. These powerful fey have felled a number of shamans and druids, collecting each victim's *totem of the night* as a trophy of the kill. The Circle has asked for assistance in destroying the hags.

Nightheart Cave: This grotto lies near the edge of the Endless Swamp. Within is the Heart of Night, a black flame that must be extinguished on each winter solstice to prevent the opening of a permanent portal into the Shadowfell. It is taboo for members of the Circle of the Bat to enter the Nightheart Cave, so they must seek a champion from outside their order to perform this task. The Circle is willing to arm that champion with a *totem of the night*.

Totem of the night

Totem of the Night   Level 12+

This totem of blackened wood is shaped like a stylized bat and allows you to pierce the veil of night.

Lvl 12	+3	13,000 gp	Lvl 22	+5	325,000 gp
Lvl 17	+4	65,000 gp	Lvl 27	+6	1,625,000 gp

Implement (Totem)
Enhancement: Attack rolls and damage rolls
Critical: +1d6 damage per plus
Property: You gain low-light vision. If you already have low-
   light vision, you instead gain darkvision.
Power (Daily): Minor Action. Until the end of your turn,
   your attacks using this totem ignore cover and conceal-
   ment, but not superior cover or total concealment.

LUCIO PARRILLO

Totem of the Ravenous Beast — Level 9+

This hideous bloodstained totem gorges itself on the life energy of your foes.

Lvl 9	+2	4,200 gp	Lvl 24	+5	525,000 gp
Lvl 14	+3	21,000 gp	Lvl 29	+6	2,625,000 gp
Lvl 19	+4	105,000 gp			

Implement (Totem)

Enhancement: Attack rolls and damage rolls

Critical: +1d6 damage per plus, or +1d10 damage per plus against a target granting combat advantage to you

Power (Daily): Free Action. *Trigger:* You reduce an enemy to 0 hit points with a primal power using this totem. *Effect:* You take a move action.

Totem of the Satyr's Dance — Level 8+

This gnarled branch, carved to look like a horn, channels the frenetic dance of reveling satyr spirits.

Lvl 8	+2	3,400 gp	Lvl 23	+5	425,000 gp
Lvl 13	+3	17,000 gp	Lvl 28	+6	2,125,000 gp
Lvl 18	+4	85,000 gp			

Implement (Totem)

Enhancement: Attack rolls and damage rolls

Critical: +1d6 damage per plus

Property: When an ally regains hit points from a primal power used through this totem, he or she gains a +1 bonus to speed until the end of his or her next turn.

Power (Daily): Free Action. *Trigger:* You hit with a primal attack power using this totem. *Effect:* An ally you can see within 10 squares of you gains a +1 power bonus to speed until the end of the encounter.

Totem of the Scouring Wind — Level 15+

Used by desert-dwelling centaur tribes, this totem shaped from sandstone summons the power of the terrible simoom.

Lvl 15	+3	25,000 gp	Lvl 25	+5	625,000 gp
Lvl 20	+4	125,000 gp	Lvl 30	+6	3,125,000 gp

Implement (Totem)

Enhancement: Attack rolls and damage rolls

Critical: +1d6 damage per plus, and the target takes ongoing 10 damage (save ends).
Level 25 or 30: Ongoing 15 damage (save ends).

Power (Daily): Standard Action. You push each creature that is adjacent to you 2 squares. Until the end of your next turn, you gain a +2 power bonus to all defenses against ranged and area attacks.

Totem of the World Tree — Level 20+

The rich wood of this totem is warm to the touch. You can feel the life of the world pulsing through it.

Lvl 20	+4	125,000 gp	Lvl 30	+6	3,125,000 gp
Lvl 25	+5	625,000 gp			

Implement (Totem)

Enhancement: Attack rolls and damage rolls

Critical: Each ally within 3 squares of you gains 1d6 temporary hit points per plus (roll once and apply the result to each ally).

Power (Daily): Free Action. *Trigger:* You hit an enemy with a primal attack power using this totem. *Effect:* You or an ally within 3 squares of you makes a saving throw with a bonus equal to the totem's enhancement bonus.

Totem of Thunder's Keeper — Level 2+

A stylized face carved into this totem animates with an angry growl to rebuff those who harm your allies.

Lvl 2	+1	520 gp	Lvl 17	+4	65,000 gp
Lvl 7	+2	2,600 gp	Lvl 22	+5	325,000 gp
Lvl 12	+3	13,000 gp	Lvl 27	+6	1,625,000 gp

Implement (Totem)

Enhancement: Attack rolls and damage rolls

Critical: +1d6 thunder damage per plus

Power (Daily ✦ Thunder): Immediate Reaction. *Trigger:* An enemy hits your spirit companion or an ally within 5 squares of you with a melee attack. *Effect:* The triggering enemy takes thunder damage equal to your Wisdom modifier. In addition, you push it a number of squares equal to the totem's enhancement bonus.

Totem of Winter's Scorn — Level 9+

Carved from a branch of winterfir tree, this totem channels the bitter cold of the tundra.

Lvl 9	+2	4,200 gp	Lvl 24	+5	525,000 gp
Lvl 14	+3	21,000 gp	Lvl 29	+6	2,625,000 gp
Lvl 19	+4	105,000 gp			

Implement (Totem)

Enhancement: Attack rolls and damage rolls

Critical: +1d6 cold damage per plus, and the target is slowed until the end of your next turn.

Power (Daily): Free Action. *Trigger:* You hit an enemy with a primal cold power using this totem. *Effect:* That enemy is immobilized and grants combat advantage (save ends).

Vengeful Spirit Totem — Level 8+

Infused with the rage of a thousand vicious beasts, this totem makes your spirit companion intimidating in battle.

Lvl 8	+2	3,400 gp	Lvl 23	+5	425,000 gp
Lvl 13	+3	17,000 gp	Lvl 28	+6	2,125,000 gp
Lvl 18	+4	85,000 gp			

Implement (Totem)

Enhancement: Attack rolls and damage rolls

Critical: +1d6 damage per plus, or +1d10 per plus with a primal spirit attack power

Power (Daily): Minor Action. Until the end of the encounter, each enemy adjacent to your spirit companion takes a -2 penalty to attack rolls.

Wildfire Totem — Level 4+

This charred totem grows hot to the touch as your enemy erupts in hungry flames.

Lvl 4	+1	840 gp	Lvl 19	+4	105,000 gp
Lvl 9	+2	4,200 gp	Lvl 24	+5	525,000 gp
Lvl 14	+3	21,000 gp	Lvl 29	+6	2,625,000 gp

Implement (Totem)

Enhancement: Attack rolls and damage rolls

Critical: +1d6 fire damage per plus

Property: You gain a +2 bonus to saving throws against ongoing fire damage.

Power (Daily ✦ Fire): Free Action. *Trigger:* You hit an enemy with a primal fire power using this totem. *Effect:* Each enemy adjacent to you takes ongoing 5 fire damage (save ends).
Level 14 or 19: Ongoing 10 fire damage (save ends).
Level 24 or 29: Ongoing 15 fire damage (save ends).

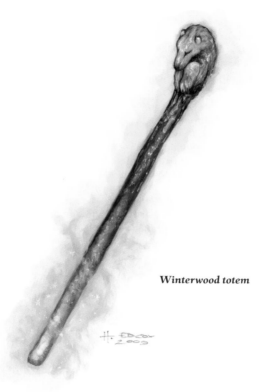

Winterwood totem

If you are a member of a class that can wield a wand as an implement, you can add the wand's enhancement bonus to the attack rolls and the damage rolls of implement powers from that class that you use through the wand, and you can use its properties and powers. Members of other classes gain no benefit from wielding a wand.

Cursing Wand			Level 14+

You curse your foe when you channel your spite through this dark yew wand.

Lvl 14	+3	21,000 gp	Lvl 24	+5	525,000 gp
Lvl 19	+4	105,000 gp	Lvl 29	+6	2,625,000 gp

Implement (Wand)
Enhancement: Attack rolls and damage rolls
Critical: +1d6 damage per plus
Property: When you score a critical hit with the *unluck* power using this wand, the target also takes a -2 penalty to attack rolls, skill checks, ability checks, and saving throws (save ends).
Power (Daily ✦ Arcane, Implement, Necrotic): Standard Action. As the bard's *unluck* power (*Player's Handbook 2*, page 72).

Winterwood Totem			Level 4+

Fashioned from trees perpetually coated in primal frost, this totem is surrounded by a cloud of freezing mist.

Lvl 4	+1	840 gp	Lvl 19	+4	105,000 gp
Lvl 9	+2	4,200 gp	Lvl 24	+5	525,000 gp
Lvl 14	+3	21,000 gp	Lvl 29	+6	2,625,000 gp

Implement (Totem)
Enhancement: Attack rolls and damage rolls
Critical: +1d6 cold damage per plus
Power (Daily): Free Action. *Trigger:* You hit an enemy with a primal cold power using this totem and deal damage to it. *Effect:* That enemy gains vulnerable 3 cold until the end of your next turn.
Level 14 or 19: Vulnerable 5 cold.
Level 24 or 29: Vulnerable 10 cold.

WANDS

Wands only look like they're too fragile to be deadly.

Wands are often considered the most popular arcane implements because nearly all arcane heroes can use them.

Wands are used to store spells, but they can also modify the spells cast through them. Perhaps the best aspect to these implements is their versatility, since they allow a bard and a wizard, for example, to explore each other's magic.

Except in rare cases, a wand is not large enough or strong enough to be used as a weapon. If a wand can function as either a weapon or an implement, that fact is noted in the item's description.

CURSING WAND

This wand is cut from yew wood and stained black with the ashes of those who suffered accidental deaths. A string of curses crawls around the implement, spiraling toward its tip. Starting with large lettering in the lokharic script, the words gradually shrink until they can be seen only through close inspection. The curses themselves change with the reader, pinpointing the wielder's flaws, fears, and failures.

The *cursing wand* originated in the hands of a jilted lover—a young minstrel spurned for another, younger woman. Her heart broken, she poured all her malice and hate into her wand, imbuing it with the darkest and most sinister curses imaginable. With the implement complete, she hunted down her former paramour and put a curse on him that turned everything he touched to ash until the day he died under mysterious circumstances.

The *cursing wands* found in the world today are reproductions of the original and, although potentially powerful in their own right, lack the full weight of the original creator's malevolence. Still, things have a way of going wrong when a *cursing wand* is present.

Defeat the Renegade Minstrel: Zasterly, a middling performer of little talent, holds a town hostage, living as a lord and compelling the locals to leap to his every whim. Those who have refused have found themselves the targets of his acid tongue and cruel spells delivered through a *cursing wand*. Over time, each of Zasterly's enemies has died in a lethal accident. The townsfolk are terrified of the minstrel and will pay someone well to remove him from power.

ED COX

Diamond Wand — Level 4+

This gem-topped wand's fragile appearance belies its strength.

Lvl 4	+1	840 gp	Lvl 19	+4	105,000 gp
Lvl 9	+2	4,200 gp	Lvl 24	+5	525,000 gp
Lvl 14	+3	21,000 gp	Lvl 29	+6	2,625,000 gp

Implement (Wand)

Enhancement: Attack rolls and damage rolls

Critical: +1d6 damage per plus

Property: When you hit an enemy with an arcane force power using this wand, the next attack that hits that enemy deals 1 extra force damage.
Level 14 or 19: 2 extra force damage.
Level 24 or 29: 3 extra force damage.

Power (Daily): Standard Action. As the artificer's *spike wire* power (EBERRON *Player's Guide*, page 48), which is reproduced below.

Spike Wire — Artificer Attack 1

You throw a bundle of barbed wire that bites into your enemy's flesh, digging deeper and deeper.

Encounter ✦ Arcane, Force, Implement
Standard Action   **Ranged** 10
Target: One creature
Attack: Intelligence vs. Fortitude
Hit: 1d8 + Intelligence modifier force damage. Until the end of your next turn, any attack deals extra damage to the target equal to your Wisdom modifier.

Hawthorn Wand — Level 9+

This pale wand harnesses fate and makes it your servant.

Lvl 9	+2	4,200 gp	Lvl 24	+5	525,000 gp
Lvl 14	+3	21,000 gp	Lvl 29	+6	2,625,000 gp
Lvl 19	+4	105,000 gp			

Implement (Wand)

Enhancement: Attack rolls and damage rolls

Critical: +1d6 damage per plus

Property: When you use an arcane power through this wand to grant yourself or an ally a bonus to saving throws and the saving throw roll is lower than this wand's enhancement bonus, you or the ally can reroll the saving throw and use either result.

Power (Daily): Standard Action. As the artificer's *altered luck* power (EBERRON *Player's Guide*, page 49), which is reproduced below.

Altered Luck — Artificer Attack 3

Your magic blasts an enemy and transfers its luck to a nearby ally.

Encounter ✦ Arcane, Implement
Standard Action   **Area** burst 2 within 10 squares
Target: One creature in burst
Attack: Intelligence vs. Will
Hit: 1d6 + Intelligence modifier damage, and the target takes a -2 penalty to saving throws until the end of your next turn.
Effect: One ally within the burst gains temporary hit points equal to 5 + your Wisdom modifier and a +2 bonus to an attack roll, a skill check, an ability check, or a saving throw before the end of your next turn. The ally can use the bonus after determining the result of a roll.

Iron Wand — Level 24+

This thick pry bar does double duty as a weapon and an implement.

| Lvl 24 | +5 | 525,000 gp | Lvl 29 | +6 | 2,625,000 gp |

Implement (Wand)

Enhancement: Attack rolls and damage rolls

Critical: +1d6 damage per plus

Property: You gain an item bonus to Strength checks to break open doors or chests equal to the wand's enhancement bonus.

Property: This wand can be used as a melee weapon, functioning as a mace. You can add its enhancement bonus to the attack rolls and damage rolls of melee weapon attacks.

Power (Daily): Minor Action. As the artificer's *iron-hide infusion* power (EBERRON *Player's Guide*, page 53), which is reproduced below.

Iron-Hide Infusion — Artificer Utility 16

You crush a bit of iron in your hand, infusing it with protective magic. You then cast the dust onto your allies' armor.

Encounter ✦ Arcane
Minor Action   **Close** burst 5
Target: You and each ally in burst
Effect: Each target gains a +4 bonus to AC until the end of your next turn.

IRON WAND

A thick length of iron easily mistaken for a pry bar, an *iron wand* is an unlikely implement. The wand's tip is a flattened wedge with a notch in the middle; its base is a hooked wedge ideal for prying open doors, chests, and just about anything else that needs opening. An *iron wand* can also be used as a weapon, since its weight and size are perfect for clobbering enemies.

For the mage who divides her time between flinging spells at enemies and building servants to fight on her behalf, an *iron wand* is an invaluable accessory, useful for battering enemies and focusing one's concentration when working with arcane magic.

Defeat the Iron Mage: A warforged artificer known only as the Iron Mage wields an *iron wand* in battle to great effect. Surrounded by a legion of lesser warforged, golems, and other constructs, he resides in a great fortress in the heart of a blasted wilderness where nothing grows and the corpses of those who oppose him swell beneath a merciless sun. Adventurers who defeat him can wrest control over his followers and his wand.

Join the Forgesmiths: The Forgesmiths were the first artificers to fashion *iron wands*. Shunned by their fellows for their dubious experiments in blending flesh with machines, the Forgesmiths developed these wands as a means of protection against assassins and hostile rivals. Although the tensions between them and their peers have cooled somewhat, the Forgesmiths are famously xenophobic and reluctant to admit new members into their secretive society. Still, those who do join are often given their own *iron wands*.

Master's wand of eyes of the vestige

HAWTHORN WAND

Where hawthorn grows, evil fears to tread. Favored by the fey spirits, hawthorn wood is reputed to be a great conduit for arcane energy—some of the best wands are made from this wood. A *hawthorn wand* is an 18-inch wand that tapers to a fine point. Varnished to give the implement an amber finish, it's smooth to the touch. When used in an implement, the wood grows warm and a faint light shines from within, revealing great power.

Simply carrying a *hawthorn wand* brings about good fortune in subtle ways. An owner might win a few extra hands in a game of *Three-Dragon Ante* or receive a small windfall in coin or opportunity. The wand's true power, however, is to bend reality in its wielder's favor so that he or she can slip free from dire situations.

Befriend the Green Sisters: The most famous makers of *hawthorn wands* are the Green Sisters, a small circle of dryads who dwell deep in the Western Wood. One who stumbles across the dryads are certain to find death, unless the hapless traveler sings a song that moves the trees themselves. If the singer succeeds, the dryads have been known to bestow a boon in the form of a *hawthorn wand* to the performer who so impressed them.

Save the Famous Minstrel: Aloysius, a famous warrior and minstrel, is a bard of unequaled skill and daring. When not confronting dragons with his keen wit and keener blade, he entertains kings and emperors, and he is a favored presence in any court. For all his success, he has also gained a number of enemies who would gladly see him brought low. So when he went missing, a call rose up through the land to find the legendary singer and bring him back to safety. The king has promised to bestow a *hawthorn wand* to whomever brings back the bard, or at least proof of his death.

Master's Wand of Eyes of the Vestige — Level 4+

This ebony wand strikes your targets with devastating power.

Lvl 4	+1	840 gp	Lvl 19	+4	105,000 gp
Lvl 9	+2	4,200 gp	Lvl 24	+5	525,000 gp
Lvl 14	+3	21,000 gp	Lvl 29	+6	2,625,000 gp

Implement (Wand)
Enhancement: Attack rolls and damage rolls
Critical: +1d8 damage per plus
Property: When you hit with the *eyes of the vestige* power using this wand, the second creature can be within 5 squares of the target instead of 3 squares, and you gain a +1 bonus to your Warlock's Curse extra damage for that attack.
Power (Encounter): Standard Action. As the warlock's *eyes of the vestige* power (*Arcane Power*, page 73), which is reproduced below.

Eyes of the Vestige — Warlock Attack 1

Your enemy's eyes glow with an eldritch light as your vestige takes hold and scours that foe's mind while you curse another nearby foe.

At-Will ✦ Arcane, Implement, Psychic; Varies
Standard Action   **Ranged 10**
Target: One creature
Attack: Constitution vs. Will
Hit: 1d6 + Constitution modifier psychic damage. Choose the target or a creature within 3 squares of the target and within the target's line of sight. You place your Warlock's Curse on that creature; if the creature is already cursed by you, you can deal your Warlock's Curse extra damage to that creature instead of to the target.
Level 21: 2d6 + Constitution modifier psychic damage.

Master's Wand of Illusory Ambush — Level 4+

With this red palm wand, your phantoms continue to harass your enemies.

Lvl 4	+1	840 gp	Lvl 19	+4	105,000 gp
Lvl 9	+2	4,200 gp	Lvl 24	+5	525,000 gp
Lvl 14	+3	21,000 gp	Lvl 29	+6	2,625,000 gp

Implement (Wand)
Enhancement: Attack rolls and damage rolls
Critical: +1d8 damage per plus
Property: After you hit an enemy with the *illusory ambush* power using this wand, when that enemy attacks while it's taking the penalty to attack rolls, it takes psychic damage equal to 3 + this wand's enhancement bonus.
Power (Encounter): Standard Action. As the wizard's *illusory ambush* power (*Arcane Power*, page 101), which is reproduced below.

Illusory Ambush — Wizard Attack 1

You create an illusion of swirling spectral assailants that swarm over your enemy.

At-Will ✦ Arcane, Illusion, Implement, Psychic
Standard Action   **Ranged 10**
Target: One creature
Attack: Intelligence vs. Will
Hit: 1d6 + Intelligence modifier psychic damage, and the target takes a -2 penalty to attack rolls until the end of your next turn.
Level 21: 2d6 + Intelligence modifier psychic damage.

KALMAN ANDRASOFSZKY

Master's Wand of Misdirected Mark · Level 4+

Disaster awaits those beguiled by this crooked hickory wand.

Lvl 4	+1	840 gp	Lvl 19	+4	105,000 gp
Lvl 9	+2	4,200 gp	Lvl 24	+5	525,000 gp
Lvl 14	+3	21,000 gp	Lvl 29	+6	2,625,000 gp

Implement (Wand)

Enhancement: Attack rolls and damage rolls

Critical: +1d8 damage per plus

Property: When you hit with the *misdirected mark* power using this wand, the ally that marked a target gains a +1 bonus to attack rolls against that target until the end of your next turn.

Power (Encounter ✦ Arcane, Implement): Standard Action. As the bard's *misdirected mark* power (*Player's Handbook 2*, page 68).

Master's Wand of Phantom Bolt · Level 4+

Your illusory bolts become more ominous with this smoky amber wand.

Lvl 4	+1	840 gp	Lvl 19	+4	105,000 gp
Lvl 9	+2	4,200 gp	Lvl 24	+5	525,000 gp
Lvl 14	+3	21,000 gp	Lvl 29	+6	2,625,000 gp

Implement (Wand)

Enhancement: Attack rolls and damage rolls

Critical: +1d8 damage per plus

Property: When you hit an enemy with the *phantom bolt* power using this wand, you can slide that enemy 1 extra square.

Power (Encounter): Standard Action. As the wizard's *phantom bolt* power (*Arcane Power*, page 101), which is reproduced below.

Phantom Bolt · Wizard Attack 1

You wave your hand, and your foe sees a bolt of fire streaking toward it. The enemy dives away from the imagined threat.

At-Will ✦ Arcane, Illusion, Implement, Psychic
Standard Action   **Ranged** 10
Target: One creature
Attack: Intelligence vs. Will
Hit: 1d8 + Intelligence modifier psychic damage, and you slide the target 1 square.
Level 21: 2d8 + Intelligence modifier psychic damage.

Master's Wand of Spiteful Glamor · Level 4+

This wand is especially deadly to creatures you haven't harmed yet.

Lvl 4	+1	840 gp	Lvl 19	+4	105,000 gp
Lvl 9	+2	4,200 gp	Lvl 24	+5	525,000 gp
Lvl 14	+3	21,000 gp	Lvl 29	+6	2,625,000 gp

Implement (Wand)

Enhancement: Attack rolls and damage rolls

Critical: +1d8 psychic damage per plus

Property: When you hit an enemy at maximum hit points that is affected by your Warlock's Curse with the *spiteful glamor* power using this wand, you deal an extra die of Warlock's Curse damage to that enemy.

Power (Encounter): Standard Action. As the warlock's *spiteful glamor* power (*Forgotten Realms* Player's Guide, page 35), which is reproduced below.

Spiteful Glamor · Warlock (Dark) Attack 1

The mere sight of you is anathema to your enemy.

At-Will ✦ Arcane, Implement, Psychic
Standard Action   **Ranged** 10
Target: One creature
Attack: Charisma vs. Will
Hit: 1d8 + Charisma modifier psychic damage, or 1d12 + Charisma modifier psychic damage to a target at maximum hit points.
Level 21: 2d8 + Charisma modifier psychic damage, or 2d12 + Charisma modifier psychic damage to a target at maximum hit points.

Master's Wand of Vicious Mockery · Level 4+

Wielding this hackberry wand sharpens your tongue and hones your wit.

Lvl 4	+1	840 gp	Lvl 19	+4	105,000 gp
Lvl 9	+2	4,200 gp	Lvl 24	+5	525,000 gp
Lvl 14	+3	21,000 gp	Lvl 29	+6	2,625,000 gp

Implement (Wand)

Enhancement: Attack rolls and damage rolls

Critical: +1d8 damage per plus

Property: When you hit with the *vicious mockery* power using this wand, choose a different enemy within 2 squares of the target. That enemy takes a penalty to attack rolls equal to your Intelligence modifier until the end of your next turn.

Power (Encounter ✦ Arcane, Charm, Implement, Psychic): Standard Action. As the bard's *vicious mockery* power (*Player's Handbook 2*, page 69).

DIAMOND WAND

A sparkling diamond the size of a human's thumb caps the base of this wand. The smooth holly wood tapers from the gemstone until it terminates at a slightly rounded tip. The gem glimmers with faint light when the wand focuses arcane energy, and shines brightly when used with a spell that creates and manipulates force.

A cabal of artificers first created this wand as a means to focus their concentration when manipulating arcane energy into the solid material they called force. The diamond aids in this process, helping the wand wielder adapt his or her magical creations to meet most circumstances on the battlefield. For this reason, *diamond wands* were valued among battlesmith artificers.

Join an Artificer Guild: One of the best ways to acquire the implements of artificers is to join one of their societies. Artificers who gather into academies and laboratories to combine their efforts sometimes provide items, such as *diamond wands*, to new members. The common test for admission is to create an item the group deems worthy of its respect.

Trawl a Battlefield: Avyn Wastel, a gnome artificer of some fame, took part in the Battle of Nine Stars, a terrible conflict that laid waste to nearly a square mile of countryside. Wastel led a detachment of warmages against a host of hideous creatures born from the nine fallen stars. Stopping the threat cost Avyn and his cohorts their lives, and their bodies were never recovered. The battlefield might still contain their weapons and gear, including Wastel's *diamond wand*.

Sharpshooter's Wand — Level 10+

You can shrink the size of your attack's area with this wand, making it more precise.

Lvl 10	+2	5,000 gp	Lvl 25	+5	625,000 gp
Lvl 15	+3	25,000 gp	Lvl 30	+6	3,125,000 gp
Lvl 20	+4	125,000 gp			

Implement (Wand)

Enhancement: Attack rolls and damage rolls

Critical: +1d6 damage per plus

Power (Encounter): Minor Action. The next area burst attack power you use through this wand has its area changed to 1 square (within the same range), and you gain a +2 power bonus to the attack roll.

Power (Daily ✦ Arcane, Implement, Lightning): Standard Action. As the wizard's *shock sphere* power (*Player's Handbook*, page 161).

Shielding Wand — Level 4+

As your spell obliterates your enemy, this heavy juniper wand creates a shimmering protective shield.

Lvl 4	+1	840 gp	Lvl 19	+4	105,000 gp
Lvl 9	+2	4,200 gp	Lvl 24	+5	525,000 gp
Lvl 14	+3	21,000 gp	Lvl 29	+6	2,625,000 gp

Implement (Wand)

Enhancement: Attack rolls and damage rolls

Critical: +1d6 damage per plus

Property: When you score a critical hit with an artificer attack power using this wand, you or one ally within 5 squares of you gains a +2 bonus to AC until the end of your next turn.

Power (Daily): Standard Action. As the artificer's *shielding cube* power (EBERRON *Player's Guide*, page 48), which is reproduced below.

Shielding Cube — Artificer Attack 1

You direct a minute cube covered in runes into the fray. Although small, the cube contains a force that bashes foes and shields allies.

Encounter ✦ Arcane, Force, Implement

Standard Action   **Ranged** 10

Target: One creature

Attack: Intelligence vs. Reflex

Hit: 2d6 + Intelligence modifier force damage.

Effect: Until the end of your next turn, any ally gains a +1 power bonus to AC while adjacent to the target.

Wand of Allure — Level 4+

Charms cast through this twinkling golden wand reach the most distant of foes.

Lvl 4	+1	840 gp	Lvl 19	+4	105,000 gp
Lvl 9	+2	4,200 gp	Lvl 24	+5	525,000 gp
Lvl 14	+3	21,000 gp	Lvl 29	+6	2,625,000 gp

Implement (Wand)

Enhancement: Attack rolls and damage rolls

Critical: +1d6 damage per plus

Property: When you use a ranged arcane charm power through this wand, the power's range increases by 2 squares, and you ignore cover and concealment.
Level 14 or 19: 5 squares.
Level 24 or 29: 10 squares.

Power (Daily ✦ Arcane, Charm, Implement): Standard Action. As the bard's *fast friends* power (*Player's Handbook 2*, page 69).

Wand of Aptitude — Level 10+

When you direct your allies with this lacewood wand, they reach beyond their normal limitations.

Lvl 10	+2	5,000 gp	Lvl 25	+5	625,000 gp
Lvl 15	+3	25,000 gp	Lvl 30	+6	3,125,000 gp
Lvl 20	+4	125,000 gp			

Implement (Wand)

Enhancement: Attack rolls and damage rolls

Critical: +1d6 damage per plus

Property: When you use the *inspire competence* power through this wand, each affected ally adds this wand's enhancement bonus to skill checks made with the skill you selected.

Power (Daily ✦ Arcane): Minor Action. As the bard's *inspire competence* power (*Player's Handbook 2*, page 70).

Wand of Thunderous Anguish — Level 14+

After you use this buzzing redwood wand, a crack of thunder indicates that your magical effect remains on an enemy.

Lvl 14	+3	21,000 gp	Lvl 24	+5	525,000 gp
Lvl 19	+4	105,000 gp	Lvl 29	+6	2,625,000 gp

Implement (Wand)

Enhancement: Attack rolls and damage rolls

Critical: +1d6 thunder damage per plus

Property: When you hit an enemy with a thunder power using this wand, until the end of your next turn that enemy takes thunder damage equal to this wand's enhancement bonus whenever one of your allies hits it.

Power (Daily ✦ Arcane, Implement, Thunder): Standard Action. As the bard's *distracting shout* power (*Player's Handbook 2*, page 72).

Wand of allure and wand of thunderous anguish

ARMS SLOT ITEMS

Shields and bracers are defensive tools, but in the language of magic, shields defend and bracers destroy.

The most iconic heroes are never seen without their shields, and bracers serve as a lesser defense for warriors who need their arms unfettered.

Enchantments on shields magnify their purpose, granting their wielders superior defenses. Some draw

ED COX

a dragon's breath into them to spare allies, while others guard their holders with a larger shield of force that falls when pierced. A set of qualities that pertains to a magic shield can be applied to a light shield, a heavy shield, or any shield, as noted in each item's description.

Bracers grant their wearers greater deftness in combat, adding power where there is already grace, and turning a simple wound into a fatal blow. They are more offensively oriented than shields.

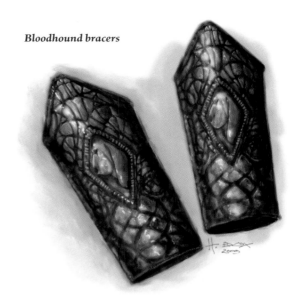

Bloodhound bracers

Absorbing Shield — Level 17

This steel shield absorbs the power from attacks, protecting both you and your allies.

Item Slot: Arms   65,000 gp
Shield: Any
Power (At-Will): Immediate Interrupt. *Trigger:* An area attack misses you and hits an ally. *Effect:* The triggering attack instead misses the ally.

Ankhmon's Bracers — Level 19

These platinum bracers are engraved with a symbol of an eye wreathed in flames.

Item Slot: Arms   105,000 gp
Property: When you hit an enemy that is granting combat advantage to you with an arcane attack power, the attack deals 1d10 extra damage against the enemy. You also regain a number of hit points equal to the extra damage roll result.

ANKHMON'S BRACERS

When the lich Ankhmon was preparing his undead army to fight the army known as the Celestial Company, he created a pair of bracers that allowed him to channel his tactical knowledge into powerful attacks that harmed his enemies and healed him. Ankhmon was eventually defeated, but his essence survived as a powerful vestige, granting power to a number of warlocks.

A lich named Revadal, who derives his power from a pact with Ankhmon, seeks the bracers but has yet to find them. He has assembled a new army of undead and has become a scourge in the south. Scholars theorize that the bracers aren't inherently malevolent, simply acting as channels for the wielder's own magic, so if someone aside from Revadal acquired them, they could be used without taint.

Thwart Revadal: Revadal doesn't have *Ankhmon's bracers*, but divinations have revealed that he is using his army to search for them. Some scholars worry that the bracers might be a key component in freeing the vestige of Ankhmon from its eternal bondage. They seek heroes to find the bracers first before Revadal can perform this terrible deed.

Barrage Bracers — Level 10

While you wear these bracers, when you attack rapidly, you can focus more power into your attacks.

Item Slot: Arms   5,000 gp
Property: When you hit an enemy with a melee attack, you gain a +1 bonus to attack rolls against that target until the end of your turn.

Bloodhound Bracers — Level 13

You can track a wounded foe and strike it down when it's most vulnerable.

Item Slot: Arms   17,000 gp
Property: Creatures that are taking ongoing damage grant combat advantage to you.
Power (Daily): Free Action. *Trigger:* You bloody an enemy. *Effect:* That enemy takes ongoing 5 damage (save ends).

Charm Bracelet — Level 8+

This simple bracelet with tiny arcane symbols dangling from it lets you share in your foes' good luck.

Lvl 8   3,400 gp   Lvl 18   85,000 gp
Item Slot: Arms
Property: You gain a +1 item bonus to saving throws against ongoing damage.
   Level 18: +2 item bonus.
Power (Daily): Immediate Reaction. *Trigger:* An enemy you can see succeeds on a saving throw. *Effect:* You make a saving throw.

Climber's Bracers — Level 16

Your hands are as effective as an animal's claws at climbing while wearing these rough leather bracers.

Item Slot: Arms   45,000 gp
Power (Daily): Minor Action. You gain a climb speed equal to your speed until the end of the encounter.

Flameward shield

Deathward Shield — Level 15+

This ebony shield with adamantine studs protects you from dark energies.

| Lvl 15 | 25,000 gp | Lvl 25 | 625,000 gp |

Item Slot: Arms
Shield: Any
Property: You gain resist 10 necrotic.
   Level 25: Resist 15 necrotic.
Power (At-Will): Immediate Interrupt. *Trigger:* You are targeted by a necrotic attack. *Effect:* All other targets of that attack gain resist 10 necrotic against the attack, and you lose resist necrotic for the attack.
   Level 25: Resist 15 necrotic.

Executioner's Bracers — Level 3+

These ornamental gold bracers help you to hit harder.

| Lvl 3 | 680 gp | Lvl 23 | 425,000 gp |
| Lvl 13 | 17,000 gp | | |

Item Slot: Arms
Property: When you score a critical hit, the attack deals 1d6 extra damage.
   Level 13: 2d6 extra damage.
   Level 23: 3d6 extra damage.

Flameward Shield — Level 16+

Stylized golden flames adorn this deep red shield.

| Lvl 16 | 45,000 gp | Lvl 26 | 1,125,000 gp |

Item Slot: Arms
Shield: Any
Property: You gain resist 10 fire.
   Level 26: Resist 15 fire.
Power (At-Will): Immediate Interrupt. *Trigger:* You are targeted by a fire attack. *Effect:* All other targets of that attack gain resist 10 fire against the attack.
   Level 26: Resist 15 fire.

LUNIA'S BRACELET

Thousands of years ago, a being known as Lunia (different stories say she was a goddess, an exarch of Sehanine, or a primal champion) blessed her followers with the ability to fight evil lycanthropes. She led them in battle against an army of werewolves that were plaguing the forest. In that conflict, an exarch of Yeenoghu was summoned to fight Lunia, and the two engaged in a massive battle. In the end, Lunia sacrificed herself in a burst of moonlight that destroyed the exarch and removed lycanthropy from the werewolves' bloodlines.

Some of Lunia's followers managed to capture a fraction of her light and turn it into a small charm bracelet. The bracelet helped them in their battle against evil lycanthropes. Though she is largely forgotten now, some still worship or pay homage to Lunia.

Stop the Lycanthropes: A small army of lycanthropes has found an ancient relic of a lost faith. The item is said to be a great bane to them, so they're trying to keep it out of the hands of their enemies. The werewolves are encroaching on civilization and are getting increasingly aggressive. Local leaders have put out a call for heroes to drive the werewolves back, possibly by claiming the item, which is said to be a bracelet.

Holy Pilgrimage: Divinations by worshipers of Sehanine have revealed that an ancient relic of Lunia lies in a temple that is under siege by werewolves. Sehanine's people say that temple priests are seeking the aid of heroes who will repel the attack and are offering the item in return.

Force Shield — Level 11

This large shield appears to be composed entirely of force. It protects you until you're struck by an attack.

Item Slot: Arms   9,000 gp
Shield: Heavy
Property: At the start of each encounter, you gain a +1 bonus to AC and Reflex until you're hit by an attack.

Frost Charger Bracers — Level 13

These metal and leather bracers have a constant sheen of frost.

Item Slot: Arms   17,000 gp
Property: When you hit an enemy with a charge attack, enemies adjacent to that enemy take cold damage equal to your Strength modifier.

Keeper's Shield — Level 9

This black iron shield with gilt edges allows your allies to make long-range attacks with less risk.

Item Slot: Arms   4,200 gp
Shield: Heavy
Property: Allies adjacent to you gain a +2 shield bonus to AC and Reflex against opportunity attacks provoked by using ranged or area powers.
Power (Daily): Immediate Interrupt. *Trigger:* An ally adjacent to you provokes an opportunity attack by using a ranged or area power. *Effect:* The opportunity attack targets you instead.

ED COX

Shield of silver light

Lunia's Bracelet — Level 3

This silver bracelet contains charms of stars and moons that hold power against lycanthropes.

Item Slot: Arms　　680 gp

Property: Treat weapons you wield (including ammunition, thrown weapons, and the like) as silvered (*Player's Handbook*, page 220).

Power (Daily): Free Action. *Trigger:* You hit a shapechanger with a weapon attack. *Effect:* The creature reverts to its natural form and can't use polymorph powers (save ends).

Preservation Shield — Level 2

This light wood shield displays an insignia of two crossed arrows, one fletched green and the other red.

Item Slot: Arms　　520 gp

Shield: Light

Power (Daily): Minor Action. You and each ally within 5 squares of you gain temporary hit points equal to the number of healing surges you have remaining.

Rhino Bracers — Level 15

These gray leather bracers let you charge with the strength of a great beast, using more powerful attacks than you ordinarily could.

Item Slot: Arms　　25,000 gp

Power (Encounter): Free Action. *Trigger:* You charge an enemy. *Effect:* You can use an at-will melee attack power instead of a melee basic attack against that enemy.

Serpentine Bracers — Level 18

Resembling coiled snakes, these bracers snap at your victim when you attack with surprise.

Item Slot: Arms　　85,000 gp

Property: While you're hidden from the target of your attack, you deal 1d8 extra poison damage on attacks against that target.

Shield of Silver Light — Level 4

This polished shield gleams with moonlight, even in the middle of the day.

Item Slot: Arms　　840 gp

Shield: Any

Power (At-Will): Minor Action. The shield sheds bright light 5 squares in all directions. You can end this effect as a minor action. You and your allies within the light treat your weapons (including ammunition, thrown weapons, and the like) as silvered (*Player's Handbook*, page 220).

Shield of Ultimate Protection — Level 30

This gold and silver shield protects you from every attack imaginable.

Item Slot: Arms　　3,125,000 gp

Shield: Any

Property: You gain a +1 shield bonus to Fortitude and Will. If this item is a heavy shield, the shield bonus increases to +2.

Power (Daily): Minor Action. You gain a +5 bonus to all defenses until the end of the encounter.

MATÍAS TAPIA

Stormward Shield — Level 16+

Trimmed in copper, this azure shield tapers to a sharp point.

Lvl 16   45,000 gp   Lvl 26   1,125,000 gp

Item Slot: Arms

Shield: Any

Property: You gain resist 10 lightning.
Level 26: Resist 15 lightning.

Power (At-Will): Immediate Interrupt. *Trigger:* A lightning attack targets you. *Effect:* All other targets of the triggering attack gain resist 5 lightning against that attack.
Level 26: Resist 10 lightning.

Trapping Shield — Level 24

This shield opens like a portal at your command, briefly trapping your enemy inside.

Item Slot: Arms   525,000 gp

Shield: Any

Property: When you grab a creature, it takes a -2 penalty to Athletics checks or Acrobatics checks to escape the grab and to attack rolls against targets other than you.

Power (Daily): Immediate Reaction. *Trigger:* An enemy adjacent to you misses you with a melee attack. *Effect:* The triggering enemy disappears until the end of its next turn. Then it reappears in any unoccupied space of its choice within 5 squares of you.

SHIELD OF SILVER LIGHT

The township of Brocada was being preyed upon by lycanthropes who controlled the sewers and who had managed to capture most of the city's silver supply. A group of halfling heroes descended into the sewers to face the beasts, and one of them created this shield as their ace in the hole.

After their success, the creator of the shield set it aside as a curiosity, thinking it was too specialized to be of much use to anyone else. It sat on a shelf for many years, and likely would have been forgotten. But a vengeful wererat stole it and was about to kill its creator when a handful of knights who had been pursuing the beast rescued the old halfling. In the aftermath, they found out about the shield, and the halfling was surprised at how enthusiastic these adventurers were to see it replicated.

By Silver Command: A local bandit is using a *shield of silver light* to keep his werewolf underlings in line, and they have been very successful in their raids. Claiming the shield would be only one reward for stopping these bandits.

The Wererats Return: Brocada is once again menaced by wererats. The city gates have been closed, and its citizens live in fear. A descendant of the original shield's creator has a map to a cache of silver weapons, one of which is a *shield of silver light*, stashed in the sewers below the city. He will give the map to heroes who pledge to end the menace.

WINTERWARD SHIELD

The Snowfang tribe lived in the far north, free to roam the ice without fear or constraint. That changed when a white dragon began to raid their homes, usually claiming their wealth, but sometimes kidnapping and eating their children. A courageous band of tribesfolk led by the hero Ice Elk took the fight to the dragon.

The heroes struck great blows, but eventually the dragon released his powerful breath. In an act of self-sacrifice, Ice Elk held forth his shield, protecting his companions from the brunt of the blast but taking it upon himself. Ice Elk was frozen solid, but his sacrifice gave his companions time to land a killing blow on the dragon, and his shield was returned to the village as a tribute to his courage.

Slay the Dragon: The Snowfang tribe is now gone, and rumor says the shield was reclaimed by another white wyrm. This dragon is plaguing the scattered tribes that arose from the remnants of the Snowfang people, taunting them with the knowledge that he possesses a symbol of their diminished culture. He has even gone so far as to defile some of the ancient cairns of the people. They are again looking for heroes to defeat the wyrm and restore their glory.

Vortex Shield — Level 14

Arcane runes form a spiral pattern on the surface of this shield, which serves to draw large attacks toward it.

Item Slot: Arms   21,000 gp

Shield: Any

Power (Daily): Immediate Interrupt. *Trigger:* An enemy targets you with a burst or blast attack. *Effect:* The triggering enemy takes a -4 penalty to attack rolls against all other targets of the attack.

Winterward Shield — Level 16+

This icy white shield with a silver rim is chill to the touch as it draws the cold to itself.

Lvl 16   45,000 gp   Lvl 26   1,125,000 gp

Item Slot: Arms

Shield: Any

Property: You gain resist 10 cold.
Level 26: Resist 15 cold.

Power (At-Will): Immediate Interrupt. *Trigger:* You are targeted by a cold attack. *Effect:* All other targets of the attack gain resist 10 cold against that attack, and you lose your resistance to cold for the attack.
Level 26: Resist 15 cold.

FEET SLOT ITEMS

Footgear might neutralize impediments or step you through time, but the best boots also make a fashion statement.

Magic footgear almost always affects speed or movement. Whether your boots, shoes, or sandals let you dash away when wounded or avoid opportunity attacks, they do their job by getting you around the battlefield.

Clearing cleats

Boots of Blood — Level 16
These red leather boots come alive when your blood is spilled.

Item Slot: Feet   45,000 gp
Property: You gain a +1 item bonus to Reflex.
Power (Daily): Immediate Reaction. *Trigger:* An enemy bloodies you. *Effect:* You shift your speed.

Boots of Bounding — Level 6
These lightweight canvas boots are perfect for athletes, greatly increasing the length of leaps.

Item Slot: Feet   1,800 gp
Property: You gain a +2 item bonus to Athletics checks to jump.
Power (Encounter): Move Action. You make an Athletics check to jump as if you had a running start. You add 3 squares to the distance jumped for a long jump, or 2 squares for a high jump.

Boots of Rapid Motion — Level 5
With these polished leather boots, you are hard to slow down.

Item Slot: Feet   1,000 gp
Power (Encounter): Immediate Reaction. *Trigger:* An effect slows you. *Effect:* You make a saving throw against the triggering effect. On a save, the effect ends.
Power (Daily): Minor Action. You gain a +1 power bonus to speed until the end of the encounter.

Boots of Surging Speed — Level 7
These springy boots let you get out of harm's way when you need to catch your breath.

Item Slot: Feet   2,600 gp
Property: When you use your second wind, you can shift 2 squares.

Boots of Unchecked Passage — Level 12
Your foes will make way for you while you're wearing these steel boots.

Item Slot: Feet   13,000 gp
Power (Daily): Minor Action. Until the end of your turn, you can move through enemy spaces, and you don't provoke opportunity attacks when moving.

Clearing Cleats — Level 26
These knobby-soled boots temporarily warp the terrain around you, clearing an easy path.

Item Slot: Feet   1,125,000 gp
Property: You ignore difficult terrain.
Power (Daily): Minor Action. Each ally within 5 squares of you ignores difficult terrain until the end of the encounter, even if that ally moves more than 5 squares from you.

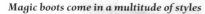

Magic boots come in a multitude of styles

Fey Warrior's Boots — Level 24

Step in and out the Feywild with this leaf-weight footwear.

Item Slot: Feet 525,000 gp
Property: You gain a +2 item bonus to Reflex.
Power (At-Will ✦ Teleportation): Immediate Reaction.
Trigger: An attack misses you. *Effect:* You teleport 3 squares.

Greaves of Fortunate Falling — Level 8

These plain gray bands guide your landing when you topple.

Item Slot: Feet 3,400 gp
Property: When you're knocked prone (including when you fall unconscious), you can fall into any unoccupied adjacent space instead of your current space. Being prone does not grant enemies combat advantage.

Riding Boots — Level 4

These stylish knee-high boots let you look good while they spur your steed.

Item Slot: Feet 840 gp
Property: While you ride a mount, it gains a +1 item bonus to speed.

Sandwalker Boots — Level 14

These supple buckskin boots let you glide through the desert sand like a dolphin through water.

Item Slot: Feet 21,000 gp
Property: You gain a burrow speed of 6 in sand. You can breathe sand as if it were air.

SANDWALKER BOOTS

Deep below the Endless Desert are the remnants of an ancient civilization. At its height, the area was the center of a fruitful nation in a verdant valley. Then, the mountains were pulled down upon it and the life force of the land was drained by the inhabitants' own magic.

Determined to find the ruins of this ancient civilization and study its culture, the adventurer and self-styled archeologist Thaigan Thornburn led an expedition to the Endless Desert. He had boots crafted for the trek that would allow him to swim through the sand like it was water.

Thaigan led his expedition into the desert and was never heard from again. Some believe that the group was waylaid by bandits. Others think that the archeologist was slain by one of his guards for his new boots.

Thornburn, I Presume: The explorers who went searching for the ancient civilization are most likely dead, but their loved ones have promised a reward to anyone who brings back the bodies, or at least locates them. They have implied that the explorer owned a powerful item that allowed its wearer to master the desert. Perhaps that item was a pair of *sandwalker boots.*

Capture the Murderer: Thaigan Thornburn's murderer is rumored to have escaped the desert with the archeologist's *sandwalker boots.* Whoever hunts down this murderer can avenge the explorer's death, prevent the killer from perpetrating further evil, and lay claim to the magic boots.

Survivor's Boots — Level 16

These rough hide boots are clearly well used, but they never wear out.

Item Slot: Feet 45,000 gp
Property: While bloodied, you don't provoke opportunity attacks when moving, using ranged powers, or using area powers.

HANDS SLOT ITEMS

An adventurer's gloves do more than just keep her hands warm.

Any task performed with the hands can be improved with magical handwear. Enchanted gauntlets allow warriors to unleash devastating attacks or disrupt those of enemies. Magic gloves have many purposes but often improve the use of skills that require fine control or subtlety or help with tasks that require the hands, such as healing.

Feinting Gloves — Level 7

These black silk gloves help you misdirect your opponent's attention.

Item Slot: Hands 2,600 gp
Property: You gain a +2 item bonus to Bluff checks to gain combat advantage.
Power (Daily): Minor Action. You gain combat advantage against the next creature you attack this turn.

Gauntlets of Blood — Level 4+

The blood of wounded foes streams along the joints of these rusty-looking steel gauntlets.

Lvl 4	840 gp	Lvl 24	525,000 gp
Lvl 14	21,000 gp		

Item Slot: Hands
Property: You gain a +2 bonus to damage rolls against bloodied targets.
Level 14: +4 bonus.
Level 24: +6 bonus.

Gauntlets of Discontinuity — Level 13

Arcane energy crackles over these gauntlets, disrupting teleportation.

Item Slot: Hands 17,000 gp
Power (Daily): Immediate Interrupt. *Trigger:* An enemy within 2 squares of you teleports. *Effect:* You negate the teleport, and the triggering enemy can't teleport until the end of your next turn.

Gloves of Dimensional Grasp — Level 16

With these skin-tight gloves you can create a small portal through which to manipulate objects.

Item Slot: Hands 45,000 gp
Property: You gain a +4 item bonus to Thievery checks.
Power (Daily): Standard Action. You make a Thievery check against a target up to 5 squares away from you. You must have line of sight to the target.

Gloves of Grace — Level 5

While wearing these gloves, you help a companion recover quickly with but a touch.

Item Slot: Hands   1,000 gp

Power (Daily): Minor Action. An ally adjacent to you makes a saving throw.

Gloves of Ice — Level 11

Encrusted with elemental ice, these gloves don't freeze your hands while worn.

| Lvl 11 | 9,000 gp | Lvl 21 | 225,000 gp |

Item Slot: Hands

Property: Choose one: Your cold attacks gain a +2 bonus to damage rolls, or your cold attacks ignore 5 of the target's resistance to cold. You can switch between properties as a minor action.

Level 21: +4 bonus, or ignore 10 resistance to cold.

Gloves of Missile Avoidance — Level 11

These black leather gloves are limned with an aura of force that shatters or deflects projectiles aimed at you.

Item Slot: Hands   9,000 gp

Power (Daily): Immediate Interrupt. *Trigger:* A ranged attack that targets AC or Reflex hits you. *Effect:* You gain a +4 power bonus to AC and Reflex against the triggering attack.

Great Hero's Gauntlets — Level 27

These heavy steel gauntlets reward great risk and heroism.

Item Slot: Hands   1,625,000 gp

Property: When you spend an action point to make an attack, you gain a +2 bonus to attack rolls for that attack.

Property: When you spend an action point to make an attack and the attack deals damage, you gain temporary hit points equal to your healing surge value.

Grizzly Gauntlets — Level 8

These gauntlets, covered with bear fur, make your grab attacks and escapes more effective.

Item Slot: Hands   3,400 gp

Property: You gain a +3 item bonus to Strength checks to grab a creature and to Athletics checks or Acrobatics checks to escape a grab.

Hero's Gauntlets — Level 17

These steel gauntlets reward risk and heroism.

Item Slot: Hands   65,000 gp

Property: When you spend an action point to make an attack, you gain a +1 bonus to attack rolls for that attack.

Property: When you spend an action point to make an attack and the attack deals damage, you gain temporary hit points equal to one-half your healing surge value.

Hrothmar's gauntlets

HROTHMAR'S GAUNTLETS

During the ancient war between the primordials and the gods, the mammoth titan Hrothmar was a powerful weapon. He could take the form of a comet, slamming into the ground to disrupt the divine forces with tremendous earthquakes.

The gods couldn't win without eliminating Hrothmar, but they were unable to defeat him in combat. So they devised a magic trap that contained the titan in his comet form, transforming him into a meteorite. They forged magic gauntlets from the meteorite's metal, then distributed them among their forces. Thus equipped, the front lines of the divine army started battles by slamming their gauntleted fists against the earth, sending shock waves through the primordial troops.

Since the end of the war, the gauntlets are thought to have been lost, but rumors abound that some have survived. Some warlocks of the vestige pact (see *Arcane Power*) believe a shred of Hrothmar's sentience still exists, and they seek these gauntlets in an attempt to contact him as a vestige.

Investigate the Ruins: Divinations have revealed that a set of *Hrothmar's gauntlets* might be buried in a city that was destroyed by a meteorite strike centuries ago. Other treasure hunters have heard the same rumors. Only the first to arrive can claim the prize.

Rumors of War: A band of primordial worshipers seek to rekindle the conflict between their kind and those who worship the gods. They have been terrorizing towns, using an item that causes minor earthquakes. Preventing war requires confronting the band and wresting away the item, a set of *Hrothmar's gauntlets.*

KALMAN ANDRASOFSZKY

Gloves of dimensional grasp

ILLUSIONIST'S GLOVES

Many illusionists are content to spend their lives performing simple tricks, whether to cheat and steal or to amuse people for profit. Zalian, one of these minor wizards, owned a pair of magic gloves handed down through his family from a powerful illusionist of ages past. However, being far less skilled at magic than his talented ancestor, Zalian earned a meager living.

Kellevec was a traveling illusionist who sought inexperienced spellcasters to exploit. He noticed Zalian's gloves and coveted them. Kellevec trapped the lesser illusionist in a maze of false visions, where Zalian wandered until he collapsed from dehydration and starvation. Kellevec stole the *illusionist's gloves* and what little coin his victim had amassed, then moved on with his ill-gotten prize.

Find Kellevec: Although Zalian was a minor wizard, the story of his robbery has become well known. Kellevec is rumored to be in the local area, committing more thefts with the help of the *illusionist's gloves*. He has yet to be caught, but if someone were to take his magic gloves, he'd have a harder time escaping.

A Greater Master: Kellevec was secretly working for a shadowy drow mage who seeks magic to boost his own spells. The drow runs a criminal organization in a nearby city and is an even more formidable challenge now that he has the gloves.

Hrothmar's Gauntlets — Level 18

These massive, black iron gauntlets are dotted with red metal studs. They create shock waves that hurl foes to the ground.

Item Slot: Hands   85,000 gp

Property: Prone creatures don't gain the normal +2 bonus to all defenses against your ranged attacks.

Power (Daily): Minor Action. Make an attack: Close burst 5; targets each enemy in burst; Constitution or Charisma +4 vs. Reflex; on a hit, you knock the target prone. You gain an additional +2 bonus to the attack roll against any target affected by your Warlock's Curse.

Illusionist's Gloves — Level 9

These shimmering gloves enhance your illusion spells and let you quickly alter an illusion that would otherwise be ineffective.

Item Slot: Hands   4,200 gp

Property: When you hit an enemy granting combat advantage to you with an illusion attack power, that enemy takes a -2 penalty to saving throws against the power's effects.

Power (Daily): Free Action. *Trigger:* You miss with an illusion attack power. *Effect:* You reroll the attack roll and must use the second result.

JASON A. ENGLE

Many-Fingered Gloves — Level 20

You seem to have more than the normal allotment of fingers while wearing these simple gloves.

Item Slot: Hands   125,000 gp
Property: You can wear and gain the benefit of one additional magic ring while wearing these gloves.

Poison Gloves — Level 4

You can store a nasty surprise in these plain-looking gloves to envenom a weapon at a moment's notice.

Item Slot: Hands   840 gp
Power (At-Will): Standard Action. You store one dose of poison that can be applied to a weapon in these gloves. The gloves can hold only one dose of poison at a time.
Power (At-Will): Minor Action. You apply the stored poison to a weapon you're holding; doing so consumes that dose of poison.

HEAD SLOT ITEMS

A circlet to clear the mind, a helmet to command the weak-willed, an Ioun stone to grant esoteric powers—the possibilities are nearly limitless.

The head holds the mind and the majority of the senses, and magic items that take up the head slot follow that theme. Among other things, they improve an arcanist's focus on magic, protect a hero from mental intrusions, or bear testament to the wearer's nobility and glory.

Bear Headdress — Level 9

This tanned and cured bear head aids you while you are transformed.

Item Slot: Head   4,200 gp
Property: You gain a +2 item bonus to Nature checks.
Property: While you're affected by a primal polymorph power, you gain a +1 bonus to Will.

Chimera Headdress — Level 16

Three miniature heads of a chimera stare out from this headgear, granting you the multifaceted abilities of that beast.

Item Slot: Head   45,000 gp
Property: You can use only one of the headdress's powers each day.
Power (Daily): Free Action. *Trigger:* You score a critical hit against an enemy. *Effect:* That enemy takes ongoing 10 damage (save ends).
Power (Daily): Free Action. *Trigger:* You hit with a charge attack. *Effect:* The charge attack deals 2d10 extra damage.
Power (Daily): Minor Action. You gain resist 15 acid, resist 15 cold, resist 15 lightning, or resist 15 poison (chosen when the item is created) until the end of the encounter.

Circlet of Continuity — Level 11

This platinum band sparkles with embedded golden topazes, guarding against mental disruption.

Item Slot: Head   9,000 gp
Property: You gain a +2 item bonus to saving throws against dazing or stunning effects.
Power (Encounter): No Action. *Trigger:* You are dazed or stunned at the start of your turn. *Effect:* You sustain a power that normally requires a minor action to sustain.

Crown of Equilibrium — Level 12

As your foes shake off disabling effects, this thick copper headband grants your allies similar relief.

Item Slot: Head   13,000 gp
Property: When an enemy saves against an effect you created, this item's power recharges.
Power (Daily): Minor Action. An ally you can see within 10 squares of you makes a saving throw.

Crown of Victory — Level 29

This majestic platinum crown is fit only for the greatest of heroes.

Item Slot: Head   2,625,000 gp
Property: You can spend two action points in an encounter.

Cyclops Helm — Level 18

The gemlike eye that stares from the brow of this finely wrought mithral helm reveals what is hidden.

Item Slot: Head   85,000 gp
Property: You gain a +4 item bonus to Perception checks.
Power (Daily): Minor Action. You can see invisible creatures until the end of your next turn. Also, choose one invisible creature that you can see. That creature becomes visible and can't become invisible again until the end of your next turn.

Essence of the Wisp — Level 21

A glowing ball of light buzzes around your head, drawing in foes that attack you from a distance.

Item Slot: Head   225,000 gp
Property: You gain a +2 item bonus to Will.
Power (At-Will): Immediate Reaction. *Trigger:* An enemy hits you with a ranged attack. *Effect:* You pull the triggering enemy 2 squares.

Chimera headdress

ED COX

Essence of the wisp

GIBBERING LUMP

A floating mass of twisting flesh, this grotesque item continually reshapes itself, growing eyes and mouths and losing them just as quickly. A rambling stream of nonsense words spouts from its mouths; baleful stars issue from its eyes. These features give the item an appearance of life, but it lacks even the twisted intelligence of a gibbering beast.

Those who wear a gibbering lump are often thought mad, though some adventurers acquire one for just that purpose.

Gibbering Marauders: Several gibbering abominations have been wreaking havoc across a wide peninsula, moving randomly between the scattered settlements and ruins. A group of slaads follows them, reveling in the chaos being created. If those dangers can be overcome, it's said that slicing off a bit of flesh from an abomination creates a gibbering lump.

Escapees from the Far Realm: Stories tell of a sporadic portal to the Far Realm that opens atop a mountain in the Underdark of the Feywild, in an area stripped of life by fomorians. The chaotic material of the Far Realm is said to spew from that portal, along with aberrant creatures, bizarre oozes, and scraps of flesh. A gibbering lump might be found among the leavings. Regardless, sealing the portal is probably best for all.

Fey-Blessed Circlet — Level 8

This slender silver and moonstone circlet grants you a small measure of fey grace.

Item Slot: Head   3,400 gp
Property: At the start of each encounter, you gain temporary hit points equal to your Charisma modifier.

Firebird — Level 27

A small fiery bird orbits your shoulders, warding against flame and burning those who strike you at range.

Item Slot: Head   1,625,000 gp
Property: You gain a +4 item bonus to damage rolls with fire implement attack powers.
Property: Any enemy that hits you with a ranged attack takes 1d12 fire damage.

Gibbering Lump — Level 20+

This tiny hunk of mottled flesh warps constantly, growing and losing eyes and mouths as it sits atop your head.

Lvl 20	125,000 gp	Lvl 30	3,125,000 gp

Item Slot: Head
Property: You gain a +1 item bonus to Will.
Level 30: +2 item bonus.
Power (Encounter ✦ Psychic): Immediate Reaction.
Trigger: An enemy hits you with an attack that targets Will for the first time in an encounter. *Effect:* The triggering enemy takes 2d12 psychic damage.
Level 30: 3d12 psychic damage.

Lenses of the Luminary — Level 23

These varicolored lenses orbit around your head at eye level, improving your vision as needed.

Item Slot: Head   425,000 gp
Property: You gain darkvision and a +5 item bonus to Perception checks.
Property: You can use these lenses as a focus for scrying rituals that require a focus worth 425,000 gp or less.
Power (At-Will, 3 Charges/Day): Minor Action. You spend the number of charges indicated and gain the special sense described until the end of the encounter.

Charges	Sense
1	You learn the resistances and vulnerabilities of any creature you look at (but not the values of those resistances or vulnerabilities).
1	You gain a +5 power bonus to Perception checks to spot traps.
2	You gain truesight 10.

Philosopher's Crown — Level 7+

This intricate golden crown ensures that the breadth of your knowledge is unparalleled.

Lvl 7	2,600 gp	Lvl 27	1,625,000 gp
Lvl 17	65,000 gp		

Item Slot: Head
Property: You gain a +1 item bonus to Arcana, Dungeoneering, History, Nature, and Religion checks.
Level 17: +2 item bonus.
Level 27: +3 item bonus.
Power (Daily): Free Action. *Trigger:* You make an Arcana, Dungeoneering, History, Nature, or Religion check and dislike the result. *Effect:* You reroll the check and use either result.

JASON A. ENGLE

LENSES OF THE LUMINARY

In all of Bael Turath, the great library at Taru Maaj held the most extensive store of knowledge. The tieflings jealously guarded their knowledge and entrusted a figure they called the Luminary with the job of gatekeeper of the library. The *lenses of the Luminary* were originally created to allow this august personage to see through the disguises of anyone who tried to sneak in. This item was presented to the Luminary by a school of tiefling magical crafters. Over time, more lenses were added to suit different needs. Eventually, a plethora of different lenses, composed of special types of glass and crystal, made up the array.

After the fall of Bael Turath, the library at Taru Maaj was lost—buried, burned, or perhaps even ripped from the world and hidden on another plane. Legend has it that the *lenses of the Luminary* survived.

Loot the Luminary: The Luminary was an enigmatic figure who lived a long life. Some records say the librarian lives still, guarding the repository (or what remains of it). Heroes who find the library might be able to steal or win the *lenses of the Luminary*.

Gather the Lenses: An old tiefling has been telling a story about a vault hidden near where the *lenses of the Luminary* are kept. He says the lenses have been dismantled and concealed in a chamber full of valuable gemstones, all similar in appearance to the lenses. For a share of gems, he's willing to reveal the vault's location, but solving the riddle of which lenses are true and reconstructing them is a job for heroes.

Sacred Mask · Level 8

This white porcelain mask with gold inlay is the bane of undead.

Item Slot: Head   3,400 gp

Property: When you use a Channel Divinity class feature, until the end of your next turn, you deal 1d6 extra radiant damage against undead enemies and can score a critical hit against undead enemies on a roll of 18–20.

NECK SLOT ITEMS

Adornment or life-saving magic? Can't it be both?

Most people never realize the great value of a simple cloak or amulet. Such magic items are second only to magic armor in terms of defensive worth. The enhancement bonus of neck slot items improves Fortitude, Reflex, and Will, and most items offer other benefits related to defense or health.

Amulet of Double Fortune · Level 2+

Good luck begets even better luck when you wear this amulet.

Lvl 2	+1	520 gp	Lvl 17	+4	65,000 gp
Lvl 7	+2	2,600 gp	Lvl 22	+5	325,000 gp
Lvl 12	+3	13,000 gp	Lvl 27	+6	1,625,000 gp

Item Slot: Neck

Enhancement: Fortitude, Reflex, and Will

Property: When you score a critical hit, you make a saving throw against one effect that a save can end. You gain an item bonus to that saving throw equal to the amulet's enhancement bonus.

Amulet of Elegy · Level 2+

This amulet allows you to infuse your voice with a sadness that grips the hearts of your foes.

Lvl 2	+1	520 gp	Lvl 17	+4	65,000 gp
Lvl 7	+2	2,600 gp	Lvl 22	+5	325,000 gp
Lvl 12	+3	13,000 gp	Lvl 27	+6	1,625,000 gp

Item Slot: Neck

Enhancement: Fortitude, Reflex, and Will

Power (Daily): Free Action. *Trigger:* You use a power to produce an effect that a save can end. *Effect:* Each target of the power takes a penalty to its first saving throw against the effect equal to the amulet's enhancement bonus.

Amulet of Vigor · Level 9+

This silver amulet bears an engraved prayer for health and healing on its back.

Lvl 9	+2	4,200 gp	Lvl 24	+5	525,000 gp
Lvl 14	+3	21,000 gp	Lvl 29	+6	2,625,000 gp
Lvl 19	+4	105,000 gp			

Item Slot: Neck

Enhancement: Fortitude, Reflex, and Will

Property: Your healing surge value increases by an amount equal to the amulet's enhancement bonus –1.

Power (Daily ✦ Healing): Free Action. *Trigger:* You spend a healing surge to regain hit points. *Effect:* You regain additional hit points as if you had spent another healing surge.

Amulet of Warding · Level 3+

Polished to a mirror finish, this bronze disk reflects light upon those closest to you, warding them against danger.

Lvl 3	+1	680 gp	Lvl 18	+4	85,000 gp
Lvl 8	+2	3,400 gp	Lvl 23	+5	425,000 gp
Lvl 13	+3	17,000 gp	Lvl 28	+6	2,125,000 gp

Item Slot: Neck

Enhancement: Fortitude, Reflex, and Will

Power (Daily): Immediate Interrupt. *Trigger:* An ally adjacent to you is hit by an attack. *Effect:* The ally gains a power bonus to all defenses equal to the amulet's enhancement bonus until the start of your next turn.

BADGE OF THE BERSERKER

This tangled knot of teeth, bone, and leathery flesh forms a screaming savage's face, twisted in insane wrath. Each piece captures the essence of fallen warriors famed for their reckless courage and thirst for violence. When pinned to clothing or armor, the spirit the badge contains transfers to the wearer, protecting her from the blades and arrows of lesser foes as she seeks an enemy worthy of her attention.

Among certain primitive tribes, shamans fashion these badges to protect their favored champions, binding the spirits of fallen warriors into the fetishes to lend their strength and insight to that war leader. The badges are worn with honor, marking that warrior's duty to the tribe.

Explore the Khittean Barrows: In bygone times, once each generation, the Khittean clans formed into vast hordes and spread across the land to slaughter all in their path. Surviving warriors returned with the corpses of their greatest champions and interred them in great tombs. It's said that the remains of those warriors can be used to create a potent *badge of the berserker*, but the barrows have remained untouched for centuries, because the champions' spirits guard the dead.

Defeat a Tribal Champion: The Skulltaker clan gained its name from the members' habit of cutting off the heads of their victims for perverse rituals. The clan's greatest warrior is Tusk, a vile orc said to have ogre blood in his veins. Stories say that when he charges into battle, no weapon can touch him. They also say that he wears a *badge of the berserker*.

Assassin's Cloak			Level 14+

This voluminous cloak swallows you up, deadening the sounds you make and concealing your movements.

Lvl 14	+3	21,000 gp	Lvl 24	+5	525,000 gp
Lvl 19	+4	105,000 gp	Lvl 29	+6	2,625,000 gp

Item Slot: Neck
Enhancement: Fortitude, Reflex, and Will
Property: When you make a Stealth check, you roll twice and use either result.
Power (Daily ✦ Illusion): Minor Action. Make an attack: Close burst 2; Charisma + the amulet's enhancement bonus vs. Will; on a hit, you're invisible to the target (save ends).

Badge of the Berserker			Level 2+

This fearsome badge, crafted from bits of bone and leathery flesh, is favored by those who savor taking the fight to the enemy.

Lvl 2	+1	520 gp	Lvl 17	+4	65,000 gp
Lvl 7	+2	2,600 gp	Lvl 22	+5	325,000 gp
Lvl 12	+3	13,000 gp	Lvl 27	+6	1,625,000 gp

Item Slot: Neck
Enhancement: Fortitude, Reflex, and Will
Property: When you charge, your movement made as part of the charge doesn't provoke opportunity attacks.

KALMAN ANDRASOFSZKY

Bloodgem Shard
Level 20+

This blood-red crystal absorbs the life force of your defeated foes, bolstering your defenses.

Lvl 20	+4	125,000 gp	Lvl 30	+6	3,125,000 gp
Lvl 25	+5	625,000 gp			

Item Slot: Neck

Enhancement: Fortitude, Reflex, and Will

Property: When you reduce a nonminion creature to 0 hit points, you gain a cumulative +1 item bonus to Fortitude, Reflex, and Will (maximum +3) until the end of the encounter.

Bralani Cloak
Level 20+

This cloak lets you slip through the Feywild and call upon its winds to move you off the ground.

Lvl 20	+4	125,000 gp	Lvl 30	+6	3,125,000 gp
Lvl 25	+5	625,000 gp			

Item Slot: Neck

Enhancement: Fortitude, Reflex, and Will

Property: You gain resist 15 psychic.
Level 30: Resist 20 psychic.

Power (Daily ✦ Teleportation): Move Action. You teleport a number of squares equal to your speed + this cloak's enhancement bonus. You don't have to end the teleport on the ground. You gain a fly speed of 8 (hover) until the end of your next turn.

Chaos Cloak
Level 14+

This cloak is brightly colored and covered in nodules, like the skin of a slaad, and its effects are just as chaotic.

Lvl 14	+3	21,000 gp	Lvl 24	+5	525,000 gp
Lvl 19	+4	105,000 gp	Lvl 29	+6	2,625,000 gp

Item Slot: Neck

Enhancement: Fortitude, Reflex, and Will

Property: You gain resist 10 to all damage from elemental creatures.
Level 24 or 29: Resist 15 to all damage from elemental creatures.

Power (Daily ✦ Teleportation): Immediate Reaction.
Trigger: An enemy hits you with an attack that targets Fortitude, Reflex, or Will. *Effect:* Roll a d6 and apply the appropriate result.
1–2: You take half damage from the triggering enemy's attack.
3–4: You teleport 1d8 squares.
5–6: The triggering enemy takes damage equal to the damage it dealt you.

Cloak of the Bat
Level 14+

Donning this dark brown cloak lets you perceive the world from a different perspective.

Lvl 14	+3	21,000 gp	Lvl 24	+5	525,000 gp
Lvl 19	+4	105,000 gp	Lvl 29	+6	2,625,000 gp

Item Slot: Neck

Enhancement: Fortitude, Reflex, and Will

Power (Daily ✦ Polymorph): Standard Action. You assume the form of an ordinary bat and gain a fly speed equal to your speed until the end of the encounter or until you end the effect as a minor action. You can't attack, carry anything, or manipulate objects while in this form. If you end this effect while you're still airborne, you float to the ground without taking falling damage.

Chaos cloak

Cloak of the Desert
Level 13+

This tan cloak blends in perfectly with the desert sand.

Lvl 13	+3	17,000 gp	Lvl 23	+5	425,000 gp
Lvl 18	+4	85,000 gp	Lvl 28	+6	2,125,000 gp

Item Slot: Neck

Enhancement: Fortitude, Reflex, and Will

Power (Daily): Minor Action. You gain concealment until the end of the encounter as sand swirls around you. Until the end of the encounter, you can unleash the sand in an attack: Standard action; Close burst 3; targets each enemy in burst; Constitution + the cloak's enhancement bonus vs. Fortitude; on a hit, the target takes 1d6 damage per plus and is blinded until the end of its next turn. If you make this attack, the concealment granted by this power ends.

Cloak of the Shadowthief
Level 19+

This cloak enwraps you in a veil of shadows, keeping your enemies constantly guessing.

Lvl 19	+4	105,000 gp	Lvl 29	+6	2,625,000 gp
Lvl 24	+5	525,000 gp			

Item Slot: Neck

Enhancement: Fortitude, Reflex, and Will

Power (Encounter): Minor Action. Until the end of your next turn, each enemy that you have concealment or cover against grants combat advantage to you.

LUCIO PARRILLO

Cloak of Translocation | Level 9+

*This silver-white cloak glimmers and shimmers when you tele-
port, hampering your enemy's ability to locate you.*

Lvl 9	+2	4,200 gp	Lvl 24	+5	525,000 gp
Lvl 14	+3	21,000 gp	Lvl 29	+6	2,625,000 gp
Lvl 19	+4	105,000 gp			

Item Slot: Neck

Enhancement: Fortitude, Reflex, and Will

Property: When you use a teleportation power, you gain a
+2 bonus to AC and Reflex until the end of your next turn.

Power (Daily): Minor Action. You regain the use of an encounter teleportation power that you have already used
during this encounter.

Courtier's Cape | Level 8+

*You have uncommon confidence while this short silk cape hangs
from your shoulders.*

Lvl 8	+2	3,400 gp	Lvl 23	+5	425,000 gp
Lvl 13	+3	17,000 gp	Lvl 28	+6	2,125,000 gp
Lvl 18	+4	85,000 gp			

Item Slot: Neck

Enhancement: Fortitude, Reflex, and Will

Property: You gain a +2 item bonus to saving throws against
charm and fear effects.

Power (Daily ✦ Charm): Immediate Interrupt. *Trigger:* An
enemy targets you with a charm or fear power. *Effect:*
You change the target of that power from yourself to any
other creature within 5 squares of you.

CLOAK OF THE DESERT

The Empire of Sand, which ruled over the great desert,
greatly abused the nomadic tribes that traveled in its
lands. Out of this abuse was born the nomadic people's
greatest hero, Shelani. She rose from a destitute background to become the most desirable courtesan in the
empire. From this exalted position, she hatched the plot
that brought down the empire and all of its abuses.

When all the Imperial Mages were gathered in front of
the emperor, Shelani struck with a secret weapon made
for her by the desert witches. Her cloak transformed her
into a swirling sandstorm that flayed the flesh from the
emperor and the mages. With the mages' demise, the
magic that protected the empire from the encroaching
desert was released, and the empire, along with Shelani
and her cloak, was buried under millions of tons of sand.

Lamia Lair: A group of lamias has taken up residence
in the desert above the buried empire. The lamias have
found Shelani's *cloak of the desert* and are using it to flay
the flesh of any who come near their lair. Several merchants who have lost caravans to the lamias are looking
to hire someone to take care of the problem.

Thaigan's Research: The explorer Thaigan Thornburn learned about a group of ruins on the edge of the
desert. He was on his way to another site and never got
to explore the ruins, but he made notes that both magic
and monsters thrived in the area, including rumors of a
cloak of the desert.

MEDALLION OF THE MIND

Medallions of the mind were first fashioned by the mystics
of Tellac Moh, an order of psychics and sages devoted to
unlocking the mysteries of the mind. Designed as small
pendants fashioned from nickel-silver with a stylized
eye set with an amethyst disk for the pupil, the medallions were given to acolytes as tools to aid the wearers in
learning the order's methods and practices. They were
reportedly all lost when Tellac Moh was reduced to rubble
and ash, but a few have surfaced now and then, each a
cherished prize from an enlightened time.

Defeat a Mastermind: Though it's unknown how they
acquire them, mind flayers often give *medallions of the
mind* as rewards to particularly useful servants. Finding
and defeating a mind flayer infiltrator or, better yet, a
mind flayer mastermind, would be a way to acquire such
an amulet.

Locate the Dream of Tellac Moh: Although Tellac
Moh is no more, its dream lives on. Sequestered away in
a dim corner of the Plane of Dreams are the dreams of the
order's finest minds, each held in perfect stasis. Explorers
who reach this distant plane sometimes leave tokens of
respect for their fallen heroes. It's said that those who
reside there sometimes give a *medallion of the mind* to
heroes who survive the journey.

Demon Amulet | Level 14+

*This simple amulet consists of a cord wrapped around a chunk
of bone or horn from a demon.*

Lvl 14	+3	21,000 gp	Lvl 24	+5	525,000 gp
Lvl 19	+4	105,000 gp	Lvl 29	+6	2,625,000 gp

Item Slot: Neck

Enhancement: Fortitude, Reflex, and Will

Power (Daily): Minor Action. Choose acid, cold, fire,
lightning, or thunder. You gain resist 10 to the chosen
damage type until the end of the encounter.

Frostwolf Pelt | Level 4+

The icy white fur of this cloak protects you against frost.

Lvl 4	+1	840 gp	Lvl 19	+4	105,000 gp
Lvl 9	+2	4,200 gp	Lvl 24	+5	525,000 gp
Lvl 14	+3	21,000 gp	Lvl 29	+6	2,625,000 gp

Item Slot: Neck

Enhancement: Fortitude, Reflex, and Will

Property: You gain resist 5 cold.

Level 14 or 19: Resist 10 cold.

Level 24 or 29: Resist 15 cold.

Power (Daily): Immediate Reaction. *Trigger:* An enemy
adjacent to you hits you. *Effect:* The triggering enemy is
knocked prone.

Lifesaving Brooch — Level 2+

This small white and red pin helps those who seek to aid you.

Lvl 2	+1	520 gp	Lvl 17	+4	65,000 gp
Lvl 7	+2	2,600 gp	Lvl 22	+5	325,000 gp
Lvl 12	+3	13,000 gp	Lvl 27	+6	1,625,000 gp

Item Slot: Neck

Enhancement: Fortitude, Reflex, and Will

Property: Allies gain a +5 bonus to Heal checks to administer first aid to you.

Lucky Charm — Level 4+

Monkey's paw or rabbit's foot, this lucky charm helps you snatch victory from the jaws of defeat.

Lvl 4	+1	840 gp	Lvl 19	+4	105,000 gp
Lvl 9	+2	4,200 gp	Lvl 24	+5	525,000 gp
Lvl 14	+3	21,000 gp	Lvl 29	+6	2,625,000 gp

Item Slot: Neck

Enhancement: Fortitude, Reflex, and Will

Power (Daily): No Action. *Trigger:* You miss with an attack or fail a skill check, ability check, or saving throw. *Effect:* Roll a d6 and add the result to the attack roll, skill check, ability check, or saving throw.
Level 14 or 19: Roll a d6 twice and add either result.
Level 24 or 29: Roll a d6 three times and add any of those results.

Medallion of the Mind — Level 14+

The amethyst pupil on this medallion glows softly when your thoughts take root in the minds of those around you.

| Lvl 14 | +3 | 21,000 gp | Lvl 24 | +5 | 525,000 gp |
| Lvl 19 | +4 | 105,000 gp | Lvl 29 | +6 | 2,625,000 gp |

Item Slot: Neck

Enhancement: Fortitude, Reflex, and Will

Property: You gain an item bonus to Insight checks equal to the medallion's enhancement bonus.

Property: You can communicate telepathically with any creature you can see. Those willing to communicate with you can send thoughts back to you, allowing two-way communication. This telepathic communication fulfills the requirement of a class feature or power that a target be able to hear you.

Power (Daily): Free Action. *Trigger:* An enemy you grant combat advantage to hits or misses you. *Effect:* The triggering enemy grants combat advantage to your allies until the start of your next turn.

Medic's Amulet — Level 9+

This amulet helps healers staunch wounds.

Lvl 9	+2	4,200 gp	Lvl 24	+5	525,000 gp
Lvl 14	+3	21,000 gp	Lvl 29	+6	2,625,000 gp
Lvl 19	+4	105,000 gp			

Item Slot: Neck

Enhancement: Fortitude, Reflex, and Will

Property: You gain an item bonus to Heal checks equal to the amulet's enhancement bonus.

Property: When you use a healing power on an ally or succeed on a Heal check to perform first aid on an ally, that ally also makes a saving throw against an ongoing damage effect.

Necklace of Keys — Level 3+

Each key threaded through this leather cord necklace can unlock a portal, even one you haven't detected yet.

Lvl 3	+1	680 gp	Lvl 18	+4	85,000 gp
Lvl 8	+2	3,400 gp	Lvl 23	+5	425,000 gp
Lvl 13	+3	17,000 gp	Lvl 28	+6	2,125,000 gp

Item Slot: Neck

Enhancement: Fortitude, Reflex, and Will

Property: You gain an item bonus to Thievery checks to open locks equal to the necklace's enhancement bonus.

Power (Daily ✦ Teleportation): Minor Action. If you're grabbed or restrained, you can teleport 3 squares.
Level 13 or 18: Teleport 5 squares.
Level 23 or 28: Teleport 10 squares.

Orc's-Eye Amulet — Level 8+

This amulet, consisting of a magic eye within a cloth pouch, has the power to fortify you.

Lvl 8	+2	3,400 gp	Lvl 23	+5	425,000 gp
Lvl 13	+3	17,000 gp	Lvl 28	+6	2,125,000 gp
Lvl 18	+4	85,000 gp			

Item Slot: Neck

Enhancement: Fortitude, Reflex, and Will

Power (Encounter): Immediate Reaction. *Trigger:* An ally within 10 squares of you bloodies an enemy. *Effect:* The ally gains temporary hit points equal to 3 + the amulet's enhancement bonus.
Level 18 or 23: 6 + the amulet's enhancement bonus.
Level 28: 9 + the amulet's enhancement bonus.

Periapt of Proof against Poison — Level 4+

The black gem on this thin silver chain turns white when you're exposed to poison.

Lvl 4	+1	840 gp	Lvl 19	+4	105,000 gp
Lvl 9	+2	4,200 gp	Lvl 24	+5	525,000 gp
Lvl 14	+3	21,000 gp	Lvl 29	+6	2,625,000 gp

Item Slot: Neck

Enhancement: Fortitude, Reflex, and Will

Property: You gain resist 5 poison.
Level 14 or 19: Resist 10 poison.
Level 24 or 29: Resist 20 poison.

Power (Daily): Immediate Interrupt. *Trigger:* You take damage from a poison attack. *Effect:* Your resistance to poison increases by 15 until the end of your next turn.

Periapt of Wound Closure — Level 25+

This bright red stone on a golden chain bleeds freely when you overcome a terrible injury.

| Lvl 25 | +5 | 625,000 gp | Lvl 30 | +6 | 3,125,000 gp |

Item Slot: Neck

Enhancement: Fortitude, Reflex, and Will

Property: You gain an item bonus to saving throws against untyped ongoing damage equal to the periapt's enhancement bonus.

Power (Daily ✦ Healing): No Action. *Trigger:* An attack reduces you to 0 hit points or fewer. *Effect:* You spend a healing surge and regain additional hit points equal to your healing surge value + 10.
Level 30: Your healing surge value + 15.

TIMELESS LOCKET

This platinum disk features numeric engravings, geometric shapes, and arcing lines on both sides. Opening a clasp at the bottom reveals a glass face atop a set of gauges. Each gauge is a circle of runes and numbers arranged around a central post that has moving hands attached to it, which point to a rune, sigil, or number. Dials set around the edges allow the user to adjust the hands to different positions as desired.

A *timeless locket* is an accurate timepiece that shows what time it is in the user's location. The locket also steals a bit of time each day, storing those borrowed moments for use when the owner needs them most.

Explore the Timeless Sanctuary: According to sages, the Timeless was an order of mages who had the power to move backward and forward through time, watching or altering events to suit their purposes. Some calamity wiped out the order, but stories say that the mages' abandoned dominions floating in the Astral Sea still exist, and that *timeless lockets* have been recovered from some of them.

Reach the Plane of Moments: In addition to the Plane of Dreams, the Plane of Mirrors, and the Far Realm, there are a myriad of strange realities, pocket dimensions, and alternate worlds where the impossible becomes possible. Legends speak of one such world where countless golden threads stretch across infinity, each a reality in itself, and the march of history can be seen by reading these strands. In the thickest tangles, representing those monumental events that shape the world and reality, strange and terrible guardians are said to safeguard the strands from tampering. These beings reputedly guard lost treasures from another time, including such items as a *timeless locket*.

Possum Amulet — Level 23+

When you're deeply wounded, this amulet stems the flow of blood to prevent you from dying.

Lvl 23	+5	425,000 gp	Lvl 28	+6	2,125,000 gp

Item Slot: Neck
Enhancement: Fortitude, Reflex, and Will
Power (Daily): No Action. *Trigger:* An attack reduces you to 0 hit points or fewer. *Effect:* You are instead reduced to 1 hit point and knocked prone. Enemies believe that you have been reduced to 0 hit points, and you gain total concealment from them until the end of your next turn.

Seashimmer Cloak — Level 13+

Phantom rivulets of water stream down this cloak, and when you're submerged, the cloak is indistinguishable from the water around it.

Lvl 13	+3	17,000 gp	Lvl 23	+5	425,000 gp
Lvl 18	+4	85,000 gp	Lvl 28	+6	2,125,000 gp

Item Slot: Neck
Enhancement: Fortitude, Reflex, and Will
Property: You gain a swim speed equal to your speed and can breathe underwater.
Power (Daily): Immediate Interrupt. *Trigger:* An enemy hits you. *Effect:* You become insubstantial until the start of your next turn.

ORC'S-EYE AMULET

A follower of Gruumsh might pluck out an eye to look more like the orc deity. By ritually treating a removed eye, an orc can turn it into a useful magic item and an even stronger symbol of devotion to Gruumsh. Orcs waste no words on creatures bearing one of these amulets who aren't followers of Gruumsh—they speak with their blades.

Slay an Eye of Gruumsh: Orc raiders led by an eye of Gruumsh who has an *orc's-eye amulet* are causing trouble for a nearby village. Heroes are needed to slay the orc leader, a deed that will earn the amulet but also the enmity of his tribe and family.

Adventuring Trophy: Word on the street says that a local adventurer who is a great orc hunter took an *orc's-eye amulet* as a trophy from a nearby orc clan. She might be willing to sell it, or she might be "persuaded" to give it up.

Shroud of Ravens — Level 13+

Pulling this cloak's black hood over your head transforms you into a murder of ravens.

Lvl 13	+3	17,000 gp	Lvl 23	+5	425,000 gp
Lvl 18	+4	85,000 gp	Lvl 28	+6	2,125,000 gp

Item Slot: Neck
Enhancement: Fortitude, Reflex, and Will
Power (Daily ✦ Polymorph): Immediate Reaction. *Trigger:* You take damage from an attack. *Effect:* You transform into a cloud of screaming ravens until the start of your next turn. While transformed, you become insubstantial and gain a fly speed equal to your speed. In addition, you shift a number of squares equal to the shroud's enhancement bonus.

SOUL SHARD TALISMAN

Death giants and death titans are known for their soul shrouds, composed of souls they have torn from fallen foes. Small pieces of a slain death giant's or death titan's armor can be enchanted to make *soul shard talismans*, which emulate the nature of the soul shroud. When an enemy of a talisman's wearer falls in combat, its soul is temporarily trapped inside the talisman. This is both a boon and a burden to the wearer. The talisman's wearer can release the soul to heal himself. But until he does so, unpleasant mental impressions from the trapped soul seep through the amulet into the wearer's mind, ending only when the soul is released.

Shard for Sale: Markets in the Shadowfell carry exotic assortments of goods, including relics of battles both ancient and recent. Interested parties can track down a *soul shard talisman* by asking the right people, though the denizens of the Shadowfell aren't too chatty with strangers (or anyone, for that matter).

Soul Shard Talisman — Level 24+

Heavy for its size, this black metal pendant emanates a wisp of blue smoke when a soul is trapped inside it.

Lvl 24	+5	525,000 gp	Lvl 29	+6	2,625,000 gp

Item Slot: Neck
Enhancement: Fortitude, Reflex, and Will
Property: When you reduce a nonminion enemy to 0 hit points, this talisman gains a charge. There is no limit to the number of charges it can gain, but it resets to 1 charge after an extended rest.
Power (Daily ✦ Healing): Minor Action. You expend 1 charge from this talisman and regain 3d6 hit points plus additional hit points equal to 4 times the number of charges remaining in the talisman.
Level 29: 3d8 hit points plus 6 times the number of charges remaining in the talisman.

Talisman of Terror — Level 7+

This amulet depicts a face with an expression of abject terror.

Lvl 7	+2	2,600 gp	Lvl 22	+5	325,000 gp
Lvl 12	+3	13,000 gp	Lvl 27	+6	1,625,000 gp
Lvl 17	+4	65,000 gp			

Item Slot: Neck
Enhancement: Fortitude, Reflex, and Will
Property: When you use a fear power, each target takes a –1 penalty to saving throws against any ongoing effects of the power.
Level 12 or 17: –2 penalty.
Level 22 or 27: –3 penalty.

Timeless Locket — Level 14+

This golden locket helps you make the most out of each moment.

Lvl 14	+3	21,000 gp	Lvl 24	+5	525,000 gp
Lvl 19	+4	105,000 gp	Lvl 29	+6	2,625,000 gp

Item Slot: Neck
Enhancement: Fortitude, Reflex, and Will
Property: You gain an item bonus to initiative checks equal to the locket's enhancement bonus.
Power (Daily): Minor Action. You take a standard action.

RINGS

After choosing two rings of power carefully, adventurers often wear a number of other nonmagical rings to disguise the fact that they are magically equipped.

A magic ring is unobtrusive, easily explained away as mere jewelry, and portable.

Most rings have a property or a power that improves when the wearer reaches a milestone. Beyond that, rings vary widely.

Alliance Band — Level 15

This silver ring is inset with complex interlocking decorations and provides healing to your allies.

Item Slot: Ring   25,000 gp
Property: When you use your second wind, one ally adjacent to you regains 10 hit points.
Power (Daily ✦ Healing): Minor Action. You spend a healing surge but regain no hit points. Instead, one ally adjacent to you regains hit points equal to your healing surge value.
    If you've reached at least one milestone today, the ally regains additional hit points equal to your level.

Crown of the Dream King — Level 15

This ornate golden ring looks like a tiny crown, complete with miniature jewels.

Item Slot: Ring   25,000 gp
Property: You gain a +1 item bonus to all defenses against illusion or psychic powers.
Power (Daily): Immediate Interrupt. *Trigger:* You are hit by an illusion, a psychic, or a sleep power. *Effect:* You gain a +4 bonus to all defenses against the triggering power.
    If you've reached at least one milestone today, the bonus to all defenses lasts until the end of your next turn.

KIERAN YANNER

Dauntless Champion's Ring Level 30

Supernal, Iokharic, and Barazhad characters entwine about this thick mithral band, rearranging themselves when the ring's magic is activated.

Item Slot: Ring   3,125,000 gp
Property: You gain a +4 item bonus to your healing surge value.
Power (Daily): Minor Action. If you have expended all of your encounter attack powers, you regain the use of one of them, determined randomly.
     If you've reached at least one milestone today and have expended all of your daily attack powers, you regain the use of one of them, determined randomly.

Death Song Ring Level 19

The soft songs chanted by this ring in times of need are of those buried alive, hummed with fading breath to hold off the final night.

Item Slot: Ring   105,000 gp
Property: When you make a death saving throw, each enemy within 3 squares of you takes 5 necrotic damage.
Power (Encounter ✦ Necrotic): Immediate Reaction. *Trigger:* An ally makes a death saving throw. *Effect:* One enemy within 3 squares of that ally takes 10 necrotic damage.
     If you've reached at least one milestone today, each enemy, instead of one, within 3 squares of that ally takes 10 necrotic damage.

Death Spiral Ring Level 16

This ring's dizzying black spirals seem to bend space and time.

Item Slot: Ring   45,000 gp
Property: You gain resist 5 necrotic.
Power (Daily ✦ Teleportation): Immediate Reaction. *Trigger:* A creature within 10 squares of you drops to 0 hit points or fewer. *Effect:* You teleport into the creature's space or to a square adjacent to it.
     If you've reached at least one milestone today, you can use the power a second time during this encounter. This second use doesn't count as a use of a daily magic item power.

Grace Ring of Lightning Level 14

The gold and silver weave of this ring is cut with sparkling channels. Lightning arcs from it to protect you when you're incapacitated.

Item Slot: Ring   21,000 gp
Property: You gain a +1 item bonus to saving throws against dazing or stunning effects.
Power (Encounter): No Action. *Trigger:* You are conscious and end your turn without having made an attack during it. *Effect:* One creature within 5 squares of you takes lightning damage equal to your highest ability modifier.

Grace Ring of Prowess Level 19

The magic within this ring is visible as a gold and silver spiral, swirling around your hand until it's released.

Item Slot: Ring   105,000 gp
Property: You gain a +1 item bonus to saving throws against dazing or stunning effects.
Power (Encounter): No Action. *Trigger:* You are conscious and end your turn without having made an attack during it. *Effect:* You gain a +2 power bonus to attack rolls during your next turn.

Grace Ring of Salvation Level 14

When hope has fled, this ring's pulsing blue sapphire might recapture it.

Item Slot: Ring   21,000 gp
Property: You gain a +1 item bonus to saving throws against dazing or stunning effects.
Power (Encounter): No Action. *Trigger:* You are conscious and end your turn without having made an attack during it. *Effect:* You gain a +5 power bonus to your next saving throw before the end of the encounter.

Grace Ward Ring Level 14

This understated gold and silver weave holds a sliver of ivory carved into a ram's head.

Item Slot: Ring   21,000 gp
Property: You gain a +1 item bonus to saving throws against dazing or stunning effects.
Power (Encounter): No Action. *Trigger:* You are conscious and end your turn without having made an attack during it. *Effect:* You push one creature adjacent to you 1 square.

CROWN OF THE DREAM KING

This ring's name comes from a tale told to human children for centuries. In the tale, a young girl named Sharnanda rescues the King of Dreams from the nightmares that haunt his kingdom, and he gives his crown to her in gratitude. Because the King of Dreams is no bigger than Sharnanda's hand, the crown is just large enough for her to wear as a ring, and it protects her dreams from that night on.

When a plague of nightmares comes to Sharnanda's town, the ring protects her, and she uses it to rescue a prince who has fallen under a spell. Together, they defeat the threat, and as such stories go, they marry and live happily ever after.

Many suspect there is some truth to this story, since the rings associated with it seem to have originated in the Feywild, said by some eladrin sages to be the dream of the natural world. Some magic-using jewelers in the world have learned the craft of making these rings, but their versions are never as lovely as the ones given as gifts by the eladrin to those who have earned their favor.

A Hop, a Skip, and a Jump: According to a recently discovered map, a traitorous knight in a magical slumber lies just on the other side of a portal to the Feywild. It's dangerous to go there, but a *crown of the dream king* is supposedly among his possessions.

Greater Ring of Invisibility — Level 23

This onyx band makes it easier for you to conceal your comings and goings.

Item Slot: Ring   425,000 gp
Property: You gain a +5 item bonus to Stealth checks.
Power (Encounter ✦ Illusion): Minor Action. You become invisible until the end of your next turn.
   If you've reached at least one milestone today, you also gain concealment until the end of the encounter.

Ring of Action Reversal — Level 20

This golden band holds a small diamond hourglass, which inverts each time the ring is used.

Item Slot: Ring   125,000 gp
Property: You gain a +4 item bonus to initiative checks.
Power (Daily): Free Action. If the next encounter attack power you use this turn misses all its targets, you regain the use of that power.
   If you've reached at least one milestone today, you can apply this power to the last encounter attack power you used this turn, rather than the next.

Ring of Agile Thought — Level 20

While you wear this ring, your thoughts seem clearer, and you recover from mental attacks quickly.

Item Slot: Ring   125,000 gp
Property: You gain a +4 item bonus to Diplomacy checks. In addition, you gain an item bonus to Will equal to the number of milestones you've reached today.
Power (Daily): No Action. *Trigger:* An attack hits your Will and dazes or stuns you. *Effect:* You make a saving throw against the effect that dazed or stunned you, even if a save can't normally end that effect. The effect ends if you save.

Ring of Battlements — Level 24

This steel band is carved to suggest crenellations—a sign of its protective magic.

Item Slot: Ring   525,000 gp
Property: When you have cover, attackers take a -3 penalty to attack rolls against you instead of a -2 penalty.
Power (Daily ✦ Zone): Minor Action. You create a zone of protection in a close burst 2. The zone lasts until the end of your next turn. While within the zone, you and your allies have cover against enemies outside the zone and can move 1 extra square when they shift. *Sustain Minor:* The zone persists.
   If you've reached at least one milestone today, you can increase the size of the zone by 1.

Ring of Eladrin Grace — Level 16

The silver and gold weave of this grace ring recalls the heraldry of the Spiral Tower.

Item Slot: Ring   45,000 gp
Property: You gain a +1 item bonus to saving throws against dazing or stunning effects.
Power (Encounter ✦ Teleportation): No Action. *Trigger:* You are conscious and end your turn without having made an attack during it. *Effect:* You teleport 5 squares.

Ring of Enduring Earth — Level 20

While you wear this ring, your hand takes on the appearance of stone, signifying that you possess the durability of earth.

Item Slot: Ring   125,000 gp
Property: You gain a +4 item bonus to Endurance checks. In addition, you gain an item bonus to Fortitude equal to the number of milestones you've reached today.
Power (Daily): Free Action. *Trigger:* You're pulled, pushed, slid, or knocked prone. *Effect:* You ignore the forced movement and aren't knocked prone.

Ring of Fearlessness — Level 28

This thin ivory band wards your mind from fear.

Item Slot: Ring   2,125,000 gp
Property: You gain a +4 bonus to all defenses against fear attacks.
Power (Daily): Immediate Interrupt. *Trigger:* An enemy within your line of sight makes a fear attack. *Effect:* Each ally within 5 squares of you gains a +4 power bonus to all defenses against that attack.
   If you've reached at least one milestone today, each ally within 10 squares of you gains the bonus instead.

Ring of Focus — Level 24

This ornate platinum and gold band is dotted with seven different gems.

Item Slot: Ring   525,000 gp
Property: You gain a +1 item bonus to Will.
Power (Daily): Minor Action. Once per round until the end of the encounter, you can use a free action on your turn to sustain an effect of yours that requires a minor action to sustain.
   If you've reached at least one milestone today, you can sustain a power once per round on your turn using no action, rather than a free action.

Ring of Guarded Will — Level 26

This band is made of sculpted force. It occasionally hums faintly in your mind.

Item Slot: Ring   1,125,000 gp
Property: You gain a +2 item bonus to Will.
Power (Daily ✦ Psychic): Immediate Reaction. *Trigger:* An enemy hits you with an attack that targets Will. *Effect:* The triggering enemy takes ongoing 10 psychic damage (save ends).
   If you've reached at least one milestone today, the triggering enemy instead takes ongoing 15 psychic damage (save ends).

Ring of Heroic Health — Level 21

This heavy gold ring is set with a large amethyst, which shimmers faintly with healing magic.

Item Slot: Ring   225,000 gp
Property: When you spend an action point, you regain hit points equal to your Constitution modifier.
Power (Daily ✦ Healing): Standard Action. You spend a healing surge.
   If you've reached at least one milestone today, you don't spend a healing surge. You instead regain hit points as if you had spent one.

Ring of the Fallen — Level 18

This gold ring is engraved with the crossed-axes symbol of a long-dead army.

Item Slot: Ring   85,000 gp

Property: When you use your second wind, you regain additional hit points equal to your Constitution modifier. In addition, you regain additional hit points equal to your Constitution modifier for each healing surge you spend at the end of a short rest.

Power (Daily ✦ Healing): Free Action. Use this power during a short rest. You and each ally within your line of sight regain additional hit points equal to one-half your level when you spend healing surges during that rest.

    If you've reached at least one milestone today, the number of additional hit points equals your level + your Constitution modifier.

Ring of the Risen — Level 23

This simple silver ring makes it easier for your allies to revive you.

Item Slot: Ring   425,000 gp

Property: When you have 0 hit points or fewer and spend a healing surge, you regain 2d6 additional hit points.

Power (Daily ✦ Healing): No Action. *Trigger:* You spend a healing surge as a result of an ally's action. *Effect:* You spend another healing surge.

    If you've reached at least one milestone today, you don't spend another healing surge. You instead regain hit points as if you had spent one.

Ring of the Zealous — Level 15

This gold ring is inlaid with mother-of-pearl blessed by priests of old.

Item Slot: Ring   25,000 gp

Property: When you use the *turn undead power,* you can increase the size of the burst by 1.

Power (Daily): Free Action. *Trigger:* You use *turn undead. Effect:* Each target you hit with that power is restrained instead of immobilized.

    If you've reached at least one milestone today, you can increase the size of the burst by 1 (in addition to the increase from the ring's property).

Ring of Influence — Level 21

This ornate white gold and sapphire ring grants you sway over the minds of others.

Item Slot: Ring   225,000 gp

Property: You gain a +2 item bonus to Charisma-based skill checks and ability checks.

Power (Daily): Minor Action. Until the end of your next turn, you gain a +2 power bonus to attack rolls against Will.

    If you've reached at least one milestone today, the bonus to attack rolls increases to +4.

Ring of Sympathy — Level 15

These copper rings are shared by those who work well together.

Item Slot: Ring   25,000 gp

Property: Once per round, when you save, one ally within 5 squares of you who is also wearing a *ring of sympathy* can make a saving throw.

Power (Daily): Minor Action. One ally within 10 squares of you can make a saving throw. If that ally is wearing a *ring of sympathy,* he or she gains a +2 power bonus to the saving throw.

    If you've reached at least one milestone today, you can instead use this power to grant an ally within 10 squares who is wearing a *ring of sympathy* a saving throw (including the +2 power bonus) against each effect on him or her that a save can end.

Ring of Traded Knowledge — Level 21

The knowledge seems as if it has always been within you, instead of gathered in the slim rune-carved band on your finger.

Item Slot: Ring   225,000 gp

Property: This ring contains one at-will attack power from your class. You choose this power when you acquire the ring and can't change it later.

Power (Daily): Minor Action. Until the end of the encounter, you can use the at-will attack power contained in the ring. If you do so, choose one of your other at-will attack powers from your class. You can't use that power during the encounter.

    If you've reached at least one milestone today, you gain a +2 power bonus to attack rolls and damage rolls when you use the power contained in the ring.

KALMAN ANDRASOFSZKY

Ring of Unfettered Motion — Level 20

When you use this ring, you move so quickly that you're a blur.

Item Slot: Ring   125,000 gp

Property: You gain a +4 item bonus to Acrobatics checks. In addition, you gain an item bonus to Reflex equal to the number of milestones you've reached today.

Power (Daily): Immediate Reaction. *Trigger:* An attack hits your Reflex and immobilizes, restrains, or slows you. *Effect:* You make a saving throw against the effect that immobilized, restrained, or slowed you, even if a save can't normally end that effect. The effect ends if you save.

Ring of Unwelcome Gifting — Level 17

This gold band feeds on things that assail you, spitting them out on your enemy.

Item Slot: Ring   65,000 gp

Property: You gain resist 3 against ongoing damage.

Power (Daily): Free Action. *Trigger:* You hit an enemy with a basic attack. *Effect:* You transfer one ongoing damage effect from yourself to that enemy.

If you've reached at least one milestone today, you can use this power after hitting with an at-will attack that isn't a basic attack.

SHADOWFELL SIGNET

Many generations ago, servants of the Raven Queen raised a temple within the Shadowfell and called it the Monastery of Dire Remembrance. It served the goddess well and helped the dead cast aside the shackles of their past lives to move on to what lay beyond. The temple's priests, who were fierce enemies of the undead, forged *Shadowfell signets* out of the dark metal they mined from beneath the temple and used them as tokens of passage through certain lands of the dead.

Endings come to all things in the Shadowfell, and the temple was no different. Some say the priests were subverted when they opened the temple's gates to servants of Vecna who came bearing stolen signets. Others say that they dug too deep and woke something that was best left asleep.

With the fall of the temple, much of its lore was lost, but a handful of devotees kept the secret of the signets safe and shared it with those who would strike against the undead.

A New Blasphemy: Attacks by undead have ravaged a town in the mountains. The undead have a leader, a female vampire who carries a black metal ring that bears the symbol of the Raven Queen, enemy of all undead. The Raven Queen's worshipers are anxious to end this blasphemy and are looking for heroes who can help them do so.

What Once Was Lost: A paladin who escaped the fall of the temple passed through the area recently. He had one of those fancy rings known as *Shadowfell signets* and said he was going to rebuild the temple in the nearby mountains, but no one ever heard from him again. Of course, a lot of nasty things live up in those mountains, so no one's been brave enough to find out what happened to him.

Ring of Windows — Level 28

This simple wooden ring allows you to go places no one else can, and you can use it to open and close dimensional windows.

Item Slot: Ring   2,125,000 gp

Property: When you teleport and no creature automatically moves into the space you left, that space is filled with a spatial flux that prevents any creature from entering it until the end of your next turn.

Power (Daily ✦ Teleportation): Free Action. *Trigger:* You use a teleportation power. *Effect:* You don't need line of sight to the destination space.

If you've reached at least one milestone today, the distance of the teleportation increases by 4.

Shadowfell Signet — Level 19

This black ring of unknown metal bears the symbol of the Raven Queen in silver.

Item Slot: Ring   105,000 gp

Property: You gain resist 10 necrotic, and if an enemy's attack causes you to lose a healing surge, you can take 10 damage instead of losing that healing surge.

Power (Daily ✦ Stance): Minor Action. Until the stance ends, you gain a +4 bonus to all defenses against opportunity attacks from undead creatures, and you don't grant combat advantage when flanked by undead.

If you've reached at least one milestone today, you don't provoke opportunity attacks from undead creatures.

RING OF THE FALLEN

Centuries ago, a company of dwarf soldiers was garrisoned in an outpost at the edge of the frontier. The soldiers were assigned to guard the edges of civilization from the encroachment of monsters. When a white dragon attacked the outpost, the dwarves were driven away. Ashamed of themselves, they reconvened and went back to the outpost to try to best the dragon.

The dwarves fought a good fight, but the dragon was victorious. Their frozen bodies weren't found until an army arrived and destroyed the dragon. The dwarves' military rings were collected and used as special medals that were handed out for bravery. Since the dissolution of the army, the rings have dispersed throughout the land.

Buried Cache: Rumor has it that a cache of *rings of the fallen* is buried deep within a forest overrun by brigands. The brigands are an uncommon lot, using monsters and magic to prey on nearby townsfolk. Perhaps the brigands know where the cache is.

Mad Oracle: Divinations have revealed that a mad oracle in the mountains knows the location of one or more *rings of the fallen*. Numerous obstacles and monsters block the path to the oracle, but the promise of one of these rings would be worth the dangers.

Stone Band | Level 17

This ring of basalt becomes more polished and intricately carved each time you use it.

Item Slot: Ring   65,000 gp
Property: You gain resist 5 against critical hits. If you've reached at least one milestone today, you gain resist 10 instead.
Power (Daily): Minor Action. You gain resist 5 to all damage until the end of your next turn. *Sustain Minor:* The effect persists.

Stormcatcher Ring | Level 17

This copper ring has a setting but no gemstone. When you use the ring, sparks fill the setting.

Item Slot: Ring   65,000 gp
Property: You gain resist 10 lightning and resist 10 thunder.
Power (Daily): Immediate Interrupt. *Trigger:* An enemy hits you with a lightning attack. *Effect:* The triggering enemy makes the attack again, but against itself.
    If you've reached at least one milestone today, you can pick a second enemy within 5 squares of you. The triggering enemy makes the attack against the second enemy too.

Traveler's Ring | Level 18

This tarnished silver ring set with a muddied stone looks mundane. When you wear it, it tugs you in the right direction.

Item Slot: Ring   85,000 gp
Property: You gain a +4 item bonus to Streetwise checks.
Power (Daily): Free Action. You gain a success in a skill challenge in which Streetwise is a primary or secondary skill.
    If you've reached at least one milestone today, you also gain a +5 power bonus on your next Streetwise check before the end of the day.

Unvanquished Grace Ring | Level 14

The distinctive gold and silver weave of this grace ring is carved with feathers.

Item Slot: Ring   21,000 gp
Property: You gain a +1 item bonus to saving throws against dazing or stunning effects.
Power (Encounter): No Action. *Trigger:* You are conscious and end your turn without having made an attack during it. *Effect:* You or an ally within 5 squares of you can stand up as a free action.

WAIST SLOT ITEMS

No hero wears a girdle. If anyone asks, it's a belt.

Waist slot items, whether baldrics, bandoliers, belts, or sashes, are hard to pin down to one mystical theme. Many waistline wraps benefit the health of the wearer, but some bands serve other purposes altogether. Those belts that hold weapons or other tools can be enchanted to enhance those items.

Acrobat's Harness | Level 14

These cloth straps help you to twist and dive out of dangerous situations.

Item Slot: Waist   21,000 gp
Property: When you make an Acrobatics check, you roll twice and use either result.

Baldric of Assault | Level 11

This gray leather baldric lets you supplant your enemy when you use your aegis of assault.

Item Slot: Waist   9,000 gp
Property: When an enemy triggers your *aegis of assault* power, you can slide the enemy 1 square and then teleport into that enemy's space, instead of teleporting to a space adjacent to the enemy.

Baldric of Shielding | Level 19

This marcasite-studded baldric aids you when you use your aegis of shielding.

Item Slot: Waist   105,000 gp
Property: When you use your *aegis of shielding* power to reduce the damage dealt to an ally, you gain temporary hit points equal to the amount of damage you prevented.

Baldric of Time | Level 6+

This rough-textured belt seems to be coated in the sands of time.

| Lvl 6 | 1,800 gp | Lvl 16 | 45,000 gp |

Item Slot: Waist
Property: When you roll a 20 on your initiative check, you gain an extra move action during the first turn of the encounter.
Level 16: You instead gain an extra standard action.

Belt of Fragile Guard | Level 9

This wide leather band toughens your skin but weakens your resilience.

Item Slot: Waist   4,200 gp
Power (At-Will): Minor Action. Until the end of your next turn, you gain a +1 power bonus to AC and vulnerability to all damage equal to half your level.

Belt of the witch king

Belt of Nourishment | Level 7

This comfortable leather belt is worked with images of foodstuffs that nourish you.

Item Slot: Waist   2,600 gp
Property: You gain a +3 item bonus to Endurance checks.
Property: You don't need to eat. You must wear the belt for 24 consecutive hours before this property functions.

ED COX

Belt of the Witch King — Level 18

The links of this slim silver chain are separated by small spheres of arcane-enhanced obsidian.

Item Slot: Waist   85,000 gp

Property: You gain a +2 item bonus to Fortitude.

Power (Daily ✦ Healing): Free Action. *Trigger:* You become bloodied. *Effect:* You regain hit points equal to twice the level of the highest-level arcane power you have not expended.

Diamond Cincture — Level 10+

The diamonds on this platinum band grant great fortitude, which you can sacrifice for health.

Lvl 10	5,000 gp	Lvl 30	3,125,000 gp
Lvl 20	125,000 gp		

Item Slot: Waist

Property: This belt holds one diamond and you gain a +1 item bonus to Fortitude.

Level 20: Two diamonds, +2 item bonus to Fortitude.
Level 30: Three diamonds, +3 item bonus to Fortitude.

Power (At-Will ✦ Healing): Minor Action. When you use this power, one diamond on the belt cracks and darkens, becoming worthless. You regain hit points as if you had spent a healing surge, and the belt's item bonus is reduced by one. If there are no diamonds on the belt, you can't use this power. After an extended rest, each diamond destroyed by this power is restored.

Phoenix Sash — Level 18

This brilliant orange wrap restores life to the vanquished.

Item Slot: Waist   85,000 gp

Property: You gain a +1 item bonus to Fortitude.

Power (Daily ✦ Healing): No Action. *Trigger:* An enemy reduces you to 0 hit points or fewer. *Effect:* You spend a healing surge and are dazed until the end of your next turn.

Potion Bandolier — Level 8

This wide brown leather baldric keeps potions in easy reach.

Item Slot: Waist   3,400 gp

Property: This belt can hold up to six potions. You can retrieve a potion from the belt as a free action.

Sash of Heroic Inspiration — Level 28

This flashy, embroidered red sash proclaims your heroism to all.

Item Slot: Waist   2,125,000 gp

Property: When you spend an action point, one ally within your line of sight can spend a healing surge as a free action.

Sash of Regeneration — Level 28

While you wear this heavy brown hide sash, you heal at a tremendous rate.

Item Slot: Waist   2,125,000 gp

Property: You gain regeneration 5 while you're bloodied.

BELT OF THE WITCH KING

Long ago in the nation of Pak Suth, the king died without an heir. Driven by a warrior tradition and the need for a strong, imposing ruler to maintain the borders, the ministers of the kingdom proclaimed that any person who could endure a series of daily tests of the body would become absolute ruler.

Many soldiers, generals, and heroes succumbed to the trials before Tulari claimed his right to be tested. Despite his slight frame, he endured each day's test and eventually became king. Tulari was a great ruler, holding the boundaries of Pak Suth firmly and ruling wisely. Today, the legend of the Witch King Tulari remains strong in the region, and the nation's ruler wears a belt of office—the same one that Tulari wore when he passed the tests.

Nation in Exile: Much has changed since Witch King Tulari set Pak Suth on the path to greatness. Today, the people of Pak Suth flee their homeland en masse. The king's lineage has ended, and rebels have stolen Tulari's belt—or so the rumor goes. What authority remains has offered a prize for the defeat of the violent rebels that plague the exodus: the *belt of the Witch King* and possibly rulership of the kingdom.

Political Ploy: The current ruler of Pak Suth needs to make a political statement regarding her strength and the nation's direction. She wants to give away Tulari's belt as part of that declaration, but she requires worthy recipients so as not to dishonor the Witch King's memory. To that end, she commissioned the construction of a labyrinth of dangers, reminiscent of the challenges Tulari defeated. The labyrinth is all that stands between a group of heroes and this belt.

Stonewall Belt — Level 8

This rough gray belt covered in stone plates grants stability to its wearer.

Item Slot: Waist   3,400 gp

Power (Daily): Minor Action. You can ignore push, pull, or slide effects until the end of your next turn.

Waistband of the Grappler — Level 13

This fur-lined wrap channels the strength and the recklessness of an accomplished wrestler.

Item Slot: Waist   17,000 gp

Power (At-Will): Minor Action. You gain a +5 power bonus to damage rolls and to grab attempts, but take a -2 penalty to attack rolls. You also grant combat advantage to all enemies. This effect lasts until you end it as a minor action.

Wraith's Cord — Level 30

You become wraithlike when you wear this worn rope band.

Item Slot: Waist   3,125,000 gp

Property: When you score a critical hit, the target is weakened until the end of your next turn.

Power (Daily ✦ Illusion): Minor Action. Until the end of your next turn, you become invisible and insubstantial and gain phasing.

Phoenix sash

PHOENIX SASH

Fenelon was an eladrin warrior of the Feywild who was known for his ability to live through anything. In the war with the fomorians, he was crushed under a pile of rock, thrown off a cliff, and speared by the giant warrior Morgkash, surviving each and every event. For his ability to rise from the ashes of tragedy and defeat, Fenelon became known as the Phoenix.

Fenelon eventually died of old age, and his magic sash passed into the hands of other eladrin. Eventually it made its way into the world, where it has been worn by a number of heroes, though none as worthy as Fenelon. Learning of this disgrace, the eladrin seek a fey warrior of great prowess who can find and reclaim the sash, returning it to glory and honor.

Reclaim the Sash: The eladrin court has put out a call for fey warriors to seek out the *Phoenix sash*. They believe that it can be found in the hands of a mad archmage by the name of Killias. The archmage has been oppressing the villagers in a small kingdom in the north.

Fomorian Clutches: Rumors suggest that Skrad, a descendant of the fomorian Morgkash, has found the *Phoenix sash* and is keeping it in his stronghold. He guards the sash closely and attacks any who would take it. It's also said that on more than one occasion, the sash has saved his life when fey assassins attempted to kill him.

WONDROUS ITEMS

If you think you have too many wondrous items, you're wrong. In truth, you have too few pockets.

The catchall category for enchanted objects, a wondrous item isn't worn or wielded, and it can have myriad enchantments. Adventurers hoard wondrous items because their effects cover such a wide spectrum and not having the right one can be the difference between success and failure.

This section described various wondrous items to help you out of jams, wondrous lair items to enhance your base of operations, and wondrous tattoos that are always with you, even if your other items aren't.

Blessed Book	Level 1

This leather tome, bound in iron and silver, contains far more pages than naturally possible.

Wondrous Item   360 gp
Property: This ritual book has the dimensions and weight of a standard ritual book, but holds 1,000 pages.

Deepfarer's Pouch	Level 5

This oilskin pouch holds more than it should, including a small breathing tube that extends from the inside.

Wondrous Item   1,000 gp
Property: This belt pouch contains 1 hour's worth of air, which remains fresh indefinitely. Once the air in the pouch has been consumed, you can refresh the supply by exposing the open pouch to any supply of breathable air during a short rest.

Ghostlight Candle	Level 15

This plain white wax candle can burn every day without diminishing.

Wondrous Item   25,000 gp
Property: This candle sheds dim light 2 squares in all directions and never burns down (but can be extinguished).
Power (Daily): Standard Action. Use this power while the candle is lit. Until the end of the encounter, creatures within 2 squares of the candle lose the insubstantial quality and can't become invisible.

Horn of Dismissal	Level 12

The sound of this black-studded bronze horn dispels conjurations.

Wondrous Item   13,000 gp
Power (Daily): Standard Action. You end each conjuration within 3 squares of you.

Ioun's Parchment	Level 1

This thin sheet of bronze, the size of a roll of parchment, is embossed with Ioun's symbol in one corner.

Wondrous Item   360 gp
Property: This material can be written on like paper or parchment, and the writing can't be erased until the parchment's owner wills it blank. It's flexible enough to roll. Creating a ritual scroll using this item fills it with text, but takes half the usual time. Once the ritual is performed, the piece of *Ioun's parchment* turns blank and can be reused.

JASON A. ENGLE

GHOSTLIGHT CANDLE

The shadar-kai's service to the Raven Queen has earned them numerous enemies over the years. One of the most persistent foes was Antala Longscar, a priest of the Raven Queen who strongly disagreed with the shadar-kai's philosophy and methodology and who had stymied a number of their plans. She was enough of a thorn in their side that the shadar-kai felt she deserved an accelerated audience with the goddess she and they both served.

Antala spent her life dealing with regular visits from shadar-kai assassins, and she developed a number of defenses and protections to minimize their threat, including the *ghostlight candle*.

Internal Matters: The shadar-kai are as given to politics and infighting as any other intelligent people. A caravan of them arrived in town with a number of *ghostlight candles* and other treasures. These shadar-kai are willing to use the candles as payment for escort to someplace safe, but others of their kind are willing to pay a similar price to see that the caravan doesn't leave. One way or another, these events offer a good chance to acquire one of the candles.

The Light under the Hill: Every night for the past 10 years, the light from a single candle has been seen from the top of a hill outside town. Stories say it's a *ghostlight candle*, lit by a girl trapped by the fey, who is badly in need of rescue.

Map of Unseen Lands	Level 7

Protected by a sturdy scroll tube, this sheet of vellum is ringed with symbols of travel: wagon wheels, footsteps, and rafts.

Wondrous Item   2,600 gp

Property: You gain a +2 item bonus to Nature checks and Perception checks to navigate through areas mapped by this item's power (including checks made during skill challenges).

Power (Daily): Standard Action. You command this map to redraw itself, depicting the surface area within a 10-mile radius around you. The map doesn't go into precise detail, but it's accurate. It shows only aboveground terrain, not underground areas.

     The map includes the following features:

✦ General terrain features, such as mountains, rivers, and lakes;

✦ Structures 5,000 square feet or larger in size;

✦ Structures important for travel, such as bridges and portals;

✦ Lairs of creatures that are significant threats;

✦ Names or general descriptions for any of the above features, if such information is well known.

The sketch remains on the map until this power is used again.

HORN OF DISMISSAL

The conjurers of the group known as the Immaculate Star enforced their will through a virtual army of magic creatures composed of cool blue flame. With such troops, a small number of conjurers were able to conquer the city of Alb and hold it for over a year. Their yoke was thrown off only when a resistance group managed to put an enchantment on the great bell of the cathedral. When it sounded, it shattered, but the note dispelled the phantom army in the city. Shards of the bell were forged into a variety of weapons to use against the conjurers, including horns that had an enchantment similar to that of the original bell. Within a few months, the Immaculate Star was no more.

The pieces of the original bell have long since been used up, but clever artisans have found ways to duplicate its functionality.

Immortal Immaculate: The Immaculate Star analyzed some of the weapons made from the bell in an attempt to counteract their effect. They were unsuccessful, but even now immortal summoned guardians stand watch over their empty laboratories. A map to one of these locations has surfaced—a real find, if it's accurate. Perhaps one of the labs holds a *horn of dismissal*.

Ribbon of Limitless Questions	Level 13

When this blue, silky ribbon is unrolled, a new question appears on it in glowing gold and silver runes.

Wondrous Item   17,000 gp

Property: When you perform a divination ritual that allows you to ask a number of questions, such as Hand of Fate, Speak with Dead, or Consult Oracle, you can ask one extra question. This effect can allow you to exceed the normal maximum number of questions allowed.

Power (Daily): Free Action. *Trigger:* You fail an Intelligence- or Charisma-based skill check during a skill challenge. *Effect:* Reroll the skill check with a +2 power bonus and use either result.

RIBBON OF LIMITLESS QUESTIONS

Legend says the first *ribbon of limitless questions* was inscribed on cloth woven by Corellon, the ink mixed from golden sunlight and mithral dust. Even if this tale is true, most such ribbons are considerably more modest.

The questions that appear on a ribbon are useful in many ways. Some present questions the ribbon's user can ask of someone else. Other questions are directed at the ribbon's holder, and prompt him or her to think about a situation and come up with new solutions.

A Temple's Gift: Few *ribbons of limitless questions* are found in the hands of normal people. The majority of these magic items are held by high priests in various temples, especially those of Ioun and Vecna. One way to gain access to a ribbon is to convince the priests of such a deity that it will be used against their enemies.

Seed of War
Level 15

When you release this black metal acorn, it grows into a fierce soldier.

Wondrous Item   25,000 gp

Power (Daily ✦ Conjuration): Standard Action. You conjure a Medium metal soldier, equipped with sword and shield, by tossing this item into an unoccupied square within 5 squares of you. The soldier occupies its square and can be attacked. It shares your defenses with a +2 bonus to AC and Reflex. It has hit points equal to your healing surge value. When it takes damage, you can spend a healing surge as a free action to negate that damage.

The soldier is treated as one of your allies, can flank enemies, and deals 10 damage to an enemy adjacent to it that is hit by an ally's attack. As a move action, you can cause the soldier to shift 1 square or move 4 squares. When reduced to 0 hit points, or at the end of the encounter, the soldier disappears, and the *seed of war* reappears in its square.

Vagabond's Die
Level 8

This die is well used—the images on its faces are almost worn away.

Wondrous Item   3,400 gp

Power (Daily ✦ Varies): Minor Action. You target a creature of your choice within 10 squares and roll a d6.
1: *Drunkard's Mug.* The target takes a -2 penalty to attack rolls until the end of its next turn.
2: *Gambler's Dice.* Roll a d20. If the result is even, the target takes damage equal to the result. If the result is odd, the target regains hit points equal to the result.
3: *Jester's Chair.* The target falls prone.
4–5: *Soldier's Fist.* The first attack that hits the target before the end of your next turn deals 2d6 extra damage.
6: *Storm's Fury.* The target and all creatures adjacent to it take 1d10 lightning damage.

Versatile Spellbook
Level 11

The pages of this spellbook are magically treated, allowing you to quickly draw on their arcane power.

Wondrous Item   9,000 gp

Property: Wizards can use this item as a spellbook.

Power (At-Will): Free Action. *Trigger:* You finish a short rest. *Effect:* Replace one wizard utility power you prepared with a wizard utility power of the same level or lower from your spellbook that you didn't prepare. If it's an encounter power, you must replace it with another encounter power, and if it's a daily power, you must replace it with another daily power.

MAP OF UNSEEN LANDS

When a *map of unseen lands* is activated, it plots out the nearby area, with excellent accuracy but poor detail. Followers of Avandra, deity of travel and adventure, claim that *maps of unseen lands* call upon her knowledge. Others say the maps flow from the memories of people (living and dead) who have visited the area, pulling on psychic ties that still linger.

Wealthy connoisseurs who understand magic items seek out different *maps of unseen lands*, since each draws maps in a unique artistic style. Some items use jagged lines, others produce thin strokes; in a few, the maps bleed out into the vellum like ink washes.

The Halflings' Reward: Tribes of river-wandering halflings carry *maps of unseen lands* as they explore new areas. Despite the maps, the small ones wind up in dangerous places quite often. In fact, a brother and sister recently went missing near some old ruins. Whoever helps them out might be given a *map of unseen lands* as a reward, or they might collect one from one of the halflings' corpses, if the aid comes too late.

Beg, Borrow, or Steal: The merchant Phineas Ollune is proud of his collection of rare items, which includes a *map of unseen lands*. Unfortunately for those who covet it, he refuses to sell it. Phineas lives in a town full of superstitious folk, and rumors abound that he is a werewolf. Whether the rumor is true or not, this information might be used to persuade him to give up the map.

Whistle of Warning
Level 8

This small, unremarkable-looking silver whistle gives off a shrill noise when sounded.

Wondrous Item   3,400 gp

Power (Encounter): Minor Action. Each ally within 10 squares of you who can hear the whistle can shift 1 square and draw a weapon or retrieve an implement as a free action.

Woundstitch Powder
Level 1

This worn leather pouch contains a quantity of life-saving yellow powder.

Wondrous Item   360 gp

Power (At-Will): Standard Action. You sprinkle this dust on an adjacent dying creature. That creature stops making death saving throws until it takes damage, and any untyped ongoing damage on the creature ends.

WONDROUS LAIR ITEMS

Lair items are a class of wondrous item that adventurers can add to their base of operations (or "lair"). Unlike most magic items, lair items aren't portable; they must be left behind when a hero goes exploring. They provide comforts when the party returns home after a difficult adventure, and a home-field advantage against enemies who would dare assault them in their sanctum.

Alchemist's Workshop — Level 8

This set of tools, worktable, vials, beakers, distillery, and other alchemical apparatuses is enchanted to aid in the creation of powerful alchemical items.

Wondrous Item   3,400 gp

Property: When you use this workshop to create alchemical items, you can create items of a level equal to or less than your level + 2.

All-Seeing Eye — Level 22

This multifaceted diamond is usually placed in the eye socket of a statue or an idol, or atop a tripod that overlooks a room. It sees all and reports back to its master what it learns.

Wondrous Item   325,000 gp

Property: This eye can see invisible creatures and objects within 20 squares of it. When a creature enters the eye's line of sight, the eye telepathically warns its owner of the creature's presence and provides a description. It can communicate with its owner across planar boundaries.

Arcane Laboratory — Level 23

Spirits of past arcane masters are bound to this well-equipped laboratory. Their aid allows you to refocus your magic for other purposes.

Wondrous Item   425,000 gp

Property: When you spend 24 hours studying in this laboratory, you can replace one arcane power as if you had gained a level and retrained. After you use this property, you can't use it again until you gain a level.

Austere Dojo — Level 23

This dojo is complete with punching bags, a weapon rack, fencing equipment, and training automatons impressed with the personalities of history's greatest masters. Working with them allows you to refocus your fighting style.

Wondrous Item   425,000 gp

Property: When you spend 24 hours in training at the dojo, you can replace one martial power as if you had gained a level and retrained. After you use this property, you can't use it again until you gain a level.

VAGABOND'S DIE

This stone die with a symbol on each of its faces is carried by well-traveled tricksters who court Lady Luck. Gamblers use a *vagabond's die* as both a randomizer and a item to wager in games of chance, so a die could pass from person to person repeatedly. Exceptionally lucky gamblers (or exceptional cheats) amass a sizable collection of these dice.

Some people who carry a *vagabond's die* consider it a tool of fate and use it to make decisions on what course of action to take. Each face's image has a theme.

Drunkard's Mug: The image of a frothing tankard represents leisure and friendship. You should take some time to relax, and visit a tavern if you can find one.

Gambler's Dice: This face implies risk and fate, and suggests that you should take a risky course of action.

Jester's Chair: Buffoonery and foolishness are symbolized by this image. Don't take things too seriously right now.

Soldier's Fist: Strength of arms can solve a current problem. Two faces hold this symbol—if you make decisions using this die, be prepared for a lot of fights.

Storm's Fury: The sublime power of nature is represented by this face. Spend some time outdoors, and explore.

The Arcane Cheat: Audren, a gambling wizard, is rumored to have never lost a game of chance and has acquired at least a dozen *vagabond's dice*. Of course, rumors abound that he cheats. Whoever discovers his secret might be able to defeat him and claim a *vagabond's die*. The rumors don't indicate whether or not he's a sore loser. . . .

Bed of Rapid Rest — Level 4

This comfortable bed speeds your rest but is too large to cart around in the dungeon.

Wondrous Item   840 gp

Property: When you take an extended rest in this bed, you can spend 4 hours (instead of the usual 6) to gain the benefit of that rest.

Brilliant Scrying Basin — Level 12

The brilliantly clear water of this large bronze basin greatly aids scrying rituals.

Wondrous Item   13,000 gp

Property: When you use this basin as a focus for a scrying ritual, the duration of your scrying sensor increases by 2 rounds.

Cask of Liquid Gold — Level 3

This cask contains a never-ending supply of dwarven ale.

Wondrous Item   680 gp

Property: At the start of each day, the cask fills to its full volume with dwarven ale. Any ale taken from the cask evaporates if it has not been consumed when the cask refills.

Chandelier of Revelation — Level 24

This chandelier reveals that which is hidden in the room.

Wondrous Item   525,000 gp

Property: You can command this chandelier to shed bright light either 10, 20, or 40 squares in all directions as a free action. Within that area, creatures can't benefit from concealment or total concealment.

Deceptive Scrying Basin — Level 16

This etched silver basin makes it more difficult for creatures you observe to detect your prying gaze.

Wondrous Item   45,000 gp

Property: When you use this basin as a focus for a scrying ritual, creatures take a −5 penalty to checks to notice your scrying sensor.

Dimensional Anchor — Level 16

This statue appears in many guises, but each binds nearby creatures to their locations in the world.

Wondrous Item   45,000 gp

Property: Any creature within 10 squares of this statue can't teleport.

Diplomat's Table — Level 12

This majestic darkwood table enhances your position in negotiations.

Wondrous Item   13,000 gp

Property: You and your allies gain a +3 item bonus to Bluff, Diplomacy, and Intimidate checks during skill challenges while sitting at this table.

WHISTLE OF WARNING

These whistles have been used by bodyguards and watch soldiers for generations, so it comes as a surprise to many citizens that they were first created for use by thieves. When a particularly brutal conflict between two halfling crime families spun out of control, each side invested in magic to tip things to their advantage. One clever member conceived the *whistle of warning* to protect the family from ambushes.

The feud continued to escalate until the two crime syndicates discovered that the entire conflict was being prolonged by the artificers who were providing each side with magic items. The enemies reached a truce and shortly thereafter assumed joint control over the magic item market in town.

Good Doggie: The local lizardfolk have been getting more aggressive lately, and one of their leaders has been using a distinctive-sounding whistle to direct his "hounds." Perhaps it's a *whistle of warning*.

Watching the Watch: The city watch might be corrupt to some degree, but its members try to do their job, at least until they come across something they can't handle. Well, "something" has been eating people and leaving bits near the south canal. The watch doesn't have the personnel to deal with it or the cash to pay heroes. But it can arrange for some supplies, including a *whistle of warning*, to go off the books if the problem stops.

Door of Alarm — Level 2

This seemingly innocuous door issues a shrill alarm when an unknown creature walks through it.

Wondrous Item   520 gp

Property: You can spend 1 minute to attune any number of individuals to this door. When a creature other than an attuned individual walks through the door, a shrill alarm sounds and doesn't stop for 1 hour, until that creature leaves through the door, or you command the door to be silent.

Door Warden — Level 12

The ornamental face on this door interrogates and introduces your visitors.

Wondrous Item   13,000 gp

Property: Cast in the shape of a face, this door ornament is aware of its surroundings and able to speak. When you install a *door warden* on a portal, the door gains resist 10 to all damage and 40 additional hit points, and can be opened or closed at will by the warden as a minor action. The *door warden* judges when to open the door or keep it sealed based on your instructions and can communicate with you telepathically if you're on the same plane.

Feast Table — Level 9

This magnificent round oak table seats twelve and provides a magnificent banquet for all present.

Wondrous Item   4,200 gp

Power (At-Will): Standard Action. A delicious feast for twelve people appears on the table.

Power (At-Will): Standard Action. All remnants of the feast vanish, and the table sparkles with cleanliness.

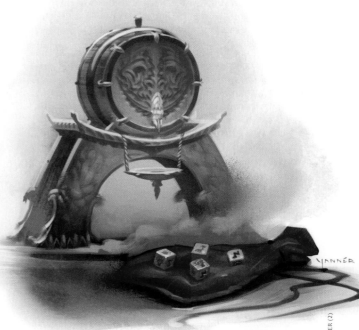

Cask of liquid gold and vagabond's dice

KIERAN YANNER (2)

Door warden

Gorgonblood Mortar — Level 22

Integrating this special mortar into your wall grants it a meta-physical denseness.

Wondrous Item   325,000 gp

Property: You can use this mortar in the construction of up to 10 contiguous squares of a wall. Creatures that have phasing can't pass through walls so constructed.

Holy Shrine — Level 23

Minor angels attend this shrine, allowing you to refocus your divine power for other purposes.

Wondrous Item   425,000 gp

Property: When you spend 24 hours in prayer at the shrine, you can replace one divine power as if you had gained a level and retrained. After you use this property, you can't use it again until you gain a level.

Loadstone Statue — Level 14

This statue usually takes the form of a dwarf paladin crouched in a defensive stance.

Wondrous Item   21,000 gp

Property: Any creature within 5 squares of this statue can't shift.

Property: Any marked creature within 5 squares of this statue takes a –3 penalty (instead of the normal –2 penalty) to attack rolls when making an attack that doesn't include the creature that marked it.

Magic Drawbridge — Level 13

This iron-banded drawbridge resizes to fit the portal it's placed in, then raises or lowers with a single word.

Wondrous Item   17,000 gp

Property: You can command this drawbridge to raise or lower as a free action. You must be able to see the drawbridge to activate it, and it neither rises if any creature is on it nor lowers if any creature is under it.

Magic Weapon Rack — Level 25

This heavy oak weapon rack recharges weapons and implements stored on it.

Wondrous Item   625,000 gp

Power (Daily): Use this power during a short rest. The daily power of a single weapon or implement stored on the rack is recharged.

Mirror of Deception — Level 18

When you stand before this wrought-iron framed mirror, you can change your looks to reflect your every whim.

Wondrous Item   85,000 gp

Power (At-Will ✦ Illusion): Standard Action. You gain the appearance of a member of any humanoid race of the same size category as you. Your clothing and equipment alter appearance as you desire. The illusion doesn't alter sound or texture, so a creature listening to you or touching you might detect the illusion. The illusion lasts until you leave the lair where the mirror resides, or until you end the effect as a free action.

Ritualist's Lectern — Level 12

This heavy teak lectern is engraved with runes and patterns of arcane power.

Wondrous Item   13,000 gp

Property: When you use this lectern to master a ritual, reduce the time necessary to 4 hours, and you can master rituals of a level equal to or less than your level + 2.

Power (At-Will): Standard Action. Use this power before performing a ritual that you have mastered. Performing the ritual takes half the normal time. This power has no effect on the time it takes to perform a ritual from a scroll.

Sacred Glade — Level 23

This clearing surrounds a sacred tree. When you meditate by the tree, you can refocus your primal powers.

Wondrous Item   425,000 gp

Property: When you spend 24 hours in contemplation in the glade, you can replace one primal power as if you had gained a level and retrained. After you use this property, you can't use it again until you gain a level.

Shiftstone — Level 8

Building these stones into your home removes handholds from would-be intruders.

Wondrous Item   3,400 gp

Property: The DC of Athletics checks to climb a building incorporating *shiftstone* increases by 10. To gain this benefit, a house requires one batch of *shiftstone* during construction, a mansion requires five batches, and a castle or larger structure requires twenty-five batches.

Holy shrine

Shining Sundial
Level 10

This gem-studded silver sundial reflects light brilliantly, amplifying radiant effects.

Wondrous Item   5,000 gp

Property: This sundial must be placed in a location where it receives natural light while the sun is up. When you use a radiant attack power, until the end of your next turn, creatures within 10 squares of the sundial gain a +1 bonus to attack rolls and a +3 bonus to damage rolls.

Silence-Warded Room
Level 4

This lush chamber offers privacy for your conversations.

Wondrous Item   840 gp

Property: When you speak a command word as a free action, creatures outside the room attempting to listen to sounds originating in the room take a -10 penalty to Perception checks until you end the effect with another free action. Creatures within the room can hear sounds originating outside the room as normal.

Spying Mirrors (pair)
Level 18

You look into one mirror and see out of its twin.

Wondrous Item   85,000 gp

Power (At-Will): Standard Action. When each of these mirrors is affixed to a solid structure and you're adjacent to one of the mirrors, you can see and hear through the other mirror as if you were in its square until the start of your next turn. If you choose, creatures adjacent to the other mirror can also see and hear through yours.

Special: Spying mirrors are generally created as a matched pair, each mirror attuned to the other. One or more other mirrors can be attuned to both mirrors of a pair, allowing you to use this item's at-will power to look out through any one of the mirrors of the set (add 42,500 gp to the price for each additional mirror attuned). A single mirror can belong to only one set of *spying mirrors*.

Sun Globe
Level 1

After being installed in a socket on the wall or ceiling, these fist-sized crystal globes shed light when commanded.

Wondrous Item   360 gp

Property: You can command this item to shed bright or dim light either 5 or 10 squares in all directions as a free action (or to shed no light).

HOWARD LYON

Teleportation Disk — Level 14

Usually set in the floor, this large, ornately inscribed teleportation circle moves you quickly around your domicile.

Wondrous Item   21,000 gp

Power (At-Will ✦ Teleportation): Move Action. When you speak a command word while standing on the disk, you teleport to any location in the same residence or structure as a move action.

Throne of Dominion — Level 12

This throne is carved with ornate filigree and reliefs showing a king ruling over subjects that span the chair's entire surface.

Wondrous Item   13,000 gp

Property: While you sit on the throne, when a creature you can see attempts to deceive, disobey, or betray you, it is stunned (save ends). All creatures you can see take a -3 penalty to attack rolls that target your Will.

Power (Daily ✦ Charm): Standard Action. Make an attack: Ranged sight; Charisma + 5 vs. Will; on a hit, the target is dominated until the end of your next turn.

Throne of Grandeur — Level 18

This magnificent carved stone throne is decorated with symbols and images of nobility and heroism.

Wondrous Item   85,000 gp

Property: While you sit on the throne, you gain a +4 item bonus to Diplomacy checks, Insight checks, and Intimidate checks.

Vigilant Gargoyle — Level 17

This ghastly stone gargoyle looks like a typical church decoration, but it's much more than that.

Wondrous Item   65,000 gp

Power (At-Will): Minor Action. You can perform this action from anywhere on the same plane as the structure in which this gargoyle is installed. Until the end of your next turn, you see through the eyes of the *vigilant gargoyle* as though you were in its square. While under the effect of this power, you're considered blinded in your current location.

THRONE OF DOMINION

For ages, monarchs and despots have used *thrones of dominion* to sway the thoughts and opinions of their subjects. Stories of the first throne's creation are inconsistent—it's a defining characteristic of the item that it inspires loyalty in followers, who refuse to believe that any other ruler but their own could have produced such a marvel. Prominent in places where rulers have or had few qualms about maintaining control using magic, *thrones of dominion* were an integral part of the tiefling empire of Bael Turath, and they can be found today in many drow cities and githyanki citadels.

Depose the Tyrant: Anyone who has a number of loyal followers in sway might have a *throne of dominion*. It's said that Ravel the Ruthless sits on an expensive throne in his hold, and should he be dethroned, none would be saddened.

Watchful Eye — Level 12

Taking the form of some lesser gem in the eye socket of an idol, or just stuck in the middle of a wall, this spy reports all that it sees back to its master.

Wondrous Item   13,000 gp

Property: When a creature enters this eye's line of sight, the eye telepathically warns you of the creature's presence and provides a description, as long as you are on the same plane as the eye.

Window of Deception — Level 3

A glance through this fine glass window reveals whatever you desire.

Wondrous Item   680 gp

Power (At-Will ✦ Illusion): Standard Action. You create an illusion seen by any creature looking through the window. The illusion is static and remains until the window is broken or opened, or until you or another creature changes the illusion or ends it with another standard action. When no illusion is presented, creatures see through the window normally. The window can maintain a separate illusion in each direction, and a character using the window can change either or both at once.

Window of Escape — Level 2

When you need to get out of a room in a hurry, this unremarkable window is your best escape.

Wondrous Item   520 gp

Property: When you jump or fall out of this window, you take no damage when you hit the ground, regardless of the distance.

TATTOOS

Whether you call them tats, ink, or body art, magic tattoos are far more than simple aesthetics.

As a mark of group identity, tattoos help distinguish and empower sects, tribes, guilds, and philosophies. As a personal art form, tattoos can be as aggressive, flamboyant, or delicate as you desire. Given how much a tattoo can represent to the person wearing it, it's no surprise that various cultures have learned to infuse those tattoos with magic.

Choosing a magic tattoo entails more than picking out an enchanted tool that is easy to hide and difficult to remove. It changes something about your nature in a subtle way. Magic tattoo effects interact with a character's intrinsic properties, such as healing surges or action points.

One's mortal form can contain only a small amount of foreign magic, however, so a character can have only one magic tattoo at a time.

OBTAINING A TATTOO

Magic tattoos are created in a fashion similar to other body art—special inks, enchanted needles, or both are used in the performance of an Enchant Magic Item ritual. A ritual performer can imbue a pattern being tattooed in his or her skin by another creature as well.

Although some cultures consider the act of creating the art with a needle to be central to activating the magic of a tattoo, other means to acquire ink exist. Eladrin are known for their habit of altering the skin through magic rather by using needles and ink. Other creatures avoid the needle by painting a tattoo on with a delicate brush, then magically fusing it with the skin.

Tattoo stones can be discovered in treasure hoards and lost cities. Each displays a pattern or image on a flat surface. To transfer the tattoo, a character presses that surface against his or her skin and activates it as part of an extended rest. The tattoo appears on the character's skin where it was applied, and the tattoo stone loses its magic.

Characters can also acquire magic tattoos through agencies other than their own. A captive hero can wake up bearing a magic tattoo; another character might be forced to accept one through extortion. Such gifts are still magical and beneficial but almost always serve another purpose as well.

Magic tattoos can be removed only through the use of the Disenchant Magic Item ritual (*Player's Handbook*, page 304), which requires the bearer of the tattoo to be willing or helpless for the duration of the ritual. At the ritual performer's discretion, the ritual can dissolve the magic and leave the tattoo, or it can remove the art completely.

TATTOOS OF BLOOD

Tattoos of blood react when you take severe wounds. They are worn over important channels of life energy, such as the jugular, wrist, heart, or the body's various meridians.

Backlash Tattoo — Level 9

Boars, sharks, and other creatures that enter a frenzy when wounded are used for this tattoo.

Wondrous Item   4,200 gp

Property: The first time you're bloodied during an encounter, you can make a basic attack as an immediate reaction.

Backlash tattoo

Escape Tattoo — Level 3

Broken chains and skeleton keys are popular images for this tattoo.

Wondrous Item   680 gp

Property: When a nonminion enemy scores a critical hit against you and deals damage, you can teleport 3 squares as a free action.

Reinforcement Tattoo — Level 9

Kobolds, rabbits, and other quick-breeding creatures are shown in this tattoo.

Wondrous Item   4,200 gp

Property: When a nonminion enemy scores a critical hit against you and deals damage, you can teleport each ally you can see to a space within 3 squares of you as a free action.

Resurgence Tattoo — Level 27

Creatures that return from defeat, such as the phoenix, are popular images for this tattoo.

Wondrous Item   1,625,000 gp

Property: When a nonminion enemy scores a critical hit against you and deals damage, you regain the use of an encounter attack power that you have already used during this encounter.

Strikeback Tattoo — Level 9

A viper is commonly part of this tattoo.

Wondrous Item   4,200 gp

Property: When a nonminion enemy scores a critical hit against you and deals damage, you gain a +2 bonus to attack rolls against that enemy until the end of the encounter.

Tattoo of Arcane Blood — Level 4+

Rods, orbs, the eye of Ioun, and other images symbolic of magic are used for this tattoo.

Lvl 4	840 gp	Lvl 24	525,000 gp
Lvl 14	21,000 gp		

Wondrous Item

Property: The first time you're bloodied during an encounter, you deal 3 force damage to the enemy that bloodied you.
Level 14: 6 force damage.
Level 24: 14 force damage.

Tattoo of the Escape Artist — Level 8

Broken handcuffs and torn straitjackets are popular for this tattoo.

Wondrous Item   3,400 gp

Property: When a nonminion enemy scores a critical hit against you and deals damage, you gain the ability to teleport 1 square as a minor action until the end of the encounter.

ED COX

Tattoo of the Wolverine — Level 7+

This tattoo is invariably a wolverine, snarling and bloody.

Lvl 7	2,600 gp	Lvl 27	1,625,000 gp
Lvl 17	65,000 gp		

Wondrous Item

Property: The first time you're bloodied during an encounter, you gain a +1 bonus to your next attack roll and a +2 bonus to your next damage roll before the end of the encounter.
Level 17: +4 bonus to your next damage roll.
Level 27: +6 bonus to your next damage roll.

Tattoo of Vengeance — Level 5+

This tattoo shows wicked-looking blades and bolts of lightning, representing the comeuppance you will extract.

Lvl 5	1,000 gp	Lvl 25	625,000 gp
Lvl 15	25,000 gp		

Wondrous Item

Property: When a nonminion enemy scores a critical hit against you and deals damage, you gain a +3 bonus to damage rolls against that enemy until the end of the encounter.
Level 15: +6 bonus to damage rolls.
Level 25: +9 bonus to damage rolls.

TATTOOS OF BOND

Bonding tattoos bring a tight-knit group even closer. They're a way of declaring permanent allegiance above all else and are worn in visible locations, such as the neck, face, or hands. Tattoos of bond borrow mechanics and appearances from other sorts of tattoos, but more than one character must have the same tattoo for any mark to work. Each character's tattoo bears the same image or follows a clear symbolic theme.

Quick-Step Tattoo — Level 7

Cheetahs, panthers, and other fast predators serve well for these tattoos.

Wondrous Item 2,600 gp

Property: When you spend an action point to take an extra action, each ally you can see who also has a *quick-step tattoo* can shift 1 square as a free action.

Tattoo of Bonded Defense — Level 6

One hero standing before a wounded ally is perfect for these tattoos.

Wondrous Item 1,800 gp

Property: The first time you're bloodied during an encounter, each ally you can see who also has a *tattoo of bonded defense* can shift 1 square closer to you as an immediate reaction.

Tattoo of Bonded Escape — Level 6

The image of a surly dwarf holding a corridor while allies escape works well for these tattoos.

Wondrous Item 1,800 gp

Property: The first time you're bloodied during an encounter, each ally you can see who also has a *tattoo of bonded escape* can shift 1 square farther from you as an immediate reaction.

Tattoo of Shared Consequence — Level 10

These tattoos usually display a hero taking a wound for another.

Wondrous Item 5,000 gp

Property: When a nonminion enemy scores a critical hit against you and deals damage, one ally who also has a *tattoo of shared consequence* and is in the attack's range can choose to reduce the damage you take from that attack by any amount and take that amount of damage.

Tattoo of Shared Vengeance — Level 10

Swords, axes, implements, or other tools of war crossed in brotherhood serve well for these tattoos.

Wondrous Item 5,000 gp

Property: When a nonminion enemy scores a critical hit against you and deals damage, each ally you can see who also has a *tattoo of shared vengeance* can make a basic attack against that enemy as a free action.

Tattoos of shared vengeance

WAYNE ENGLAND

Tattoo of the Shared Heart — Level 14+

These marks resemble something dear, something to fight on for.

Lvl 14	21,000 gp	Lvl 24	525,000 gp

Wondrous Item

Property: When you use your second wind, each ally you can see who also has a *tattoo of the shared heart* regains 5 hit points.
Level 24: 10 hit points.

Teamstrike Tattoo — Level 11

These tattoos frequently show wolves acting as a pack.

Wondrous Item 9,000 gp

Property: When you spend an action point to make an attack, each ally you can see who also has a *teamstrike tattoo* gains a +2 bonus to attack rolls against the first target of your attack until the end of your next turn.

Tattoos of Heart

Tattoos of heart deal with health and healing surges. They're generally worn over the heart or the waist chakra, an area that most cultures consider the seat of the body's energy.

Eager Hero's Tattoo — Level 10+

Scenes showing one warrior against many or a lone victorious hero are popular for this tattoo.

Lvl 10	5,000 gp	Lvl 30	3,125,000 gp
Lvl 20	125,000 gp		

Wondrous Item

Property: When you take a short rest, you gain temporary hit points equal to 5 + the number of healing surges you have spent since your last extended rest.
Level 20: 10 + twice the number of healing surges you have spent since your last extended rest.
Level 30: 15 + three times the number of healing surges you have spent since your last extended rest.

Ironheart Tattoo — Level 8+

Ironheart tattoos represent in symbol or image how the bearer can't be conquered.

Lvl 8	3,400 gp	Lvl 28	2,125,000 gp
Lvl 18	85,000 gp		

Wondrous Item

Property: When you spend a healing surge, you gain resistance against the next damage dealt to you equal to the number of healing surges you have spent since your last extended rest.
Level 18: Twice the number of healing surges you have spent since your last extended rest.
Level 28: Three times the number of healing surges you have spent since your last extended rest.

Long-Battle Tattoo — Level 7

This tattoo is often depicted as a shield surrounded by weapons.

Wondrous Item 2,600 gp

Property: When you hit with a daily attack power, you gain a bonus to the damage roll equal to the number of healing surges you have spent since your last extended rest.

Curse eye tattoo

Strongheart Tattoo — Level 8+

This image shows why the hero fights on.

Lvl 8	3,400 gp	Lvl 28	2,125,000 gp
Lvl 18	85,000 gp		

Wondrous Item

Property: When you spend a healing surge, you regain extra hit points equal to the number of healing surges you have spent since your last extended rest.
Level 18: Twice the number of healing surges you have spent since your last extended rest.
Level 28: Three times the number of healing surges you have spent since your last extended rest.

Tattoo of the Unlucky — Level 7

Broken coins, three-leaf clovers, mirror shards, or all three do nicely for this tattoo.

Wondrous Item 2,600 gp

Property: When you miss with a daily attack power that has an effect on a miss, that effect deals extra damage equal to the number of healing surges you have spent since your last extended rest.

Tattoos of Spirit

Tattoos of spirit grant manifest heroism in moments when a character strives for greatness, adding effect to action points. They are worn in many places and have great variety.

HOWARD LYON

Breakchain Tattoo — Level 13+

One broken link is enough for the symbolism, but many use a full chain.

Lvl 13	17,000 gp	Lvl 23	425,000 gp

Wondrous Item

Property: When you spend an action point to take an extra action, you ignore immobilizing, restraining, and slowing effects on you until the end of your turn.
Level 23: You can also end one effect on you that is immobilizing, restraining, or slowing you.

Curse Eye Tattoo — Level 8

This tattoo is a small eye, often in the center of the forehead, which blinks when used.

Wondrous Item   3,400 gp

Property: When you spend an action point to take an extra action, one enemy within 10 squares of you that you can see takes a –2 penalty to saving throws (save ends).

Demonskin Tattoo — Level 3+

Not all societies understand that tattooing a portion of demonskin onto your body isn't an evil act.

Lvl 3	680 gp	Lvl 23	425,000 gp
Lvl 13	17,000 gp		

Wondrous Item

Property: When you spend an action point to take an extra action, choose acid, cold, fire, lightning, or thunder. You gain resist 5 to the chosen damage type until the end of the encounter.
Level 13: Resist 10.
Level 23: Resist 15.

Distracting Tattoo — Level 6

Any small, bright image in a highly visible place is sufficient.

Wondrous Item   1,800 gp

Property: When you spend an action point to take an extra action, you end any mark affecting you.

Fireheart Tattoo — Level 4+

As you call upon its power, flames flare and twist around the heart at the center of this tattoo.

Lvl 4	840 gp	Lvl 24	525,000 gp
Lvl 14	21,000 gp		

Wondrous Item

Property: When you spend an action point to take an extra action, you gain 5 temporary hit points.
Level 14: 10 temporary hit points.
Level 24: 15 temporary hit points.

Fleet Hero Tattoo — Level 8+

This mark often takes the form of wings tattooed on the ankles.

Lvl 8	3,400 gp	Lvl 28	2,125,000 gp
Lvl 18	85,000 gp		

Wondrous Item

Property: When you spend an action point to take an extra action, you gain a +1 bonus to speed until the end of your next turn.
Level 18: +2 bonus to speed.
Level 28: +3 bonus to speed.

Ghostwalk Tattoo — Level 26

Artists paint this tattoo using vague or amorphous designs and avoiding color.

Wondrous Item   1,125,000 gp

Property: When you spend an action point to take an extra action, until the end of your turn you gain phasing and become insubstantial.

Greatwing Tattoo — Level 18+

A wing, a feather, or any winged creature—dragons or couatls are popular—will do for this tattoo.

Lvl 18	85,000 gp	Lvl 28	2,125,000 gp

Wondrous Item

Property: When you spend an action point to take an extra action, you also gain a fly speed equal to your speed until the end of your turn.
Level 28: You gain a fly speed equal to your speed + 6.

CONSUMABLES

An experienced adventurer keeps an unpredictable assortment of magic nearby. It helps counter the unpredictable trouble that predictably befalls him.

Use it, and it's gone. That's the nature of a consumable item, and for that reason some put off using such an item because it could be useful in the future. But because there might be no tomorrow— sometimes literally—the bold adventurer knows that a dead hero drinks no potions and quaffs the draught when he or she has the chance.

This section is divided into three groups. First are potions, elixirs, and other sundry one-shot items. Second are reagents that can be used to improve specific types of powers. Third are immurements, which are powerful one-shot items that reshape the landscape when used.

REAGENTS

Clay of Creation — Level 7+

Your summoned creatures are tougher when you use this material.

Lvl 7	100 gp	Lvl 27	65,000 gp
Lvl 17	2,600 gp		

Reagent

Power (Consumable): Free Action. You expend this reagent when you use a summoning power of up to 5th level. The summoned creature gains 5 temporary hit points, and the first time it misses with an attack, you reroll that attack roll but must use the second result.
Level 17: Power of up to 15th level, 10 temporary hit points.
Level 27: Power of up to 25th level, 15 temporary hit points.

Flash Flower — Level 11+

This flower, which is sometimes found near lightning-struck ground, contains electrical magic.

Lvl 11	350 gp	Lvl 21	9,000 gp

Reagent

Power (Consumable): Free Action. You expend this reagent when you hit with a lightning power of up to 7th level. You choose one target hit by the attack. It's also blinded until the end of your next turn. This reagent has no effect if the power already blinds the target.

Level 21: Power of up to 17th level.

Rust Bark — Level 11+

When ground into a fine dust, this reddish tree bark expands the area of your powers.

Lvl 11	350 gp	Lvl 21	9,000 gp

Reagent

Power (Consumable): Free Action. You expend this reagent when you use an area burst power of up to 5th level that has a damage keyword. The size of the burst increases by 1.

Level 21: Power of up to 15th level.

Silver Sand — Level 8+

Your healing powers become more effective after you coat your hands with this fine sand.

Lvl 8	125 gp	Lvl 28	85,000 gp
Lvl 18	3,400 gp		

Reagent

Power (Consumable ✦ Healing): Free Action. You expend this reagent when you use a healing power of up to 6th level. The target of the power regains 5 additional hit points.

Level 18: Power of up to 16th level, 10 additional hit points.

Level 28: Power of up to 26th level, 15 additional hit points.

Silver sand

Vortex Stone — Level 8+

This stone from the Shadowfell imbues your conjurations with a magical field that saps your foes' strength.

Lvl 8	125 gp	Lvl 28	85,000 gp
Lvl 18	3,400 gp		

Reagent

Power (Consumable): Free Action. You expend this reagent when you use a conjuration power of up to 6th level. While the conjuration is in effect, enemies adjacent to it take a -2 penalty to attack rolls.

Level 18: Power of up to 16th level.

Level 28: Power of up to 26th level.

IMMUREMENTS

An immurement is a rare form of magical prison that contains a place that has been sealed away from the rest of the world. The enchantments placed on immurements are fragile; when an immurement's power is expended in a blast, it releases the terrain and effects contained within it into the blast area for a short time.

Each immurement description provides the features of the terrain and effects contained within it. Refer to the illustration of each immurement for placement of specific terrain.

DMs should be careful with allowing immurements into a game, because they can render lovingly crafted set pieces less memorable. For a group using one, it's useful to have the new terrain prepared in advance and ready for use, whether it's printed out, drawn on a battle mat, or laid out in D&D™ *Dungeon Tiles.*

IMMUREMENT OF BALEFUL GOSSAMER

Skasshaa was a demonweb terror spider of great age, might, and arrogance. She ruled her domain with eager ruthlessness, allowing no creature to enter her lair and live.

When she returned from a week-long hunt one morning, she discovered a mortal of noble mien waiting for her amid her trophies. He declared that his people had hunted her for generations, and now her punishment was at hand. The mortal was prepared, and their battle was short. He fashioned the clear sphere of one of her many eyes into an immurement that contained her domain, sealing away the heart of the region's evil so that the land could recover.

Skasshaa Returns: Less one eye and a century's worth of pride, Skasshaa hunts again for what was taken from her body and from her domain. She seeks those who have an *immurement of baleful gossamer* and is tearing through mortal civilization in her search.

Protect the Immurement: The mortal who created the immurement concealed it within a temple in an altar to Sehanine. Stories say that the immurement waits for a new hero to release it from the altar when Skasshaa returns to the world. But rumors also hint that the temple is now guarded by blackspawn gloomwebs and an elder black dragon that rules over them.

CHRIS SEAMAN

Immurement of arcane suspension

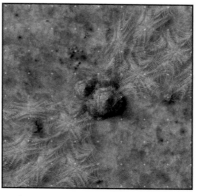

Immurement of baleful gossamer

Immurement of Arcane Suspension — Level 24

This chunk of earth feels as light as a feather.

Other Consumable   21,000 gp

Power (Daily): Move Action. You can move 4 squares verti-cally and then 1 square horizontally. At the start of your next turn, you float safely to the ground. This power is lost when you use the immurement's consumable power.

Power (Consumable): Standard Action. You destroy this immurement and change the terrain in a close blast 8 until the end of the encounter. Replace the terrain in the blast with the following terrain and effects.

✦ The marked areas tear themselves free of the ground (and any moorings they're attached to) and rise to float 4 squares above the ground. A creature on one of these floating sections has cover against creatures on the ground.

✦ There are shallow pits where the ground pulls away. Treat these areas as difficult terrain.

✦ At the start of your turn, shift each floating object 1 square in any direction. Creatures on the object move with it.

✦ The other terrain in the area doesn't change.

Special: Using this item counts as a use of a magic item daily power.

Immurement of Baleful Gossamer — Level 28

A tree surrounded by cobwebs is visible within this soft, clear sphere.

Other Consumable   85,000 gp

Power (Consumable): Standard Action. You expend this immurement and change the terrain in a close blast 8 until the end of the encounter. Replace the terrain in the blast with the following terrain and effects.

✦ Squares filled with webs are difficult terrain.

✦ The tree in the center of the area is difficult terrain that costs 2 extra squares to enter and provides cover.

✦ When a creature starts its turn in a web square, you make an attack against that creature: +27 vs. Reflex; on a hit, the target is immobilized until the start of its next turn. On a miss, the target is slowed until the start of its next turn.

Special: Using this item counts as a use of a magic item daily power.

Immurement of Seething Scoria — Level 26

You transplant a section of a great lava lake into the battlefield by shattering this hunk of obsidian.

Other Consumable   45,000 gp

Power (Consumable): Standard Action. You expend this immurement and change the terrain in a close blast 4 until the end of the encounter. Replace the terrain in the blast with the following terrain and effects.

✦ Squares of lava are difficult terrain.

✦ When a creature starts its turn in a lava square, you make an attack against that creature: +30 vs. Reflex; on a hit, the target takes 3d8 fire damage, and ongoing 10 fire damage (save ends).

Special: Using this item counts as a use of a magic item daily power.

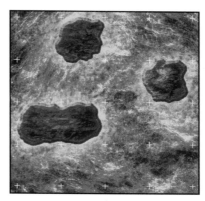

Immurement of seething scoria

RPGA PLAY ADVICE

When participating in an RPGA® event, a player who wants to use an immurement has a responsibility to the other players, the DM, and the event organizers to make this complex item operate as efficiently as possible. The responsibility is on the player to have a usable map, either drawn clearly to scale or constructed from *Dungeon Tiles*, to place on the table when he or she invokes the power of the immurement. Otherwise, play slows as a new map must be constructed and the game threatens to exceed its allotted time. Players can find printable maps for the items described in this section on the *D&D™ Insider* web site at www.dndinsider.com.

Immurement of the abandoned throne

Immurement of the Abandoned Throne   Level 24

This marred bronze scepter has had the sigil of the kingdom it once represented scratched off its surface.

Other Consumable   21,000 gp

Power (Consumable): Standard Action. You expend this immurement and change the terrain in a close blast 4 until the end of the encounter. Replace the terrain in the blast with the following terrain and effects.

✦ The dais is 1 square higher than the ground. Entering the dais from the ground costs 1 extra square of movement.

✦ Any creature that starts its turn within 2 squares of the throne is dazed until the end of its turn.

Special: Using this item counts as a use of a magic item daily power.

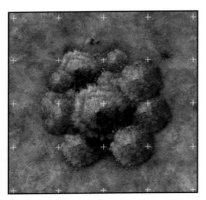
Immurement of the blood vine

Immurement of the Blood Vine   Level 24

When this branch from the holly tree that always bears new growth is snapped, it spawns what was once the heart of a forest.

Other Consumable   21,000 gp

Power (Consumable): Standard Action. You expend this immurement and change the terrain in a close blast 4 until the end of the encounter. Replace the terrain in the blast with the following terrain and effects.

✦ Small tree squares provide cover to creatures in them. The large tree square is a solid obstacle.

✦ At the start of your turn, you can have vines on the tree wrap up a creature. Make an attack against one enemy within 2 squares of the tree: +27 vs. Reflex; on a hit, the target is pulled adjacent to the tree, and is restrained and takes ongoing 10 damage (save ends both).

Special: Using this item counts as a use of a magic item daily power.

Immurement of the Dragon Boneyard   Level 25

A miniature boneyard, complete with a massive dragon skull in the center, is visible within this crystal sphere.

Other Consumable   25,000 gp

Power (Consumable): Standard Action. You expend this immurement and change the terrain in a close blast 4 until the end of the encounter. Replace the terrain in the blast with the following terrain and effects.

✦ The area has natural illumination providing dim light.

✦ The squares filled with bones on the ground level are difficult terrain.

✦ The dragon skull platform is 2 squares higher than the ground (Athletics DC 26 to climb).

✦ At the start of your turn, make an attack against each enemy on a bone square: +30 vs. AC; on a hit, the target takes 2d10 + 5 damage, and you slide the target 1 square (as bones shift and move it).

Special: Using this item counts as a use of a magic item daily power.

Immurement of the dragon boneyard

IMMUREMENT OF THE DRAGON BONEYARD

Arnod the Loyal returned to his home of Greatfalls one late spring to discover that disaster had befallen the town. A dragon had passed through, slaying the living and destroying the crypt that contained all the town's ancestors.

After overcoming his grief, Arnod succumbed to vengeance. At great risk, he sought out the remains of the dragon's ancestors and bound their bones, piece by piece, within a small crystal sphere. His task complete, he made his desecration known to the dragon and then concealed the immurement.

Acquire Musty Maps: Rumors say that Arnod the Loyal changed the sphere into a pile of maps, each depicting a portion of the realm contained within the sphere, and then scattered the scraps of paper across the world. If true, collecting and reuniting all the maps would reveal an *immurement of the dragon boneyard*.

Continued Vengeance: The dragon that Arnod sought vengeance against has recovered the sphere containing her ancestors and is pondering the best way to safely retrieve the remains. Arnod's descendants are looking for a band of heroes to retrieve the sphere and dare her displeasure.

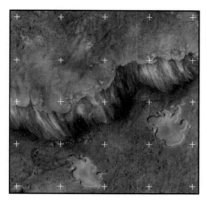

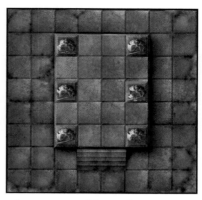

Immurement of the mordant hideaway

Immurement of the strident statuary

Immurement of the Mordant Hideaway Level 28

This hunk of stone contains a cavern interior dotted with small pools of bubbling acid that occasionally geyser.

Other Consumable   85,000 gp

Power (Consumable): Standard Action. You expend this immurement and change the terrain in a close blast 4 until the end of the encounter. Replace the terrain in the blast with the following terrain and effects.
- ✦ The upper shelf is 2 squares higher than the lower section of ground (Athletics DC 28 to climb)
- ✦ The pools of acid are difficult terrain, and any creature moving into a pool or starting its turn in one takes 3d6 acid damage.
- ✦ At the start of your turn, roll a d6 for each acid pool. On a 6, make an attack: Close burst 1; +32 vs. Reflex; on a hit, the target takes 3d8 + 5 acid damage, and a –4 penalty to AC and ongoing 10 acid damage (save ends both).

Special: Using this item counts as a use of a magic item daily power.

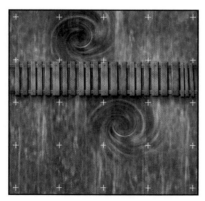

Immurement of the vengeful river

Immurement of the Strident Statuary Level 28

A finely appointed hall shimmers into existence, surrounding combatants with sentient statues that carry vicious swords.

Other Consumable   85,000 gp

Power (Consumable): Standard Action. You expend this immurement and change the terrain in a close blast 8 until the end of the encounter. Replace the terrain in the blast with the following terrain and effects.
- ✦ The platform is 1 square higher than the ground. Entering a platform square from the ground costs 1 extra square of movement.
- ✦ Healing effects used on you or your allies within the blast heal an additional 4d6 hit points.
- ✦ Your enemies' movement provokes opportunity attacks from the statues. Make an attack: +35 vs. AC; on a hit, the target takes 2d8 + 8 damage, and if the target is moving, it ends its movement.

Special: Using this item counts as a use of a magic item daily power.

Immurement of the Vengeful River Level 26

When you use this immurement, it spawns a roaring river that appears from an unknown source and runs off in all directions.

Other Consumable   45,000 gp

Power (Consumable): Standard Action. You expend this immurement and change the terrain in a close blast 4 until the end of the encounter. Replace the terrain in the blast with the following terrain and effects.
- ✦ The water squares are 2 squares deep. A DC 20 Athletics check is required to swim in this water.
- ✦ At the start of your turn, slide each creature in the water 1 square toward the south end of the area. Then slide each creature adjacent to a whirlpool into a whirlpool square. Then pull each creature in a whirlpool square down 1 square.
- ✦ The bridge is 1 square above the water. It's normal terrain and provides cover against creatures in the water.
- ✦ The water disperses normally after the encounter.

Special: Using this item counts as a use of a magic item daily power.

IMMUREMENT OF THE MORDANT HIDEAWAY

The rocky cave contained in this pitted ball of stone was once the seat of power for the black dragon Akzosial. According to legend, the dragon was away from its lair when a group of heroes stole the heart of the cave, which contained the power to make Akzosial immortal. Though the dragon raged, the immurement was never recovered .

Theft of Akzosial's Power: A famed dragon slayer and her followers seek an *immurement of the mordant hideaway*, believing they can use it in a ritual to steal Akzosial's might. The dragon who currently holds the immurement approaches the heroes. He asks the group to keep the immurement from falling into the dragonslayer's hands.

ITEM SETS

SOME MAGIC items were made to work together. When all the items belonging to a set are collected and wielded in unison, their power becomes greater than the sum of their parts. Depending on how much of a magic item set has been assembled, its collective items can grant additional qualities, different properties, and new powers to their wielders.

A magic item set contains four or more items that a character or a party can collect. Each set has at least one set benefit that is revealed when a minimum number of the set's items are used together. Some set items also have individual properties or effects that depend on the number of other set items being used.

When a set benefit grants a daily power, using that power doesn't count toward the limit of magic item daily powers a character can use in a day.

To qualify for an item set's benefits, a character must be wielding or wearing one or more items from the set. A stowed item (for example, a magic cloak stuffed in a pack) doesn't count toward a set's benefits (though a sheathed weapon is considered to be worn). Wondrous items are an exception and need only be carried in order for a character to gain an item set's benefits.

Each magic item in a set can stand alone. No item needs to be used with another of its set to function.

This chapter provides item sets in four varieties.

✦ **Heroic Tier Item Sets:** A character just starting his or her adventuring career can benefit from the additional power granted by these item sets.

✦ **Paragon Tier Item Sets:** As a character becomes an elite representative of a chosen path, one of these item sets can add to his or her reputation.

✦ **Epic Tier Item Sets:** The mightiest heroes deserve the most fantastic panoply of items.

✦ **Group Item Sets:** These item sets are meant to be used by an entire party at various levels of play.

SEAN "MUTTONHEAD" MURRAY

These item sets are suitable for PCs at the beginning of their adventuring careers.

ALEHEART COMPANIONS' GEAR

The Aleheart Companions' Gear is a set of items first crafted for a legendary Underdark adventuring group. The items in the set were designed by dwarves for the benefit of their nondwarf allies, so that those allies might be gifted with the innate qualities of the dwarf race.

LORE

History DC 7: The Aleheart Companions were members of an adventuring party that owed its start to three time-honored dwarven traditions: drinking, complaining, and taking a dare. A group of dwarf miners fed up with working for the profit of others grumbled once too often to their human, elf, and dragonborn drinking companions. The nondwarves challenged their friends to strike out and set up their own mine rather than endlessly complaining. The dwarves agreed to the challenge, provided that their friends joined them in their efforts.

History DC 12: Calling themselves the Aleheart Companions, the friends set off on a mission of exploration into the Underdark. However, rather than the mother lode they hoped to find, they ran into Lolth-bound goblins and bugbear raiders striking out from an area of deadly caverns known as the Howling Warrens. Using their dungeoneering knowledge to good effect, the dwarves managed to defeat their foes through cunning and ambush.

When the battle was done, the companions realized that looting their enemies yielded more profit than their honest labor ever had. Thus did this mixed bag of miners and drinkers take their first steps toward becoming legendary adventurers.

History DC 17: With the profits of their new trade, the dwarves of the companions commissioned magic items to help their nondwarf allies survive the Underdark. Though the Aleheart Companions have passed into history, adventuring parties specializing in the exploration of ancient ruins and the underground covet the items that bear the Companions' name.

Collecting all the Aleheart Companions' Gear enhances a dwarf's innate racial abilities, or grants dwarflike abilities to other races. Some stories suggest that a bearer of these items becomes more like a dwarf in manner and appearance, but these are most likely idle rumors.

ALEHEART COMPANIONS' GEAR ITEMS

Lvl	Name	Price (gp)	Item Slot
2+	Armor of dwarven vigor	520	Armor
5+	Rousing hammer	1,000	Weapon
8	Hammer shield	3,400	Arms
9	Clear-blood baldric	4,200	Waist

ALEHEART COMPANIONS' GEAR BENEFITS

Pieces	Benefit
2	You gain a +2 item bonus to Dungeoneering checks and Endurance checks.
4	You gain resist poison equal to 10 + your Constitution modifier.

Armor of Dwarven Vigor — Level 2+

This armor, which appears to be crafted of chiseled stone, grants you the endurance of a dwarf warrior.

Lvl 2	+1	520 gp	Lvl 17	+4	65,000 gp
Lvl 7	+2	2,600 gp	Lvl 22	+5	325,000 gp
Lvl 12	+3	13,000 gp	Lvl 27	+6	1,625,000 gp

Armor: Chain, scale, plate
Enhancement: AC
Power (Daily ✦ Healing): Minor Action. You use your second wind and regain an additional 1d6 hit points per plus.
Special: If you're a dwarf, you can use this armor's power as a free action on your turn.

CHRIS SEAMAN

Clear-Blood Baldric — Level 9

The protective power of this belt guarantees that foes who hide behind the cowardice of poison will regret it.

Item Slot: Waist   4,200 gp
Property: Nondwarf allies within 3 squares of you gain a +5 item bonus to saving throws against poison effects.

Hammer Shield — Level 8

The hammer sigil emblazoned on this steel shield strengthens the arm that wields a hammer in battle.

Item Slot: Arms   3,400 gp
Shield: Any
Property: When you hit an enemy with an attack power using a hammer while wielding this shield, you gain a +1 bonus to all defenses until the start of your next turn.

Rousing Hammer — Level 5+

The wrath you deal out with this dwarven hammer instills vigor in your allies.

Lvl 5	+1	1,000 gp	Lvl 20	+4	125,000 gp
Lvl 10	+2	5,000 gp	Lvl 25	+5	625,000 gp
Lvl 15	+3	25,000 gp	Lvl 30	+6	3,125,000 gp

Weapon: Hammer
Enhancement: Attack rolls and damage rolls
Critical: +1d6 damage per plus
Property: When you hit an enemy with this weapon, each ally you can see can stand up as a free action.

ARMS OF WAR

The Arms of War were once wielded by four generals who led their human kingdoms in battle against a great hobgoblin empire. Each general was known as the master of a different aspect of martial strategy, and the warrior who owns all their treasures gains a measure of their skill.

LORE

History DC 7: In ages past, allied human kingdoms fought a hobgoblin empire in a great war that created legendary heroes on both sides. The fierce clan lords of the hobgoblin armies were opposed by four human generals, each of whom exemplified a different area of combat prowess. Korra was an expert in counterattacks. Teron's forces were unequalled in the defensive tactics of the shield wall. Juhana's troops were legendary for their skill at flanking and positioning. Mandu was the undisputed master of martial weapon training.

Though they came from different lands that had fought each other in the past, all four leaders worked together to present a unified response to the hobgoblin forces.

History DC 12: Through the combined efforts of the four generals, the human armies defeated the hobgoblins, though at great loss. Teron and Juhana fell while holding off the hobgoblin lines single-handedly, granting the forces they led time to regroup behind them. Korra and Mandu survived to be honored by their kingdoms and the soldiers who served them.

Over time, the human kingdoms were consolidated and their armies placed under the leadership of a single general gifted with the arms and armor of the four who had come before him. However, wars of strife and succession eventually shattered the kingdom once more, and the Arms of War were scattered across new lands.

History DC 17: Despite their rank, Korra, Teron, Juhana, and Mandu made it their mission to fight alongside the troops who served them, even when doing so put their own lives in danger. Collecting all the Arms of War enhances the wielder's ability to take advantage of opponents' vulnerabilities and to protect allies.

ARMS OF WAR ITEMS

Lvl	Name	Price (gp)	Item Slot
5+	Weapon of great opportunity	1,000	Weapon
6	Helm of exemplary defense	1,800	Head
7	Dual-threat gauntlets	2,600	Hands
8	Pincer shield	3,400	Arms

ARMS OF WAR BENEFITS

Pieces	Benefit
2	For each two items you have from this set, you gain a +1 bonus to opportunity attack rolls.
4	You gain the *ally's opportunity* power, described below.

Ally's Opportunity — Item Set Power

When your enemy drops its guard, you lash out at your foe, distracting it further to allow a nearby ally to freely fire upon it.

Daily
Free Action   **Close** burst 5
Trigger: You make an opportunity attack
Target: One ally in burst
Effect: The target makes a ranged basic attack against the target of your opportunity attack as a free action.

Dual-Threat Gauntlets — Level 7

When you and an ally fight together, the power of these gauntlets heightens both your attacks.

Item Slot: Hands   2,600 gp
Power (Daily): Minor Action. Until the end of the encounter, while you're flanking an enemy, you and the ally flanking with you gain an additional +1 bonus to attack rolls against that enemy.

Helm of Exemplary Defense — Level 6

The power of this helm grants you and your allies an advantage against foes who leave themselves open.

Item Slot: Head   1,800 gp
Property: You and each ally within 3 squares of you deal 2 extra damage when you hit with opportunity attacks.

Pincer Shield — Level 8

This shield extends its protection from you to your flanking ally.

Item Slot: Arms   3,400 gp
Shield: Heavy
Property: While you're flanking an enemy with an ally, that ally gains a +1 shield bonus to AC and Reflex.

Weapon of Great Opportunity — Level 5+

You take advantage of a foe's vulnerability to deliver a devastating strike with this weapon.

Lvl 5	+1	1,000 gp	Lvl 20	+4	125,000 gp
Lvl 10	+2	5,000 gp	Lvl 25	+5	625,000 gp
Lvl 15	+3	25,000 gp	Lvl 30	+6	3,125,000 gp

Weapon: Any melee
Enhancement: Attack rolls and damage rolls
Critical: +1d8 damage per plus
Power (Encounter): Free Action. *Trigger:* You hit with an opportunity attack. *Effect:* Deal 1d8 extra damage per plus of the weapon.

BLADE DANCER'S REGALIA

The origin of the mysterious combat art known as the blade dance is hotly contested among those who study and perform it. This manner of fighting is known for its grace and control, and practitioners of the blade dance can be found among all races and cultures. Each group of blade dancers can be easily distinguished by the details of their unique style. However, the underlying similarities of the form remain apparent.

LORE

History DC 5: The blade dance is an ancient combat art whose origins are shrouded in mystery. Practiced by a wide variety of cultures and races, this distinctive two-weapon style incorporates flowing dancelike moves into its attacks and defenses. Most blade dancers consider their own style to be original and definitive, marking all others as mere imitators. Blade dancers are quick to fight among themselves to establish their superiority. However, regardless of their chosen school, blade dancers all covet a set of specialized regalia whose origins are as old as the form.

History DC 10: Among dwarves, the blade dance is called Moradin's Drums. It favors steady rhythms and heavy weapons such as hammers and axes. Among the eladrin and other beings of the Feywild, the fighting style is known as Corellon's War Chant and is practiced with longswords. The elves have adapted it to lighter blades, and it's said that the drow have their own version of the blade dance incorporating the cruel weapons of that race.

Other schools have a wider following. The Drunkard's Waltz features knife fighting and is favored by humans and halflings. The Jester's Prance school uses mismatched weapons and was said to have been created in the training halls of the tiefling empire,

though it's now practiced by humans, tieflings, and dragonborn in equal measure.

History or Religion DC 15: According to legend, the blade dance was invented as the result of a wager between Kord and Erathis. Erathis created the fighting style to demonstrate to Kord that not all combat need be crude and brutal. Stories tell of a warrior-priest of Erathis who traveled among many of the cultures and races that claim to have originated the blade dance. It's thought that this priest was the first to teach the legendary style.

BLADE DANCER'S REGALIA ITEMS

Lvl	Name	Price (gp)	Item Slot
2	Bracers of enforced regret	520	Arms
3+	Baffling cape	680	Neck
3+	Rhythm blade	680	Weapon
4+	Harmony blade	840	Weapon
5	Gloves of recovery	1,000	Hands

BLADE DANCER'S REGALIA BENEFITS

Pieces	Benefit
2	You gain a bonus to AC against opportunity attacks equal to the number of items you have from this set.
5	You can use your Hunter's Quarry class feature as a free action instead of a minor action.

Baffling Cape — Level 3+

This rippling cape allows you to slip past an attacking foe.

Lvl 3	+1	680 gp	Lvl 18	+4	85,000 gp
Lvl 8	+2	3,400 gp	Lvl 23	+5	425,000 gp
Lvl 13	+3	17,000 gp	Lvl 28	+6	2,125,000 gp

Item Slot: Neck
Enhancement: Fortitude, Reflex, and Will
Power (Daily ✦ Teleportation): Immediate Reaction. *Trigger:* An enemy adjacent to you misses you with a melee attack. *Effect:* Swap positions with the triggering enemy.

Bracers of Enforced Regret — Level 2

When an enemy presses you, the power of these simple steel bracers lets you turn the tables.

Item Slot: Arms   520 gp
Property: While you're marked, you gain a +2 bonus to attack rolls and damage rolls against the enemy that marked you.

Gloves of Recovery — Level 5

When you fumble in combat, these gloves allow you to recover and strike again.

Item Slot: Hands   1,000 gp
Power (Daily): Free Action. *Trigger:* You miss an enemy with a melee attack power. *Effect:* Make a melee basic attack against that enemy.

Harmony Blade — Level 4+

Though you wield it as your primary weapon, this blade lends its power to your off-hand attacks.

Lvl 4	+1	840 gp	Lvl 19	+4	105,000 gp
Lvl 9	+2	4,200 gp	Lvl 24	+5	525,000 gp
Lvl 14	+3	21,000 gp	Lvl 29	+6	2,625,000 gp

Weapon: Heavy blade

Enhancement: Attack rolls and damage rolls

Critical: +1d6 damage per plus, and you can make a melee basic attack with your off-hand weapon.

Property: When you hit an enemy with both this weapon and your off-hand weapon during the same turn, that enemy takes a –2 penalty to attack rolls against you until the end of your next turn.

Rhythm Blade — Level 3+

Fighting with this off-hand weapon improves your defense.

Lvl 3	+1	680 gp	Lvl 18	+4	85,000 gp
Lvl 8	+2	3,400 gp	Lvl 23	+5	425,000 gp
Lvl 13	+3	17,000 gp	Lvl 28	+6	2,125,000 gp

Weapon: Light blade

Enhancement: Attack rolls and damage rolls

Critical: +1d6 damage per plus

Property: While you wield this weapon in your off hand, your shield bonus to AC and Reflex increases by 1.

GADGETEER'S GARB

Characters drawn to the inner workings of traps and alchemy covet this set of items. The items of the Gadgeteer's Garb bestow a wide range of utilitarian magic, combat boons, and power over traps and alchemical devices. All the items of the set share a skillful synthesis of mechanical and magical design.

Artificers and rogues most often seek out and collect the items of this set, though they can benefit any character.

LORE

Arcana DC 7: Created through constant tinkering and experimentation, the items of the Gadgeteer's Garb were developed, then perfected by a number of ingenious inventors. Some parts of the set were first crafted by dwarf artificers, others by human arcane practitioners, and some by fomorians and other fey. Despite their disparate origins, however, each of the items of the set represented a singular advance in magical and mechanical design.

Arcana DC 12: An artificer known as Morton the Gadgeteer is said to have been the first to unify these once-disparate items, seeing the common thread of ingenuity in each and imbuing the set with its unique benefits. With the power of the Gadgeteer's Garb, Morton became a legendary arcanist and trapfinder, and the item set that bears his moniker is his enduring legacy.

GADGETEER'S GARB ITEMS

Lvl	Name	Price (gp)	Item Slot
5+	Shockweave armor	1,000	Armor
6	Alchemy gloves	1,800	Hands
7+	Deep-pocket cloak	2,600	Neck
8	Gadgeteer's goggles	3,400	Head

GADGETEER'S GARB BENEFITS

Pieces	Benefit
2	When you or an ally within 5 squares of you spends a healing surge, you or that ally regains additional hit points equal to the number of items you have from this set.
4	You gain a +4 bonus to all defenses against traps.

Alchemy Gloves — Level 6

When you use an alchemical item, these gloves charge it with magical power.

Item Slot: Hands   1,800 gp

Property: You gain a +2 item bonus to attack rolls with alchemical items.

Deep-Pocket Cloak — Level 7+

The hundreds of magically hidden pockets on this cloak allow you to keep a wealth of items close at hand.

Lvl 7	+2	2,600 gp	Lvl 22	+5	325,000 gp
Lvl 12	+3	13,000 gp	Lvl 27	+6	1,625,000 gp
Lvl 17	+4	65,000 gp			

Item Slot: Neck

Enhancement: Fortitude, Reflex, and Will

Property: The pockets of this cloak can hold up to 1,000 pounds in weight or 100 cubic feet in volume, but the cloak always weighs only 1 pound. Each item stored within one of the cloak's pockets can weigh no more than 10 pounds.

Drawing an item from a *deep-pocket cloak* is a minor action.

Level 22 or 27: The cloak can hold 2,000 pounds in weight or 200 cubic feet in volume.

Power (At-Will): Free Action, 1/round. You draw an item from the cloak or store an item within it.

Gadgeteer's Goggles — Level 8

The residuum suspended in these lenses helps you see through the complexities of the deadliest traps.

Item Slot: Head   3,400 gp

Property: You gain a +4 item bonus to Perception checks and Thievery checks to detect and disable traps.

Power (Encounter): Minor Action. You make a Thievery check to disable a trap.

Shockweave Armor
Level 5+

Metal studs on this armor magically protect you from lightning, and then unleash that same power against your foes.

Lvl 5	+1	1,000 gp	Lvl 20	+4	125,000 gp
Lvl 10	+2	5,000 gp	Lvl 25	+5	625,000 gp
Lvl 15	+3	25,000 gp	Lvl 30	+6	3,125,000 gp

Armor: Cloth, leather
Enhancement: AC
Property: You gain resist 5 lightning.
  Level 15 or 20: Resist 10 lightning.
  Level 25 or 30: Resist 15 lightning.
Power (Encounter): Free Action. *Trigger:* You take lightning damage. *Effect:* Until the end of the encounter, this armor's daily power gains a +1 bonus to the attack roll and deals 1d10 extra lightning damage.
Power (Daily ✦ Lightning): Immediate Interrupt. *Trigger:* An enemy adjacent to you targets you with an attack. *Effect:* Make an attack against the triggering enemy: +8 vs. Fortitude; on a hit, deal 2d10 lightning damage, and the enemy is dazed until the end of your next turn.
  Level 10: +13 vs. Fortitude.
  Level 15: +18 vs. Fortitude, 3d10 lightning damage.
  Level 20: +23 vs. Fortitude.
  Level 25: +28 vs. Fortitude, 4d10 lightning damage.
  Level 30: +33 vs. Fortitude.

GOLDEN LION'S BATTLE REGALIA

A legendary barbarian chieftain of the great deserts, the Golden Lion of Summer was a warrior renowned for her single-minded ferocity and military cunning. Her cloak, gauntlets, and boots were fashioned from the hide of a desert lion, and her weapons bore the mark of that fearsome beast.

Barbarian characters, particularly thaneborn barbarians, benefit the most from the Golden Lion's Battle Regalia. However, defenders and melee strikers can also make good use of these legendary items.

LORE

History DC 7: The Golden Lion took her name from the gauntlets, cloak, and boots she wore—crafted from the pelt of a lion she slew when she was only a child.

History DC 12: Despite her reputation as a scourge of Nerath, the Golden Lion and her folk came to the aid of the empire in the face of a gnoll invasion. The power of her regalia helped her slay the gnoll war chief, but in that fierce final battle, the Golden Lion fell.

History DC 17: The relics that bear the Golden Lion's name are now scattered across all lands, though the desert cairn marking her grave has long been lost to time. However, it's said that anyone who can find the site is then visited by the spirit of the Golden Lion, who will reveal the location of one or more item from her battle regalia to a worthy successor.

GOLDEN LION'S BATTLE REGALIA ITEMS

Lvl	Name	Price (gp)	Item Slot
2+	Hungry spear	520	Weapon
3	Swiftpad boots	680	Feet
4+	Cloak of the lion's mane	840	Neck
5	Lion's claw gauntlets	1,000	Hands
5+	Thane blood weapon	1,000	Weapon

GOLDEN LION'S BATTLE REGALIA BENEFITS

Pieces	Benefit
3	When you're adjacent to three or more enemies you can see, you gain a +1 bonus to attack rolls.
5	Your *roar of triumph* power increases to a close burst 7. When you use your *swift charge* power, you gain a +2 bonus to speed until the end of your next turn.

Cloak of the Lion's Mane
Level 4+

This lionskin cloak bestows the majesty of that desert predator upon you to strike fear into the hearts of your foes.

Lvl 4	+1	840 gp	Lvl 19	+4	105,000 gp
Lvl 9	+2	4,200 gp	Lvl 24	+5	525,000 gp
Lvl 14	+3	21,000 gp	Lvl 29	+6	2,625,000 gp

Item Slot: Neck
Enhancement: Fortitude, Reflex, and Will
Property: When you use your *roar of triumph* power, you and each ally adjacent to you can shift 1 square as a free action.
Power (Daily ✦ Fear): Free Action. *Trigger:* You reduce an enemy to 0 hit points. *Effect:* Each enemy within 5 squares of you takes a −2 penalty to attack rolls until the end of your next turn.

Hungry Spear
Level 2+

A roaring lion engraved on the head of this spear pins your foe in place while you close for the kill.

Lvl 2	+1	520 gp	Lvl 17	+4	65,000 gp
Lvl 7	+2	2,600 gp	Lvl 22	+5	325,000 gp
Lvl 12	+3	13,000 gp	Lvl 27	+6	1,625,000 gp

Weapon: Spear
Enhancement: Attack rolls and damage rolls
Critical: +1d6 damage per plus
Property: This weapon has the heavy thrown property and a range of 10/20.
Power (Encounter): Standard Action. Make a ranged basic attack with this spear. On a hit, the target is also immobilized (save ends). The spear doesn't return to you until the immobilized effect on the target imposed by this weapon is ended.

Lion's Claw Gauntlets
Level 5

These gauntlets, crafted from a lion's paws, help overcome the toughest adversaries.

Item Slot: Hands   1,000 gp
Property: When you make a weapon attack that targets Fortitude and your attack roll is 20 or lower, add a +1 item bonus to the roll.

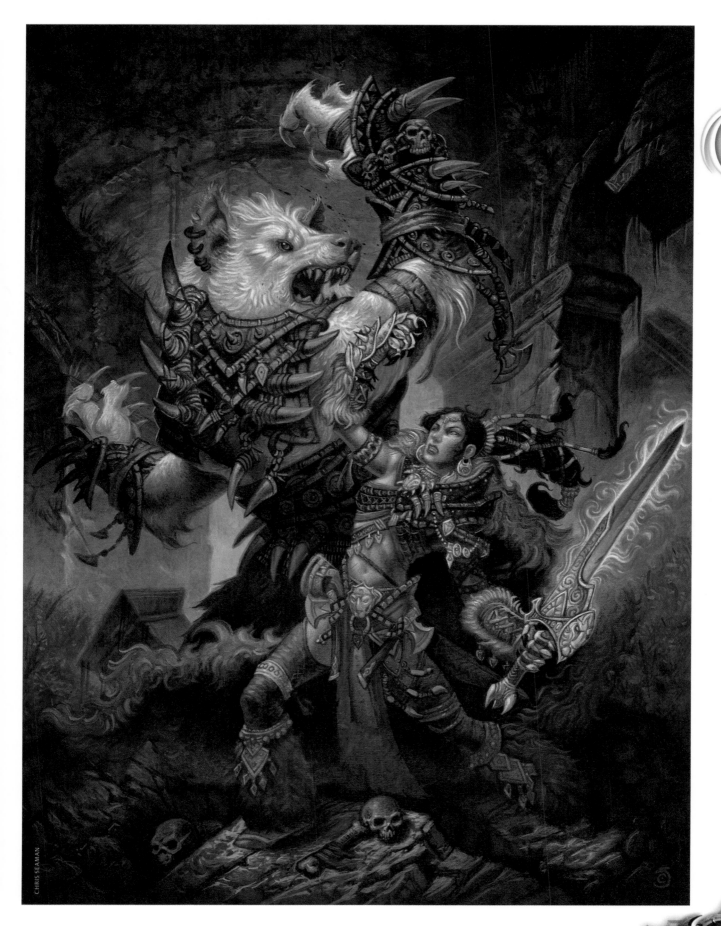

CHRIS SEAMAN

Swiftpad Boots — Level 3

These supple boots lend a lion's strength to your leaps.

Item Slot: Feet   680 gp
Property: You gain a +2 item bonus to Athletics checks to jump.
Power (Daily): Move Action. You jump a number of squares equal to your Strength modifier.

Thane Blood Weapon — Level 5+

Each time you drop an enemy, the bloodlust in your allies mounts.

Lvl			Lvl		
5	+1	1,000 gp	20	+4	125,000 gp
10	+2	5,000 gp	25	+5	625,000 gp
15	+3	25,000 gp	30	+6	3,125,000 gp

Weapon: Any melee
Enhancement: Attack rolls and damage rolls
Critical: +1d6 damage per plus
Property: When you use this weapon to reduce an enemy to 0 hit points, you and each ally adjacent to you gain a +2 item bonus to your next attack roll before the end of the encounter.

KAMESTIRI UNIFORM

The city-state of Nageo was once a major port and trade hub, but its great wealth made it a target for goblin raiders, competing city-states, and pirates. In response, the Nageos created a defensive force to protect the city and its lucrative shipping trade, and also to provide seaborne mercenary forces for traders and neighboring states. These legendary warriors called the Kamestiri are little more than a memory now, but the force's legacy lives on in the magical panoply its members once wore.

This item set is most useful for rangers, but it can be utilized by any character who favors long-range attacks and mobility in combat.

LORE

History DC 8: The elite soldiers of the city-state of Nageo trained with light armor suited to mobility and shipboard combat. The long-range crossbows that were their signature weapon had first been created by a local tribe known as the kamesti. The Kamestiri, as these soldiers called themselves, soon became the dominant fighting force in the region. Their effectiveness in battle on both land and sea soon became legendary, and helped maintain a decades-long peace between Nageo and its powerful neighbors.

History DC 14: At the height of Nageo's power, rumors began to circulate that the Kamestiri captains had been keeping much of the wealth they had liberated from the area's pirates. A new prince, uncertain in his position, grew jealous of the Kamestiri's power. Deciding to take steps to remove them, he sent the bulk of the Kamestiri forces on a doomed voyage of exploration from which few returned. Within the year, however, the prince was assassinated—slain by a single crossbow bolt fired from a great distance. With no clear heir and no defenders, Nageo quickly fell to its neighbors.

No trace of the Kamestiri's rumored riches was ever found. However, even if the tales of ill-gotten gains were unfounded, the group's legitimate earnings were said to have gone unaccounted for in the

STANDARD ITEMS IN ITEM SETS

Some item sets include magic items found in the *Player's Handbook* and other supplements. Such items can be found in a campaign in both their default (free) and item set (bound) versions. Items bound to a set exhibit qualities that link it to that set, and a character can learn that a magic item is bound in the same way he or she learns the item's properties or powers.

Magic items created in bound form as part of a magic item set use the normal rules for creating magic items. Set items in their free form (for example, an *endless quiver* not created as part of a Kamestiri uniform) can be incorporated into an item set. A character can perform the Enchant Magic Item ritual with no component cost to bind such a free magic item into a set. At the DM's discretion, binding an item into a set might require effort or special components: the blood of a descendant of the original set creator, taking the item to a special location, or the like.

An item that is bound into an item set can't later be unbound.

ERIC L. WILLIAMS

chaos after the death of the prince. The ultimate fate of that treasure remains a matter of great interest to scholars and adventurers alike.

History DC 19: The few survivors of the Kamestiri are said to have gone on to found mercenary troops in far-flung lands. These wandering companies are thought to have been the source of the first Kamestiri uniforms to appear in the wider world. Countless modern mercenary companies trace their origins to the Kamestiri, though in many cases, this claim is little more than spurious boasting.

Streetwise DC 19: Rumors in the larger cities of the land speak of lone assassins who specialize in murder at long range, and of the unique crossbows they bear. Some call these killers the last of the Kamestiri, though they're careful to not say so too loudly.

KAMESTIRI UNIFORM ITEMS

Lvl	Name	Price (gp)	Item Slot
7+	Infighting blade	2,600	Weapon
7+	Shipboard armor	2,600	Armor
8	Boarding boots	3,400	Feet
8+	Pavise charm	3,400	Neck
9	Endless quiver	4,200	Wondrous item
9+	Kamesti crossbow	4,200	Weapon

KAMESTIRI UNIFORM BENEFITS

Pieces	Benefit
2	The short range of a crossbow you wield increases by a number of squares equal to the number of items you have from this set. The long range of your crossbow increases by twice that amount.
3	You gain a +1 bonus to damage rolls on melee attacks while you are adjacent to two or more enemies.
5	When you reduce an enemy to 0 hit points, you can shift 1 square.

Boarding Boots — Level 8

These hard boots of black leather keep you moving in combat, to deadly effect.

Item Slot: Feet   3,400 gp

Property: You ignore difficult terrain on a boat, ship, or other watercraft.

Power (Daily): Standard Action. You jump a number of squares equal to your speed and use one of your at-will attack powers with a +1 power bonus to the attack roll.

Endless Quiver — Level 9

This elven-styled quiver can create an endless supply of normal arrows or bolts.

Wondrous Item   4,200 gp

Power (At-Will ✦ Conjuration): Free Action. Use this power when you attack with a bow or crossbow. When you reach into the *endless quiver*, it automatically produces a single arrow or bolt, as appropriate. Ammunition created by the quiver that is not used within 1 round of its creation disappears.

Infighting Blade — Level 7+

The closer your foes press, the more deadly this quick blade becomes.

Lvl 7	+2	2,600 gp	Lvl 22	+5	325,000 gp
Lvl 12	+3	13,000 gp	Lvl 27	+6	1,625,000 gp
Lvl 17	+4	65,000 gp			

Weapon: Light blade, axe (one-handed only)

Enhancement: Attack rolls and damage rolls

Critical: +1d6 damage per plus

Power (Daily): Minor Action. Until the end of your turn, when you attack with this weapon, you gain a bonus to damage rolls equal to the number of enemies adjacent to you when you make the attack. If you're wielding another *infighting blade* in your off hand, this bonus also applies to damage rolls with that weapon.

Special: If you're wielding two *infighting blades*, the first use per day of the weapon's daily power doesn't count toward the limit of magic item daily powers you can use in a day.

Kamesti Crossbow — Level 9+

This exceptionally crafted crossbow can target even the farthest foes.

Lvl 9	+2	4,200 gp	Lvl 24	+5	525,000 gp
Lvl 14	+3	21,000 gp	Lvl 29	+6	2,625,000 gp
Lvl 19	+4	105,000 gp			

Weapon: Crossbow

Enhancement: Attack rolls and damage rolls

Critical: +1d6 damage per plus

Property: Attacks with this crossbow don't take the -2 penalty for long range.

Power (Daily): Free Action. *Trigger:* You miss every target with an attack you make using this crossbow. *Effect:* You don't expend the use of that power. The power also has no effect on a miss, even if it normally does.

Pavise Charm — Level 8+

This shield-shaped charm surrounds you with protective energy.

Lvl 8	+2	3,400 gp	Lvl 23	+5	425,000 gp
Lvl 13	+3	17,000 gp	Lvl 28	+6	2,125,000 gp
Lvl 18	+4	85,000 gp			

Item Slot: Neck

Enhancement: Fortitude, Reflex, and Will

Power (Daily): Minor Action. You gain a +2 power bonus to AC and Reflex until you leave your current space.

Shipboard Armor — Level 7+

This black leather armor allows you to stand steady in the face of uncertain footing or a possible fall.

Lvl 7	+2	2,600 gp	Lvl 22	+5	325,000 gp
Lvl 12	+3	13,000 gp	Lvl 27	+6	1,625,000 gp
Lvl 17	+4	65,000 gp			

Armor: Leather

Enhancement: AC

Property: When you make a saving throw to avoid forced movement, you gain an item bonus to the saving throw equal to the armor's enhancement bonus. On a save, you don't fall prone.

MARJAM'S DREAM

A faithless mercenary driven by prophetic visions given to him by Melora collected the items of Marjam's Dream. With those relics, he trained the first in a long line of warriors taught to balance their martial prowess with arcane power.

Though the items of this set are usable by any class, they're most highly coveted by swordmages.

LORE

History DC 7: Marjam was a vain and boastful mercenary warrior who was disdainful of magic his entire life. In his later years, however, Marjam had a dream in which Melora instructed him to collect a number of powerful relics in her name. Initially resistant to what he perceived as the product of an age-addled brain and a healthy love of strong ale, Marjam tried to ignore this prophetic vision, but the dream increased in frequency and intensity. Fearing for his sanity in the end, the warrior strapped on mail and sword once more and undertook an epic quest that saw him collect the five relics that his dream had showed him.

History DC 12: By the time his quest was complete, a change had come over Marjam. Attuned to the arcane energy that permeated the world, the warrior had a final vision in which he saw a succession of heroes who would wield arcane and martial power in equal measure. He knew that it was the destiny of his final years to train the first of these heroes.

At the nearby temple of Melora, Marjam sought out a child he had seen in his final vision—an orphan named Alora, who had grown up under the care of the temple faithful and who showed great promise as a spellcaster. The child became Marjam's charge, and for long years at the temple he raised and trained her. From Marjam, Alora learned the ways of combat, even as the relics of Marjam's Dream allowed her to balance that martial skill with the magical ability taught to her by Melora's faithful.

History DC 17: Even before Marjam's death, Alora had left the temple to become an adventuring swordmage. A powerful symbol of Melora's faith, she was known by her reputation and the distinctive weapons and raiment of Marjam's Dream. When Alora died, the items of Marjam's Dream quickly spread across the world and beyond the bounds of Melora's faith. However, sages believe that Melora still seeks out chosen champions on whom to bestow the items of this set.

MARJAM'S DREAM ITEMS

Lvl	Name	Price (gp)	Item Slot
2	Boots of jaunting	520	Feet
3	Gauntlets of arcane might	680	Hands
4+	Weapon of arcane bonds	840	Weapon
5	Circlet of arcane extension	1,000	Head
6	Warded vambraces	1,800	Arms

MARJAM'S DREAM BENEFITS

Pieces	Benefit
2	When you make Arcana checks to detect magic, you gain a bonus equal to the number of items you have from this set.
5	The area affected by your Swordmage Aegis class feature increases to a close burst 3.

Boots of Jaunting — Level 2

These comfortable leather boots allow you to slip past obstacles unhindered.

Item Slot: Feet   520 gp
Power (Daily ✦ Teleportation): Minor Action. You teleport 1 square.

Circlet of Arcane Extension — Level 5

This golden circlet extends the range of your arcane power to strike at distant foes.

Item Slot: Head   1,000 gp
Power (Daily): Minor Action. Until the end of your turn, the range of your ranged arcane powers increases by 5 squares.

Gauntlets of Arcane Might — Level 3

When a foe you have challenged reels from your arcane power, these gauntlets grant you increased vigor.

Item Slot: Hands   680 gp
Property: When you hit an enemy marked by you with an arcane attack power, you gain 2 temporary hit points.

Warded Vambraces — Level 6

These leather armbands let you share your arcane defenses with others.

Item Slot: Arms   1,800 gp
Power (Encounter): Minor Action. Until the end of your next turn, each ally adjacent to you gains a power bonus to AC equal to the bonus provided by your Swordmage Warding class feature.

Weapon of Arcane Bonds — Level 4+

Effects you cause with this blade bind your enemies to you.

Lvl 4	+1	840 gp	Lvl 19	+4	105,000 gp
Lvl 9	+2	4,200 gp	Lvl 24	+5	525,000 gp
Lvl 14	+3	21,000 gp	Lvl 29	+6	2,625,000 gp

Weapon: Heavy blade, light blade
Enhancement: Attack rolls and damage rolls
Critical: +1d6 damage per plus
Power (Encounter): Free Action. *Trigger:* You hit an enemy with an arcane attack power using this weapon. *Effect:* That enemy is marked by you (save ends).

RADIANT TEMPLE TREASURES

Many cultures tell versions of the myth of the Radiant Temple—a great bastion of light created during the ancient war between the gods and the primordials. Though the temple was taken to the celestial realms by the gods in the aftermath of their victory, a number of its faithful stayed behind in the mortal realm. The treasures they bore became their legacy.

Any character can wield the Radiant Temple Treasures, but they're most useful to avengers.

LORE

History or Religion DC 8: In the final years of the war between the gods and the primordials, a great number of mortal clerics, paladins, and other servants of the gods came together to create a mighty bastion of light. This act greatly pleased the gods, and it's said that the devotion of the temple helped turn the tide of war in their favor.

History or Religion DC 14: In the end, the gods were victorious. In a glorious cataclysm that shook the mortal world, the Radiant Temple and the souls that had forged it were taken to the Astral Sea. However, in the moments before the temple's ascendance, a number of the faithful stepped forth from its towers of light, chosen by the gods to remain behind as protectors of the new-made world. These faithful are said by some to be the first avengers—divine champions of the deities themselves.

History or Religion DC 19: The items of the Radiant Temple Treasures are spread across all cultures, even those where the secret rituals of the avengers are all but unknown. Some believe that the appearance of these relics is a sign meant to inspire worshipers to take up the path of the avenger.

RADIANT TEMPLE TREASURES ITEMS

Lvl	Name	Price (gp)	Item Slot
7+	Radiant temple uniform	2,600	Armor
8+	Blade of vengeance	3,400	Weapon
8+	Warding blade	3,400	Weapon
9+	Bracers of zeal	4,200	Arms

RADIANT TEMPLE TREASURES BENEFITS

Pieces	Benefit
2	When your *oath of enmity* reduces a target to 0 hit points, you gain temporary hit points equal to twice the number of items you have from this set.
4	You gain a +10 bonus to your first death saving throw each day.

Blade of Vengeance — Level 8+

Your foe's attack bites deep, but your counterstrike hits even harder.

Lvl 8	+2	3,400 gp	Lvl 23	+5	425,000 gp
Lvl 13	+3	17,000 gp	Lvl 28	+6	2,125,000 gp
Lvl 18	+4	85,000 gp			

Weapon: Heavy blade, light blade
Enhancement: Attack rolls and damage rolls
Critical: +1d6 radiant damage per plus
Power (Daily): Immediate Reaction. *Trigger:* An enemy adjacent to you bloodies you with a melee attack. *Effect:* Make a melee basic attack against the triggering enemy with this blade. On a hit, the enemy is also pushed 5 squares, and you can move 5 squares. You must end your movement in a space adjacent to that enemy.
Special: If you have the *oath of enmity* power, you can shift 5 squares instead of moving 5 squares.

Bracers of Zeal — Level 9+

These golden bracers let you channel your own resiliency into a punishing attack.

Lvl 9	+2	4,200 gp	Lvl 24	+5	525,000 gp
Lvl 14	+3	21,000 gp	Lvl 29	+6	2,625,000 gp
Lvl 19	+4	105,000 gp			

Item Slot: Arms
Power (Encounter): Free Action. *Trigger:* You hit an enemy adjacent to you with a melee attack power, and you have temporary hit points. *Effect:* You lose up to 5 temporary hit points and deal that amount of extra damage to that enemy.
Level 19 or 24: Lose up to 10 temporary hit points and deal that amount of damage.
Level 29: Lose any number of temporary hit points and deal that amount of damage.

Radiant Temple Uniform — Level 7+

This muted gray uniform protects you from watchful eyes and lets you skillfully slip past your foes in combat.

Lvl 7	+2	2,600 gp	Lvl 22	+5	325,000 gp
Lvl 12	+3	13,000 gp	Lvl 27	+6	1,625,000 gp
Lvl 17	+4	65,000 gp			

Armor: Cloth
Enhancement: AC
Property: You gain a +2 item bonus to Stealth checks.
Power (Encounter): Free Action. *Trigger:* You shift 1 or more squares. *Effect:* You shift an additional number of squares equal to half of this armor's enhancement bonus.

Warding Blade — Level 8+

This silvery blade seems to move of its own accord, protecting you from harm.

Lvl 8	+2	3,400 gp	Lvl 23	+5	425,000 gp
Lvl 13	+3	17,000 gp	Lvl 28	+6	2,125,000 gp
Lvl 18	+4	85,000 gp			

Weapon: Light blade
Enhancement: Attack rolls and damage rolls
Critical: +1d6 damage per plus
Property: While you wield this weapon in your off hand, you gain an item bonus to AC against opportunity attacks equal to the blade's enhancement bonus.

RESPLENDENT FINERY

Only the most fashionable adventurers seek out the clothing that makes up the set known as Resplendent Finery. The items of the Resplendent Finery grant potent defenses and mental abilities to any character, but these garments are favored by bards, fey pact warlocks, and illusionist wizards.

LORE

History DC 7: The magic items known as the Resplendent Finery are as legendary for their fine styling as for their powers. Adventurers who want their heroic status to be known adopt the finery as a kind of status symbol, with the items of the set granting their wearers a measure of control over their interactions with others.

Though versions of the finery can appear in any number of styles, many sets feature fey touches that echo the fashion and art of the eladrin.

History DC 12: The items of the Resplendent Finery are said to have threads of glamor and illusion woven into them, giving their wearer the power to influence minds. These legendary garments have appeared throughout the ages, indistinguishable from other fine clothing unless the magic within them is detected.

History DC 17: The first prominent set of Resplendent Finery was a gift from an eladrin lord to a powerful dwarf clan chief. Over time, the magical enhancements in the garments were revealed and stealthily copied, though the benefits and core powers of all sets remain the same.

RESPLENDENT FINERY ITEMS

Lvl	Name	Price (gp)	Item Slot
5+	Resplendent gloves	1,000	Hands
6	Resplendent boots	1,800	Feet
7	Resplendent circlet	2,600	Head
8+	Resplendent cloak	3,400	Neck

RESPLENDENT FINERY BENEFITS

Pieces	Benefit
2	You gain an item bonus to Bluff checks equal to the number of items you have from this set.
4	Each ally within 10 squares of you gains a +1 item bonus to checks involving any skill you're trained in.

Resplendent Boots — Level 6

These intricately embroidered boots let you fade from sight for a moment to slip past your foes.

Item Slot: Feet   1,800 gp

Property: You gain an item bonus to all defenses against opportunity attacks equal to the number of items you have from this set.

Power (Daily ✦ Illusion): Move Action. You become invisible and move your speed. You become visible again at the end of this action.

Resplendent Circlet — Level 7

This gold and mithral circlet masks your thoughts and grants an ally favor in combat.

Item Slot: Head   2,600 gp

Property: Enemies within 10 squares of you take a –2 penalty to Insight checks. Those enemies are not aware of this effect.

Power (Encounter): Minor Action. Choose one ally within 5 squares of you. One enemy adjacent to that ally grants combat advantage to him or her.

Resplendent Cloak — Level 8+

This richly colored cloak shields you and your allies from powers that affect the mind.

Lvl 8	+2	3,400 gp	Lvl 23	+5	425,000 gp
Lvl 13	+3	17,000 gp	Lvl 28	+6	2,125,000 gp
Lvl 18	+4	85,000 gp			

Item Slot: Neck

Enhancement: Fortitude, Reflex, and Will

Property: You and each ally within 10 squares of you gain a +2 bonus to Will against charm, fear, and illusion attacks.

Resplendent Gloves — Level 5+

These fine calfskin gloves increase the potency of powers that break a foe's will.

Lvl 5	1,000 gp	Lvl 25	625,000 gp
Lvl 15	25,000 gp		

Item Slot: Hands

Property: When you hit an enemy with an attack power that targets Will, the attack deals 2 extra damage. If it's an illusion attack, one target you hit (your choice) also grants combat advantage to you until the end of your next turn.

Level 15: 3 extra damage.

Level 25: 5 extra damage.

SHADOWDANCER'S GARB

The clothing that makes up the Shadowdancer's Garb is elegant and well crafted, but also stern and forbidding. While you wear these items, you're cloaked in silence and shadow. Even in bright daylight, your features are obscured, and the shadows cast by your body seem to exude tendrils of darkness.

The items of the Shadowdancer's Garb are most useful for rogues, but the set appeals to any character who understands the benefits of stealth.

LORE

Arcana or History DC 10: Creators of the Shadowdancer's Garb imbue each item of clothing with shadow magic, wrapping the wearer in a cloak of magical darkness. Shadowdancer's Garb items are popular among rogues and other characters who value stealth both in and out of combat. Additionally, the garb has a reputation as the raiment of choice for assassins and spies.

Arcana or History DC 16: The items that make up the Shadowdancer's Garb were first crafted as individual magic items for the use of elite shadar-kai warriors. Originally, the cloak, mask, gloves, and boots of the set were signature gear for the leaders of four shadar-kai regiments in the service of a powerful Shadowfell lord. These companies were known as the shadowdancers, and their exploits in the Shadowfell and the mortal world are legendary.

Arcana or History DC 21: Razman-kash was the leader of a powerful Shadowfell assassin's guild—a former member of the shadowdancers passed over for a regimental command that he believed was his by right. After nurturing his hate for years, Razman-kash staged a coup in which the four regimental leaders and the Shadowfell lord were killed. Not content with merely claiming leadership of the shadowdancers, Razman-kash had the combined regalia enchanted to provide even greater power when the four pieces were worn together. His original design has long since spread across the Shadowfell and into the world.

SHADOWDANCER'S GARB ITEMS

Lvl	Name	Price (gp)	Item Slot
9+	Shadowdancer's cloak	4,200	Neck
10	Shadowdancer's mask	5,000	Head
11	Shadowdancer's gloves	9,000	Hands
12	Shadowdancer's boots	13,000	Feet

SHADOWDANCER'S GARB BENEFITS

Pieces	Benefit
2	You gain an item bonus to Athletics, Stealth, and Thievery checks equal to the number of items you have from this set.
4	At the start of each encounter, if you aren't surprised, you have concealment until the end of your first turn.

Shadowdancer's Boots — Level 12

These sleek boots lighten your steps, particularly while shadow conceals you.

Item Slot: Feet   13,000 gp
Property: You gain a +1 bonus to speed while you're wearing light armor. This bonus increases to +2 when you start your turn in dim light or darkness.

Shadowdancer's Cloak — Level 9+

This flowing cloak obscures your movement while you are hidden.

Lvl 9	+2	4,200 gp	Lvl 24	+5	525,000 gp
Lvl 14	+3	21,000 gp	Lvl 29	+6	2,625,000 gp
Lvl 19	+4	105,000 gp			

Item Slot: Neck
Enhancement: Fortitude, Reflex, and Will
Power (Daily): Free Action. *Trigger:* You hit or miss an enemy you're hidden from. *Effect:* You make a Stealth check against that enemy's passive Perception check to remain hidden from it. You are no longer hidden from other creatures, as normal.

Shadowdancer's Gloves — Level 11

While you're hidden, these supple gloves make your attacks more deadly.

Item Slot: Hands   9,000 gp
Property: When you hit an enemy you're hidden from, you deal 1d6 extra damage.

Shadowdancer's Mask — Level 10

This featureless black mask aids your efforts to fool or hide from your foes.

Item Slot: Head   5,000 gp
Power (Daily): Free Action. *Trigger:* You make a Bluff check or Stealth check and dislike the result. *Effect:* Reroll the check with a +3 power bonus and use either result.

SKIN OF THE PANTHER

This item set was first crafted in the deep jungle, where the druids venerate the spirit of the panther. Crafted from the hide of these stealthy hunters, the items that make up the Skin of the Panther grant their wearer the hunting prowess and demeanor of this noble beast.

This magic item set is most commonly sought out by predator druids, though any character who wears hide armor and seeks to excel in stealth and hard-hitting attacks can benefit from it.

LORE

Arcana or Nature DC 7: In the untamed jungles, human tribes give honor and respect to the panther. Jungle warriors model their combat tactics on the strength and stealthy power of these great hunting cats, whose spirits are said to live on within the mightiest hunters and the magic relics they wield.

Arcana or Nature DC 12: The components of this item set are carefully crafted from the hide of the panther—both the great cats of the mortal world and their Feywild cousins. To hunt the Feywild panther is an honor accorded only to the most powerful warriors of a tribe, and the locations of the hidden jungle portals that lead to that plane are carefully guarded secrets known only to high-ranking druids.

Arcana or Nature DC 17: Animals fated to supply the raw materials for the Skin of the Panther are given great reverence by the tribes, and are hunted in accordance with ancient rituals. Warriors who take up the hunt must follow a strict regimen of training, fasting, and prayer—traditions designed to ensure that the spirits of these great cats form the foundation of the Skin of the Panther's powerful magic.

SKIN OF THE PANTHER ITEMS

Lvl	Name	Price (gp)	Item Slot
2+	Shadow hunter hide	520	Armor
3+	Death fang totem	680	Implement
4	Claw gloves	840	Hands
5	Panther slippers	1,000	Feet
6	Cat's-eye headband	1,800	Head

SKIN OF THE PANTHER BENEFITS

Pieces	Benefit
2	You gain an item bonus to Stealth checks equal to the number of items you have from this set.
5	The first time you use *wild shape* to take on your beast form during an encounter, you become invisible until the end of your next turn or until you attack.

Cat's-Eye Headband — Level 6

Two fragments of green jade set in this black leather headband open up the shadows to your sight.

Item Slot: Head   1,800 gp

Power (Encounter): Minor Action. You gain darkvision until the end of your next turn.

Claw Gloves — Level 4

These gloves incorporate the claws of a panther, granting you additional power in your beast form.

Item Slot: Hands   840 gp

Property: When you're in beast form and an enemy grants combat advantage to you, your melee attacks deal 1d10 extra damage against that enemy.

Death Fang Totem — Level 3+

A wounded or vulnerable foe grants you advantage while you wield this totem of bone, teeth, and sinew.

Lvl 3	+1	680 gp	Lvl 18	+4	85,000 gp
Lvl 8	+2	3,400 gp	Lvl 23	+5	425,000 gp
Lvl 13	+3	17,000 gp	Lvl 28	+6	2,125,000 gp

Implement (Totem)

Enhancement: Attack rolls and damage rolls

Critical: +1d6 damage per plus, plus 1d6 extra damage against a target that is granting combat advantage to you.

Power (Daily): Free Action. *Trigger:* You bloody an enemy with an attack. *Effect:* That enemy grants combat advantage to you (save ends).

Panther Slippers — Level 5

These soft, clawed shoes help you stay within striking range of your prey.

Item Slot: Feet   1,000 gp

Enhancement: Fortitude, Reflex, and Will

Power (Daily): Immediate Reaction. *Trigger:* An enemy adjacent to you shifts. *Effect:* You shift 1 square. If you're in beast form, you instead shift 3 squares.

Shadow Hunter Hide — Level 2+

This shimmering black hide armor allows you to get the drop on your foes.

Lvl 2	+1	520 gp	Lvl 17	+4	65,000 gp
Lvl 7	+2	2,600 gp	Lvl 22	+5	325,000 gp
Lvl 12	+3	13,000 gp	Lvl 27	+6	1,625,000 gp

Armor: Hide

Enhancement: AC

Property: You can move 4 squares during an action while you're hidden (instead of 2 squares) without taking a –5 penalty to your Stealth check.

TOOLS OF ZANE'S VENGEANCE

Fate can be cruel, as the legendary shaman Zane knew all too well. After a despot slaughtered his people and had his eyes put out, the blind Zane spent years in pursuit of bloody revenge. The Tools of Zane's Vengeance are the weapons and raiment he crafted in the course of achieving that lifelong goal.

This item set is most useful to shamans.

LORE

History or Nature DC 8: As a mystic and elder of his tribe, the shaman Zane brought his people into harmony with their totem spirits. However, an ambitious king shattered the peace when he turned hungry eyes toward the tribe's rich lands. Driven by greed, his armies laid waste to the tribe's hunting grounds. Zane's people were slaughtered, and he was brought before the king. Sensing the shaman's authority and wanting to set a harsh example, the king ordered Zane's eyes put out, then set him free.

History or Nature DC 14: Though blinded, Zane vowed that he would visit upon the despot the same horrors his people had suffered. After the soldiers had moved on, he returned and harvested from his fallen kin the items with which he would make good on his vow, infusing each with blood magic and dire curses.

For the remainder of his days, Zane walked the land, hearing the spirits of his fallen tribesfolk calling for vengeance. Each time he took a life, the shaman placed the victim's eyes in his own ruined sockets, regaining his sight for a short time by the use of dark rituals.

History or Nature DC 19: The Tools of Zane's Vengeance were spread across all lands after his

ED COX

death. Even now, it's said that Zane's spirit lingers in the world, ready to aid the downtrodden in their struggles against tyranny and injustice. Characters who follow in his path are sometimes gifted with the knowledge of where the Tools of Zane's Vengeance can be found.

TOOLS OF ZANE'S VENGEANCE ITEMS

Lvl	Name	Price (gp)	Item Slot
6	Savage mask	1,800	Head
7+	Cloak of the crimson path	2,600	Neck
8+	Blood harvest blade	3,400	Weapon
9+	Totem of the bleeding eye	4,200	Implement

TOOLS OF ZANE'S VENGEANCE BENEFITS

Pieces	Benefit
2	You gain an item bonus to Intimidate checks equal to the number of items you have from this set.
4	While you're bloodied, you gain blindsight 5.

Blood Harvest Blade   Level 8+

When you drop an enemy with this bloodstained blade, your spirit companion takes on a horrifying visage that shakes your foes.

Lvl 8	+2	3,400 gp	Lvl 23	+5	425,000 gp
Lvl 13	+3	17,000 gp	Lvl 28	+6	2,125,000 gp
Lvl 18	+4	85,000 gp			

Weapon: Light blade
Enhancement: Attack rolls and damage rolls
Critical: +1d6 damage per plus, plus 1[W] extra damage
Power (Encounter ✦ Fear): Free Action. *Trigger:* You reduce an enemy to 0 hit points with an attack power using this weapon. *Effect:* Each enemy adjacent to your spirit companion grants combat advantage to you until the end of your next turn.

Cloak of the Crimson Path   Level 7+

When you're injured, this blood-crusted cloak allows you and your allies to take advantage of an enemy's error.

Lvl 7	+2	2,600 gp	Lvl 22	+5	325,000 gp
Lvl 12	+3	13,000 gp	Lvl 27	+6	1,625,000 gp
Lvl 17	+4	65,000 gp			

Item Slot: Neck
Enhancement: Fortitude, Reflex, and Will
Power (Daily ✦ Teleportation): Immediate Reaction. *Trigger:* While you're bloodied, an enemy adjacent to you or your spirit companion misses with a melee attack. *Effect:* You and your spirit companion swap positions, and the triggering enemy grants combat advantage to you until the end of your next turn.

Savage Mask   Level 6

The savage spirit whose visage marks this mask grants you strength against attacks that would sap your will.

Item Slot: Head   1,800 gp
Property: You gain a +2 item bonus to Will against close and area attacks.

Totem of the Severed Eye   Level 9+

The severed eyes placed upon this totem can blind a foe or expose invisible creatures to your sight.

Lvl 9	+2	4,200 gp	Lvl 24	+5	525,000 gp
Lvl 14	+3	21,000 gp	Lvl 29	+6	2,625,000 gp
Lvl 19	+4	105,000 gp			

Implement (Totem)
Enhancement: Attack rolls and damage rolls
Critical: +1d6 damage per plus, and the target is blinded until the end of your next turn.
Property: You can see any invisible creatures adjacent to your spirit companion.

ZY TORMTOR'S TRINKETS

Zy Tormtor is a legend among the drow of Erelhei-Cinlu, particularly to other dark pact warlocks. Millennia after his betrayal and execution at the hands of House Kilsek, his life and exploits are revered by the drow, though the details of that life vary with the affiliations of the teller.

The weapons and tools that Zy used in his exploits are almost as famous as the warlock himself– particularly the *prison of Salzacas*, a black iron jar within which was bound a powerful spirit. Though the full secrets of Zy's power are said to have died with him, the item set that bears his name has since spread from the Underdark and across the surface world. Warlocks, wizards, and rogues covet these items for their power, and for the symbolic value of following in the path of the legendary warlock who crafted them.

LORE

Arcana or History DC 5: A minor scion of his house, Zy Tormtor used his arcane talents for intelligence gathering, skulduggery, and outright larceny. Though he worked frequently in the service of House Tormtor, Zy's chief motivations were to sow chaos and increase his own infamy. During his career, the warlock was responsible for countless daring burglaries, complex acts of sabotage, and the murder of dozens of nobles from rival houses–including the matron mother of House Kilsek.

Arcana or History DC 10: Zy's activities were aided by a powerful spirit named Salzacas, bound in an enchanted black iron flask. Some claim that Zy had summoned and held a demon within the prison, while others say that the *prison of Salzacas* was an ancient relic he found during one of his adventures. Darker rumors suggest that Salzacas was the spirit of Zy's twin brother, bound to the warlock after being slain by him in the womb.

Arcana or History DC 15: Zy Tormtor's Trinkets have passed through the hands of numerous scoundrels seeking to claim the long-dead warlock's power or fame. However, if the legends of Zy Tormtor are to be believed, the items that bear his name today vary in power from the tools the warlock once wielded. It

remains unknown whether later copies of the trinkets have lost the originals' power or whether unseen power lies latent within the trinkets and waits to be claimed.

ZY TORMTOR'S TRINKETS ITEMS

Lvl	Name	Price (gp)	Item Slot
2	Prison of Salzacas	520	Wondrous item
3+	Pact blade	680	Weapon
3+	Spidersilk mantle	680	Neck
4	Blackleaf gloves	840	Hands

ZY TORMTOR'S TRINKETS BENEFITS

Pieces	Benefit
2	The *prison of Salzacas* gains the following property: Your Thievery checks are always treated as if you're using thieves' tools, and you gain an additional +2 item bonus to Thievery checks.
4	You gain the *hand of Salzacas* power, described below.

Hand of Salzacas — Item Set Power

Your bond with the spirit of the prison is strong, allowing you to channel your arcane energies through the item even when it's not with you.

Daily
Free Action   **Personal**
Trigger: You use a warlock power
Effect: The power uses the location of the *prison of Salzacas* instead of your location as the origin square.

Blackleaf Gloves — Level 4

Made from the leaves of an ancient Feywild oak, these well-preserved black gloves increase the utility of your pact boon.

Item Slot: Hands   840 gp
Power (Encounter ✦ Teleportation): Free Action. *Trigger:* Your pact boon triggers. *Effect:* You teleport 3 squares in addition to the other effect of your pact boon.

Pact Blade — Level 3+

Warlocks favor this wickedly sharp blade.

Lvl 3	+1	680 gp	Lvl 18	+4	85,000 gp
Lvl 8	+2	3,400 gp	Lvl 23	+5	425,000 gp
Lvl 13	+3	17,000 gp	Lvl 28	+6	2,125,000 gp

Weapon: Light blade (usually daggers and sickles)
Enhancement: Attack rolls and damage rolls
Critical: +1d6 damage per plus
Property: This blade functions as a warlock implement, adding its enhancement bonus to attack rolls and damage rolls for warlock powers that use implements.
Property: When a creature you have cursed with your Warlock's Curse makes a melee attack against you, deal damage to the creature equal to the *pact blade*'s enhancement bonus.
Special: You do not gain your weapon proficiency bonus to the attack roll when using a *pact blade* as an implement.

ERIC L. WILLIAMS

Prison of Salzacas
Level 2

The spirit bound within this rune-scribed black metal flask manipulates objects at your command.

Wondrous Item   520 gp

Power (Encounter ✦ Conjuration): Minor Action. You conjure the spirit contained within the prison in an unoccupied space within 10 squares of you. The spirit can pick up, move, or manipulate an object adjacent to it weighing 20 pounds or less and can carry it 10 squares. If you're holding the object when you use this power, the spirit can move the object into a pack, a pouch, a sheath, or a similar container and simultaneously move any one object carried or worn anywhere on your body into your hand.

     As a move action, you can move the spirit 10 squares. As a free action, you can cause the spirit to drop an object it's holding. As a minor action, you can cause the spirit to pick up or manipulate a different object.
     Sustain Minor: The spirit persists.

Spidersilk Mantle
Level 3+

Spun from the silk of a demonweb terror, this mantle grants you a spider's effortless ability to climb.

Lvl 3	+1	680 gp	Lvl 18	+4	85,000 gp
Lvl 8	+2	3,400 gp	Lvl 23	+5	425,000 gp
Lvl 13	+3	17,000 gp	Lvl 28	+6	2,125,000 gp

Item Slot: Neck

Enhancement: Fortitude, Reflex, and Will

Power (Encounter): Minor Action. You gain a climb (spider climb) speed equal to your speed until the end of your turn.

PARAGON TIER ITEM SETS

Characters in the paragon tier seek magic arms, implements, and other items that can reflect and complement their increasing notoriety.

ARMS OF UNBREAKABLE HONOR

Paladins, bards, and commoners alike know the songs of the legendary hero Bradaman. She was a knight of one of the ancient human kingdoms on whose bones the empire of Nerath was built—a warrior whose exploits shaped the items and powers of the Arms of Unbreakable Honor. Bradaman's legend isn't a part of any particular faith, race, or culture. Rather, the weapons and armor she wore are said to seek out any whose valor and pure heart reflect the ideals of a lost age.

The magic items of this set are closely associated with paladins, though other defenders can benefit from their power.

LORE

History DC 11: The legend of Bradaman is first recorded at the height of the Empire of Nerath, where it was told as the story of an earlier age of nobility. Lady Bradaman was a paladin of great repute, one of many free knights who served and defended the common folk of her land. When her three brothers were falsely accused of murder, Bradaman swore to secure their pardon by undertaking three tasks set for her by the high king.

History DC 18: For her first task, Bradaman reclaimed a temple to Moradin and Melora that had fallen under the control of worshipers of Zehir. With her brothers, she fought her way to the altar of the temple and sounded her horn, staggering the cult's yuan-ti leaders so that her brothers could strike them down.

For the second task, Bradaman vanquished the titan Shixzan, whose hammer brought down deadly storms. By tricking Shixzan to go underground where he could not swing his hammer, Bradaman forced the titan to swear loyalty to the king with unbreakable oaths.

For her final task, Bradaman was ordered to unhorse the Crow Knight, an undead warrior whose lance brought death. When the two knights clashed, the Crow Knight's lance passed through Bradaman's shield, armor, body, and soul, but the paladin did not waver from her goal. The Crow Knight was unhorsed, though Bradaman paid with her life.

History DC 23: Her brothers returned Bradaman's body to the high king, who declared she would be buried with the honor she had in life. Shixzan raised up a great tomb for her, hiding it away in the mountains. The weapons, armor, and gear she bore at death became known as the Arms of Unbreakable Honor, their magic grown more powerful by her heroic sacrifice. Though many have searched for it, Bradaman's crypt remains as much a legend as she.

ARMS OF UNBREAKABLE HONOR ITEMS

Lvl	Name	Price (gp)	Item Slot
12+	Unbroken lance	13,000	Weapon
13+	Bradaman's weapon	17,000	Weapon
13+	Mirrored plate	17,000	Armor
14	Pennant helm	21,000	Head
15	Shield of fellowship	25,000	Arms
16	Bridle of flame	45,000	Mount

ARMS OF UNBREAKABLE HONOR BENEFITS

Pieces	Benefit
2	When you or a mount you ride charges an enemy, you or your mount gains an item bonus to speed equal to the number of items you have from this set.
5	When you use your *lay on hands* power, the target regains an additional 5 hit points.

Bradaman's Weapon

Level 13+

This elegantly crafted weapon draws on your own reserves of valor to take the fight to your foes.

Lvl 13	+3	17,000 gp	Lvl 23	+5	425,000 gp
Lvl 18	+4	85,000 gp	Lvl 28	+6	2,125,000 gp

Weapon: Heavy blade, axe, hammer
Enhancement: Attack rolls and damage rolls
Critical: +1d6 damage per plus, and you can spend a healing surge.
Property: Divine characters can use this weapon as a holy symbol implement for divine powers.
Power (Encounter): Minor Action. Until the end of the encounter, your *divine challenge* power targets two creatures in the burst instead of one.

Bridle of Flame

Level 16

This black leather bridle decorated with a flame motif grants healing power and can transform your mount into a fiery steed.

Item Slot: Mount   45,000 gp
Property: When you spend a healing surge to regain hit points, your mount also regains hit points as if it had spent a healing surge.
Power (Daily ✦ Fire, Polymorph): Minor Action. Your mount transforms into a creature of wind and flame. The mount gains resist 20 fire. Any creature other than you that starts its turn on or adjacent to the mount takes 2d6 fire damage. Your mount retains this form until the end of the encounter, until you end the power as a free action, or until you are no longer mounted on it.

Mirrored Plate

Level 13+

This gleaming plate mail lends authority to your voice and can blind foes with its brilliance.

Lvl 13	+3	17,000 gp	Lvl 23	+5	425,000 gp
Lvl 18	+4	85,000 gp	Lvl 28	+6	2,125,000 gp

Armor: Plate
Enhancement: AC
Property: You gain an item bonus to Diplomacy checks equal to the armor's enhancement bonus.
Property: When an enemy scores a critical hit against you, it is blinded until the end of its next turn.

Pennant Helm

Level 14

This brightly decorated helmet grants you strength of will and helps revitalize your allies.

Item Slot: Head   21,000 gp
Property: You gain a +1 item bonus to Will.
Power (Daily ✦ Healing): Minor Action. Spend a healing surge. You don't regain hit points as normal. Instead, each ally who can see you can spend a healing surge.

Shield of Fellowship

Level 15

Polished to a bright sheen, this shield has magic that helps you share your resilience with allies.

Item Slot: Arms   25,000 gp
Shield: Any
Property: When you gain temporary hit points, you can transfer those temporary hit points + 3 additional temporary hit points to an adjacent ally as a free action.

CHRIS SEAMAN

Unbroken Lance — Level 12+

This weapon glows with the power of your righteousness when you charge.

| Lvl 12 | +3 | 13,000 gp | Lvl 22 | +5 | 325,000 gp |
| Lvl 17 | +4 | 65,000 gp | Lvl 27 | +6 | 1,625,000 gp |

Weapon: Spear
Enhancement: Attack rolls and damage rolls
Critical: +1d6 damage per plus
Property: When you hit an enemy with a charge attack while you're mounted, that enemy is knocked prone.
Power (Daily): Standard Action. Your mount shifts 3 squares and you make a charge attack.

ASPECT OF THE RAM

Tenacious, stalwart, and sure-footed, the mountain ram is revered by many wielders of primal power. Totems of the ram adorn the armor of the hunters and warriors of the mountains, and adventurers draw inspiration from the visage and spirit of these nimble and fearless beasts.

Wardens and martial-minded druids benefit the most from this magic item set, particularly those guardians who enjoy being at the front of the fray.

LORE

Arcana or Nature DC 10: The items of the Aspect of the Ram were first created by members of the druid orders that haunt the high mountain passes. Made of leather-stitched fur and decorated with dangling fetishes in the shape of a ram's head, this set's crude outward appearance is in sharp contrast to its true power.

Arcana or Nature DC 16: The druids of the Dawnforge Mountains believe that the noblest of the mountain rams move on to the spirit realm after death. When they do, the rams discard their physical forms on the rocks of their favorite peaks. The raiment that makes up the Aspect of the Ram is crafted from these rare finds.

ASPECT OF THE RAM ITEMS

Lvl	Name	Price (gp)	Item Slot
10+	Stern mountain totem	5,000	Implement
11	Steady boots of the ram	9,000	Feet
12	Charger's headdress	13,000	Head
13+	Fleece of renewal	17,000	Neck

ASPECT OF THE RAM BENEFITS

Pieces	Benefit
2	You gain a +1 bonus to attack rolls with charge attacks.
4	When you hit an enemy with a charge attack, one ally within 5 squares of you can make a saving throw as a free action.

Charger's Headdress — Level 12

Fashioned from a mountain ram's horns, this headdress lets you charge unhindered through the spirit world.

Item Slot: Head   13,000 gp
Property: You gain a +1 bonus to attack rolls with charge attacks.
Power (Daily ✦ Teleportation): Standard Action. Make a charge attack, but instead of moving your speed before the attack, you teleport the same number of squares.

Fleece of Renewal — Level 13+

This fleece cloak gives you a boost of vigor each time you charge.

| Lvl 13 | +3 | 17,000 gp | Lvl 23 | +5 | 425,000 gp |
| Lvl 18 | +4 | 85,000 gp | Lvl 28 | +6 | 2,125,000 gp |

Item Slot: Neck
Enhancement: Fortitude, Reflex, and Will
Property: Free Action. When you charge an enemy, you gain temporary hit points equal to your Constitution modifier until the start of your next turn.

Steady Boots of the Ram — Level 11

These fur-lined leather boots give you the sure-footed step of the mountain ram.

Item Slot: Feet   9,000 gp
Property: You gain the earth walk ability (*Monster Manual*, page 283).
Property: You gain a +2 item bonus to Athletics checks to climb.

THOMAS DENMARK

Stern Mountain Totem Level 10+

The strength of the mountain beneath the ram's hooves flows into your attacks.

Lvl 10	+2	5,000 gp	Lvl 25	+5	625,000 gp
Lvl 15	+3	25,000 gp	Lvl 30	+6	3,125,000 gp
Lvl 20	+4	125,000 gp			

Implement (Totem)
Enhancement: Attack rolls and damage rolls
Critical: +1d8 per plus, or +1d10 per plus with charge attacks
Power (Daily ✦ Healing): Free Action. *Trigger:* You hit with a primal attack power using this totem. *Effect:* You regain hit points as if you had spent a healing surge.

AYRKASHNA ARMOR

Crafted by an ancient civilization of devas, Ayrkashna Armor grants its full power only to members of that race. Many devas are drawn to seek out the scattered pieces of this armor, delving into their subconscious and journeying to strange locales in an attempt to unearth the secrets of their own past.

LORE

History or Religion DC 10: The city-state of Ayrkashna was once the site from which good devas set out on their quests among the mortals they had sworn to defend. Though the city's location was lost to history long ago, Ayrkashna Armor remains a potent reminder of the power from which the devas sprang.

History or Religion DC 16: When the first angels tied themselves to the mortal realm to become devas, they crafted the Ayrkashna Armor to represent the five principles most important to their kind to bolster them against the evil of their ancient enemies, the rakshasas. When a deva in possession of this item set dies, the armor vanishes to be scattered in nearby locations.

History or Religion DC 21: Devas who come into contact with items from the Ayrkashna Armor often believe that they owned these items in a previous life. By undertaking a quest of self-discovery, they hope to reacquire the rest of the set—seeking out the places where their previous incarnations lived and died.

AYRKASHNA ARMOR ITEMS

Lvl	Name	Price (gp)	Item Slot
10+	Weapon of evil undone	5,000	Weapon
11	Helm of vision unclouded	9,000	Head
12	Crest of vigilance eternal	13,000	Arms
13+	Armor of essence inviolate	17,000	Armor
14	Sash of vitality ceaseless	21,000	Waist

AYRKASHNA ARMOR BENEFITS

Pieces	Benefit
2	You gain resistance to fire equal to the resistance to radiant granted by your Astral Resistance racial trait.
5	You gain the *strength of Ayrkashna* power, described below.

Strength of Ayrkashna Item Set Power

You use the power locked within the items of this set to recover from the minor wounds your enemies inflict upon you.

Daily ✦ Healing
Minor Action   **Personal**
Effect: Until the end of the encounter, you gain regeneration 5 while you're not bloodied.

Armor of Essence Inviolate Level 13+

The strength of your unending spirit surges through this armor, reinforcing your defenses when you call upon it.

| Lvl 13 | +3 | 17,000 gp | Lvl 23 | +5 | 425,000 gp |
| Lvl 18 | +4 | 85,000 gp | Lvl 28 | +6 | 2,125,000 gp |

Armor: Any
Enhancement: AC
Property: When you use your *memory of a thousand lifetimes* racial power, you gain an item bonus to AC equal to the result of the 1d6 roll until the end of your next turn.

Crest of Vigilance Eternal Level 12

The undying courage of the deva race fuels the power of this item to keep you focused in combat.

Item Slot: Arms   13,000 gp
Special: This item can be either bracers, a light shield, or a heavy shield.
Power (Daily): Immediate Interrupt. *Trigger:* An effect dazes or stuns you. *Effect:* You make a saving throw against the triggering effect. On a save, the effect ends.

Helm of Vision Unclouded Level 11

A band of platinum encircles this helmet, sharpening your senses and showing you things unseen.

Item Slot: Head   9,000 gp
Property: You gain a +2 item bonus to Insight checks and Perception checks.
Power (Daily): Free Action. You can see invisible creatures and objects until the end of your next turn.

Sash of Vitality Ceaseless Level 14

This sash's red and white coloring represents harm and healing, granting you increased vitality when you need it most.

Item Slot: Waist   21,000 gp
Property: When you spend a healing surge while you're bloodied, you regain additional hit points equal to your Wisdom modifier.

Weapon of Evil Undone   Level 10+

The power and purity of this weapon lays into your foe and leaves it stricken on the battlefield.

Lvl 10	+2	5,000 gp	Lvl 25	+5	625,000 gp
Lvl 15	+3	25,000 gp	Lvl 30	+6	3,125,000 gp
Lvl 20	+4	125,000 gp			

Weapon: Any
Enhancement: Attack rolls and damage rolls
Critical: +1d6 damage per plus, or +1d12 damage per plus against rakshasas
Property: Divine characters can use this weapon as a holy symbol implement for divine powers.
Property: When you use your *memory of a thousand lifetimes* racial power, you gain an item bonus to your next attack roll before the end of your next turn equal to the result of the 1d6 roll.
Power (Daily): Free Action. *Trigger:* You hit an enemy with this weapon. *Effect:* Until the end of your next turn, that enemy takes 2d10 damage whenever it attacks (3d10 damage if the enemy is a rakshasa).
Level 25 or 30: 3d10 damage (4d10 damage if a rakshasa).

CHAMPION'S FLAME

Even the most beneficent faith must take a hard line against threats. Whether devils undermining the clergy of a good deity, heroes infiltrating dark cults, or the temples of a large city engaging in mundane espionage, the dangers facing the faithful are sought out and eliminated by elite champions of good.

A legendary priest charged with uncovering corruption within his faith first developed the items of the Champion's Flame. They're most often sought out by clerics, but any who defend their faith can make use of these items.

LORE

Religion DC 11: One of the most legendary champions of good was Connor Valis, "The Flame of Bahamut." He earned that epithet when he uncovered the corruption of the previous high priest, whose office he purged with faith and holy fire. Valis singlehandedly broke a half-dozen cults of Vecna, Orcus, and Asmodeus that had been infiltrating Bahamut's temples.

Religion DC 18: At the height of his success, Valis resigned his post and disappeared from public view. Some whisper that he himself became corrupted by so long staring into the dark heart of evil, while others suggest that he came to loathe the violence required by his office.

Religion DC 23: After Valis vanished, the tools of the Champion's Flame were lost for a number of years. However, the items of this set have since appeared within the orders of numerous faiths, all clearly derived from the designs of Valis's original panoply. Some even say that the high priest still lives, seeding his legacy even as he searches for a worthy successor.

CHAMPION'S FLAME ITEMS

Lvl	Name	Price (gp)	Item Slot
13+	Champion's hauberk	17,000	Armor
14+	Weapon of cruel persuasion	21,000	Weapon
15+	Champion's symbol	25,000	Implement
16	Restorative gauntlets	45,000	Hands
17	Pursuer's boots	65,000	Feet

CHAMPION'S FLAME BENEFITS

Pieces	Benefit
2	You gain an item bonus to Insight checks and Intimidate checks equal to the number of items you have from this set.
5	When a creature lies to you and fails a Bluff check against your opposed Insight check, you gain a +1 bonus to attack rolls against that creature until the end of the encounter.

Champion's Hauberk   Level 13+

Fitted to be worn under a priest's robe, this shirt of black mail lets you focus the power of your faith.

| Lvl 13 | +3 | 17,000 gp | Lvl 23 | +5 | 425,000 gp |
| Lvl 18 | +4 | 85,000 gp | Lvl 28 | +6 | 2,125,000 gp |

Armor: Chain, scale
Enhancement: AC
Power (Encounter): Free Action. You expend a use of your *healing word* power to use your Channel Divinity class feature an additional time during this encounter. You can't use the same Channel Divinity power twice in the same encounter.

Champion's Symbol   Level 15+

Inscribed with stylized flames, this holy symbol grants you control over the will of your foes.

| Lvl 15 | +3 | 25,000 gp | Lvl 25 | +5 | 625,000 gp |
| Lvl 20 | +4 | 125,000 gp | Lvl 30 | +6 | 3,125,000 gp |

Implement (Holy Symbol)
Enhancement: Attack rolls and damage rolls
Critical: The target is dominated until the end of your next turn.
Power (Daily ✦ Charm): Free Action. *Trigger:* You hit an enemy with a fire or radiant power and deal damage to it using this holy symbol. *Effect:* That enemy is dominated until the end of your next turn and takes a –5 penalty to Bluff checks until the end of the encounter.

Pursuer's Boots   Level 17

The magic of these fine leather boots sharpens your reflexes and lets you stay close to a fleeing foe.

Item Slot: Feet   65,000 gp
Property: You gain a +1 item bonus to Reflex.
Power (Encounter): Immediate Reaction. *Trigger:* An enemy adjacent to you moves. *Effect:* You shift 3 squares.

Restorative Gauntlets
Level 16

These black leather gloves flare with crimson flames, their potent energy allowing an ally to return to fighting form.

Item Slot: Hands   45,000 gp

Power (Encounter): Standard Action. One willing ally adjacent to you takes damage equal to half his or her level and ends one effect on him or her that a save can end (ally's choice).

Weapon of Cruel Persuasion
Level 14+

The menacing cut of this weapon keeps your foes at bay.

Lvl 14	+3	21,000 gp	Lvl 24	+5	525,000 gp
Lvl 19	+4	105,000 gp	Lvl 29	+6	2,625,000 gp

Weapon: Any melee

Enhancement: Attack rolls and damage rolls

Critical: +1d6 damage per plus

Power (Daily ✦ Fear): Free Action. *Trigger:* You hit an enemy with this weapon. *Effect:* That enemy can't attack you until the end of your next turn.

ELDRITCH PANOPLY

In the dying days of Nerath, the swordmages known as the eldritch knights were said to be the most elite force in the empire. None fought harder to stave off Nerath's fall than this dedicated group of warrior-arcanists. Their legend survives today in the Eldritch Panoply—a set of magic arms, armor, and gear that supported their impressive fighting talents.

Swordmages benefit the most from owning the Eldritch Panoply, but warlocks, other strikers, and some defenders can make use of these powerful relics.

LORE

Arcana or History DC 13: The eldritch knights were a distinguished order of swordmages who fought in the service of Nerath.

Arcana or History DC 20: Items in the Eldritch Panoply have precious metals and other special materials woven or fused into them, allowing the wearer to channel arcane energy for use in combat maneuvers or spellcasting. The pieces of the panoply were scattered across the world when the eldritch knights fell, and they remain highly sought after by swordmages and other arcane warriors.

ELDRITCH PANOPLY ITEMS

Lvl	Name	Price (gp)	Item Slot
14+	Swift-step boots	21,000	Feet
15+	Blade of the eldritch knight	25,000	Weapon
17+	Eldritch medallion	65,000	Neck
18	Rebuking bracers	85,000	Arms
19	Belt of breaching	105,000	Waist
20	Dimensional gauntlets	125,000	Hands

ELDRITCH PANOPLY BENEFITS

Pieces	Benefit
2	When you use a teleportation power, you can use a minor action in the same turn to teleport again a number of squares equal to the number of items you have from this set.
4	When an enemy marked by you triggers your Swordmage Aegis class feature by attacking a target other than you, your next attack against that enemy deals extra damage equal to the number of items you have from this set.
6	You gain a +1 item bonus to AC while you're wearing light armor or no armor.

Belt of Breaching
Level 19

Even as your foe falls, this plain leather belt sends you across the battlefield, refreshed and ready to fight on.

Item Slot: Waist   105,000 gp

Property: When you reduce an enemy to 0 hit points, you can spend a healing surge to regain hit points and then teleport 5 squares.

Blade of the Eldritch Knight
Level 15+

Mystic runes shimmer along the length of this blade. The weapon enables you to attack a distant enemy.

Lvl 15	+3	25,000 gp	Lvl 25	+5	625,000 gp
Lvl 20	+4	125,000 gp	Lvl 30	+6	3,125,000 gp

Weapon: Heavy blade

Enhancement: Attack rolls and damage rolls

Critical: +1d6 damage per plus

Property: When you use a standard action to make a melee attack with this blade, your melee reach increases to 5 for that attack.

Dimensional Gauntlets
Level 20

These light mail gauntlets allow you to lash out at nearby foes.

Item Slot: Hands   125,000 gp

Power (Daily): Minor Action. Until the start of your next turn, your melee reach increases by 1 and you gain threatening reach.

If you're wielding the *blade of the eldritch knight*, your melee reach increases by 2 and you gain threatening reach.

Eldritch Medallion
Level 17+

When you're injured, the power of this intricately engraved medallion lets you slip away from your foes.

Lvl 17	+4	65,000 gp	Lvl 27	+6	1,625,000 gp
Lvl 22	+5	325,000 gp			

Item Slot: Neck

Enhancement: Fortitude, Reflex, and Will

Power (Daily ✦ Teleportation): Immediate Reaction. *Trigger:* An enemy bloodies you. *Effect:* You teleport a number of squares equal to the medallion's enhancement bonus.

Rebuking Bracers — Level 18

These gem-studded bracers flare with blue light as your devastating attack sends an enemy away from you.

Item Slot: Arms   85,000 gp

Property: When you score a critical hit with a melee attack, you can teleport the target 3 squares. If you're wielding the *blade of the eldritch knight*, the target is also dazed until the end of your next turn.

Swift-Step Boots — Level 14+

These nondescript leather boots let you run past any obstacle.

Lvl 14	+3	21,000 gp	Lvl 24	+5	525,000 gp
Lvl 19	+4	105,000 gp	Lvl 29	+6	2,625,000 gp

Item Slot: Feet

Property: When you run, you can teleport the last 2 squares of your move.

    Level 24 or 29: Teleport the last 4 squares of your move plus 1 extra square.

GIFTS FOR THE QUEEN

This item set is spoken of in the legends of humans and eladrin, though its origins remain shrouded in mystery. The tales tell of Isathrain—a queen of old who was kidnapped and taken to the Shadowfell—and of the powerful relics that aided her lover on his dangerous quest to rescue her.

Over long centuries, these Gifts for the Queen have found their way back to the world. Though most useful to sorcerers, they are coveted by other characters who undertake adventures in the Shadowfell or who hunt the undead.

LORE

Arcana or History DC 11: Isathrain, the queen of a powerful border kingdom, became betrothed to Giryon, a sorcerer from a distant land. Days before the wedding, Giryon's enemies struck from the Shadowfell and stole Isathrain away. Giryon and the queen's court responded by turning what had been planned as a wedding reception into a war council. Gifts that had been intended as courtly vestments for the queen were transformed into powerful weapons and implements in preparation for an assault into the Shadowfell.

Arcana or History DC 18: According to legend, Giryon and Isathrain were reunited in the Shadowfell after many trials. However, though the Gifts for the Queen were soon seen in the mortal world, the two lovers never returned to the queen's court. Some say they traveled to the Feywild to escape Giryon's enemies; others claim that the lovers remained in the Shadowfell, searching for other mortals that had been stolen away by the denizens of that dark land.

Arcana or History DC 23: Those who believe that Queen Isathrain still fights for the lives of mortals trapped in the Shadowfell say that a character who assembles a full set of the Gifts for the Queen can seek her there.

GIFTS FOR THE QUEEN ITEMS

Lvl	Name	Price (gp)	Item Slot
13	Bracelet of the radiant storm	17,000	Arms
14	Crown of the brilliant sun	21,000	Head
15+	Queen's staff	25,000	Implement
16	Spark slippers	45,000	Feet
17	Ring of the radiant storm	65,000	Ring

GIFTS FOR THE QUEEN BENEFITS

Pieces	Benefit
2	When you hit with a lightning or radiant attack power, you gain a bonus to damage rolls on that attack equal to the number of items you have from this set.
5	The resistances granted by the *bracelet of the radiant storm* increase to 10. In addition, when you take lightning or radiant damage, you can make a saving throw as an immediate reaction to negate that damage.

Bracelet of the Radiant Storm — Level 13

Seemingly composed of pure energy, this bracelet keeps you safe from energy attacks.

Item Slot: Arms   17,000 gp

Property: You gain resist 5 radiant and resist 5 lightning.

Crown of the Brilliant Sun — Level 14

This crown flares with brilliant energy that you can unleash in place of a lightning attack.

Item Slot: Head   21,000 gp

Property: When you hit an enemy with a lightning power and deal damage to it, you can deal radiant damage instead.

Ring of the Radiant Storm — Level 17

A gem of pure energy set into this platinum ring sharpens your mastery of light and lightning.

Item Slot: Ring   65,000 gp

Property: When you hit an enemy with a lightning or radiant power and deal damage to it, you can roll the damage twice and use either result.

Power (Daily): Free Action. *Trigger:* You attack an enemy with an encounter lightning or radiant power and miss. *Effect:* You regain the use of the power.

    If you've reached at least one milestone today, a daily lightning or radiant power can trigger this power instead.

Spark Slippers — Level 16

When you wear these magically supple glass slippers, foes who step too close to you pay the price.

Item Slot: Feet   45,000 gp

Property: When a creature moves adjacent to you, you can deal lightning damage to that creature equal to your Charisma modifier.

JASON A. ENGLE

CHAPTER 2 | *Item Sets*

Queen's Staff | Level 15+

Your lightning attacks and arcane defenses are more potent while you wield this staff.

Lvl 15	+3	25,000 gp	Lvl 25	+5	625,000 gp
Lvl 20	+4	125,000 gp	Lvl 30	+6	3,125,000 gp

Implement (Staff)
Enhancement: Attack rolls and damage rolls
Critical: +1d6 damage per plus, and if the attack gives you a bonus to AC from your Chaos Burst class feature, that bonus increases to +3.
Property: When you hit an enemy with an arcane lightning power using this staff and deal damage to it, you gain a +2 bonus to your attack rolls against that enemy until the end of your next turn.

OFFERINGS OF CELESTIAN

Once in a dozen generations, a fiery comet called the Far Wanderer traverses the night sky. Legend holds that the Far Wanderer is a sign of salvation and a portent of the watchful eyes of the gods of good. In ages past, a great sorcerer secured a fragment of the Far Wanderer for use in the creation of a set of powerful items—the Offerings of Celestian.

The Offerings of Celestian are best suited for cosmic sorcerers, but any character can make use of the items of this set.

LORE

Arcana, History, or Religion DC 13: When the comet known as the Far Wanderer last traversed the skies centuries ago, it is said that fragments of its essence split off and rained white fire across the land. Adventurers and scholars roamed far and wide in search of these fragments, but only one was ever recovered. Collected by an arcanist and astronomer named Celestian, this strange piece of metal was found to carry potent levels of magical power.

Arcana, History, or Religion DC 20: Believing this magical fragment to be a gift from the good deities, Celestian sought to honor them. After smelting the fragment down, the arcanist spun a thin metallic thread that was stronger than steel. By stitching this thread into fine silk and leather and embedding pieces of it in other materials, he crafted a set of magic items as his offering to the gods.

OFFERINGS OF CELESTIAN ITEMS

Lvl	Name	Price (gp)	Item Slot
17+	Mooncloth robes	65,000	Armor
17+	Staff of the Far Wanderer	65,000	Implement
18+	Star-strewn scarf	85,000	Neck
19	Gloves of the wandering star	105,000	Hands
20	Sun sphere	125,000	Head

OFFERINGS OF CELESTIAN BENEFITS

Pieces	Benefit
2	When you have resistance to cold, psychic, or radiant, that resistance increases by an amount equal to the number of items you have from this set.
4	When you teleport, you can also teleport a number of allies equal to the number of items you have from this set. The allies must begin and end the teleport adjacent to you.

Gloves of the Wandering Star | Level 19

The magic of these supple gloves sends forth a burst of starlight to blind your foes.

Item Slot: Hands   105,000 gp
Property: The range of your ranged attack powers increases by 2 squares.
Power (Daily ✦ Implement, Radiant): Free Action. *Trigger:* You hit or miss an enemy with a ranged attack. *Effect:* Make a secondary attack: Area burst 1 centered on that enemy; Charisma + 4 vs. Fortitude; targets enemies; on a hit, the attack deals 2d8 + Charisma modifier radiant damage, and the target is blinded until the start of your next turn.

Mooncloth Robes | Level 17+

A would-be attacker is shunted away from you by the protective power of these shimmering robes.

Lvl 17	+4	65,000 gp	Lvl 27	+6	1,625,000 gp
Lvl 22	+5	325,000 gp			

Armor: Cloth
Enhancement: AC
Power (Encounter): Free Action. *Trigger:* An enemy adjacent to you misses you with a melee attack. *Effect:* You slide the triggering enemy 1 square.
Special: If you have the Cosmic Magic class feature, you slide the triggering enemy 2 squares.

Staff of the Far Wanderer | Level 17+

When you burn your foes with radiant power, the four white stars set at the head of this staff send you effortlessly across the battlefield.

Lvl 17	+4	65,000 gp	Lvl 27	+6	1,625,000 gp
Lvl 22	+5	325,000 gp			

Implement (Staff)
Enhancement: Attack rolls and damage rolls
Critical: +1d8 radiant damage per plus
Power (Daily ✦ Teleportation): Free Action. *Trigger:* You use a radiant power. *Effect:* You teleport to a space adjacent to any target of the triggering power.
Special: If you have the Cosmic Magic class feature and are in the phase of the stars, you gain a power bonus to AC equal to the staff's enhancement bonus until the start of your next turn.

Star-Strewn Scarf — Level 18+

This shimmering black scarf protects your vision even as it hinders your enemies' attacks.

| Lvl 18 | +4 | 85,000 gp | Lvl 28 | +6 | 2,125,000 gp |
| Lvl 23 | +5 | 425,000 gp | | | |

Item Slot: Neck

Enhancement: Fortitude, Reflex, and Will

Property: You gain a +2 item bonus to saving throws against the blinded condition.

Power (Daily): Minor Action. Until the start of your next turn, you are blinded, and each enemy that can see you takes a -5 penalty to attack rolls for attacks that include you as a target.

Sun Sphere — Level 20

This tiny sphere in the shape of the sun circles your head, burning foes who move too close.

Item Slot: Head   125,000 gp

Property: You gain a +1 item bonus to Will.

Power (Encounter ✦ Fire, Radiant): Minor Action. Each enemy adjacent to you takes fire and radiant damage equal to your Strength modifier.

Special: If you have the Cosmic Magic class feature and are in the phase of the sun, this power affects each enemy within 2 squares of you.

PANOPLY OF THE SHEPHERDS OF GHEST

Ancient legends tell of the floating city of Ghest and of its spectacular destruction. Less well known is the tale of those who survived that destruction, and how a handful of heroes—the shepherds of Ghest—successfully led their people through countless dangers to make new lives. Though Ghest is little more than a memory now, its name lives on in the arms and armor those heroes wore.

This item set is favored by defenders and characters charged with protecting others from harm.

LORE

Arcana or History DC 11: The floating city of Ghest was a magical marvel said to have been built by mighty archmages and demigods. For centuries, Ghest was a center of learning, peace, and prosperity— and then disaster struck. When its magic was shut down by unknown forces, the floating city fell to earth. Through the efforts and sacrifice of Ghest's powerful priests and wizards, a fraction of the city's population survived the cataclysm. However, those survivors were left alone in a hostile land, their leaders and champions dead.

Arcana or History DC 18: From the broken wreckage of their once-mighty city, the exiles salvaged some of the arcane wonders of Ghest to help them survive. A handful of self-appointed "shepherds" wielding weapons and armor of sacred crystal led the people of Ghest through many trials, eventually finding a safe home in new lands. The relics they

had created were passed to new generations of shepherds and eventually spread to the wider world.

Arcana or History DC 23: When the shepherds led their people from the fallen city, they took only the panoply they had created. Fearing that Ghest's powerful magic might fall into the wrong hands, the survivors allowed the city's great arcane engines to destroy themselves and the surrounding ruins. For centuries, sages and adventurers have sought the location of the fallen city, to no avail. However, some believe that the descendants of the first shepherds still guard the ruins, and that characters who successfully collect the panoply can attempt to find them.

PANOPLY OF THE SHEPHERDS OF GHEST ITEMS

Lvl	Name	Price (gp)	Item Slot
12	Shepherd's battle standard	13,000	Wondrous item
13+	Shepherd's arms	17,000	Weapon
14	Helm of able defense	21,000	Head
15+	Crystalline breastplate	25,000	Armor

PANOPLY OF THE SHEPHERDS OF GHEST BENEFITS

Pieces	Benefit
2	Each ally adjacent to you gains resistance to all damage equal to the number of items you have from this set.
4	Each ally adjacent to you gains a +1 item bonus to all defenses.

Crystalline Breastplate — Level 15+

Thumb-sized crystals set into this armor absorb certain types of damage, but at the expense of increased vulnerability.

| Lvl 15 | +3 | 25,000 gp | Lvl 25 | +5 | 625,000 gp |
| Lvl 20 | +4 | 125,000 gp | Lvl 30 | +6 | 3,125,000 gp |

Armor: Leather, hide, chain, scale, plate

Enhancement: AC

Property: After an extended rest, choose one of the following pairs: cold and fire, lightning and thunder, or necrotic and radiant. You gain resist 10 to one of the chosen damage types and gain vulnerable 10 to the other type.

Level 25 or 30: Resist 15, vulnerable 15.

Helm of Able Defense — Level 14

Lifelike crystal eyes in the back of this helmet focus your will and bolster your defenses.

Item Slot: Head   21,000 gp

Property: You gain a +1 item bonus to Will.

Property: At the start of each encounter, you gain a +2 bonus to all defenses until you take damage for the first time after the end of your first turn (not including a surprise round).

Shepherd's Arms — Level 13+

The protective magic of this crystal-bladed weapon hinders a foe's attacks against your allies.

Lvl 13	+3	17,000 gp	Lvl 23	+5	425,000 gp
Lvl 18	+4	85,000 gp	Lvl 28	+6	2,125,000 gp

Weapon: Polearm, spear
Enhancement: Attack rolls and damage rolls
Critical: +1d6 damage per plus
Property: An enemy adjacent to you can't flank your allies.

Shepherd's Battle Standard — Level 12

Set with scores of shining crystals, this banner inspires bravery in your allies and keeps enemies at bay.

Wondrous Item   13,000 gp

Power (Encounter ✦ Zone): Standard Action. When you plant this battle standard in your space or an adjacent square, it creates a zone in a close burst 5. While within the zone, you and your allies gain a +2 power bonus to Will against fear effects. It costs enemies 3 extra squares of movement to enter the zone.

    This effect lasts until the end of the encounter or until the battle standard is removed from the ground. Any character in or adjacent to a battle standard's square can remove it from the ground as a standard action.

RAIMENT OF SHADOWS

Created by a militant order of warlocks, the Raiment of Shadows is a set of battle garb crafted from the hides and scales of extraplanar creatures dwelling in the Shadowfell. Though the warlock order no longer exists, pieces of the raiment still circulate, and many warlocks seek to complete a set for themselves.

LORE

Arcana DC 10: The Blades of Shadow were an elite order of warlocks who strove to overcome the philosophical barriers arising between warlocks of different pacts. The Raiment of Shadows—a set of magic relics crafted with the power of the Shadowfell—was their uniform and was designed to obscure any differences of race, creed, or pact.

Arcana DC 16: Despite their dedication to unifying the eldritch arts, the Blades of Shadow eventually fell. Over time, the divisions between warlocks of different pacts turned to conflict, with smaller groups within the Blades accusing each other of withholding the order's most powerful secrets.

Arcana DC 21: Sages know that the fall of the Blades of Shadow was due to more than mere infighting. The beings and powers to whom the warlocks had sworn fealty feared that the Blades were on the verge of discovering the means to tap directly into the eldritch power that was their lifeblood. By doing so, they would be able to bypass their traditional patrons of the Feywild, the Far Realm, the Nine Hells, and other powers. These patrons forged a short-term alliance that shattered the Blades of Shadow and destroyed its teachings.

MATIAS TAPIA

RAIMENT OF SHADOWS ITEMS

Lvl	Name	Price (gp)	Item Slot
3+	Pact blade	680	Weapon
11	Razordark bracers	9,000	Arms
12+	Darkstrike armor	13,000	Armor
14	Tenebrous mask	21,000	Head
15+	Cloak of burgeoning shadow	25,000	Neck

RAIMENT OF SHADOWS BENEFITS

Pieces	Benefit
2	You gain an item bonus to Stealth checks equal to the number of items you have from this set.
5	When an enemy affected by your Warlock's Curse drops to 0 hit points, you become invisible until the end of your next turn.

Cloak of Burgeoning Shadow — Level 15+

This dark cloak helps obscure your allies when you stay close.

Lvl 15	+3	25,000 gp	Lvl 25	+5	625,000 gp
Lvl 20	+4	125,000 gp	Lvl 30	+6	3,125,000 gp

Item Slot: Neck

Enhancement: Fortitude, Reflex, and Will

Power (Daily): Minor Action. Until the end of the encounter, each ally adjacent to you while you have concealment from your Shadow Walk class feature also has concealment.

Darkstrike Armor — Level 12+

Shadowy runes shift across the surface of this black armor, protecting you when you single out a foe with your attacks.

Lvl 12	+3	13,000 gp	Lvl 22	+5	325,000 gp
Lvl 17	+4	65,000 gp	Lvl 27	+6	1,625,000 gp

Armor: Leather, hide

Enhancement: AC

Property: When you hit an enemy with an attack power, if you gained a bonus to your ranged attack roll against that enemy from your Prime Shot class feature, you gain a +2 bonus to AC against that enemy until the end of your next turn.

Pact Blade — Level 3+

Warlocks favor this wickedly sharp blade.

Lvl 3	+1	680 gp	Lvl 18	+4	85,000 gp
Lvl 8	+2	3,400 gp	Lvl 23	+5	425,000 gp
Lvl 13	+3	17,000 gp	Lvl 28	+6	2,125,000 gp

Weapon: Light blade (usually daggers and sickles)

Enhancement: Attack rolls and damage rolls

Critical: +1d6 damage per plus

Property: This blade functions as a warlock implement, adding its enhancement bonus to attack rolls and damage rolls for warlock powers that use implements.

Property: When a creature you have cursed with your Warlock's Curse makes a melee attack against you, deal damage to the creature equal to the *pact blade's* enhancement bonus.

Special: You do not gain your weapon proficiency bonus to the attack roll when using a *pact blade* as an implement.

Razordark Bracers — Level 11

Lashed with lines of glass-sharp shadow, these bracers allow you to strike at range without letting your guard down.

Item Slot: Arms   9,000 gp

Property: Your warlock at-will ranged attack powers don't provoke opportunity attacks from adjacent enemies.

Tenebrous Mask — Level 14

This thin slip of black silk allows you to target foes shrouded from your sight.

Item Slot: Head   21,000 gp

Power (Encounter): Minor Action. Until the end of your next turn, you ignore the –2 penalty to attack rolls against creatures within 10 squares of you that have concealment.

RAIMENT OF THE WORLD SPIRIT

The Raiment of the World Spirit is a magic item set of ancient design and primal power. To the untrained eye, the items in this set appear as the relics of some primitive tribe—a shield, necklace, mask, and ring fashioned from wood, bark, and other materials of the forest. However, closer scrutiny reveals that the pieces of the raiment are untouched by mortal tools, appearing instead as though they were grown as living objects.

Wardens benefit the most from the Raiment of the World Spirit set, but defenders and classes that grant access to polymorph powers will find these items useful as well.

LORE

Arcana or Nature DC 11: Primal power infuses the Raiment of the World Spirit set, binding it to nature. Spellcasting crafters create each component as part of an ancient ceremony passed down through the ages. Each piece of the set is grown as the offshoot of a living tree—an avatar of the mysterious World Spirit. The tree gives up a portion of its heartwood to serve as a shield, forms the mask from its bark, provides its seed pods for the necklace, and manifests the ring as an extension of its primal spirit.

Arcana or Nature DC 18: The Raiment of the World Spirit was first fashioned in the earliest age of the mortal world. Sensing looming threats that might disrupt the fragile cycle of life and death, shamans, wardens, and druids came together to request aid from the primal power they sought to protect. With these now-ancient rites, the keepers of the old ways continue to craft these relics, both to honor the champions who once carried them and as a boon to new heroes dedicated to defending the natural world.

When an item from the raiment is worn, it releases tiny seeds that take root in the wearer's clothing and sprout vines that weave about that person's body. The tendrils staunch wounds and supplement strength to allow the wearer to keep fighting past the point when others would fall.

Arcana or Nature DC 23: The crafters of the raiment treat its creation as a sacred trust, and they take care to ensure that the relics don't fall into the wrong hands. The raiment is a gift of nature, and that gift can be withdrawn if its wearer abuses its power. Dark tales abound of primal spirits visiting calamity on heroes who misuse the raiment, and of whole lands scourged by blight and disease in response to the power of the World Spirit being betrayed.

RAIMENT OF THE WORLD SPIRIT ITEMS

Lvl	Name	Price (gp)	Item Slot
12	Necklace of fate	13,000	Neck
13	Shield of the World Tree	17,000	Arms
14	Mask of the vengeful spirit	21,000	Head
15	Ring of many forms	25,000	Ring

RAIMENT OF THE WORLD SPIRIT BENEFITS

Pieces	Benefit
2	You gain an item bonus to saving throws against ongoing damage equal to the number of items you have from this set.
4	Your healing surge value increases by 4.

Mask of the Vengeful Spirit — Level 14

This wooden mask takes on the appearance of a snarling beast, causing a selected foe to be overcome by fear.

Item Slot: Head   21,000 gp
Power (Daily ✦ Fear): No Action. When you roll initiative, you mark one enemy you can see, and that enemy grants combat advantage to you until the end of your next turn.

Necklace of Fate — Level 12

This necklace of acorns and woven vines tethers your spirit to nature, helping you shake off the effects of combat.

Lvl 12	+3	13,000 gp	Lvl 22	+5	325,000 gp
Lvl 17	+4	65,000 gp	Lvl 27	+6	1,625,000 gp

Item Slot: Neck
Enhancement: Fortitude, Reflex, and Will
Power (Encounter): No Action. *Trigger:* You make a saving throw at a time other than the end of your turn. *Effect:* You gain an item bonus to that saving throw equal to the necklace's enhancement bonus.

Ring of Many Forms — Level 15

This ring appears as a band of shifting energy, sharpening your combat prowess when you wield the magic of transformation.

Item Slot: Ring   25,000 gp
Property: When you use a polymorph power, you gain a +1 bonus to your next attack roll before the end of your turn.

Shield of the World Tree — Level 13

When you make use of healing energy, the magic within this solid heartwood shield protects your allies.

Item Slot: Arms   17,000 gp
Shield: Any
Property: When you spend a healing surge, each ally adjacent to you gains a +2 shield bonus to AC until the start of your next turn.

REAPER'S ARRAY

Stained with dried blood, etched with the scars of countless battles, and bearing silent witness to uncountable acts of savage slaughter, the Reaper's Array is a panoply befitting only the deadliest warriors. For those who collect the items of this set, death is a constant companion, and foes met on the field of battle are destined to find only pain and ruin.

Barbarians benefit the most from these items, though any character who yearns to be in the thick of combat will find value in this set.

LORE

Arcana or History DC 11: The crafting of a Reaper's Array set is a secret known only to a handful of arcanists, and the dark process involves the incorporation of an enemy's corporeal essence into each piece. Blood quenches the steel pulled white-hot from the forge. The hair of a foe is woven into the cloak's fabric, and its flesh is cured to provide the leather of gauntlets and belt. Most sets are made with the blood and bodies of monsters, but more than a few have been crafted using materials harvested from sentient humanoids.

Arcana or History DC 18: The legendary berserker Ygnir, a dragonborn barbarian warrior whose bloodlust and thirst for vengeance still inspires fear in the tieflings that remember his name, first created the items in the Reaper's Array. When a slave overseer murdered his family as punishment for Ygnir's refusal to kneel, the barbarian vowed to bring down the empire of Bael Turath single-handedly. Breaking his chains, Ygnir killed his master, the overseer, and a dozen guards with his bare hands.

Arcana or History DC 23: With the help of a fellow prisoner schooled in the warlock arts, Ygnir forged the first Reaper's Array set using the steel, blood, skin, and hair of the foes he had slain. With his grim helm and terrifying axe, Ygnir became a legend on ancient battlefields. Unable to slay him themselves, tiefling diabolists were said to have summoned powerful devils to finally end the warrior's threat—an act that some say might have hastened the fall of that race.

REAPER'S ARRAY ITEMS

Lvl	Name	Price (gp)	Item Slot
14+	Crimson cloak	21,000	Neck
15+	Reaper's axe	25,000	Weapon
15	Reaper's helm	25,000	Head
17	Gauntlets of brutality	65,000	Hands
18	Head-taker's belt	85,000	Waist

REAPER'S ARRAY BENEFITS

Pieces	Benefit
2	You gain an item bonus to Intimidate checks equal to the number of items you have from this set.
5	When you bloody an enemy, you can shift 1 square as a free action.

Crimson Cloak — Level 14+

This rich cloak shimmers with a blood-red sheen, defending you against the most potent attacks of your foes.

Lvl 14	+3	21,000 gp	Lvl 24	+5	525,000 gp
Lvl 19	+4	105,000 gp	Lvl 29	+6	2,625,000 gp

Item Slot: Neck
Enhancement: Fortitude, Reflex, and Will
Property: When you take untyped ongoing damage, you make a saving throw against the ongoing damage with an item bonus equal to the cloak's enhancement bonus.

Gauntlets of Brutality — Level 17

Rust and bloodstains mark these leather and steel gauntlets, which strengthen your attacks against fallen foes.

Item Slot: Hands   65,000 gp
Property: When you hit a prone enemy with a melee attack, the attack deals 5 extra damage.

Head-Taker's Belt — Level 18

This plain leather belt is set with skull-shaped steel studs, with a new one appearing each time you slay a foe.

Item Slot: Waist   85,000 gp
Property: You gain a +1 item bonus to Fortitude.
Power (Daily): Free Action. *Trigger:* You reduce an enemy to 0 hit points. *Effect:* You gain temporary hit points equal to your level.

Reaper's Axe — Level 15+

Sporting a wickedly curved blade, this steel axe draws on the death throes of your opponents to fuel its attack.

Lvl 15	+3	25,000 gp	Lvl 25	+5	625,000 gp
Lvl 20	+4	125,000 gp	Lvl 30	+6	3,125,000 gp

Weapon: Axe
Enhancement: Attack rolls and damage rolls
Critical: +1d12 damage per plus
Property: When you reduce an enemy to 0 hit points, you can shift 1 square and make a melee basic attack with this weapon.

Reaper's Helm — Level 15

Badly wounded foes can't elude your attacks while you wear this battle-scarred steel helmet.

Item Slot: Head   25,000 gp
Property: You ignore the –2 penalty to attack rolls against bloodied enemies that have concealment.

REGALIA OF THE GOLDEN GENERAL

The Golden General is an enduring figure of legend, a warlord known as one of the foremost demon slayers who ever lived. Though the fragments of the original arms, armor, and raiment wielded by the Golden General are said to lie in the depths of the Abyss where he met his end, the design of his regalia was well known even before his death. Pieces belonging to this item set can be found throughout the world and beyond it.

Resourceful warlords benefit the most from the items in this set, but all warlords can make use of them.

LORE

History or Religion DC 18: No accurate records of the Golden General's birth or death exist, nor is it known which lands were his true home. The historians of many human cultures claim this legendary warlord as their own, and at least one tale claims that the Golden General became an exarch of Pelor after he met his end. The items of the Regalia of the Golden General are usable by characters of any alignment, but it's said that an evil creature that dons these relics causes them to turn dead black in color.

History or Religion DC 23: Legend says that a hero who owns the full Regalia of the Golden General set can attempt to retrieve the fragments of the original regalia from the abyssal depths. If successful, this hero can bring the fragments to the city of Hestavar in the Astral Sea. Upon presenting the regalia to Pelor, the hero earns the right to become one of the deity's exarchs upon death.

REGALIA OF THE GOLDEN GENERAL ITEMS

Lvl	Name	Price (gp)	Item Slot
12+	Mantle of the Golden General	13,000	Neck
13+	General's weapon	17,000	Weapon
14	Golden crown of battle command	21,000	Head
15	General's belt	25,000	Waist
16	Ring of tactical brilliance	45,000	Ring

REGALIA OF THE GOLDEN GENERAL BENEFITS

Pieces	Benefit
2	You gain a +2 item bonus to Will.
5	When an ally you can see spends an action point, that ally gains a +2 bonus to Will until the end of his or her next turn.

General's Belt — Level 15

The buckle of this leather belt is a golden shield whose magic revitalizes you when you help your allies heal.

Item Slot: Waist   25,000 gp
Property: You gain a +1 item bonus to Fortitude.
Power (Daily ✦ Healing): Free Action. *Trigger:* You use a power that heals an ally. *Effect:* You spend a healing surge.

General's Weapon — Level 13+

A foe lurking out of reach will feel the magical bite of this gilded polearm.

| Lvl 13 | +3 | 17,000 gp | Lvl 23 | +5 | 425,000 gp |
| Lvl 18 | +4 | 85,000 gp | Lvl 28 | +6 | 2,125,000 gp |

Weapon: Polearm

Enhancement: Attack rolls and damage rolls

Critical: +1d6 damage per plus

Power (Encounter): Minor Action. Until the end of your next turn, your melee reach with this weapon increases by 1.

Golden Crown of Battle Command — Level 14

When you direct an ally's attack, the power of this simple circlet of beaten gold helps guide his hand.

Item Slot: Head   21,000 gp

Property: When you use a warlord power to grant a melee basic attack to an ally within your line of sight, that ally gains a +2 bonus to the attack roll and the damage roll.

Mantle of the Golden General — Level 12+

The aid you give an ally is strengthened by the power of this fur-lined amber cloak.

| Lvl 12 | +3 | 13,000 gp | Lvl 22 | +5 | 325,000 gp |
| Lvl 17 | +4 | 65,000 gp | Lvl 27 | +6 | 1,625,000 gp |

Item Slot: Neck

Enhancement: Fortitude, Reflex, and Will

Property: When you use a warlord power to grant a saving throw to an ally, that ally gains a +2 bonus to the saving throw.

Ring of Tactical Brilliance — Level 16

The power of this golden ring helps protect an ally who changes position at your command.

Item Slot: Ring   45,000 gp

Property: When you use a warlord power that lets an ally shift, that ally gains a +1 bonus to all defenses until the end of his or her next turn.

RELICS OF THE FORGOTTEN ONE

Crafted from the remains of a dead god, the Relics of the Forgotten One are a set of potent magic items from the dawn of time. Though clerics, avengers, and paladins most often seek these relics, they can be used by any class.

LORE

History or Religion DC 18: Histories and religious texts record the fates of the deities that fell in the ancient conflict between the gods and the primordials, but a few stories have escaped the scholars' quills. In centuries past, one such fallen deity was found by a mysterious order of arcanists whose members fashioned the remains of the Forgotten One into relics of incredible power.

RELICS OF THE FORGOTTEN ONE ITEMS

Lvl	Name	Price (gp)	Item Slot
13+	Skin of agonies	17,000	Armor
14+	Sword of melancholy	21,000	Weapon
15+	Mantle of regrets	25,000	Neck
16	Mask of tears	45,000	Head
17+	Symbol of the Forgotten One	65,000	Implement
18	Ring of sorrows	85,000	Ring

RELICS OF THE FORGOTTEN ONE BENEFITS

Pieces	Benefit
2	When you spend a healing surge while you are bloodied, you regain additional hit points equal to the number of items you have from this set.
5	While you are bloodied, your melee weapon attacks gain the brutal 1 property (originally described in *Adventurer's Vault*): Reroll any damage die result of 1 until the die shows 2 or higher.

Mantle of Regrets — Level 15+

This somber mantle bestows a crippling weight on your enemies.

| Lvl 15 | +3 | 25,000 gp | Lvl 25 | +5 | 625,000 gp |
| Lvl 20 | +4 | 125,000 gp | Lvl 30 | +6 | 3,125,000 gp |

Item Slot: Neck

Enhancement: Fortitude, Reflex, and Will

Power (Daily ✦ Fear, Psychic): Immediate Reaction. *Trigger:* An enemy hits you with a melee or a close attack. *Effect:* The triggering enemy takes a −2 penalty to attack rolls and saving throws (save ends both). *First Failed Saving Throw:* The enemy also takes ongoing 10 psychic damage (save ends all). *Second Failed Saving Throw:* The enemy is also stunned (save ends all).

Mask of Tears — Level 16

This bone mask captures the image of a grieving figure whose tears become a balm to you or an ally.

Item Slot: Head   45,000 gp

Power (Daily ✦ Healing): Free Action. *Trigger:* An enemy bloodies you with a melee or a close attack. *Effect:* You or an ally adjacent to you can spend a healing surge.

Ring of Sorrows — Level 18

You conjure the manifestation of sorrow from this plain silver ring, tasking your foes with the agony of the Forgotten One's demise.

Item Slot: Ring   85,000 gp

Property: You and each ally you can see gain a +1 bonus to attack rolls with fear powers.

Power (Daily ✦ Conjuration, Teleportation): Standard Action. You conjure a manifestation of sorrow in each of three unoccupied squares within 10 squares of you. The three sorrows remain until the end of your next turn. An enemy that starts its turn adjacent to a sorrow and that deals damage during that turn is teleported to another space adjacent to the sorrow (your choice) and dazed until the end of your next turn.

Skin of Agonies
Level 13+

The likeness of a screaming face is etched across this armor, which protects you from your foes' harshest attacks.

| Lvl 13 | +3 | 17,000 gp | Lvl 23 | +5 | 425,000 gp |
| Lvl 18 | +4 | 85,000 gp | Lvl 28 | +6 | 2,125,000 gp |

Armor: Leather, hide
Enhancement: AC
Property: You automatically succeed on saving throws against untyped ongoing damage.
Power (Daily): Immediate Reaction. *Trigger:* An enemy hits you with an attack that deals ongoing damage. *Effect:* The ongoing damage ends. One enemy adjacent to you takes the ongoing damage instead, and takes a −2 penalty to saving throws against that ongoing damage.

Sword of Melancholy
Level 14+

The magic of this well-notched blade fills your foe with a dread malaise that leaves it open to further attack.

| Lvl 14 | +3 | 21,000 gp | Lvl 24 | +5 | 525,000 gp |
| Lvl 19 | +4 | 105,000 gp | Lvl 29 | +6 | 2,625,000 gp |

Weapon: Heavy blade, light blade
Enhancement: Attack rolls and damage rolls
Critical: +1d8 damage per plus
Power (Daily ✦ Fear): Free Action. *Trigger:* You make a melee attack against an enemy using this weapon and miss. *Effect:* That enemy takes a −2 penalty to all defenses (save ends). *Aftereffect:* If you're adjacent to the enemy when it succeeds on its saving throw against this effect, you can make a melee basic attack using this weapon against that enemy as a free action.

Symbol of the Forgotten One
Level 17+

The divine power of this battered symbol conceals you from your foes.

| Lvl 17 | +4 | 65,000 gp | Lvl 27 | +6 | 1,625,000 gp |
| Lvl 22 | +5 | 325,000 gp | | | |

Implement (Holy Symbol)
Enhancement: Attack rolls and damage rolls
Critical: +1d8 radiant damage per plus
Power (Daily ✦ Illusion): Standard Action. By expending a use of your Channel Divinity class feature, you become invisible to each creature within 5 squares of you until the end of your next turn.

EPIC TIER ITEM SETS

Characters require the most potent arms, armor, implements, and other magic items to face the challenges of the epic levels.

MIRROR OF NESSECAR

The *mirror of Nessecar* was a unique treasure from an ancient fey empire. It held a dimensional portal within its magically silvered glass that was capable of transporting large numbers of creatures to its location. In a great battle between eladrin and fomorians, the mirror was shattered as eladrin soldiers prepared to come through it, and their souls were trapped within its shards.

LORE

History DC 17: Over a thousand years ago, a great battle was fought in the Feywild palace of Nessecar between the eladrin and the fomorians. The great behemoths laid waste to the priceless crystal relics for which the palace was known, slaying many in their wake. However, before the fomorians could triumph, the eladrin lord Ondathian unveiled a magic mirror that had the power to save his people.

History DC 26: The magic of the mirror opened a portal through which eladrin reinforcements prepared to enter the fray. But the fomorian war chief Morgkash shattered the mirror just after the portal opened, trapping the souls of the eladrin within the broken pieces. The fomorians overran the palace, slaying all within it. In an attempt at total victory, Morgkash tried to destroy the shards of the shattered mirror but couldn't affect them. Sensing the power lingering within these fragments, the fomorians scattered the pieces throughout multiple worlds.

History DC 31: Over many generations, fragments of the mirror have been collected and formed into Mirror of Nessecar sets. The items of this set are powered by the essence of the eladrin who died trapped within the mirror, granting potent abilities to the wielder.

MIRROR OF NESSECAR ITEMS

Lvl	Name	Price (gp)	Item Slot
26	Bloodshard ring	1,125,000	Ring
27	Mirrored mask	1,625,000	Head
28	Feyshard wand	2,125,000	Implement
29	Far-step amulet	2,625,000	Neck

MIRROR OF NESSECAR BENEFITS

Pieces	Benefit
2	You gain a +10 item bonus to skill checks made as part of a scrying ritual or a travel ritual.
4	You can perform the Observe Creature and True Portal rituals once per day each with no component cost.

Bloodshard Ring
Level 26

The images of eladrin nobles flicker within this circular shard of mirrored glass, which injures you even as it extends your vitality.

Item Slot: Ring　　1,125,000 gp
Property: You reduce your maximum hit points by 5. In addition, whenever you spend a healing surge, you regain 2 additional hit points.
Power (Daily ✦ Healing): Minor Action. Regain hit points as if you had spent a healing surge.
　　If you've reached at least one milestone today, you also regain a spent healing surge.

Far-Step Amulet — Level 29

This amulet appears to be the frame and shattered glass of a scrying mirror. Its magic focuses your teleportation powers.

Lvl 29   +6   2,625,000 gp

Item Slot: Neck
Enhancement: Fortitude, Reflex, and Will
Property: When you use a teleportation power, the distance you can teleport increases by 3 squares.
Power (Daily ✦ Teleportation): Move Action. You teleport 20 squares.

Feyshard Wand — Level 28

This slender mirrored shard reflects the ghostly image of eladrin battle mages and replenishes the arcane power within you.

Lvl 28   +6   2,125,000 gp

Implement (Wand)
Enhancement: Attack rolls and damage rolls
Critical: +1d6 damage per plus
Power (Daily): Free Action. You gain the use of an arcane encounter power that you or an ally has already used during this encounter. This power is lost if it is not used before the end of the encounter.

Mirrored Mask — Level 27

A jagged-cut mask of silvered glass appears to show images of eladrin scouts even as it protects you from attacks.

Item Slot: Head   1,625,000 gp
Property: You are immune to gaze attacks.
Property: You gain a +2 bonus to all defenses against ranged or area attacks.

POINTS OF THE CONSTELLATION

The Points of the Constellation are relics sacred to an ancient sect of star pact warlocks who worshiped the unknown powers of the Far Realm. Each item is named for a different alien star and allows its wielder to exert influence over mortal minds and bodies.

Though this set is most useful to warlocks, any character seeking a connection to the Far Realm can make use of its items.

LORE

History DC 17: Calling themselves the Constellation, a secret sect of warlocks in the ancient tiefling empire of Bael Turath worshiped the alien powers lurking within the Far Realm. When this practice and the resultant corruption of these star pact warlocks was discovered by the elders of the empire, retribution came swiftly.

Praying to their elder gods, the warlocks called a mighty power to the world, showering the realm with monstrous meteorites. This assault destroyed the warlocks' foes, even as it enchanted a panoply of items with power never meant to be wielded by mortal hands.

History DC 26: The dragonborn of Arkhosia finished the job that the elders of Bael Turath could not, laying siege to the sanctums and fortresses of the star pact warlocks before their taint could spread. In the aftermath, the unholy relics from beyond the stars were scattered far and wide, and they have continued to spread to various cultures over the centuries.

History DC 31: Sages speculate that the power granted by these items is given only to help reunite the items. And many think that the Points of the Constellation items send dark dreams of power to those who seek them, exacting a cost from the user for their power. It's even said that the items not only work to be reunited, but also are trying to return to the Far Realm—at the expense of those who collect them.

POINTS OF THE CONSTELLATION ITEMS

Lvl	Name	Price (gp)	Item Slot
23	Delbanian vambraces	425,000	Arms
24	Boots of Caiphon	525,000	Feet
25+	Rod of Ulban	625,000	Implement
26	Hands of Hadar	1,125,000	Hands
27	Ring of Khirad	1,625,000	Ring

POINTS OF THE CONSTELLATION BENEFITS

Pieces	Benefit
2	Your enemies take a –1 penalty to saving throws against your powers for every two pieces you have of this set.
5	You gain a +3 item bonus to Fortitude or Will. You can change the defense this bonus applies to after a short rest.

Boots of Caiphon — Level 24

A mote of purple light orbits these black leather boots, burning you even as it lets you move freely across the battlefield.

Item Slot: Feet   525,000 gp
Property: You gain a +2 item bonus to Reflex.
Power (At-Will): Minor Action. You shift your speed and take damage equal to two times the number of squares you shifted.

Delbanian Vambraces — Level 23

These ice-white bracers let you pass unseen, but their power freezes you to the marrow if left unchecked.

Item Slot: Arms   425,000 gp
Power (At-Will ✦ Cold, Illusion): Free Action. *Trigger:* You score a critical hit using a cold power or reduce an enemy to 0 hit points using a cold power. *Effect:* You become invisible until the end of your next turn. *Sustain Free:* The invisibility persists, but each time you sustain it, you take 5 cold damage that can't be reduced or prevented in any way.

Hands of Hadar — Level 26

Fire opals speckle these black gloves, which focus the power of your Warlock's Curse.

Item Slot: Hands   1,125,000 gp
Property: When you hit an enemy that is granting combat advantage to you and deal your Warlock's Curse extra damage to it, you deal an additional 2d6 extra damage.

Ring of Khirad — Level 27

This ring is set with a clouded astral diamond whose gleam reveals things seen and unseen.

Item Slot: Ring   1,625,000 gp

Property: You gain a +5 item bonus to Insight checks and Perception checks, and you can see invisible creatures and objects.

Power (Daily): Minor Action. Until the end of your next turn, creatures within 5 squares of you lose invisibility, gain a +2 power bonus to all defenses against illusion attacks, and take a -2 penalty to attack rolls with illusion powers. In addition, an affected creature that makes an attack is slowed until the end of its next turn. *Sustain Minor:* The effects persist.

    If you've reached at least one milestone today, your allies are unaffected by this power.

Rod of Ulban — Level 25+

The mind of your foe is made more susceptible to attack by the power of this blue-white crystal rod.

| Lvl 25 | +5 | 625,000 gp | Lvl 30 | +6 | 3,125,000 gp |

Implement (Rod)

Enhancement: Attack rolls and damage rolls

Critical: +1d12 psychic damage per plus

Property: While an enemy is affected by your Warlock's Curse, it gains vulnerable 10 psychic.

Relics of Creation

Each piece in the item set known as the Relics of Creation is the epitome of wondrous design and manufacture. Unflawed and unspoiled, these items demonstrate a quality of perfection that suggests creation by divine hands. Their otherworldly construction incorporates fabulous substances such as solidified flame, wood trimmed from heavenly trees, and elements now unknown in the mortal realm. It's said that the bearer of these relics is filled with the light of creation, whose energy fuels potent powers that sear enemies with divine judgment.

Invokers derive the most benefit from items of the Relics of Creation, but any divine character can make use of this set.

Lore

Arcana or Religion DC 17: In the cataclysmic war between the gods and the primordials for control of the world, each deity fashioned a powerful relic to bestow on the greatest of their chosen followers. Few relics survived the war, however; most were lost alongside their wielders in the dread battles that swept across the world and through the planes.

Arcana or Religion DC 26: The Relics of Creation found across the world today contain only six items, each holding a sliver of divine power from the deity who fashioned the original item. Though long centuries have driven rifts between these deities, and while their servants sometimes wage war with one another, it's said that a hero who brings the relics

together can remind the gods of the strength and righteousness of their once-common cause.

Arcana or Religion DC 31: The six Relics of Creation appear consistently in the contemporary historical record. However, fragments of older histories speak of other items that were once part of the set—some named for deities whose presence is still felt within the world, and others whose names and powers are drawn from gods long dead.

RELICS OF CREATION ITEMS

Lvl	Name	Price (gp)	Item Slot
24	Ioun's flame	525,000	Head
25	Zehir's gloves	625,000	Hands
27	Avandra's ring	1,625,000	Ring
28	Bane's collar	2,125,000	Neck
29	Pelor's scepter	2,625,000	Implement
30	Vecna's puzzle box	3,125,000	Wondrous item

RELICS OF CREATION BENEFITS

Pieces	Benefit
2	You gain a bonus to Arcana, History, and Religion checks equal to the number of items you have from this set.
4	When you hit an elemental creature with an invoker attack power, the attack deals 1d8 extra damage (2d8 extra damage if you have all six pieces of the set).
6	When you use a divine blast or burst attack power, you can affect 3 additional squares, each of which must be adjacent to the power's normal area.

Avandra's Ring — Level 27

This loose-fitting ring grants you the power to ignore effects that would constrain you.

Item Slot: Ring   1,625,000 gp

Property: You ignore difficult terrain.

Power (Daily): Immediate Interrupt. *Trigger:* An effect immobilizes, restrains, or slows you. *Effect:* The triggering effect ends.

    If you've reached at least one milestone today, you also gain a +5 power bonus to saving throws against immobilizing, restraining, or slowing effects until the end of the encounter.

Bane's Collar — Level 28

Your mind shrugs off the control of others while you wear this bright steel collar, but an ally pays the price.

| Lvl 28 | +6 | 2,125,000 gp |

Item Slot: Neck

Enhancement: Fortitude, Reflex, and Will

Property: When you make a saving throw against a charm or fear effect, you can roll twice and use either result.

Power (Daily): Immediate Interrupt. *Trigger:* An enemy targets you with an charm or fear attack. *Effect:* An ally within 10 squares of you becomes the target of the attack.

Ioun's Flame — Level 24

A flickering violet flame darts about your head, granting you knowledge and flaring to life at your command.

Item Slot: Head   525,000 gp

Property: You gain a +2 item bonus to Will.

Property: You gain a +8 item bonus to knowledge and monster knowledge checks.

Power (At-Will): Minor Action. You set *Ioun's flame* to shed bright light 10 squares in all directions, dim light 5 squares in all directions, or no light.

Pelor's Scepter — Level 29

This golden rod is capped with a sunburst that adds potency to your radiant powers.

Lvl 29   +6   2,625,000 gp

Implement (Rod)

Enhancement: Attack rolls and damage rolls

Critical: +1d8 radiant damage per plus

Property: Divine characters can use this rod as a holy symbol implement for divine powers.

Property: When you hit an enemy with a divine radiant power using this rod, you can reroll any damage die that shows a 1. Against elemental creatures, you can reroll any damage die that shows a 1 or a 2.

Vecna's Puzzle Box — Level 30

Great secrets are revealed to you by your possession of this fist-sized brass puzzle box.

Wondrous Item   3,125,000 gp

Property: You can perform the Loremaster's Bargain and Voice of Fate rituals as if you had mastered them.

Property: Divination rituals you perform have no component cost. When you perform a divination ritual that requires a Religion check, you can make an Arcana check instead.

Zehir's Gloves — Level 25

These black gloves bolster your powers to bypass your enemy's most potent defenses.

Item Slot: Hands   625,000 gp

Power (Daily): Free Action. *Trigger:* You hit an enemy with an attack power. *Effect:* The attack ignores the enemy's immunities and resistances.

HOWARD LYON

Time Wizard's Tools

Spellcasters manipulate the material world and the energy of the planes with ease, but time remains notoriously resistant to magical control. Few wizards and other arcanists specialize in deconstructing time and enchanting objects to manipulate its boundaries, and for good reason. Such characters often suffer the strange effects of this potent magic, disappearing into unseen realms or even coming face to face with themselves for short periods.

The item set known as the Time Wizard's Tools is legendary among arcanists who tinker with time, although the power of its items can be utilized by any character.

Lore

Arcana DC 28: The Time Wizard's Tools are powerful relics scattered across the present-day world from both the future and the past. The various items and their mysterious creators were said to have appeared in widespread locations throughout the world's history. However, given the nature of the tools, it's speculated that these relics might be the product of a single mage traveling through time with the aid of spells or items beyond the scope of mortal magic.

Arcana DC 33: Shaping time is perhaps the most daunting of the arcanist's tasks. Although the power of the Time Wizard's Tools is formidable, certain items in the set also exact a cost from the wielder as part of the unstable nature of their magic.

TIME WIZARD'S TOOLS ITEMS

Lvl	Name	Price (gp)	Item Slot
27	Time-jumping boots	1,625,000	Feet
28	Crown of stuttered time	2,125,000	Head
29	Ring of free time	2,625,000	Ring
30	Staff of time	3,125,000	Implement

TIME WIZARD'S TOOLS BENEFITS

Pieces	Benefit
2	You gain an item bonus to initiative checks equal to twice the number of items you have from this set.
4	You gain one additional use per day of magic item daily powers. Each use of a magic item daily power must come from a different magic item.

Crown of Stuttered Time — Level 28

This copper crown is set with numerous tiger's-eye gems that slip out of phase with the world even as you do.

Item Slot: Head   2,125,000 gp
Property: You gain a +2 item bonus to Will.
Power (Daily ✦ Psychic): Minor Action. Until the end of your next turn, you become insubstantial and gain phasing. *Sustain Minor:* The effect persists, and you take 10 psychic damage that can't be reduced or prevented in any way.

Ring of Free Time — Level 29

You slip the bonds of time while you wear this simple silver band, allowing you to act faster than your foes.

Item Slot: Ring   2,625,000 gp
Property: You gain resist 5 to all damage.
Power (Encounter): Free Action. You can take an additional minor action on your turn.
    If you've reached at least one milestone today, you can use this power at will once per round.

Staff of Time — Level 30

This elegant birch staff is capped with a brilliant diamond whose power can cast foes out of time.

Lvl 30   +6   3,125,000 gp
Implement (Staff)
Enhancement: Attack rolls and damage rolls
Critical: +1d12 damage per plus, and you can use the staff's power without expending its daily use, even if the power's daily use has been expended.
Power (Daily): Free Action. *Trigger:* You hit an enemy with an attack using this staff. *Effect:* That enemy disappears until the start of your next turn. Until that time, it can't take actions and can't be targeted. The enemy reappears in the space it last occupied or in the nearest unoccupied space of its choice.

Time-Jumping Boots — Level 27

For a brief moment, these nondescript boots allow you to step out of time and evade your enemies' attention.

Item Slot: Feet   1,625,000 gp
Property: You gain a +2 item bonus to Reflex.
Power (Daily): Move Action. You disappear until the start of your next turn. Until that time, you don't have line of sight or line of effect to any creature, and creatures don't have line of sight or line of effect to you. You also ignore negative ongoing effects, take no damage, and don't need to make saving throws (though you can still do so if you wish). You can take one standard action and two minor actions. At the start of your next turn, you reappear in the space you last occupied or in the nearest unoccupied space of your choice, and you are dazed until the end of your turn.

Tinkerer's Inventions

A legendary adventuring artificer known only as the Tinkerer originally crafted this set of magical and mechanical items. These Tinkerer's Inventions were a triumph of magic and craft, though the pieces have an unpredictable quality consistent with their creator's work.

Lore

Arcana or History DC 16: Artificers favor the light armor that grants them easier use of their numerous tools, but one artificer and inventor wasn't content with cloth and leather. Considered mad by his peers, the legendary crafter known only as the Tinkerer created a set of items designed to provide unique benefits for his chosen profession.

Arcana or History DC 24: After the Tinkerer's death, his assistants divided the pieces of his masterpiece set among themselves, and so his inventions were copied and spread. Relatively few artificers have access to a whole set of Tinkerer's Inventions, however, and many artificers actively seek set items lost by adventuring artificers in years past.

TINKERER'S INVENTIONS ITEMS

Lvl	Name	Price (gp)	Item Slot
21	Artificer's belt	225,000	Waist
22	Gauntlets of magical interchange	325,000	Hands
23+	Tinkersuit	425,000	Armor
24	Propellant boots	525,000	Feet

TINKERER'S INVENTIONS BENEFITS

Pieces	Benefit
2	When you use your Healing Infusion class feature to allow an ally to regain hit points, that ally regains additional hit points equal to the number of items you have from this set.
4	You gain the *tinkerer's disjunction* power, described below.

ERIC L. WILLIAMS

Tinkerer's Disjunction — Item Set Power

With but a thought, you disable an effect that threatens the area where you stand.

At-Will
Standard Action   Personal
Effect: One zone you're within or one conjuration you're adjacent to ends. In addition, all its effects end, including those that normally last until a target saves.

Artificer's Belt — Level 21

This multipocketed belt charges your healing infusions with potent power.

Item Slot: Waist   225,000 gp
Property: You can use your Healing Infusion class feature twice in the same round.
Power (Daily): Free Action. *Trigger:* You use your Healing Infusion class feature on an ally. *Effect:* The ally gains one additional use of a magic item daily power.

Gauntlets of Magical Interchange — Level 22

These gauntlets magically extrude a variety of useful tools and allow you to restore the magic of other items in the thick of combat.

Item Slot: Hands   325,000 gp
Power (At-Will ✦ Polymorph): Free Action. The gauntlets transform to incorporate the form and function of any mundane handheld tool, as found in the equipment list of the *Player's Handbook* and other supplements. The tool must be one normally usable by a creature of your size.
Power (Daily): Minor Action. You use your Arcane Empowerment class feature on an item held by you or an adjacent ally.

Propellant Boots — Level 24

These boots contain a self-replenishing alchemical fuel that launches you through the air.

Item Slot: Feet   525,000 gp
Power (Daily): Minor Action. You gain a fly speed equal to your speed + 2 until the end of the encounter.

Tinkersuit — Level 23+

This armor's magic lets you store an abundance of gear, even as it generates a defensive field in response to attack.

Lvl 23   +5   425,000 gp   Lvl 28   +6   2,125,000 gp
Armor: Leather
Enhancement: AC
Property: The many pockets of this armor can hold up to 2,000 pounds in weight or 200 cubic feet in volume, but items stored in the armor add only 1 pound to its weight. Each item stored within one of the armor's pockets can weigh no more than 20 pounds.
Drawing an item from a *tinkersuit* is a minor action.
Power (Encounter): Immediate Interrupt. *Trigger:* An enemy hits you with a melee or a ranged attack. *Effect:* You gain a +2 power bonus to all defenses until the end of your next turn.

GROUP SETS

Some item sets are designed to be borne not by a single character, but by the members of an entire party. When a party collects the items of a group item set, the set benefits are determined by the number of allies who possess items from the set. Each character wearing or wielding an item from the set qualifies for the set benefits.

ARMORY OF THE UNVANQUISHED

The Armory of the Unvanquished is a set of favored items used by the Unvanquished Company, a band of legendary adventurers who were active centuries ago. Stories of their adventures are a mainstay in travelers' camps and in front of tavern fires, inspiring would-be heroes of each new generation. Many of those who would follow in the footsteps of the Unvanquished seek out the items of the armory, though not all who find them are stalwart enough to wield them.

LORE

History DC 11: Two hundred years ago, the heroes of the Unvanquished Company made a glorious name for themselves. Adventurers, mercenaries, and ne'er-do-wells, the Unvanquished plundered tombs, foiled deadly plots, and engaged in legendary exploits from one side of the globe to the other.

History DC 18: How the Unvanquished met their end is uncertain. Some say they fell fighting demons in the Abyss, while others suggest they quit this world to seek new adventures in realms beyond. Regardless, the weapons and implements with which they made their reputation survived them, and these items soon spread to all corners of the world.

History DC 23: When claimed by a new master, each item in the Armory of the Unvanquished manifests a tattoo on the wielder's body—a storm for the *tempest staff*, a dragon for the *dragontooth blade*, a scorpion for the *scorpion tail blade*, a lion for the *lion's heart hammer*, and a snake for the *serpent's kiss bow*. As more items in the set are claimed, each tattoo grows larger and more resplendent—the legend of the Unvanquished Company manifesting in a new generation.

ARMORY OF THE UNVANQUISHED ITEMS

Lvl	Name	Price (gp)	Item Slot
13+	Scorpion tail blade	17,000	Weapon
14+	Dragontooth blade	21,000	Weapon
15+	Tempest staff	25,000	Implement
17+	Lion's heart hammer	65,000	Weapon
18+	Serpent's kiss bow	85,000	Weapon

ARMORY OF THE UNVANQUISHED BENEFITS

Wielders*	Benefit
2	When you spend a healing surge, each ally who wields an item from this set and can see you gains temporary hit points equal to his or her item's enhancement bonus (ally's choice of items, if more than one).
4	When two or more allies who wield items from this set flank the same target, each flanker can score a critical hit against the flanked target on a roll of 19-20.

*The number of allies who wield one or more items from the set.

Dragontooth Blade — Level 14+

The fury of dragon fire powers your attacks with this bone-handled blade.

Lvl 14	+3	21,000 gp	Lvl 24	+5	525,000 gp
Lvl 19	+4	105,000 gp	Lvl 29	+6	2,625,000 gp

Weapon: Heavy blade

Enhancement: Attack rolls and damage rolls

Critical: Each enemy marked by you takes ongoing fire damage equal to 3 + the blade's enhancement bonus (save ends).

Property: While you're bloodied, you can score a critical hit with this weapon on a roll of 19-20.

Power (Daily ✦ Fire): Free Action. *Trigger:* You score a critical hit. *Effect:* Make an attack: Close burst 1; targets enemies; Strength vs. Reflex; on a hit, the attack deals 2d6 extra fire damage and the target takes ongoing 10 fire damage (save ends).

Lion's Heart Hammer — Level 17+

When you wield this hammer, an attack that bloodies you sends your foes stumbling back in fear.

Lvl 17	+4	65,000 gp	Lvl 27	+6	1,625,000 gp
Lvl 22	+5	325,000 gp			

Weapon: Hammer

Enhancement: Attack rolls and damage rolls

Critical: +1d6 damage per plus, and each ally within 5 squares of you gains 10 temporary hit points. *Level 22 or 27:* 15 temporary hit points.

Property: Divine characters can use this hammer as a holy symbol implement for divine powers.

Power (Daily ✦ Fear): Immediate Reaction. *Trigger:* An enemy bloodies you. *Effect:* Make an attack: Close burst 5; targets enemies; Wisdom vs. Will; on a hit, the target is pushed 1 square and takes a −2 penalty to attack rolls until the end of your next turn.

Scorpion Tail Blade — Level 13+

This magically envenomed blade leaves foes at your mercy.

Lvl 13	+3	17,000 gp	Lvl 23	+5	425,000 gp
Lvl 18	+4	85,000 gp	Lvl 28	+6	2,125,000 gp

Weapon: Light blade

Enhancement: Attack rolls and damage rolls

Critical: The target is slowed and takes ongoing 10 poison damage (save ends both).

Level 18: Ongoing 12 poison damage.

Level 23: Ongoing 15 poison damage.

Level 28: Ongoing 17 poison damage.

Power (Daily ✦ Poison): Free Action. *Trigger:* You hit an enemy with a melee attack power using this weapon. *Effect:* That enemy is immobilized (save ends). *Aftereffect:* The enemy is slowed (save ends).

Serpent's Kiss Bow — Level 18+

This bow bestows a kiss of toxic venom to its attacks, making your foes more vulnerable.

Lvl 18	+4	85,000 gp	Lvl 28	+6	2,125,000 gp
Lvl 23	+5	425,000 gp			

Weapon: Bow

Enhancement: Attack rolls and damage rolls

Critical: +1d6 poison damage per plus, and the target can't shift until the end of your next turn.

Property: This weapon has the brutal 1 property (originally described in *Adventurer's Vault*): Reroll any damage die result of 1 until the die shows 2 or higher.

Power (Encounter ✦ Poison): Free Action. *Trigger:* You hit an enemy with a ranged attack power using this weapon. *Effect:* That enemy grants combat advantage to your allies until the start of your next turn.

Tempest Staff — Level 15+

The power of the storm drives your foe back and blasts enemies pressing your allies.

Lvl 15	+3	25,000 gp	Lvl 25	+5	625,000 gp
Lvl 20	+4	125,000 gp	Lvl 30	+6	3,125,000 gp

Implement (Staff)

Enhancement: Attack rolls and damage rolls

Critical: +1d6 lightning damage per plus against each enemy adjacent to you, and each other enemy within 3 squares of you takes thunder damage equal to half the amount of lightning damage.

Power (Daily ✦ Lightning, Thunder): Immediate Reaction. *Trigger:* An enemy hits you with a melee or close attack. *Effect:* The triggering enemy takes 2d6 lightning damage and is pushed 1 square. Each enemy adjacent to an ally you can see takes 1d6 thunder damage.

LUCIO PARRILLO

CAELYNNVALA'S BOONS

Drow, eladrin, and elves are all children of the Fey-wild, and many maintain hope that these estranged races might one day unite in a culture of peace. Caelynnvala's Boons are useful to eladrin, elf, or drow characters of any class, but their potency is greatest when a group of wielders includes members of all three races.

LORE

History DC 14: Caelynnvala is a legendary archfey—one of the godlike spirit-avatars of the Fey-wild. An immortal eladrin noble, she hopes to end the ages-long conflict between drow, eladrin, and elf. To this end, she crafted a set of magic items whose powers define the bond she seeks to forge between the sibling races. Caelynnvala's Boons have a habit of finding their way into the hands of champions who embody the ideal of reconciliation and peace.

CAELYNNVALA'S BOONS ITEMS

Lvl	Name	Price (gp)	Item Slot
7+	Scarf of reconciliation	2,600	Neck
8	Bowstring of accuracy	3,400	Wondrous item
9	Darkfire gloves	4,200	Hands
10	Circlet of revelations	5,000	Head
11	Feystride boots	9,000	Feet

CAELYNNVALA'S BOONS BENEFITS

Wielders*	Benefit
3	Each drow, eladrin, or elf who wears or wields an item from this set gains a +1 item bonus to speed.
5	When a drow, eladrin, or elf who wears or wields an item from this set uses a racial power, any other drow, eladrin, or elf who wears or wields an item from this set gains a +1 bonus to all defenses until the end of the next turn of the creature using the racial power.

*The number of allies who wear or wield one or more items from the set.

Bowstring of Accuracy — Level 8

This silver cord makes your bow strike true when you fight alongside allies of your sibling races.

Wondrous Item   3,400 gp
Property: When you use your *elven accuracy* racial power while you have a drow or eladrin ally within 10 squares of you, you gain a +2 bonus to the reroll.
Power (Encounter): Free Action. *Trigger:* You miss with an attack using the bow this bowstring is fitted to while you have an elf ally within 10 squares of you. *Effect:* You expend your *fey step* racial power or your use of the Lolthtouched racial trait and reroll the attack roll.

Circlet of Revelations — Level 10

This slender mithral circlet grants you the unique abilities of your sibling-race allies.

Item Slot: Head   5,000 gp
Property: While you have an eladrin ally within 10 squares of you, you gain a +5 item bonus to saving throws against charm effects.
Property: While you have an elf ally within 10 squares of you, each ally within 5 squares of you gains a +1 item bonus to Perception checks.
Property: While you have a drow ally within 10 squares of you, you gain darkvision.

Darkfire Gloves — Level 9

These leather gloves are imbued with the darkfire power of the drow.

Item Slot: Hands   4,200 gp
Property: When you hit an enemy with your *darkfire* racial power, your eladrin and elf allies gain a +2 bonus to damage rolls against that enemy until the end of your next turn.
Power (Encounter): Minor Action. While you have a drow ally within 10 squares of you, you can expend your *elven accuracy* racial power or your *fey step* racial power to use the *darkfire* racial power (FORGOTTEN REALMS *Player's Guide*, page 8).

Feystride Boots — Level 11

These supple gray boots help you close the distance across the battlefield.

Item Slot: Feet   9,000 gp
Property: While you have a drow or elf ally within 10 squares of you, the range of your *fey step* racial power increases by 2 squares.
Power (Encounter ✦ Teleportation): Move Action. While you have an eladrin ally within 10 squares of you, you can expend your *elven accuracy* racial power or your use of the Lolthtouched racial trait to teleport 5 squares.

Scarf of Reconciliation — Level 7+

The shifting colors of this scarf reflect a common legacy, granting you power in the presence of your sibling-race allies.

Lvl 7	+2	2,600 gp	Lvl 22	+5	325,000 gp
Lvl 12	+3	13,000 gp	Lvl 27	+6	1,625,000 gp
Lvl 17	+4	65,000 gp			

Item Slot: Neck
Enhancement: Fortitude, Reflex, and Will
Property: While you have a drow ally within 10 squares of you, you gain a +2 item bonus to Intimidate checks and Stealth checks.
Property: While you have an eladrin ally within 10 squares of you, you gain a +2 item bonus to Arcana checks and History checks.
Property: While you have an elf ally within 10 squares of you, you gain a +2 item bonus to Perception checks and Nature checks.

FORTUNE STONES

Nonmagical fortune stones were first created by devotees of Avandra, god of luck. As simple talismans and tokens of faith, the stones provided common folk with a reminder that Avandra's favor must be earned by deed, not bought by magical means such as divination and prophecy. However, for followers who best exemplified her ideals, Avandra bestowed the power of luck into magic Fortune Stones. This set of relics regularly comes into the possession of adventurers and others who epitomize the tenet that luck favors the bold.

LORE

History or Religion DC 10: From dealing cards to casting dice to reading entrails, divination has long had a powerful allure. The monk Askar Rei was a follower of Avandra and an expert on the subject, though most of his effort centered on exposing false soothsayers and charlatans. Askar labored to impress upon others that fortune must be earned, not made by magical means.

History or Religion DC 16: In an effort to undermine the prevalence of false prophets and diviners among his people, Askar Rei and his followers fashioned and distributed symbolic tokens called fortune stones. These stones had no magical power, but were meant to provide the bearer with a focus for his or her actions in the present, thus increasing the chance of Avandra's favor for the future.

History or Religion DC 21: Askar Rei has long since passed on into history, but it's said that his piety inspired Avandra to create sets of magic Fortune Stones for him and his closest followers. These enchanted stones provide a boon of luck to their bearers—a sign of the gifts of fortune that Avandra bestows on the boldest and bravest.

FORTUNE STONES ITEMS

Lvl	Name	Price (gp)	Item Slot
12	Stone of earth	13,000	Wondrous item
12	Stone of flame	13,000	Wondrous item
12	Stone of light	13,000	Wondrous item
12	Stone of shadow	13,000	Wondrous item
12	Stone of spirit	13,000	Wondrous item
12	Stone of storms	13,000	Wondrous item
12	Stone of wind	13,000	Wondrous item

FORTUNE STONES BENEFITS

Wielders*	Benefit
2	Each ally who bears a *fortune stone* gains an item bonus to the reroll granted by the stone's power equal to the number of allies who bear one or more items from this set.
5	Each ally who bears a *fortune stone* gains a +2 item bonus to initiative and a +1 item bonus to saving throws.

*The number of allies who bear one or more items from the set.

Stone of Earth	Level 12

This smooth brown agate is warm to the touch, and the arcane symbol for "earth" adorns it.

Wondrous Item   13,000 gp
Power (Daily): Free Action. *Trigger:* You miss an enemy with a melee weapon attack. *Effect:* Reroll the attack roll.

Stone of Flame	Level 12

The arcane symbol for "fire" smolders within this chunk of red-tinged anthracite.

Wondrous Item   13,000 gp
Power (Daily): Free Action. *Trigger:* You miss an enemy with a fire attack power. *Effect:* Reroll the attack roll.

Stone of Light	Level 12

This oval bead of white quartz has the arcane symbol for "radiance" on its surface.

Wondrous Item   13,000 gp
Power (Daily): Free Action. *Trigger:* You miss an enemy with a radiant attack power. *Effect:* Reroll the attack roll.

Stone of Shadow	Level 12

The arcane symbol for "darkness" etched across this nugget of glossy hematite seems to absorb all light.

Wondrous Item   13,000 gp
Power (Daily): Free Action. *Trigger:* You miss an enemy with a necrotic attack power. *Effect:* Reroll the attack roll.

Stone of Spirit	Level 12

This swirled teardrop of lapis is scribed with the arcane symbol for "spirit."

Wondrous Item   13,000 gp
Power (Daily): Free Action. *Trigger:* You miss an enemy with a psychic attack power. *Effect:* Reroll the attack roll.

Stone of Storms	Level 12

The arcane symbols for "thunder" and "lightning" are scribed on opposite faces of this piece of rough obsidian.

Wondrous Item   13,000 gp
Power (Daily): Free Action. *Trigger:* You miss an enemy with a lightning or thunder attack power. *Effect:* Reroll the attack roll.

Stone of Wind	Level 12

This pale blue zircon is scribed with the arcane symbol for "air."

Wondrous Item   13,000 gp
Power (Daily): Free Action. *Trigger:* You miss an enemy with a ranged weapon attack. *Effect:* Reroll the attack roll.

HEIRLOOMS OF MAZGORAX

At the height of the dragonborn empire of Arkhosia, the legendary artisan Mazgorax first crafted the items of this set as gifts for his children. When his children were slain by a ruthless copper dragon, the Heirlooms of Mazgorax were scattered and sold, spreading the names of their bearers far and wide. Characters who claim these relics can gain some measure of the heroic nature of the dragonborn whom the items were named for.

LORE

History DC 14: The famed dragonborn crafter Mazgorax created the items of this set. In ancient Arkhosia, he and his family were members of the nobility, famed for their dedication and service to the empire. Each item in the Heirlooms of Mazgorax set is named for one of his children, all legendary dragonborn heroes whose success owed itself in no small part to their father's craft.

History DC 19: Long before the fall of Arkhosia, the House of Mazgorax was brought down by the machinations of a copper dragon named Salingrazi. Seeking power over the dragonborn, Salingrazi struck at the empire's strongest families in an effort to sow fear and unrest. Some say the copper dragon still lives, and that he harbors a particular enmity for individuals who wear the heirlooms.

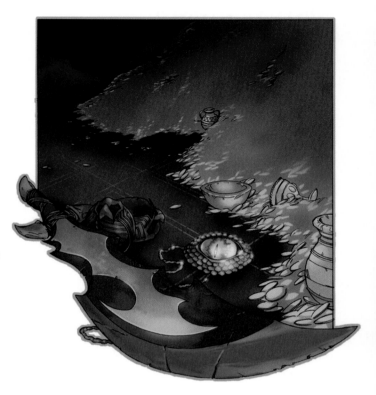

HEIRLOOMS OF MAZGORAX ITEMS

Lvl	Name	Price (gp)	Item Slot
7+	Symbol of Gajz	2,600	Implement
8+	Rovikar's weapon	3,400	Weapon
9+	Keicha's amulet	4,200	Neck
10	Skaivani's anklets	5,000	Feet
11	Matrakk's lenses	9,000	Head

HEIRLOOMS OF MAZGORAX BENEFITS

Wielders*	Benefit
2	Each ally who wears or wields an item from this set gains an item bonus to Athletics, Bluff, Diplomacy, Endurance, and Religion checks equal to the number of allies who wear or wield one or more items from this set.
4	When a creature who wears or wields an item from this set would spend a healing surge, that creature can allow an ally who wears or wields an item from this set to spend a healing surge instead.

*The number of allies who wear or wield one or more items from the set.

Keicha's Amulet
Level 9+

The gemstone scales of this amulet grant you resistance against your enemies' harshest attacks.

Lvl 9	+2	4,200 gp	Lvl 24	+5	525,000 gp
Lvl 14	+3	21,000 gp	Lvl 29	+6	2,625,000 gp
Lvl 19	+4	105,000 gp			

Item Slot: Neck

Enhancement: Fortitude, Reflex, and Will

Property: After an extended rest, choose acid, cold, fire, lightning, or poison. You gain resist 5 to the chosen damage type.
Level 14 or 19: Resist 10.
Level 24 or 29: Resist 15.

Power (Encounter): Minor Action. You grant an ally within 5 squares of you the resistance from the amulet (losing that resistance yourself) until the end of the encounter.

Matrakk's Lenses
Level 11

Lenses of perfect crystal hone your vision and protect you from attacks that target your sight.

Item Slot: Head   9,000 gp

Property: You gain an item bonus to Perception checks equal to the number of allies who wear or wield one or more items from this set.

Property: You gain a +1 bonus to all defenses against gaze attacks and a +5 bonus to saving throws against effects that cause the blinded condition.

KALMAN ANDRASOFSZKY

Rovikar's Weapon — Level 8+

Inlaid with a delicate pattern in gold leaf, this weapon allows you to channel your own strength to an ally in battle.

Lvl 8	+2	3,400 gp	Lvl 23	+5	425,000 gp
Lvl 13	+3	17,000 gp	Lvl 28	+6	2,125,000 gp
Lvl 18	+4	85,000 gp			

Weapon: Any
Enhancement: Attack rolls and damage rolls
Critical: +1d6 damage per plus
Power (Daily): Immediate Interrupt. *Trigger:* An ally you can see makes an attack roll. *Effect:* The triggering ally gains a bonus to the attack roll and damage roll equal to your Charisma modifier or your Strength modifier. If the triggering ally wears or wields one or more items from this set, the bonus increases by 2.

Skaivani's Anklets — Level 10

These anklets of leather and copper let you surge across the battlefield.

Item Slot: Feet   5,000 gp
Power (Encounter): Free Action. You gain a +2 power bonus to speed until the end of your next turn. While this bonus is in effect, when you make an Acrobatics check or Athletics check and roll 5 or lower, you can re-roll the check.

Symbol of Gajz — Level 7+

The runes that adorn this holy symbol allow your healing powers to grant resistance to your allies.

Lvl 7	+2	2,600 gp	Lvl 22	+5	325,000 gp
Lvl 12	+3	13,000 gp	Lvl 27	+6	1,625,000 gp
Lvl 17	+4	65,000 gp			

Implement (Holy Symbol)
Enhancement: Attack rolls and damage rolls
Critical: +1d6 damage per plus
Property: When you use a healing power through this holy symbol, choose acid, cold, fire, lightning, or poison. Each ally affected by the power gains resist 5 to the chosen damage type until the end of your next turn. If the ally is a dragonborn, the resistance increases by 5. If the ally wears or wields one or more items from this set, the resistance increases by 5.
Level 17 or 22: Each ally gains resist 10.
Level 27: Each ally gains resist 15.

MAZGORAX'S CHILDREN

Armed with the items crafted by their father, the scions of Mazgorax lived lives of great fame and glory.

Gajz: A devout worshiper of Bahamut, Gajz spent many years as the head of a temple in a desolate province at the northernmost reaches of the empire. Upon his father's death, he returned to take care of the estate. He surprised Salingrazi's assassins with his elusiveness, managing to stay one step ahead of them for over a year before disappearing. Most think he was killed, but rumors suggest that he left Arkhosia to proselytize in a distant land.

Keicha: With her noble bearing and elegant manner, Keicha served as a courtier in the Arkhosian capital. However, she also played a more secret role as bodyguard to the emperor's youngest daughter. She received many honors over the years and was a trusted member of the court. When a caravan transporting the emperor's daughter was ambushed, Keicha died defending her.

Matrakk: With a preference for art and literature, Matrakk lived a less conspicuous life than his siblings. His sculptures and frescoes adorned the noble's houses of the Arkhosian capital and smaller settlements. For his political power and connections, Matrakk was targeted by Salingrazi's wrath.

Rovikar: A fierce and inspiring warrior, Rovikar the Relentless led Arkhosian troops to the far reaches of the empire, conquering several new provinces in the name of the dragonborn. His standard—a golden basilisk—flew above countless fortresses of the frontier. It's said he was killed by Salingrazi's assassins while putting down a rebellion in one of his conquered territories.

Skaivani: A skilled athlete, Skaivani the Swift was a star attraction at Arkhosia's formalized sporting competitions. Eventually feeling a greater sense of duty toward the empire, she became a scout and soldier in the imperial army. However, the life of a soldier was not to her liking, and Skaivani resigned when asked to undertake missions she thought were contrary to her own moral code. Before she could make her way home, she was attacked by Salingrazi's servants. Though Skaivani ran the race of her life in an attempt to escape, she was caught and killed.

Rings of the Akarot

In dark barrows and within ancient mausoleums lie the six members of the Akarot. An archaic league of powerful lords, these tyrants once ruled the Six Cities of the Akarot, all long lost to time. The six rulers were said to have wielded potent power—power now locked within the rings that bear their names.

Lore

History DC 16: The original Rings of the Akarot were the royal signets of the mysterious rulers of six ancient city-states. Though the Akarot lords wielded considerable power, each fell over the course of long years, and their cities were lost to the ravages of time. Countless adventurers have since claimed the rings that bear their names, just as many have sought out their tombs. However, the resting places of the Akarot lords remain a mystery.

THE SIX CITIES

Each of the six cities of the Akarot was ruled by a powerful tyrant.

Hrumdar's Horn: Minotaurs living in the militaristic society of Hrumdar's Horn followed the savage minotaur lord for which their city was named. Built within a mountain spire, Hrumdar's Horn threatened a wide spread of human lands below it. Dark legends spoke of prisoners being set loose in vast labyrinths within the mountain, hunted for sport by bloodthirsty minotaur warriors.

Laga, the Smoking Waste: Built atop an ancient mineshaft, the city of Laga was perpetually shrouded in dust and smoke. Its ruler, Farndak, was a dwarf known for his greed and tyranny who enslaved the folk of nearby settlements to labor in his deadly mines.

Urual, Defier of Tides: Great walls imbued with powerful magic protected the coastal city of Urual from the pounding tides of the sea. Rom Kala the Sealord ruled here, and his privateers scoured the nearby seas for the wealth that filled his coffers. A great tide is said to have destroyed his city after his death.

Synnith Ordan: The eladrin city of Synnith Ordan was as beautiful as all the other settlements of that race. Its ruler, Haggaron, was the most secretive of the Akarot. This fomorian king manipulated the eladrin of the city with the powerful magic of his ring.

The Empty City: A twisting maze of stone and shadow, the Empty City contains gates that reach numerous places in the Shadowfell, including the dark port of Gloomwrought. Kartan, lord of the Empty City, was a shadar-kai who surrounded himself with nihilistic allies and soulless walking dead.

Aurunia Palace: A sprawling, opulent estate housing thousands of servants and slaves, Aurunia Palace was known for its wealth and the narcissism of its master, Teros the Perfect. This human lord believed that his beauty was eternal, and he was said to go to any lengths to retain his youth and vigor.

History DC 24: While they still lived, the Akarot lords made a secret pact, taking undead form to outlive the mortal races they ruled over. The six swore that when the old empires had fallen and left civilized lands undefended, they would rise once more, banding together to conquer and control the world.

History DC 29: The six cities of the Akarot were once seven cities. Whatever disaster befell the seventh was potent enough to wipe its record and its ruler from the annals of history. *Sherazuul's black band* is said to be the name of a seventh Ring of the Akarot lost in the cataclysm. Its history and power remain unknown.

RINGS OF THE AKAROT ITEMS

Lvl	Name	Price (gp)	Item Slot
21	Rom Kala's tideshield ring	225,000	Ring
22	Farndak's glittering ring	325,000	Ring
23	Ring of Hrumdar's halls	425,000	Ring
24	Golden ring of Teros	525,000	Ring
25	Haggaron's ring of control	625,000	Ring
26	Kartan's void ring	1,125,000	Ring

RINGS OF THE AKAROT BENEFITS

Wielders*	Benefit
2	Each ally wearing a ring from this set can communicate telepathically with the others, regardless of distance.
5	Each ally wearing a ring from this set gains the *blood of the Akarot* power, described below.
6	Each ally wearing a ring from this set gains the *voice of the Akarot* power, described below.

*The number of allies wearing one or more items from the set.

Blood of the Akarot   Item Set Power

You tap into your reserves to restore your vitality and that of your allies.

At-Will ✦ Healing
Free Action   **Ranged** sight
Trigger: You spend a healing surge
Target: Each ally wearing a ring from this set
Effect: Each target regains 10 hit points.
Special: Using this power does not provoke opportunity attacks.

Voice of the Akarot   Item Set Power

Channeling the power of your allies' will, you command your enemies to stop attacking, though each ally is momentarily disoriented.

Daily ✦ Charm
Standard Action   **Close** burst 5
Target: Each enemy in burst
Attack: +30 vs. Will
Hit: The target cannot attack (save ends).
Effect: Each ally wearing a ring from this set is dazed until the end of your next turn.

Farndak's Glittering Ring — Level 22

This gem-studded ring lets you draw vigor from your allies even as it pulls a foe into your grasp.

Item Slot: Ring   325,000 gp

Property: When you spend a healing surge, you regain additional hit points equal to the number of allies who wear one or more rings from this set.

   If you've reached at least one milestone today, double the number of additional hit points you regain from this property.

Power (Daily ✦ Charm): Minor Action. Choose one enemy within 5 squares of you. You pull the chosen enemy 5 squares and mark it (save ends).

Haggaron's Ring of Control — Level 25

This beautiful fey-styled ring sharpens your ability to soothe others and grants you control of their minds in combat.

Item Slot: Ring   625,000 gp

Property: You gain a +4 item bonus to Bluff checks and Diplomacy checks (+6 against fey creatures).

Power (Daily ✦ Charm): Minor Action. You choose a stunned enemy within 10 squares of you. The chosen enemy is dominated until the end of its next turn. The stunned condition is temporarily negated while the enemy is dominated, though its duration continues. If its duration allows, the stunned condition resumes once the dominated condition ends.

   If you've reached at least one milestone today, you can also use this power against enemies that are dazed, with the dazed condition temporarily negated as above.

Golden Ring of Teros — Level 24

The magic of this golden ring protects your physical perfection from harm.

Item Slot: Ring   525,000 gp

Property: You gain a +2 item bonus to AC and Fortitude while you're not bloodied.

Power (Daily): Immediate Reaction. *Trigger:* An enemy hits you while you're at maximum hit points. *Effect:* You gain a +5 power bonus to your next attack roll against the triggering enemy.

   If you've reached at least one milestone today, you also gain resist 5 to all damage until you become bloodied or until the end of the encounter.

Kartan's Void Ring — Level 26

The shifting form of this black ring allows you to draw off your enemies' vigor when one of their nearby allies drops.

Item Slot: Ring   1,125,000 gp

Power (At-Will ✦ Healing, Necrotic): Free Action. *Trigger:* You reduce an enemy within 20 squares of you to 0 hit points. *Effect:* Make an attack: Area burst 2 centered on that enemy; targets enemies; +29 vs. Fortitude; on a hit, the attack deals 1d10 necrotic damage, and you regain 2 hit points. This attack doesn't provoke opportunity attacks.

   If you've reached at least one milestone today, the attack deals 2d8 necrotic damage, and you regain 4 hit points.

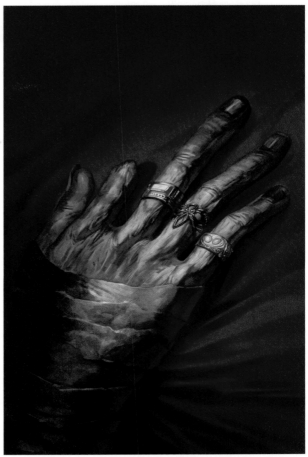

Ring of Hrumdar's Halls — Level 23

This solid iron band grants you insight into the hazards of the underground and lets you drive your foes before you.

Item Slot: Ring   425,000 gp

Property: You gain a +5 item bonus to Dungeoneering checks.

Power (Daily): Minor Action. Make an attack: Ranged 30; targets one creature you can see; +26 vs. Will; on a hit, you slide the target 10 squares.

   If you've reached at least one milestone today, you can use this power one additional time against the same target on your next turn.

Rom Kala's Tideshield Ring — Level 21

The magic of this blue-green ring protects you from the denizens of the sea and lets you stand fast in combat.

Item Slot: Ring   225,000 gp

Property: You gain resist 10 to all damage on attacks from aquatic creatures or water creatures.

Power (Daily): Immediate Interrupt. *Trigger:* You or an ally within 10 squares of you is pulled, pushed, or slid. *Effect:* You or your ally ignores the forced movement.

   If you've reached at least one milestone today, each ally within 10 squares of you reduces the distance of any forced movement by 1 square until the end of the encounter. If the ally has a ring from this set, this effect lasts until the ally takes an extended rest.

MATIAS TAPIA

APPENDIX: ITEM TABLES

The following section contains master tables for all of the items in *Adventurer's Vault 2*. Items are sorted by level and by type. Each level header indicates the price of items of that level, with the exception of ammunition, for which a price is given separately. Each entry includes the page number on which the item can be found. Weapons and armor entries include information about the category of each item. Items that are parts of sets are marked with an asterisk (*).

LEVEL 1 ITEMS   360 GP
WEAPONS

Challenge-seeking weapon +1	Any melee	17
Earth-wrought hammer +1	Hammer	17

WONDROUS ITEMS

Blessed book	76
Ioun's parchment	76
Woundstitch powder	78

WONDROUS LAIR ITEMS

Sun globe	82

LEVEL 2 ITEMS   520 GP
ARMOR

Armor of aegis expansion +1	Cloth, leather	6
*Armor of dwarven vigor +1	Chain, scale, plate	94
Coruscating armor +1	Scale, plate	7
Hero's armor +1	Chain	9
Rat killer's coat +1	Cloth, leather	11
*Shadow hunter hide +1	Hide	106

WEAPONS

Aftershock weapon +1	Any	15
Duelist's bow +1	Bow	17
Entrapping weapon +1	Bow, crossbow	17
Farbond spellblade +1	Hvy blade, lt blade	18
Guardian's call +1	Any melee	19
Harmonic songblade +1	Hvy blade, lt blade	19
*Hungry spear +1	Spear	98
Quicksilver blade +1	Lt blade	21
Rebounding weapon +1	Any ranged	21
Supremely vicious weapon +1	Any	24
Totemic spear +1	Spear	24
Totemic warclub +1	Mace	25
Whistling songbow +1	Bow, crossbow	25

AMMUNITION (25 GP PER ITEM)

Onslaught arrow +1	27

HOLY SYMBOLS

Ioun-blessed symbol +1	28
Symbol of divine force +1	29
Symbol of the first spirits +1	31

ORBS

Orb of resilient tenacity +1	33

RODS

Rod of burgeoning memory +1	34
Rod of the fickle servant +1	36

STAFFS

Staff of divinity +1	38
Staff of knives +1	39
Verdant staff +1	40

TOTEMS

Roaring bear totem +1	45
Totem of thunder's keeper +1	47

ARMS SLOT

*Bracers of enforced regret	96
Preservation shield	55

FEET SLOT

*Boots of jaunting	102

NECK SLOT

Amulet of double fortune +1	63
Amulet of elegy +1	63
Badge of the berserker +1	64
Lifesaving brooch +1	67

WONDROUS ITEMS

*Prison of Salzacas	109

WONDROUS LAIR ITEMS

Door of alarm	80
Window of escape	83

LEVEL 3 ITEMS   680 GP
ARMOR

Armor of sudden recovery +1	Cloth, leather	6
Holy adversary's armor +1	Cloth	9
Moon armor +1	Chain	10
Nightmare ward armor +1	Leather, hide	11
Predator's hide +1	Hide	11
Robe of avoidance +1	Cloth	11
Runic armor +1	Any	12
Sanguine vestments +1	Cloth	12
Spiked jacket +1	Leather, hide	13
Wall armor +1	Any	14
Warmage's uniform +1	Cloth, leather	14

WEAPONS

Aegis blade +1	Hvy blade, lt blade	15
Alfsair spear +1	Spear	15
Aura killer weapon +1	Any melee	15
Blood fury weapon +1	Axe, hvy blade	17
Flesh grinder +1	Axe, hvy blade, polearm	18
Frost fury waraxe +1	Axe	18
Great hunger weapon +1	Any melee	18
Guardian's brand +1	Any melee	19
*Pact blade +1	Lt blade	108, 120
*Rhythm blade +1	Lt blade	97
Songbow of vanishment +1	Bow, crossbow	23
Targeting weapon +1	Bow, crossbow	24

AMMUNITION (30 GP PER ITEM)

Attention-stealing bullet +1	26
Firestorm arrow +1	26
Freezing arrow +1	27
Lightning arrow +1	27

Spider bolt +1	27
Surprise bullet +1	28

HOLY SYMBOLS

Symbol of brawn +1	29

ORBS

Orb of supplementary force +1	34

RODS

Hexer's rod +1	34
Rod of divinity +1	35

STAFFS

Staff of resilience +1	39
Staff of sleep and charm +1	39

TOTEMS

Boar's charge totem +1	43
*Death fang totem +1	106
Fell beast totem +1	44

ARMS SLOT

Executioner's bracers	54
Lunia's bracelet	55

FEET SLOT

*Swiftpad boots	100

HANDS SLOT

*Gauntlets of arcane might	102

NECK SLOT

Amulet of warding +1	63
*Baffling cape +1	96
Necklace of keys +1	67
*Spidersilk mantle +1	109

WONDROUS LAIR ITEMS

Cask of liquid gold	79
Window of deception	83

TATTOOS

Demonskin tattoo	87
Escape tattoo	84

LEVEL 4 ITEMS   840 GP

ARMOR

Dazzling plate +1	Plate	7
Genasi soul armor +1	Leather, hide	8
Lifefont armor +1	Hide	10
Parchment armor +1	Cloth, leather	11
Scale of the serpent +1	Scale	12
Serpentine armor +1	Scale	12
Time link armor +1	Chain	14

WEAPONS

Avalanche hammer +1	Hammer	15
Echoing songblade +1	Hvy blade, lt blade	17
*Harmony blade +1	Hvy blade	97
Impaler's pick +1	Pick	20
Intensifying weapon +1	Any	20
Master's blade +1	Hvy blade, lt blade	20
Maw of the guardian +1	Any melee	20
Screaming bow +1	Bow	21
Stormbiter warblade +1	Hvy blade, lt blade	23
*Weapon of arcane bonds +1	Hvy blade, lt blade	102
Weapon of oaths fulfilled +1	Any melee	25

HOLY SYMBOLS

Symbol of the holy nimbus +1	32

RODS

Darkspiral rod +1	34
Rod of the pactbinder +1	36

STAFFS

Staff of iron infusion +1	38

TOMES

Tome of striking lightning +1	42

TOTEMS

Wildfire totem +1	47
Winterwood totem +1	48

WANDS

Diamond wand +1	49
Master's wand of eyes of the vestige +1	50
Master's wand of illusory ambush +1	50
Master's wand of misdirected mark +1	51
Master's wand of phantom bolt +1	51
Master's wand of spiteful glamor +1	51
Master's wand of vicious mockery +1	51
Shielding wand +1	52
Wand of allure +1	52

ARMS SLOT

Shield of silver light	55

FEET SLOT

Riding boots	58

HANDS SLOT

*Blackleaf gloves	108
*Claw gloves	106
Gauntlets of blood	58
Poison gloves	61

NECK SLOT

*Cloak of the lion's mane +1	98
Frostwolf pelt +1	66
Lucky charm +1	67
Periapt of proof against poison +1	67

WONDROUS ITEMS

Bed of rapid rest	79
Silence-warded room	82

TATTOOS

Fireheart tattoo	87
Tattoo of arcane blood	84

LEVEL 5 ITEMS   1,000 GP

ARMOR

Healer's armor +1	Hide, chain	9
*Shockweave armor +1	Cloth, leather	98
Supporting armor +1	Scale, plate	13

WEAPONS

*Rousing hammer +1	Hammer	95
Runic weapon +1	Any	21
*Thane blood weapon +1	Any melee	100
*Weapon of great opportunity +1	Any melee	96

AMMUNITION (50 GP PER ITEM)

Bending bullet +1	26

HOLY SYMBOLS

Symbol of daring +1	29

STAFFS

Staff of wind +1		40

TOTEMS

Bloodhunter totem +1		43

FEET SLOT

Boots of rapid motion		57
*Panther slippers		106

HANDS SLOT

Gloves of grace		59
*Gloves of recovery		96
*Lion's claw gauntlets		98
*Resplendent gloves		104

HEAD SLOT

*Circlet of arcane extension		102

WONDROUS ITEMS

Deepfarer's pouch		76

TATTOOS

Tattoo of vengeance		85

LEVEL 6 ITEMS   1,800 GP

ARMOR

Gambler's suit +2	Leather	8

WEAPONS

Challenge-seeking weapon +2	Any melee	17
Earth-wrought hammer +2	Hammer	17

ARMS SLOT

*Warded vambraces		102

FEET SLOT

Boots of bounding		57
*Resplendent boots		104

HANDS SLOT

*Alchemy gloves		97

HEAD SLOT

*Cat's-eye headband		106
*Helm of exemplary defense		95
*Savage mask		107

WAIST SLOT

Baldric of time		74

TATTOOS

Distracting tattoo		87
Tattoo of bonded defense		85
Tattoo of bonded escape		85

LEVEL 7 ITEMS   2,600 GP

ARMOR

Armor of aegis expansion +2	Cloth, leather	6
*Armor of dwarven vigor +2	Chain, scale, plate	94
Bastion armor +2	Scale, plate	6
Coruscating armor +2	Scale, plate	7
Death's brink armor +2	Scale, plate	7
Hero's armor +2	Chain	9
Marauder's armor +2	Leather, hide	10
*Radiant temple uniform +2	Cloth	103
Rat killer's coat +2	Cloth, leather	11
Shadow hound armor +2	Hide	12
*Shadow hunter hide +2	Hide	106
*Shipboard armor +2	Leather	101

WEAPONS

Aftershock weapon +2	Any	15
Boltshard crossbow +2	Crossbow	17
Duelist's bow +2	Bow	17
Entrapping weapon +2	Bow, crossbow	17
Farbond spellblade +2	Hvy blade, lt blade	18
Guardian's call +2	Any melee	19
Harmonic songblade +2	Hvy blade, lt blade	19
*Hungry spear +2	Spear	98
*Infighting blade +2	Lt blade, axe (one-handed only)	101
Quicksilver blade +2	Lt blade	21
Rebounding weapon +2	Any ranged	21
Supremely vicious weapon +2	Any	24
Totemic spear +2	Spear	24
Totemic warclub +2	Mace	25
Whistling songbow +2	Bow, crossbow	25

AMMUNITION (100 GP PER ITEM)

Onslaught arrow +2		27

HOLY SYMBOLS

Ioun-blessed symbol +2		28
Symbol of divine force +2		29
Symbol of foe turning +2		30
*Symbol of Gajz +2		135
Symbol of shared healing +2		30
Symbol of the first spirits +2		31
Symbol of vigor +2		32

ORBS

Orb of resilient tenacity +2		33

RODS

Rod of burgeoning memory +2		34
Rod of stolen starlt +2		35
Rod of the fickle servant +2		36

STAFFS

Moonsilver staff +2		38
Staff of divinity +2		38
Staff of knives +2		39
Summoner's staff +2		40
Verdant staff +2		40

TOMES

Dispelling tome +2		41

TOTEMS

Earthfall totem +2		44
Roaring bear totem +2		45
Totem of thunder's keeper +2		47

FEET SLOT

Boots of surging speed		57

HANDS SLOT

*Dual-threat gauntlets		95
Feinting gloves		58

HEAD SLOT

Philosopher's crown		62
*Resplendent circlet		104

NECK SLOT

Amulet of double fortune +2		63
Amulet of elegy +2		63

Badge of the berserker +2		64
*Cloak of the crimson path +2		107
*Deep-pocket cloak +2		97
Lifesaving brooch +2		67
*Scarf of reconciliation +2		132
Talisman of terror +2		69

WAIST SLOT

Belt of nourishment		74

WONDROUS ITEMS

Map of unseen lands		77

TATTOOS

Long-battle tattoo		86
Quick-step tattoo		85
Tattoo of the unlucky		86
Tattoo of the wolverine		85

CONSUMABLES (100 GP PER ITEM)

Clay of creation		87

Level 8 Items   3,400 gp

ARMOR

Armor of sudden recovery +2	Cloth, leather	6
Holy adversary's armor +2	Cloth	9
Kemstone armor +2	Scale, plate	9
Moon armor +2	Chain	10
Nightmare ward armor +2	Leather, hide	11
Predator's hide +2	Hide	11
Robe of avoidance +2	Cloth	11
Runic armor +2	Any	12
Sanguine vestments +2	Cloth	12
Slime armor +2	Scale, plate	13
Spiderweb robes +2	Cloth	13
Spiked jacket +2	Leather, hide	13
Wall armor +2	Any	14
Warmage's uniform +2	Cloth, leather	14

WEAPONS

Aegis blade +2	Hvy blade, lt blade	15
Alfsair spear +2	Spear	15
Aura killer weapon +2	Any melee	15
*Blade of vengeance +2	Hvy blade, lt blade	103
Blood fury weapon +2	Axe, hvy blade	17
*Blood harvest blade +2	Lt blade	107
Flesh grinder +2	Axe, hvy blade, polearm	18
Frost fury waraxe +2	Axe	18
Great hunger weapon +2	Any melee	18
Guardian's brand +2	Any melee	19
Hideous weapon +2	Flail, hammer, pick	19
*Pact blade +2	Lt blade	108, 120
Ravenclaw warblade +2	Hvy blade	21
*Rhythm blade +2	Lt blade	97
*Rovikar's weapon +2	Any	135
Songbow of vanishment +2	Bow, crossbow	23
Targeting weapon +2	Bow, crossbow	24
Unforgettable cudgel +2	Mace	25
*Warding blade +2	Lt blade	103
Writhing vine weapon +2	Any melee	25

AMMUNITION (125 GP PER ITEM)

Attention-stealing bullet +2		26
Bolt of clumsiness +2		26
Bolt of transit +2		26
Dispelling bolt +2		26
Firestorm arrow +2		26
Freezing arrow +2		27
Lightning arrow +2		27
Space-shifting bolt +2		27
Spider bolt +2		27
Summoning bullet +2		28
Surprise bullet +2		28

HOLY SYMBOLS

Symbol of brawn +2		29
Symbol of the champion's code +2		31
Symbol of the radiant flame +2		32

ORBS

Orb of supplementary force +2		34

RODS

Hexer's rod +2		34
Rod of divinity +2		35

STAFFS

Staff of resilience +2		39
Staff of sleep and charm +2		39
Staff of the faithful arcanist +2		40

TOMES

Gossamer tome +2		42

TOTEMS

Boar's charge totem +2		43
*Death fang totem +2		106
Fell beast totem +2		44
Iron bear totem +2		44
Totem of the satyr's dance +2		47
Vengeful spirit totem +2		47

ARMS SLOT

Charm bracelet		53
*Hammer shield		95
*Pincer shield		96

FEET SLOT

*Boarding boots		101
Greaves of fortunate falling		58

HANDS SLOT

Grizzly gauntlets		59

HEAD SLOT

Fey-blessed circlet		62
*Gadgeteer's goggles		97
Sacred mask		63

NECK SLOT

Amulet of warding +2		63
*Baffling cape +2		96
Courtier's cape +2		66
Necklace of keys +2		67
Orc's-eye amulet +2		67
*Pavise charm +2		101
*Resplendent cloak +2		104
*Spidersilk mantle +2		109

WAIST SLOT

Potion bandolier		75
Stonewall belt		75

WONDROUS ITEMS

*Bowstring of accuracy	132
Vagabond's die	78
Whistle of warnng	78

WONDROUS LAIR ITEMS

Alchemist's workshop	79
Shiftstone	81

TATTOOS

Curse eye tattoo	87
Fleet hero tattoo	87
Ironheart tattoo	86
Strongheart tattoo	86
Tattoo of the escape artist	84

CONSUMABLES (125 GP PER ITEM)

Silver sand	88
Vortex stone	88

LEVEL 9 ITEMS   4,200 GP

ARMOR

Dazzling plate +2	Plate	7
Demonscale +2	Scale	8
Genasi soul armor +2	Leather, hide	8
Lifefont armor +2	Hide	10
Magnetic armor +2	Scale, plate	10
Parchment armor +2	Cloth, leather	11
Scale of the serpent +2	Scale	12
Serpentine armor +2	Scale	12
Time link armor +2	Chain	14

WEAPONS

Avalanche hammer +2	Hammer	15
Blood drinker +2	Axe, hvy blade	16
Echoing songblade +2	Hvy blade, lt blade	17
*Harmony blade +2	Hvy blade	97
Impaler's pick +2	Pick	20
Incisive dagger +2	Dagger	20
Intensifying weapon +2	Any	20
*Kamesti crossbow +2	Crossbow	101
Master's blade +2	Hvy blade, lt blade	20
Maw of the guardian +2	Any melee	20
Screaming bow +2	Bow	21
Songbow of lullabies +2	Bow, crossbow	22
Stormbiter warblade +2	Hvy blade, lt blade	23
*Weapon of arcane bonds +2	Hvy blade, lt blade	102
Weapon of oaths fulfilled +2	Any melee	25

AMMUNITION (160 GP PER ITEM)

Arrow of revelation +2	26
Forbiddance bolt +2	26

HOLY SYMBOLS

Symbol of fire and fury +2	30
Symbol of the holy nimbus +2	32
Symbol of unified defense +2	32

RODS

Darkspiral rod +2	34
Rod of obliterating wrath +2	35
Rod of the pactbinder +2	36

STAFFS

Staff of iron infusion +2	38

TOMES

Tome of crushing force +2	42
Tome of striking lightning +2	42

TOTEMS

Panther totem +2	45
Totem of the ravenous beast +2	47
*Totem of the severed eye +2	107
Totem of winter's scorn +2	47
Wildfire totem +2	47
Winterwood totem +2	48

WANDS

Diamond wand +2	49
Hawthorn wand +2	49
Master's wand of eyes of the vestige +2	50
Master's wand of illusory ambush +2	50
Master's wand of misdirected mark +2	51
Master's wand of phantom bolt +2	51
Master's wand of spiteful glamor +2	51
Master's wand of vicious mockery +2	51
Shielding wand +2	52
Wand of allure +2	52

ARMS SLOT

*Bracers of zeal +2	103
Keeper's shield	54

HANDS SLOT

*Darkfire gloves	132
Illusionist's gloves	60

HEAD SLOT

Bear headdress	61

NECK SLOT

Amulet of vigor +2	63
*Cloak of the lion's mane +2	98
Cloak of translocation +2	66
Frostwolf pelt +2	66
*Keicha's amulet +2	134
Lucky charm +2	67
Medic's amulet +2	67
Periapt of proof against poison +2	67
*Shadowdancer's cloak +2	105

WAIST SLOT

Belt of fragile guard	74
*Clear-blood baldric	95

WONDROUS ITEMS

*Endless quiver	101

WONDROUS LAIR ITEMS

Feast table	80

TATTOOS

Backlash tattoo	84
Reinforcement tattoo	84
Strikeback tattoo	84

LEVEL 10 ITEMS   5,000 GP

ARMOR

Counterstrike armor +2	Cloth, leather, hide	7
Healer's armor +2	Hide, chain	9

Shadow warlock armor +2	Leather	12
*Shockweave armor +2	Cloth, leather	98
Supporting armor +2	Scale, plate	13

WEAPONS

*Rousing hammer +2	Hammer	95
Runic weapon +2	Any	21
Supreme skirmisher's bow +2	Bow	24
*Thane blood weapon +2	Any melee	100
*Weapon of evil undone +2	Any	113
*Weapon of great opportunity +2	Any melee	96

AMMUNITION (200 GP PER ITEM)

Bending bullet +2	26

HOLY SYMBOLS

Symbol of daring +2	29
Symbol of protection +2	30

RODS

Rod of devilry +2	35
Torch of misery +2	37

STAFFS

Blastwarp staff +2	38
Staff of wind +2	40

TOTEMS

Bloodhunter totem +2	43
Dire totem +2	43
Flameheart totem +2	44
*Stern mountain totem +2	112
Totem of nature's balm +2	45

WANDS

Sharpshooter's wand +2	52
Wand of aptitude +2	52

ARMS SLOT

Barrage bracers	53

FEET SLOT

*Skaivani's anklets	135

HEAD SLOT

*Circlet of revelations	132
*Shadowdancer's mask	105

WAIST SLOT

Diamond cincture	75

WONDROUS LAIR ITEMS

Shining sundial	82

TATTOOS

Eager hero's tattoo	86
Tattoo of shared consequence	85
Tattoo of shared vengeance	85

LEVEL 11 ITEMS   9,000 GP

ARMOR

Gambler's suit +3	Leather	8

WEAPONS

Challenge-seeking weapon +3	Any melee	17
Earth-wrought hammer +3	Hammer	17

ARMS SLOT

Force shield	54
*Razordark bracers	120

FEET SLOT

*Feystride boots	132
*Steady boots of the ram	111

HANDS SLOT

Gloves of ice	59
Gloves of missile avoidance	59
*Shadowdancer's gloves	105

HEAD SLOT

Circlet of continuity	61
*Helm of vision unclouded	112
*Matrakk's lenses	134

WAIST SLOT

Baldric of assault	74

WONDROUS ITEMS

Versatile spellbook	78

TATTOOS

Teamstrike tattoo	86

CONSUMABLES (350 GP PER ITEM)

Flash flower	88
Rust bark	88

LEVEL 12 ITEMS   13,000 GP

ARMOR

Armor of aegis expansion +3	Cloth, leather	6
*Armor of dwarven vigor +3	Chain, scale, plate	94
Bastion armor +3	Scale, plate	6
Blackflock robe +3	Cloth	6
Coruscating armor +3	Scale, plate	7
*Darkstrike armor +3	Leather, hide	120
Death's brink armor +3	Scale, plate	7
Hero's armor +3	Chain	9
Marauder's armor +3	Leather, hide	10
*Radiant temple uniform +3	Cloth	103
Rat killer's coat +3	Cloth, leather	11
Shadow hound armor +3	Hide	12
*Shadow hunter hide +3	Hide	106
*Shipboard armor +3	Leather	101
Teleporting armor +3	Scale, plate	14

WEAPONS

Aftershock weapon +3	Any	15
Boltshard crossbow +3	Crossbow	17
Duelist's bow +3	Bow	17
Entrapping weapon +3	Bow, crossbow	17
Farbond spellblade +3	Hvy blade, lt blade	18
Guardian's call +3	Any melee	19
Harmonic songblade +3	Hvy blade, lt blade	19
*Hungry spear +3	Spear	98
*Infighting blade +3	Lt blade, axe (one-handed only)	101
Quicksilver blade +3	Lt blade	21
Rebounding weapon +3	Any ranged	21
Shadowrift blade +3	Lt blade	21
Supremely vicious weapon +3	Any	24
Totemic spear +3	Spear	24
Totemic warclub +3	Mace	25
*Unbroken lance +3	Spear	111
Whistling songbow +3	Bow, crossbow	25

AMMUNITION (500 GP PER ITEM)

Onslaught arrow +3	27

HOLY SYMBOLS

Ioun-blessed symbol +3	28
Symbol of branding +3	29
Symbol of divine force +3	29
Symbol of foe turning +3	30
*Symbol of Gajz +3	135
Symbol of shared healing +3	30
Symbol of the first spirits +3	31
Symbol of vigor +3	32

ORBS

Orb of heightened imposition +3	33
Orb of resilient tenacity +3	33
Orb of visionary protection +3	34

RODS

Rod of burgeoning memory +3	34
Rod of stolen starlt +3	35
Rod of the fickle servant +3	36

STAFFS

Moonsilver staff +3	38
Staff of divinity +3	38
Staff of knives +3	39
Summoner's staff +3	40
Verdant staff +3	40

TOMES

Dispelling tome +3	41

TOTEMS

Earthfall totem +3	44
Roaring bear totem +3	45
Totem of the harrier's claws +3	46
Totem of the night +3	46
Totem of thunder's keeper +3	47

ARMS SLOT

*Crest of vigilance eternal	112

FEET SLOT

Boots of unchecked passage	57
*Shadowdancer's boots	105

HEAD SLOT

*Charger's headdress	111
Crown of equilibrium	61

NECK SLOT

Amulet of double fortune +3	63
Amulet of elegy +3	63
Badge of the berserker +3	64
*Cloak of the crimson path +3	107
*Deep-pocket cloak +3	97
Lifesaving brooch +3	67
*Mantle of the golden general +3	123
*Necklace of fate +3	121
*Scarf of reconciliation +3	132
Talisman of terror +3	69

WONDROUS ITEMS

Horn of dismissal	76
*Shepherd's battle standard	119
*Stone of earth	133
*Stone of flame	133
*Stone of light	133
*Stone of shadow	133
*Stone of spirit	133
*Stone of storms	133
*Stone of wind	133

WONDROUS LAIR ITEMS

Brilliant scrying basin	79
Diplomat's table	80
Door warden	80
Ritualist's lectern	81
Throne of dominion	83
Watchful eye	83

LEVEL 13 ITEMS 17,000 GP

ARMOR

*Armor of essence inviolate +3	Any	112
Armor of sudden recovery +3	Cloth, leather	6
*Champion's hauberk +3	Chain, scale	113
Gambit armor +3	Cloth, leather	8
Holy adversary's armor +3	Cloth	9
Kemstone armor +3	Scale, plate	9
*Mirrored plate +3	Plate	110
Moon armor +3	Chain	10
Nightmare ward armor +3	Leather, hide	11
Predator's hide +3	Hide	11
Robe of avoidance +3	Cloth	11
Runic armor +3	Any	12
Sanguine vestments +3	Cloth	12
*Skin of agonies +3	Leather, hide	124
Slime armor +3	Scale, plate	13
Snaketongue robe +3	Cloth	13
Spiderweb robes +3	Cloth	13
Spiked jacket +3	Leather, hide	13
Wall armor +3	Any	14
Warmage's uniform +3	Cloth, leather	14
Winged armor +3	Any	14

WEAPONS

Aegis blade +3	Hvy blade, lt blade	15
Alfsair spear +3	Spear	15
Aura killer weapon +3	Any melee	15
*Blade of vengeance +3	Hvy blade, lt blade	103
Blood fury weapon +3	Axe, hvy blade	17
*Blood harvest blade +3	Lt blade	107
*Bradaman's weapon +3	Hvy blade, axe, hammer	110
Flesh grinder +3	Axe, hvy blade, polearm	18
Frost fury waraxe +3	Axe	18
*General's weapon +3	Polearm	123
Great hunger weapon +3	Any melee	18
Guardian's brand +3	Any melee	19
Hideous weapon +3	Flail, hammer, pick	19
*Pact blade +3	Lt blade	108, 120
Ravenclaw warblade +3	Hvy blade	21
*Rhythm blade +3	Lt blade	97
*Rovikar's weapon +3	Any	135
*Scorpion tail blade +3	Lt blade	131

*Shepherd's arms +3	Polearm, spear	119
Shrieking songbow +3	Bow, crossbow	21
Songbow of vanishment +3	Bow, crossbow	23
Targeting weapon +3	Bow, crossbow	24
Unforgettable cudgel +3	Mace	25
*Warding blade +3	Lt blade	103
Writhing vine weapon +3	Any melee	25

AMMUNITION (650 GP PER ITEM)

Attention-stealing bullet +3	26
Bolt of clumsiness +3	26
Bolt of transit +3	26
Dispelling bolt +3	26
Firestorm arrow +3	26
Freezing arrow +3	27
Lightning arrow +3	27
Space-shifting bolt +3	27
Spider bolt +3	27
Summoning bullet +3	28
Surprise bullet +3	28

HOLY SYMBOLS

Convert's symbol +3	28
Symbol of brawn +3	29
Symbol of the champion's code +3	31
Symbol of the radiant flame +3	32

ORBS

| Orb of repeated imposition +3 | 33 |
| Orb of supplementary force +3 | 34 |

RODS

Hexer's rod +3	34
Rod of divinity +3	35
Spider rod +3	37

STAFFS

Staff of resilience +3	39
Staff of sleep and charm +3	39
Staff of the faithful arcanist +3	40

TOMES

| Gossamer tome +3 | 42 |
| Mordenkainen's tome +3 | 42 |

TOTEMS

Boar's charge totem +3	43
Bronzewood coils totem +3	43
*Death fang totem +3	106
Fell beast totem +3	44
Iron bear totem +3	44
Life river totem +3	44
Totem of the awakened bear +3	45
Totem of the satyr's dance +3	47
Vengeful spirit totem +3	47

ARMS SLOT

Bloodhound bracers	53
*Bracelet of the radiant storm	115
Executioner's bracers	54
Frost charger bracers	54
*Shield of the world tree	121

HANDS SLOT

| Gauntlets of discontinuity | 58 |

NECK SLOT

Amulet of warding +3	63
*Baffling cape +3	96
Cloak of the desert +3	65
Courtier's cape +3	66
*Fleece of renewal +3	111
Necklace of keys +3	67
Orc's-eye amulet +3	67
*Pavise charm +3	101
*Resplendent cloak +3	104
Seashimmer cloak +3	68
Shroud of ravens +3	68
*Spidersilk mantle +3	109

WAIST SLOT

| Waistband of the grappler | 75 |

WONDROUS ITEMS

| Ribbon of limitless questions | 77 |

WONDROUS LAIR ITEMS

| Magic drawbridge | 81 |

TATTOOS

| Breakchain tattoo | 87 |
| Demonskin tattoo | 87 |

LEVEL 14 ITEMS   21,000 GP

ARMOR

Armor of dark deeds +3	Leather, hide	6
Dazzling plate +3	Plate	7
Demonscale +3	Scale	8
Formidable armor +3	Hide, chain	8
Genasi soul armor +3	Leather, hide	8
Lifefont armor +3	Hide	10
Magnetic armor +3	Scale, plate	10
Parchment armor +3	Cloth, leather	11
Scale of the serpent +3	Scale	12
Serpentine armor +3	Scale	12
Spirit armor +3	Chain	13
Time link armor +3	Chain	14
Translocating armor +3	Any	14

WEAPONS

Avalanche hammer +3	Hammer	15
Banishing spellblade +3	Hvy blade, lt blade	16
Blood drinker +3	Axe, hvy blade	16
*Dragontooth blade +3	Hvy blade	130
Echoing songblade +3	Hvy blade, lt blade	17
*Harmony blade +3	Hvy blade	97
Impaler's pick +3	Pick	20
Incisive dagger +3	Dagger	20
Intensifying weapon +3	Any	20
*Kamesti crossbow +3	Crossbow	101
Master's blade +3	Hvy blade, lt blade	20
Maw of the guardian +3	Any melee	20
Screaming bow +3	Bow	21
Songbow of lullabies +3	Bow, crossbow	22
Soul drinker weapon +3	Any melee	23
Stormbiter warblade +3	Hvy blade, lt blade	23
*Sword of melancholy +3	Hvy blade, lt blade	124
*Weapon of arcane bonds +3	Hvy blade, lt blade	102

*Weapon of cruel persuasion +3	Any melee	114
Weapon of oaths fulfilled +3	Any melee	25

AMMUNITION (800 GP PER ITEM)

Arrow of revelation +3	26
Forbiddance bolt +3	26

HOLY SYMBOLS

Symbol of fire and fury +3	30
Symbol of the holy nimbus +3	32
Symbol of unified defense +3	32

ORBS

Orb of accuracy +3	33

RODS

Darkspiral rod +3	34
Rod of obliterating wrath +3	35
Rod of the hag +3	36
Rod of the pactbinder +3	36

STAFFS

Staff of iron infusion +3	38
Staff of spell blasting +3	40

TOMES

Deck of spells +3	41
Tome of crushing force +3	42
Tome of enduring creation +3	42
Tome of striking lightning +3	42

TOTEMS

Panther totem +3	45
Razor talon totem +3	45
Totem of new beginnings +3	45
Totem of the ravenous beast +3	47
*Totem of the severed eye +3	107
Totem of winter's scorn +3	47
Wildfire totem +3	47
Winterwood totem +3	48

WANDS

Cursing wand +3	48
Diamond wand +3	49
Hawthorn wand +3	49
Master's wand of eyes of the vestige +3	50
Master's wand of illusory ambush +3	50
Master's wand of misdirected mark +3	51
Master's wand of phantom bolt +3	51
Master's wand of spiteful glamor +3	51
Master's wand of vicious mockery +3	51
Shielding wand +3	52
Wand of allure +3	52
Wand of thunderous anguish +3	52

ARMS SLOT

*Bracers of zeal +3	103
Vortex shield	56

FEET SLOT

Sandwalker boots	58
*Swift-step boots +3	115

HANDS SLOT

Gauntlets of blood	58

HEAD SLOT

*Crown of the brilliant sun	115
*Golden crown of battle command	123
*Helm of able defense	118
*Mask of the vengeful spirit	121
*Pennant helm	110
*Tenebrous mask	120

NECK SLOT

Amulet of vigor +3	63
Assassin's cloak +3	64
Chaos cloak +3	65
Cloak of the bat +3	65
*Cloak of the lion's mane +3	98
Cloak of translocation +3	66
*Crimson cloak +3	122
Demon amulet +3	66
Frostwolf pelt +3	66
*Keicha's amulet +3	134
Lucky charm +3	67
Medallion of the mind +3	67
Medic's amulet +3	67
Periapt of proof against poison +3	67
*Shadowdancer's cloak +3	105
Timeless locket +3	69

RINGS

Grace ring of lightning	70
Grace ring of salvation	70
Grace ward ring	70
Unvanquished grace ring	74

WAIST SLOT

Acrobat's harness	74
*Sash of vitality ceaseless	112

WONDROUS LAIR ITEMS

Loadstone statue	81
Teleportation disk	83

TATTOOS

Fireheart tattoo	87
Tattoo of arcane blood	84
Tattoo of the shared heart	86

LEVEL 15 ITEMS   25,000 GP

ARMOR

Armor of shared valor +3	Leather, chain	6
Counterstrike armor +3	Cloth, leather, hide	7
*Crystalline breastplate +3	Leather, hide, chain, scale, plate	118
Healer's armor +3	Hide, chain	9
Holy radiance armor +3	Chain	9
Shadow warlock armor +3	Leather	12
*Shockweave armor +3	Cloth, leather	98
Supporting armor +3	Scale, plate	13

WEAPONS

Battle spirit weapon +3	Axe, flail, hammer, hvy blade, mace, spear	16
*Blade of the eldritch knight +3	Hvy blade	114
*Reaper's axe +3	Axe	122
*Rousing hammer +3	Hammer	95

Runic weapon +3	Any	21
Songbow of summoning +3	Bow, crossbow	22
Supreme skirmisher's bow +3	Bow	24
*Thane blood weapon +3	Any melee	100
*Weapon of evil undone +3	Any	113
*Weapon of great opportunity +3	Any melee	96

AMMUNITION (1,000 GP PER ITEM)
Bending bullet +3		26

HOLY SYMBOLS
*Champion's symbol +3	113
Symbol of daring +3	29
Symbol of protection +3	30

RODS
Rod of devilry +3	35
Rod of silver rain +3	35
Torch of misery +3	37

STAFFS
Blastwarp staff +3	38
*Queen's staff +3	117
Staff of wind +3	40
*Tempest staff +3	131

TOTEMS
Bloodhunter totem +3	43
Dire totem +3	43
Flameheart totem +3	44
*Stern mountain totem +3	112
Totem of nature's balm +3	45
Totem of the crashing tide +3	46
Totem of the scouring wind +3	47

WANDS
Sharpshooter's wand +3	52
Wand of aptitude +3	52

ARMS SLOT
Deathward shield	54
Rhino bracers	55
*Shield of fellowship	110

HANDS SLOT
*Resplendent gloves	104

HEAD SLOT
*Reaper's helm	122

NECK SLOT
*Cloak of burgeoning shadow +3	120
*Mantle of regrets +3	123

RINGS
Alliance band	69
Crown of the dream king	69
*Ring of many forms	121
Ring of sympathy	72
Ring of the zealous	72

WAIST SLOT
*General's belt	122

WONDROUS ITEMS
Ghostlight candle	76
Seed of war	78

TATTOOS
Tattoo of vengeance	85

LEVEL 16 ITEMS   45,000 GP
ARMOR
Gambler's suit +4	Leather	8

WEAPONS
Challenge-seeking weapon +4	Any melee	17
Earth-wrought hammer +4	Hammer	17

ARMS SLOT
Climber's bracers	53
Flameward shield	54
Stormward shield	56
Winterward shield	56

FEET SLOT
Boots of blood	57
*Spark slippers	115
Survivor's boots	58

HANDS SLOT
Gloves of dimensional grasp	58
*Restorative gauntlets	114

HEAD SLOT
Chimera headdress	61
*Mask of tears	123

MOUNT SLOT
*Bridle of flame	110

RINGS
Death spiral ring	70
Ring of eladrin grace	71
*Ring of tactical brilliance	123

WAIST SLOT
Baldric of time	74

WONDROUS LAIR ITEMS
Deceptive scrying basin	80
Dimensional anchor	80

LEVEL 17 ITEMS   65,000 GP
ARMOR
Armor of aegis expansion +4	Cloth, leather	6
*Armor of dwarven vigor +4	Chain, scale, plate	94
Bastion armor +4	Scale, plate	6
Blackflock robe +4	Cloth	6
Coruscating armor +4	Scale, plate	7
*Darkstrike armor +4	Leather, hide	120
Death's brink armor +4	Scale, plate	7
Hero's armor +4	Chain	9
Marauder's armor +4	Leather, hide	10
*Mooncloth robes +4	Cloth	117
*Radiant temple uniform +4	Cloth	103
Rat killer's coat +4	Cloth, leather	11
Shadow hound armor +4	Hide	12
*Shadow hunter hide +4	Hide	106
*Shipboard armor +4	Leather	101
Teleporting armor +4	Scale, plate	14

WEAPONS
Aftershock weapon +4	Any	15
Boltshard crossbow +4	Crossbow	17

Duelist's bow +4	Bow	17
Entrapping weapon +4	Bow, crossbow	17
Farbond spellblade +4	Hvy blade, lt blade	18
Guardian's call +4	Any melee	19
Harmonic songblade +4	Hvy blade, lt blade	19
*Hungry spear +4	Spear	98
*Infighting blade +4	Lt blade, axe (one-handed only)	101
*Lion's heart hammer +4	Hammer	130
Quicksilver blade +4	Lt blade	21
Rebounding weapon +4	Any ranged	21
Shadowrift blade +4	Lt blade	21
Supremely vicious weapon +4	Any	24
Totemic spear +4	Spear	24
Totemic warclub +4	Mace	25
*Unbroken lance +4	Spear	111
Whistling songbow +4	Bow, crossbow	25

AMMUNITION (2,600 GP PER ITEM)

Onslaught arrow +4	27

HOLY SYMBOLS

Ioun-blessed symbol +4	28
Symbol of branding +4	29
Symbol of divine force +4	29
Symbol of divine light +4	29
Symbol of foe turning +4	30
*Symbol of Gajz +4	135
Symbol of shared healing +4	30
Symbol of the first spirits +4	31
*Symbol of the forgotten one +4	124
Symbol of vigor +4	32

ORBS

Orb of heightened imposition +4	33
Orb of resilient tenacity +4	33
Orb of visionary protection +4	34

RODS

Rod of burgeoning memory +4	34
Rod of stolen starlight +4	35
Rod of the fickle servant +4	36

STAFFS

Moonsilver staff +4	38
Staff of divinity +4	38
Staff of knives +4	39
*Staff of the Far Wanderer +4	117
Summoner's staff +4	40
Verdant staff +4	40

TOMES

Dispelling tome +4	41

TOTEMS

Earthfall totem +4	44
Roaring bear totem +4	45
Totem of the harrier's claws +4	46
Totem of the night +4	46
Totem of thunder's keeper +4	47

ARMS SLOT

Absorbing shield	53
*Gauntlets of brutality	122

FEET SLOT

*Pursuer's boots	113

HANDS SLOT

Hero's gauntlets	59

HEAD SLOT

Philosopher's crown	62

NECK SLOT

Amulet of double fortune +4	63
Amulet of elegy +4	63
Badge of the berserker +4	64
*Cloak of the crimson path +4	107
*Deep-pocket cloak +4	97
*Eldritch medallion +4	114
Lifesaving brooch +4	67
*Mantle of the golden general +4	123
*Necklace of fate +4	121
*Scarf of reconciliation +4	132
Talisman of terror +4	69

RINGS

*Ring of the radiant storm	115
Ring of unwelcome gifting	73
Stone band	74
Stormcatcher ring	74

WONDROUS LAIR ITEMS

Vigilant gargoyle	83

TATTOOS

Tattoo of the wolverine	85

CONSUMABLES (2,600 GP PER ITEM)

Clay of creation	87

LEVEL 18 ITEMS   85,000 GP
ARMOR

*Armor of essence inviolate +4	Any	112
Armor of sudden recovery +4	Cloth, leather	6
*Champion's hauberk +4	Chain, scale	113
Gambit armor +4	Cloth, leather	8
Holy adversary's armor +4	Cloth	9
Kemstone armor +4	Scale, plate	9
*Mirrored plate +4	Plate	110
Moon armor +4	Chain	10
Nightmare ward armor +4	Leather, hide	11
Predator's hide +4	Hide	11
Robe of avoidance +4	Cloth	11
Runic armor +4	Any	12
Sanguine vestments +4	Cloth	12
*Skin of agonies +4	Leather, hide	124
Slime armor +4	Scale, plate	13
Snaketongue robe +4	Cloth	13
Spiderweb robes +4	Cloth	13
Spiked jacket +4	Leather, hide	13
Wall armor +4	Any	14
Warmage's uniform +4	Cloth, leather	14
Winged armor +4	Any	14

WEAPONS

Aegis blade +4	Hvy blade, lt blade	15
Alfsair spear +4	Spear	15

Aura killer weapon +4	Any melee	15
*Blade of vengeance +4	Hvy blade, lt blade	103
Blood fury weapon +4	Axe, hvy blade	17
*Blood harvest blade +4	Lt blade	107
*Bradaman's weapon +4	Hvy blade, axe, hammer	110
Flesh grinder +4	Axe, hvy blade, polearm	18
Frost fury waraxe +4	Axe	18
*General's weapon +4	Polearm	123
Great hunger weapon +4	Any melee	18
Guardian's brand +4	Any melee	19
Hideous weapon +4	Flail, hammer, pick	19
*Pact blade +4	Lt blade	108, 120
Ravenclaw warblade +4	Hvy blade	21
*Rhythm blade +4	Lt blade	97
*Rovikar's weapon +4	Any	135
*Scorpion tail blade +4	Lt blade	131
*Serpent's kiss bow +4	Bow	131
*Shepherd's arms +4	Polearm, spear	119
Shrieking songbow +4	Bow, crossbow	21
Songbow of vanishment +4	Bow, crossbow	23
Targeting weapon +4	Bow, crossbow	24
Unforgettable cudgel +4	Mace	25
*Warding blade +4	Lt blade	103
Writhing vine weapon +4	Any melee	25

AMMUNITION (3,400 GP PER ITEM)

Attention-stealing bullet +4	26
Bolt of clumsiness +4	26
Bolt of transit +4	26
Dispelling bolt +4	26
Firestorm arrow +4	26
Freezing arrow +4	27
Lightning arrow +4	27
Space-shifting bolt +4	27
Spider bolt +4	27
Summoning bullet +4	28
Surprise bullet +4	28

HOLY SYMBOLS

Convert's symbol +4	28
Symbol of brawn +4	29
Symbol of defense +4	29
Symbol of prayers recovered +4	30
Symbol of the champion's code +4	31
Symbol of the radiant flame +4	32

ORBS

Orb of repeated imposition +4	33
Orb of supplementary force +4	34

RODS

Battle-pact rod +4	34
Hexer's rod +4	34
Rod of divinity +4	35
Spider rod +4	37

STAFFS

Spellshaper's staff +4	38
Staff of resilience +4	39
Staff of sleep and charm +4	39
Staff of the faithful arcanist +4	40

TOMES

Frozen tome +4	41
Gossamer tome +4	42
Mordenkainen's tome +4	42

TOTEMS

Boar's charge totem +4	43
Bronzewood coils totem +4	43
*Death fang totem +4	106
Fell beast totem +4	44
Iron bear totem +4	44
Life river totem +4	44
Totem of the awakened bear +4	45
Totem of the satyr's dance +4	47
Vengeful spirit totem +4	47

ARMS SLOT

Charm bracelet	53
*Rebuking bracers	115
Serpentine bracers	55

HANDS SLOT

Hrothmar's gauntlets	60

HEAD SLOT

Cyclops helm	61

NECK SLOT

Amulet of warding +4	63
*Baffling cape +4	96
Cloak of the desert +4	65
Courtier's cape +4	66
*Fleece of renewal +4	111
Necklace of keys +4	67
Orc's-eye amulet +4	67
*Pavise charm +4	101
*Resplendent cloak +4	104
Seashimmer cloak +4	68
Shroud of ravens +4	68
*Spidersilk mantle +4	109
*Star-strewn scarf +4	118

RINGS

*Ring of sorrows	123
Ring of the fallen	72
Traveler's ring	74

WAIST SLOT

Belt of the Witch King	75
*Head-taker's belt	122
Phoenix sash	75

WONDROUS LAIR ITEMS

Mirror of deception	81
Spying mirrors (pair)	82
Throne of grandeur	83

TATTOOS

Fleet hero tattoo	87
Greatwing tattoo	87
Ironheart tattoo	86
Strongheart tattoo	86

CONSUMABLES (3,400 GP PER ITEM)

Silver sand	88
Vortex stone	88

LEVEL 19 ITEMS   105,000 GP

ARMOR

Armor of dark deeds +4	Leather, hide	6
Dazzling plate +4	Plate	7
Demonscale +4	Scale	8
Formidable armor +4	Hide, chain	8
Genasi soul armor +4	Leather, hide	8
Great cat armor +4	Hide	9
Lifefont armor +4	Hide	10
Magnetic armor +4	Scale, plate	10
Parchment armor +4	Cloth, leather	11
Scale of the serpent +4	Scale	12
Serpentine armor +4	Scale	12
Spirit armor +4	Chain	13
Time link armor +4	Chain	14
Translocating armor +4	Any	14

WEAPONS

Avalanche hammer +4	Hammer	15
Banishing spellblade +4	Hvy blade, lt blade	16
Blood drinker +4	Axe, hvy blade	16
*Dragontooth blade +4	Hvy blade	130
Echoing songblade +4	Hvy blade, lt blade	17
*Harmony blade +4	Hvy blade	97
Impaler's pick +4	Pick	20
Incisive dagger +4	Dagger	20
Intensifying weapon +4	Any	20
*Kamesti crossbow +4	Crossbow	101
Master's blade +4	Hvy blade, lt blade	20
Maw of the guardian +4	Any melee	20
Screaming bow +4	Bow	21
Songbow of lullabies +4	Bow, crossbow	22
Soul drinker weapon +4	Any melee	23
Space-bending weapon +4	Hvy blade, lt blade	23
Stormbiter warblade +4	Hvy blade, lt blade	23
*Sword of melancholy +4	Hvy blade, lt blade	124
*Weapon of arcane bonds +4	Hvy blade, lt blade	102
*Weapon of cruel persuasion +4	Any melee	114
Weapon of oaths fulfilled +4	Any melee	25

AMMUNITION (4,200 GP PER ITEM)

Arrow of revelation +4	26
Forbiddance bolt +4	26

HOLY SYMBOLS

Symbol of fire and fury +4	30
Symbol of the holy nimbus +4	32
Symbol of unified defense +4	32

ORBS

Orb of accuracy +4	33

RODS

Darkspiral rod +4	34
Rod of obliterating wrath +4	35
Rod of the hag +4	36
Rod of the pactbinder +4	36

STAFFS

Staff of iron infusion +4	38
Staff of spell blasting +4	40

TOMES

Deck of spells +4	41
Tome of crushing force +4	42
Tome of enduring creation +4	42
Tome of striking lightning +4	42

TOTEMS

Avalanche's wake totem +4	43
Panther totem +4	45
Razor talon totem +4	45
Totem of new beginnings +4	45
Totem of the ravenous beast +4	47
*Totem of the severed eye +4	107
Totem of winter's scorn +4	47
Wildfire totem +4	47
Winterwood totem +4	48

WANDS

Cursing wand +4	48
Diamond wand +4	49
Hawthorn wand +4	49
Master's wand of eyes of the vestige +4	50
Master's wand of illusory ambush +4	50
Master's wand of misdirected mark +4	51
Master's wand of phantom bolt +4	51
Master's wand of spiteful glamor +4	51
Master's wand of vicious mockery +4	51
Shielding wand +4	52
Wand of allure +4	52
Wand of thunderous anguish +4	52

ARMS SLOT

Ankhmon's bracers	53
*Bracers of zeal +4	103

FEET SLOT

*Swift-step boots +4	115

HANDS SLOT

*Gloves of the wandering star	117

NECK SLOT

Amulet of vigor +4	63
Assassin's cloak +4	64
Chaos cloak +4	65
Cloak of the bat +4	65
*Cloak of the lion's mane +4	98
Cloak of the shadowthief +4	65
Cloak of translocation +4	66
*Crimson cloak +4	122
Demon amulet +4	66
Frostwolf pelt +4	66
*Keicha's amulet +4	134
Lucky charm +4	67
Medallion of the mind +4	67
Medic's amulet +4	67
Periapt of proof against poison +4	67
*Shadowdancer's cloak +4	105
Timeless locket +4	69

RINGS

Death song ring	70
Grace ring of prowess	70
Shadowfell signet	73

WAIST SLOT

Baldric of shielding	74
*Belt of breaching	114

LEVEL 20 ITEMS   125,000 GP

ARMOR

Armor of shared valor +4	Leather, chain	6
Counterstrike armor +4	Cloth, leather, hide	7
*Crystalline breastplate +4	Leather, hide, chain, scale, plate	118
Healer's armor +4	Hide, chain	9
Holy radiance armor +4	Chain	9
Shadow warlock armor +4	Leather	12
*Shockweave armor +4	Cloth, leather	98
Spectral plate +4	Plate	13
Supporting armor +4	Scale, plate	13

WEAPONS

*Rousing hammer +4	Hammer	95
Battle spirit weapon +4	Axe, flail, hammer, hvy blade, mace, spear	16
*Blade of the eldritch knight +4	Hvy blade	114
*Reaper's axe +4	Axe	122
Runic weapon +4	Any	21
Songbow of summoning +4	Bow, crossbow	22
Supreme skirmisher's bow +4	Bow	24
*Thane blood weapon +4	Any melee	100
*Weapon of evil undone +4	Any	113
*Weapon of great opportunity +4	Any melee	96

AMMUNITION (5,000 GP PER ITEM)

Bending bullet +4	26

HOLY SYMBOLS

*Champion's symbol +4	113
Symbol of daring +4	29
Symbol of protection +4	30

ORBS

Orb of distance denial +4	33
Orb of petrification +4	33

RODS

Rod of devilry +4	35
Rod of silver rain +4	35
Torch of misery +4	37

STAFFS

Blastwarp staff +4	38
*Queen's staff +4	117
Staff of wind +4	40
*Tempest staff +4	131

TOTEMS

Bloodhunter totem +4	43
Dire totem +4	43
Flameheart totem +4	44
Nine furies totem +4	44
*Stern mountain totem +4	112
Totem of nature's balm +4	45
Totem of the crashing tide +4	46
Totem of the scouring wind +4	47
Totem of the world tree +4	47

WANDS

Sharpshooter's wand +4	52
Wand of aptitude +4	52

HANDS SLOT

*Dimensional gauntlets	114
Many-fingered gloves	61

HEAD SLOT

Gibbering lump	62
*Sun sphere	118

NECK SLOT

Bloodgem shard +4	65
Bralani cloak +4	65
*Cloak of burgeoning shadow +4	120
*Mantle of regrets +4	123

RINGS

Ring of action reversal	71
Ring of agile thought	71
Ring of enduring earth	71
Ring of unfettered motion	73

WAIST SLOT

Diamond cincture	75

TATTOOS

Eager hero's tattoo	86

LEVEL 21 ITEMS   225,000 GP

ARMOR

Gambler's suit +5	Leather	8

WEAPONS

Challenge-seeking weapon +5	Any melee	17
Earth-wrought hammer +5	Hammer	17

HANDS SLOT

Gloves of ice	59

HEAD SLOT

Essence of the wisp	61

RINGS

Ring of heroic health	71
Ring of influence	72
Ring of traded knowledge	72
*Rom Kala's tideshield ring	137

WAIST SLOT

*Artificer's belt	129

CONSUMABLES (9,000 GP PER ITEM)

Flash flower	88
Rust bark	88

LEVEL 22 ITEMS   325,000 GP

ARMOR

Armor of aegis expansion +5	Cloth, leather	6
*Armor of dwarven vigor +5	Chain, scale, plate	94
Bastion armor +5	Scale, plate	6
Blackflock robe +5	Cloth	6
Coruscating armor +5	Scale, plate	7
*Darkstrike armor +5	Leather, hide	120
Death's brink armor +5	Scale, plate	7
Hero's armor +5	Chain	9
Marauder's armor +5	Leather, hide	10

*Mooncloth robes +5	Cloth	117
*Radiant temple uniform +5	Cloth	103
Rat killer's coat +5	Cloth, leather	11
Shadow hound armor +5	Hide	12
*Shadow hunter hide +5	Hide	106
*Shipboard armor +5	Leather	101
Teleporting armor +5	Scale, plate	14

WEAPONS

Aftershock weapon +5	Any	15
Boltshard crossbow +5	Crossbow	17
Duelist's bow +5	Bow	17
Entrapping weapon +5	Bow, crossbow	17
Farbond spellblade +5	Hvy blade, lt blade	18
Guardian's call +5	Any melee	19
Harmonic songblade +5	Hvy blade, lt blade	19
*Hungry spear +5	Spear	98
*Infighting blade +5	Lt blade, axe (one-handed only)	101
*Lion's heart hammer +5	Hammer	130
Quicksilver blade +5	Lt blade	21
Rebounding weapon +5	Any ranged	21
Shadowrift blade +5	Lt blade	21
Supremely vicious weapon +5	Any	24
Totemic spear +5	Spear	24
Totemic warclub +5	Mace	25
*Unbroken lance +5	Spear	111
Whistling songbow +5	Bow, crossbow	25

AMMUNITION (13,000 GP PER ITEM)

Onslaught arrow +5	27

HOLY SYMBOLS

Ioun-blessed symbol +5	28
Symbol of branding +5	29
Symbol of divine force +5	29
Symbol of divine light +5	29
Symbol of foe turning +5	30
*Symbol of Gajz +5	135
Symbol of shared healing +5	30
Symbol of the first spirits +5	31
*Symbol of the forgotten one +5	124
Symbol of vigor +5	32

ORBS

Orb of heightened imposition +5	33
Orb of resilient tenacity +5	33
Orb of visionary protection +5	34

RODS

Rod of burgeoning memory +5	34
Rod of stolen starlight +5	35
Rod of the fickle servant +5	36

STAFFS

Moonsilver staff +5	38
Staff of divinity +5	38
Staff of knives +5	39
*Staff of the Far Wanderer +5	117
Summoner's staff +5	40
Verdant staff +5	40

TOMES

Dispelling tome +5	41

TOTEMS

Earthfall totem +5	44
Roaring bear totem +5	45
Totem of the harrier's claws +5	46
Totem of the night +5	46
Totem of thunder's keeper +5	47

HANDS SLOT

*Gauntlets of magical interchange	129

NECK SLOT

Amulet of double fortune +5	63
Amulet of elegy +5	63
Badge of the berserker +5	64
*Cloak of the crimson path +5	107
*Deep-pocket cloak +5	97
*Eldritch medallion +5	114
Lifesaving brooch +5	67
*Mantle of the golden general +5	123
*Necklace of fate +5	121
*Scarf of reconciliation +5	132
Talisman of terror +5	69

RINGS

*Farndak's glittering ring	137

WONDROUS LAIR ITEMS

All-seeing eye	79
Gorgonblood mortar	81

Level 23 Items   425,000 gp

ARMOR

Armor of enduring health +5	Hide, chain	6
*Armor of essence inviolate +5	Any	112
Armor of sudden recovery +5	Cloth, leather	6
*Champion's hauberk +5	Chain, scale	113
Gambit armor +5	Cloth, leather	8
Holy adversary's armor +5	Cloth	9
Kemstone armor +5	Scale, plate	9
Mind armor +5	Scale, plate	10
*Mirrored plate +5	Plate	110
Moon armor +5	Chain	10
Nightmare ward armor +5	Leather, hide	11
Predator's hide +5	Hide	11
Robe of avoidance +5	Cloth	11
Runic armor +5	Any	12
Sanguine vestments +5	Cloth	12
*Skin of agonies +5	Leather, hide	124
Slime armor +5	Scale, plate	13
Snaketongue robe +5	Cloth	13
Spiderweb robes +5	Cloth	13
Spiked jacket +5	Leather, hide	13
*Tinkersuit +5	Leather	129
Wall armor +5	Any	14
Warmage's uniform +5	Cloth, leather	14
Winged armor +5	Any	14

WEAPONS

Aegis blade +5	Hvy blade, lt blade	15

Alfsair spear +5	Spear	15
Aura killer weapon +5	Any melee	15
*Blade of vengeance +5	Hvy blade, lt blade	103
Blood fury weapon +5	Axe, hvy blade	17
*Blood harvest blade +5	Lt blade	107
*Bradaman's weapon +5	Hvy blade, axe, hammer	110
Death mark weapon +5	Any	17
Flesh grinder +5	Axe, hvy blade, polearm	18
Frost fury waraxe +5	Axe	18
*General's weapon +5	Polearm	123
Great hunger weapon +5	Any melee	18
Guardian's brand +5	Any melee	19
Hideous weapon +5	Flail, hammer, pick	19
*Pact blade +5	Lt blade	108, 120
Ravenclaw warblade +5	Hvy blade	21
*Rhythm blade +5	Lt blade	97
*Rovikar's weapon +5	Any	135
*Scorpion tail blade +5	Lt blade	131
*Serpent's kiss bow +5	Bow	131
*Shepherd's arms +5	Polearm, spear	119
Shrieking songbow +5	Bow, crossbow	21
Songbow of vanishment +5	Bow, crossbow	23
Targeting weapon +5	Bow, crossbow	24
Unforgettable cudgel +5	Mace	25
*Warding blade +5	Lt blade	103
Writhing vine weapon +5	Any melee	25

AMMUNITION (17,000 GP PER ITEM)

Attention-stealing bullet +5	26
Bolt of clumsiness +5	26
Bolt of transit +5	26
Dispelling bolt +5	26
Firestorm arrow +5	26
Freezing arrow +5	27
Lightning arrow +5	27
Space-shifting bolt +5	27
Spider bolt +5	27
Summoning bullet +5	28
Surprise bullet +5	28

HOLY SYMBOLS

Convert's symbol +5	28
Symbol of brawn +5	29
Symbol of defense +5	29
Symbol of prayers recovered +5	30
Symbol of the champion's code +5	31
Symbol of the radiant flame +5	32

ORBS

Orb of repeated imposition +5	33
Orb of supplementary force +5	34

RODS

Battle-pact rod +5	34
Hexer's rod +5	34
Rod of divinity +5	35
Spider rod +5	37

STAFFS

Spellshaper's staff +5	38
Staff of luck and skill +5	39

Staff of resilience +5	39
Staff of sleep and charm +5	39
Staff of the faithful arcanist +5	40

TOMES

Frozen tome +5	41
Gossamer tome +5	42
Mordenkainen's tome +5	42

TOTEMS

Boar's charge totem +5	43
Bronzewood coils totem +5	43
*Death fang totem +5	106
Fell beast totem +5	44
Iron bear totem +5	44
Life river totem +5	44
Totem of the awakened bear +5	45
Totem of the satyr's dance +5	47
Vengeful spirit totem +5	47

ARMS SLOT

*Delbanian vambraces	125
Executioner's bracers	54

HEAD SLOT

Lenses of the luminary	62

NECK SLOT

Amulet of warding +5	63
*Baffling cape +5	96
Cloak of the desert +5	65
Courtier's cape +5	66
*Fleece of renewal +5	111
Necklace of keys +5	67
Orc's-eye amulet +5	67
*Pavise charm +5	101
Possum amulet +5	68
*Resplendent cloak +5	104
Seashimmer cloak +5	68
Shroud of ravens +5	68
*Spidersilk mantle +5	109
*Star-strewn scarf +5	118

RINGS

Greater ring of invisibility	71
*Ring of Hrumdar's halls	137
Ring of the risen	72

WONDROUS LAIR ITEMS

Arcane laboratory	79
Austere dojo	79
Holy shrine	81
Sacred glade	81

TATTOOS

Breakchain tattoo	87
Demonskin tattoo	87

LEVEL 24 ITEMS   525,000 GP

ARMOR

Armor of dark deeds +5	Leather, hide	6
Dazzling plate +5	Plate	7
Demonscale +5	Scale	8
Formidable armor +5	Hide, chain	8
Genasi soul armor +5	Leather, hide	8
Great cat armor +5	Hide	9

Lifefont armor +5	Hide	10
Magnetic armor +5	Scale, plate	10
Parchment armor +5	Cloth, leather	11
Scale of the serpent +5	Scale	12
Serpentine armor +5	Scale	12
Spirit armor +5	Chain	13
Time link armor +5	Chain	14
Translocating armor +5	Any	14

WEAPONS

Avalanche hammer +5	Hammer	15
Banishing spellblade +5	Hvy blade, lt blade	16
Blood drinker +5	Axe, hvy blade	16
*Dragontooth blade +5	Hvy blade	130
Echoing songblade +5	Hvy blade, lt blade	17
*Harmony blade +5	Hvy blade	97
Impaler's pick +5	Pick	20
Incisive dagger +5	Dagger	20
Intensifying weapon +5	Any	20
*Kamesti crossbow +5	Crossbow	101
Master's blade +5	Hvy blade, lt blade	20
Maw of the guardian +5	Any melee	20
Screaming bow +5	Bow	21
Songbow of lullabies +5	Bow, crossbow	22
Soul drinker weapon +5	Any melee	23
Space-bending weapon +5	Hvy blade, lt blade	23
Stormbiter warblade +5	Hvy blade, lt blade	23
*Sword of melancholy +5	Hvy blade, lt blade	124
*Weapon of arcane bonds +5	Hvy blade, lt blade	102
*Weapon of cruel persuasion +5	Any melee	114
Weapon of oaths fulfilled +5	Any melee	25

AMMUNITION (21,000 GP PER ITEM)

Arrow of revelation +5	26
Forbiddance bolt +5	26

HOLY SYMBOLS

Symbol of fire and fury +5	30
Symbol of reflection +5	30
Symbol of the holy nimbus +5	32
Symbol of unified defense +5	32

ORBS

Orb of accuracy +5	33

RODS

Darkspiral rod +5	34
Rod of obliterating wrath +5	35
Rod of the hag +5	36
Rod of the pactbinder +5	36

STAFFS

Staff of iron infusion +5	38
Staff of spell blasting +5	40

TOMES

Deck of spells +5	41
Tome of crushing force +5	42
Tome of enduring creation +5	42
Tome of striking lightning +5	42
Toxic tome +5	43

TOTEMS

Avalanche's wake totem +5	43
Panther totem +5	45
Razor talon totem +5	45
Totem of new beginnings +5	45
Totem of the ravenous beast +5	47
*Totem of the severed eye +5	107
Totem of winter's scorn +5	47
Wildfire totem +5	47
Winterwood totem +5	48

WANDS

Cursing wand +5	48
Diamond wand +5	49
Hawthorn wand +5	49
Iron wand +5	49
Master's wand of eyes of the vestige +5	50
Master's wand of illusory ambush +5	50
Master's wand of misdirected mark +5	51
Master's wand of phantom bolt +5	51
Master's wand of spiteful glamor +5	51
Master's wand of vicious mockery +5	51
Shielding wand +5	52
Wand of allure +5	52
Wand of thunderous anguish +5	52

ARMS SLOT

*Bracers of zeal +5	103
Trapping shield	56

FEET SLOT

*Boots of Caiphon	125
Fey warrior's boots	58
*Propellant boots	129
*Swift-step boots +5	115

HANDS SLOT

Gauntlets of blood	58

HEAD SLOT

*Ioun's flame	127

NECK SLOT

Amulet of vigor +5	63
Assassin's cloak +5	64
Chaos cloak +5	65
Cloak of the bat +5	65
*Cloak of the lion's mane +5	98
Cloak of the shadowthief +5	65
Cloak of translocation +5	66
*Crimson cloak +5	122
Demon amulet +5	66
Frostwolf pelt +5	66
*Keicha's amulet +5	134
Lucky charm +5	67
Medallion of the mind +5	67
Medic's amulet +5	67
Periapt of proof against poison +5	67
*Shadowdancer's cloak +5	105
Soul shard talisman +5	69
Timeless locket +5	69

RINGS

*Golden ring of Teros	137

Ring of battlements		71
Ring of focus		71

WONDROUS LAIR ITEMS

Chandelier of revelation		80

TATTOOS

Fireheart tattoo		87
Tattoo of arcane blood		84
Tattoo of the shared heart		86

CONSUMABLES (21,000 GP PER ITEM)

Immurement of arcane suspension		89
Immurement of the abandoned throne		90
Immurement of the blood vine		90

LEVEL 25 ITEMS 625,000 GP

ARMOR

Armor of shared valor +5	Leather, chain	6
Counterstrike armor +5	Cloth, leather, hide	7
*Crystalline breastplate +5	Leather, hide, chain, scale, plate	118
Healer's armor +5	Hide, chain	9
Holy radiance armor +5	Chain	9
Shadow warlock armor +5	Leather	12
*Shockweave armor +5	Cloth, leather	98
Spectral plate +5	Plate	13
Supporting armor +5	Scale, plate	13

WEAPONS

*Rousing hammer +5	Hammer	95
Battle spirit weapon +5	Axe, flail, hammer, hvy blade, mace, spear	16
*Blade of the eldritch knight +5	Hvy blade	114
*Reaper's axe +5	Axe	122
Runic weapon +5	Any	21
Songbow of summoning +5	Bow, crossbow	22
Supreme skirmisher's bow +5	Bow	24
*Thane blood weapon +5	Any melee	100
*Weapon of evil undone +5	Any	113
*Weapon of great opportunity +5	Any melee	96

AMMUNITION (25,000 GP PER ITEM)

Bending bullet +5		26
Phasing arrow +5		27

HOLY SYMBOLS

*Champion's symbol +5		113
Ioun stone of divine knowledge +5		28
Symbol of daring +5		29
Symbol of protection +5		30

ORBS

Orb of distance denial +5		33
Orb of petrification +5		33

RODS

Rod of devilry +5		35
Rod of silver rain +5		35
*Rod of Ulban +5		126
Torch of misery +5		37

STAFFS

Blastwarp staff +5		38
*Queen's staff +5		117
Staff of wind +5		40
*Tempest staff +5		131

TOTEMS

Bloodhunter totem +5		43
Dire totem +5		43
Flameheart totem +5		44
Nine furies totem +5		44
*Stern mountain totem +5		112
Totem of nature's balm +5		45
Totem of the crashing tide +5		46
Totem of the scouring wind +5		47
Totem of the world tree +5		47

WANDS

Sharpshooter's wand +5		52
Wand of aptitude +5		52

ARMS SLOT

Deathward shield		54

HANDS SLOT

*Resplendent gloves		104
*Zehir's gloves		127

NECK SLOT

Bloodgem shard +5		65
Bralani cloak +5		65
*Cloak of burgeoning shadow +5		120
*Mantle of regrets +5		123
Periapt of wound closure +5		67

RINGS

*Haggaron's ring of control		137

WONDROUS LAIR ITEMS

Magic weapon rack		81

TATTOOS

Tattoo of vengeance		85

CONSUMABLES (25,000 GP PER ITEM)

Immurement of the dragon boneyard		90

LEVEL 26 ITEMS 1,125,000 GP

ARMOR

Gambler's suit +6	Leather	8

WEAPONS

Challenge-seeking weapon +6	Any melee	17
Earth-wrought hammer +6	Hammer	17

ARMS SLOT

Flameward shield		54
Stormward shield		56
Winterward shield		56

FEET SLOT

Clearing cleats		57

HANDS SLOT

*Hands of Hadar		125

RINGS

*Bloodshard ring		124
*Kartan's void ring		137
Ring of guarded will		71

TATTOOS

Ghostwalk tattoo	87

CONSUMABLES (45,000 GP PER ITEM)

Immurement of seething scoria	89
Immurement of the vengeful river	91

LEVEL 27 ITEMS   1,625,000 GP

ARMOR

Armor of aegis expansion +6	Cloth, leather	6
*Armor of dwarven vigor +6	Chain, scale, plate	94
Bastion armor +6	Scale, plate	6
Blackflock robe +6	Cloth	6
Coruscating armor +6	Scale, plate	7
*Darkstrike armor +6	Leather, hide	120
Death's brink armor +6	Scale, plate	7
Gallant armor +6	Plate	8
Hero's armor +6	Chain	9
Marauder's armor +6	Leather, hide	10
*Mooncloth robes +6	Cloth	117
*Radiant temple uniform +6	Cloth	103
Rat killer's coat +6	Cloth, leather	11
Shadow hound armor +6	Hide	12
*Shadow hunter hide +6	Hide	106
*Shipboard armor +6	Leather	101
Teleporting armor +6	Scale, plate	14

WEAPONS

Aftershock weapon +6	Any	15
Boltshard crossbow +6	Crossbow	17
Duelist's bow +6	Bow	17
Entrapping weapon +6	Bow, crossbow	17
Farbond spellblade +6	Hvy blade, lt blade	18
Guardian's call +6	Any melee	19
Harmonic songblade +6	Hvy blade, lt blade	19
*Hungry spear +6	Spear	98
*Infighting blade +6	Lt blade, axe (one-handed only)	101
*Lion's heart hammer +6	Hammer	130
Quicksilver blade +6	Lt blade	21
Rebounding weapon +6	Any ranged	21
Shadowrift blade +6	Lt blade	21
Supremely vicious weapon +6	Any	24
Totemic spear +6	Spear	24
Totemic warclub +6	Mace	25
*Unbroken lance +6	Spear	111
Whistling songbow +6	Bow, crossbow	25

AMMUNITION (65,000 GP PER ITEM)

Onslaught arrow +6	27

HOLY SYMBOLS

Ioun-blessed symbol +6	28
Symbol of branding +6	29
Symbol of divine force +6	29
Symbol of divine light +6	29
Symbol of foe turning +6	30
*Symbol of Gajz +6	135
Symbol of shared healing +6	30

Symbol of the first spirits +6	31
*Symbol of the forgotten one +6	124
Symbol of vigor +6	32

ORBS

Orb of heightened imposition +6	33
Orb of resilient tenacity +6	33
Orb of visionary protection +6	34

RODS

Rod of burgeoning memory +6	34
Rod of stolen starlight +6	35
Rod of the fickle servant +6	36
Rod of the risen dead +6	37

STAFFS

Moonsilver staff +6	38
Staff of divinity +6	38
Staff of knives +6	39
*Staff of the Far Wanderer +6	117
Summoner's staff +6	40
Verdant staff +6	40

TOMES

Dispelling tome +6	41

TOTEMS

Earthfall totem +6	44
Roaring bear totem +6	45
Totem of the harrier's claws +6	46
Totem of the night +6	46
Totem of thunder's keeper +6	47

FEET SLOT

*Time-jumping boots	128

HANDS SLOT

Great hero's gauntlets	59

HEAD SLOT

Firebird	62
*Mirrored mask	125
Philosopher's crown	62

NECK SLOT

Amulet of double fortune +6	63
Amulet of elegy +6	63
Badge of the berserker +6	64
*Cloak of the crimson path +6	107
*Deep-pocket cloak +6	97
*Eldritch medallion +6	114
Lifesaving brooch +6	67
*Mantle of the golden general +6	123
*Necklace of fate +6	121
*Scarf of reconciliation +6	132
Talisman of terror +6	69

RINGS

*Avandra's ring	126
*Ring of Khirad	126

TATTOOS

Resurgence tattoo	84
Tattoo of the wolverine	85

CONSUMABLES (65,000 GP PER ITEM)

Clay of creation	87

LEVEL 28 ITEMS   2,125,000 GP

ARMOR

Armor of enduring health +6	Hide, chain	6
*Armor of essence inviolate +6	Any	112
Armor of sudden recovery +6	Cloth, leather	6
Champion's hauberk +6	Chain, scale	113
Gambit armor +6	Cloth, leather	8
Holy adversary's armor +6	Cloth	9
Kemstone armor +6	Scale, plate	9
Mind armor +6	Scale, plate	10
Mirrored plate +6	Plate	110
Moon armor +6	Chain	10
Nightmare ward armor +6	Leather, hide	11
Predator's hide +6	Hide	11
Robe of avoidance +6	Cloth	11
Runic armor +6	Any	12
Sanguine vestments +6	Cloth	12
*Skin of agonies +6	Leather, hide	124
Slime armor +6	Scale, plate	13
Snaketongue robe +6	Cloth	13
Spidersweb robes +6	Cloth	13
Spiked jacket +6	Leather, hide	13
*Tinkersuit +6	Leather	129
Wall armor +6	Any	14
Warmage's uniform +6	Cloth, leather	14
Winged armor +6	Any	14

WEAPONS

Aegis blade +6	Hvy blade, lt blade	15
Alfsair spear +6	Spear	15
Aura killer weapon +6	Any melee	15
*Blade of vengeance +6	Hvy blade, lt blade	103
Blood fury weapon +6	Axe, hvy blade	17
*Blood harvest blade +6	Lt blade	107
*Bradaman's weapon +6	Hvy blade, axe, hammer	110
Death mark weapon +6	Any	17
Flesh grinder +6	Axe, hvy blade, polearm	18
Frost fury waraxe +6	Axe	18
*General's weapon +6	Polearm	123
Great hunger weapon +6	Any melee	18
Guardian's brand +6	Any melee	19
Hideous weapon +6	Flail, hammer, pick	19
*Pact blade +6	Lt blade	108, 120
Ravenclaw warblade +6	Hvy blade	21
*Rhythm blade +6	Lt blade	97
*Rovikar's weapon +6	Any	135
*Scorpion tail blade +6	Lt blade	131
*Serpent's kiss bow +6	Bow	131
*Shepherd's arms +6	Polearm, spear	119
Shrieking songbow +6	Bow, crossbow	21
Songbow of vanishment +6	Bow, crossbow	23
Targeting weapon +6	Bow, crossbow	24
Unforgettable cudgel +6	Mace	25
*Warding blade +6	Lt blade	103
Writhing vine weapon +6	Any melee	25

AMMUNITION (85,000 GP PER ITEM)

Attention-stealing bullet +6	26
Bolt of clumsiness +6	26
Bolt of transit +6	26
Dispelling bolt +6	26
Firestorm arrow +6	26
Freezing arrow +6	27
Lightning arrow +6	27
Space-shifting bolt +6	27
Spider bolt +6	27
Summoning bullet +6	28
Surprise bullet +6	28

HOLY SYMBOLS

Convert's symbol +6	28
Symbol of brawn +6	29
Symbol of defense +6	29
Symbol of prayers recovered +6	30
Symbol of the champion's code +6	31
Symbol of the radiant flame +6	32

ORBS

Orb of repeated imposition +6	33
Orb of supplementary force +6	34

RODS

Battle-pact rod +6	34
Hexer's rod +6	34
Rod of divinity +6	35
Spider rod +6	37

STAFFS

Spellshaper's staff +6	38
Staff of luck and skill +6	39
Staff of resilience +6	39
Staff of sleep and charm +6	39
Staff of the faithful arcanist +6	40

TOMES

Confounding tome +6	41
Frozen tome +6	41
Gossamer tome +6	42
Mordenkainen's tome +6	42

TOTEMS

Boar's charge totem +6	43
Bronzewood coils totem +6	43
*Death fang totem +6	106
Fell beast totem +6	44
Iron bear totem +6	44
Life river totem +6	44
Totem of the awakened bear +6	45
Totem of the satyr's dance +6	47
Vengeful spirit totem +6	47

WANDS

*Feyshard wand +6	125

HEAD SLOT

*Crown of stuttered time	128

NECK SLOT

Amulet of warding +6	63
*Baffling cape +6	96
*Bane's collar +6	126
Cloak of the desert +6	65

Courtier's cape +6		66
*Fleece of renewal +6		111
Necklace of keys +6		67
Orc's-eye amulet +6		67
*Pavise charm +6		101
Possum amulet +6		68
*Resplendent cloak +6		104
Seashimmer cloak +6		68
Shroud of ravens +6		68
*Spidersilk mantle +6		109
*Star-strewn scarf +6		118

RINGS
Ring of fearlessness	71
Ring of windows	73

WAIST SLOT
Sash of heroic inspiration	75
Sash of regeneration	75

TATTOOS
Fleet hero tattoo	87
Greatwing tattoo	87
Ironheart tattoo	86
Strongheart tattoo	86

CONSUMABLES (85,000 GP PER ITEM)
Immurement of baleful gossamer	89
Immurement of the mordant hideaway	91
Immurement of the strident statuary	91
Silver sand	88
Vortex stone	88

LEVEL 29 ITEMS   2,625,000 GP

ARMOR
Armor of dark deeds +6	Leather, hide	6
Dazzling plate +6	Plate	7
Demonscale +6	Scale	8
Formidable armor +6	Hide, chain	8
Genasi soul armor +6	Leather, hide	8
Great cat armor +6	Hide	9
Lifefont armor +6	Hide	10
Magnetic armor +6	Scale, plate	10
Parchment armor +6	Cloth, leather	11
Scale of the serpent +6	Scale	12
Serpentine armor +6	Scale	12
Spirit armor +6	Chain	13
Time link armor +6	Chain	14
Translocating armor +6	Any	14

WEAPONS
Avalanche hammer +6	Hammer	15
Banishing spellblade +6	Hvy blade, lt blade	16
Blood drinker +6	Axe, hvy blade	16
*Dragontooth blade +6	Hvy blade	130
Echoing songblade +6	Hvy blade, lt blade	17
*Harmony blade +6	Hvy blade	97
Impaler's pick +6	Pick	20
Incisive dagger +6	Dagger	20
Intensifying weapon +6	Any	20
*Kamesti crossbow +6	Crossbow	101
Master's blade +6	Hvy blade, lt blade	20
Maw of the guardian +6	Any melee	20

Screaming bow +6	Bow	21
Songbow of lullabies +6	Bow, crossbow	22
Soul drinker weapon +6	Any melee	23
Space-bending weapon +6	Hvy blade, lt blade	23
Stormbiter warblade +6	Hvy blade, lt blade	23
*Sword of melancholy +6	Hvy blade, lt blade	124
*Weapon of arcane bonds +6	Hvy blade, lt blade	102
*Weapon of cruel persuasion +6	Any melee	114
Weapon of oaths fulfilled +6	Any melee	25

AMMUNITION (105,000 GP PER ITEM)
Arrow of revelation +6	26
Forbiddance bolt +6	26

HOLY SYMBOLS
Symbol of fire and fury +6	30
Symbol of reflection +6	30
Symbol of the holy nimbus +6	32
Symbol of unified defense +6	32

ORBS
Orb of accuracy +6	33

RODS
Darkspiral rod +6	34
*Pelor's scepter +6	127
Rod of obliterating wrath +6	35
Rod of the hag +6	36
Rod of the pactbinder +6	36

STAFFS
Staff of iron infusion +6	38
Staff of spell blasting +6	40

TOMES
Deck of spells +6	41
Tome of crushing force +6	42
Tome of enduring creation +6	42
Tome of striking lightning +6	42
Toxic tome +6	43

TOTEMS
Avalanche's wake totem +6	43
Panther totem +6	45
Razor talon totem +6	45
Totem of new beginnings +6	45
Totem of the ravenous beast +6	47
*Totem of the severed eye +6	107
Totem of winter's scorn +6	47
Wildfire totem +6	47
Winterwood totem +6	48

WANDS
Cursing wand +6	48
Diamond wand +6	49
Hawthorn wand +6	49
Iron wand +6	49
Master's wand of eyes of the vestige +6	50
Master's wand of illusory ambush +6	50
Master's wand of misdirected mark +6	51
Master's wand of phantom bolt +6	51
Master's wand of spiteful glamor +6	51

Master's wand of vicious mockery +6	51
Shielding wand +6	52
Wand of allure +6	52
Wand of thunderous anguish +6	52

ARMS SLOT

*Bracers of zeal +6	103

FEET SLOT

*Swift-step boots +6	115

HEAD SLOT

Crown of victory	61

NECK SLOT

Amulet of vigor +6	63
Assassin's cloak +6	64
Chaos cloak +6	65
Cloak of the bat +6	65
*Cloak of the lion's mane +6	98
Cloak of the shadowthief +6	65
Cloak of translocation +6	66
*Crimson cloak +6	122
Demon amulet +6	66
*Far-step amulet +6	125
Frostwolf pelt +6	66
*Keicha's amulet +6	134
Lucky charm +6	67
Medallion of the mind +6	67
Medic's amulet +6	67
Periapt of proof against poison +6	67
*Shadowdancer's cloak +6	105
Soul shard talisman +6	69
Timeless locket +6	69

RINGS

*Ring of free time	128

LEVEL 30 ITEMS   3,125,000 GP

ARMOR

Armor of shared health +6	Chain	6
Armor of shared valor +6	Leather, chain	6
Counterstrike armor +6	Cloth, leather, hide	7
*Crystalline breastplate +6	Leather, hide, chain, scale, plate	118
Healer's armor +6	Hide, chain	9
Holy radiance armor +6	Chain	9
Shadow warlock armor +6	Leather	12
*Shockweave armor +6	Cloth, leather	98
Spectral plate +6	Plate	13
Supporting armor +6	Scale, plate	13

WEAPONS

*Rousing hammer +6	Hammer	95
Battle spirit weapon +6	Axe, flail, hammer, hvy blade, mace, spear	16
*Blade of the eldritch knight +6	Hvy blade	114
*Reaper's axe +6	Axe	122
Runic weapon +6	Any	21
Songbow of summoning +6	Bow, crossbow	22
Supreme skirmisher's bow +6	Bow	24
*Thane blood weapon +6	Any melee	100

*Weapon of evil undone +6	Any	113
*Weapon of great opportunity +6	Any melee	96

AMMUNITION (125,000 GP PER ITEM)

Bending bullet +6	26
Phasing arrow +6	27

HOLY SYMBOLS

*Champion's symbol +6	113
Ioun stone of divine knowledge +6	28
Symbol of daring +6	29
Symbol of protection +6	30

ORBS

Orb of distance denial +6	33
Orb of petrification +6	33

RODS

Rod of devilry +6	35
Rod of silver rain +6	35
*Rod of Ulban +6	126
Torch of misery +6	37

STAFFS

Blastwarp staff +6	38
*Queen's staff +6	117
*Staff of time +6	128
Staff of wind +6	40
*Tempest staff +6	131

TOTEMS

Bloodhunter totem +6	43
Dire totem +6	43
Flameheart totem +6	44
Nine furies totem +6	44
*Stern mountain totem +6	112
Totem of nature's balm +6	45
Totem of the crashing tide +6	46
Totem of the scouring wind +6	47
Totem of the world tree +6	47

WANDS

Sharpshooter's wand +6	52
Wand of aptitude +6	52

ARMS SLOT

Shield of ultimate protection	55

HEAD SLOT

Gibbering lump	62

NECK SLOT

Bloodgem shard +6	65
Bralani cloak +6	65
*Cloak of burgeoning shadow +6	120
*Mantle of regrets +6	123
Periapt of wound closure +6	67

RINGS

Dauntless champion's ring	70

WAIST SLOT

Diamond cincture	75
Wraith's cord	75

WONDROUS ITEMS

*Vecna's puzzle box	127

TATTOOS

Eager hero's tattoo	86

SHARE YOUR ADVENTURES.
SHAPE YOUR WORLD.

Explore Faerûn with a band of adventurers gathered from around the globe and make a *real* impact on the world of Toril.

The RPGA's Living Forgotten Realms campaign offers dozens of official D&D® adventures every year—adventures that will help guide how the Realms will continue to evolve.

And best of all, you can do it wherever you play D&D—at home, your favorite game store, conventions—anywhere.

GET MORE INFORMATION AT: WIZARDS.COM/RPGA

DUNGEONS & DRAGONS®
LIVING FORGOTTEN REALMS

RPGA NETWORK

All trademarks are property of Wizards of the Coast LLC